W9-BWG-997

THE NEW KNOW-NOTHINGS

MORTON HUNT

THE NEW KNOW-NOTHINGS

THE POLITICAL FOES OF THE SCIENTIFIC STUDY OF HUMAN NATURE

Transaction Publishers
New Brunswick (U.S.A.) and London (U.K.)

Copyright © 1999 by Transaction Publishers, New Brunswick, New Jersey.

All rights reserved under International and Pan-American Copyright Conventions. No part of this book may be reproduced or transmitted in any form or by any means, electronic or mechanical, including photocopy, recording, or any information storage and retrieval system, without prior permission in writing from the publisher. All inquiries should be addressed to Transaction Publishers, Rutgers—The State University, 35 Berrue Circle, Piscataway, New Jersey 08854-8042.

This book is printed on acid-free paper that meets the American National Standard for Permanence of Paper for Printed Library Materials.

Library of Congress Catalog Number: 98-28985
ISBN: 1-56000-393-6 (cloth); 0-7658-0497-2 (paper)
Printed in the United States of America

Library of Congress Cataloging-in-Publication Data

Hunt, Morton M., 1920–
    The new know-nothings : the political foes of the scientific study of human nature / Morton Hunt.
        p. cm.
    Includes bibliographical references (p.   ) and index.
    ISBN 1-56000-393-6 (hardcover : alk. paper); 0-7658-0497-2 (pbk. : alk. paper)
    1. Psychology—Research—Political aspects. 2. Psychology—Research—Political aspects—Case studies. 3. Social sciences—Research—Political aspects. 4. Social sciences—Research—Political aspects—Case studies. I. Title.
BF76.5.H86   1998
150'.72—dc21   98-28985
                                                                                              CIP

Contents

Acknowledgments

I am deeply grateful to John Gagnon for suggesting to Andrea Tyree, chair of the sociology department at SUNY, Stony Brook, that I be named an adjunct professor in order to enable me to receive the grant that supported my work on this book, and I thank Dr. Tyree and the members of the department for giving me the appointment.

I owe thanks to more people than I can name here—to all who replied to my notices posted on various listservs on the Internet and all whom I contacted by e mail, mail, and phone for suggestions, most of whom replied and were helpful. You know who you are, and you have my gratitude.

But I must name those who gave of their time to be interviewed, or wrote to me, sent me materials, or reviewed parts of the manuscript for accuracy. With abbreviated identifications of their affiliations (some of which are identified in the glossary of acronyms), they are:

Adrienne Asch, Wellesley College; Elaine Baldwin, NIMH, Wendy Baldwin, NIH; John Bancroft, The Kinsey Institute; Jay Belsky, Pennsylvania State University; Camilla Benbow, Iowa State University; Sarah Brookhart, APS; Thomas J. Bouchard, Jr., University of Minnesota; Michael Buckley, COSSA; Merry Bullock, APA; Vern Bullough; Marilyn Carroll, University of Minnesota; Diane di Mauro, SSRC; Ann DuLaney, OPRR; Lee Ellis, Minot State University; Julia Erickson, Temple University; Sy Fisher, University of Texas Medical Branch, Galveston; Mark Frankel, AAAS; Pamela Freyd, FMS Foundation; John Gagnon, SUNY-Stony Brook; Stanton Glantz, University of California, San Francisco; Frederick Goodwin, George Washington University; Irving I. Gottesman, University of Virginia; Linda Gottfredson, University of Delaware; Diane Halpern, California State University, San Bernardino; Neil W. Hamilton, William Mitchell College of Law; Christine Hartel, APA; Ed Hatcher, ASA; Charles Honts, Boise State University; Joseph M. Horn, University of Texas, Austin; William Irons, Northwestern University; James Jasper; Arthur R. Jensen, University of California, Berkeley; David Johnson, Federation of Behavioral, Psychological and Cognitive Sciences; Lloyd Johnston, Institute of Social Research, University of Michigan; Doreen Kimura, University of Western Ontario; Robert H. Knight, Family Research Council; Patricia Kobor, APA; Alan Kraut, APS; Joshua Lederberg, Rockefeller University; Felice Levine, ASA; John C. Loehlin, University of Texas, Austin; Elizabeth Loftus, University of Washington; Irving Maltzman, University of California, Los Angeles; G. Alan Marlatt, University of Washington; Cora Marrett, NSF; Edward M. Miller, University of New Orleans; Roberta Balstad Miller, formerly of COSSA; Robert G. Morrison, Family Research Council; Richard Nakamura, NIMH; Herbert Needleman, University of Pittsburgh; Paula Niedenthal, Indiana University; Mary Utne O'Brien; Patrick O'Malley, Institute for Social Research, University of Michigan; Susan Persons, NIH; Anne Petersen, formerly of NSF; Nancy Pierce; Robert Plomin, Pennsylvania State University; Ira Reiss, University of Minnesota; Catherine Robertson, APA; Harris Rubin, Southern Illinois University; J. Philippe Rushton, University of Western Ontario; Leonard Saxe, Brandeis University; Sandra Scarr, Kinder Care, Montgomery, Alabama; Robert Schaeffer, Fair-Test; Nancy L. Segal, California State University-Fullerton; Ullica Segerstråle, Illinois Institute of Technology; Howard Silver, COSSA; Eleanor Singer, American Association for Public Opinion Research; Devendra Singh, University of Texas, Austin; Philip M. Smith, formerly of NAS; Mark and Linda Sobell, Nova Southeastern University; Andrea Solarz, NAS; Julian C. Stanley, Johns Hopkins University; Anne Thomas, NIH; Randy Thornhill, University of New Mexico; Barbara Torrey, NAS; Susan Turner-Lowe, NAS; J. Richard Udry, University of North Carolina; David Wasserman, University of Maryland; Glayde Whitney, Florida State University; David E. Williams, CAGW; Edward O. Wilson, Harvard University; Fred Wood, formerly of OTA; Ronald Wood, University of Rochester.

I thank Irving I. Gottesman and Eric Turkheimer for permission to reproduce, on page 58, Figure 1 from their article "Individual Differences and the Canalization of Human Behavior," *Developmental Psychology, 27 (1)*: 18–22.

Finally, I am grateful to Bernice Hunt, my wife, for her careful reading of the manuscript and her many valuable editorial suggestions.

Preface

Warning: Read Before Proceeding

Why the warning?

For good reason: If you continue, you may be upset and distressed by what you read, as I was when I investigated the recent growth and metastasis of political opposition to, and obstruction of, research in the behavioral and social sciences.*

Yet I hope that despite this warning (and two others that I will make in a moment), you will read what I report here, for I believe that the best safeguard against this grave danger to the social sciences, which are now so vital to our society's functioning, is increased public awareness.

And so although I am no ancient mariner—fairly ancient I am, but no mariner—I hope to hold you with my glittering eye and tell you a tale. Or, rather, a series of tales: first, a brief personal story, then a number of longer ones of larger social significance, after reading which you will be, like Coleridge's wedding guest, sadder and wiser—and, I hope, ready to support those who defend freedom of research.

So, then, to my personal story.

* * *

In August 1948, when I was a young staff writer for the McGraw-Hill magazine *Science Illustrated*, I was working on an article about H. J. Muller, the Nobel Laureate geneticist. At the time I was still sympathetic to left wing ideals and to the Soviet Union; I had clung to this position since my undergraduate days in the depth of the Great Depression, assuring myself, like many another wishful idealist, that what I had read about the suppression of freedoms and the "liquidation" of supposed enemies of the state were only the lies of reactionaries or, at worst, a gross exaggeration of the temporary safeguards that would

---

*In the interest of brevity, from here on the behavioral and social sciences will, most often, be called simply "the social sciences."

enable the fledgling utopia to survive and evolve into a classless, just, and benevolent society.

One day, just after lunch, a thick envelope arrived unexpectedly on my desk from Harrison Salisbury, McGraw-Hill's Moscow correspondent. It contained some fifty single-spaced typed pages of translations of speeches made at a genetics conference at the Lenin Academy of Agricultural Sciences. The speeches had been triggered by a one-sentence remark of Trofim Lysenko, the noted agronomist, at the end of a report he delivered late in the conference. Lysenko had, as was his wont, attacked genetic science as known in the West on the doctrinaire political grounds that Mendelian genetics was a reactionary invention (he even asserted that chromosomes have nothing to do with heredity) designed to justify the capitalist status quo by denying that social change can transform human nature.[1] Then, winding up, he sprang a surprise: With a thin-lipped smirk, he proudly announced that the Central Committee of the Communist Party had examined and approved his report.

On hearing this, the members of the audience, recognizing the import of the announcement, stood up and gave a ringing ovation to Stalin and the new party line on genetics. As soon as the demonstration subsided and they sat down, one leading Soviet geneticist rose again to confess how misguided he had been and to express regret for his error in believing in genetic science. Then, one by one, some fifty others got up and, in terms ranging from the humbled to the self-castigating, said that they too now saw the subject in its true light, denounced the science they had believed in and practiced, and apologized to all present and to the nation for their errors. The conferees then voted to send Comrade Stalin a letter of thanks for his support of "progressive Michurinist biological science...the most advanced agricultural science in the world."[2]

It took me all afternoon to read the sheaf of confessional speeches, at the end of which my political philosophy lay in shards on the floor. At closing time I lurched homeward stunned, drained, and profoundly disillusioned; the one thought with which I sought to console myself was, "It could never happen here."

* * *

I wish I could tell myself that now, but I cannot. For something malignant, and akin to what I read about that day so long ago, *has* recently been happening here. As a long-time science writer, I have lately seen and become genuinely alarmed by a rising tide of ideological opposition to certain areas of scientific research, particularly in the social sciences, the fields I specialize in. In the past decade and a half, especially in the past half dozen years, many valuable and some critically important psychological and sociological research projects have been severely impeded, and in certain cases totally halted, by the actions of activists and special-interest groups on the far right, the radical left, and all points in between along the political spectrum.

Half a dozen years ago I was galvanized by two particularly egregious cases (to be narrated in later chapters) to begin an inquiry; this book is the outcome. It presents the evidence I have gathered that political interference with social science research has become increasingly and alarmingly common. Most troubling about this development is that, unlike periods of such interference in the past, opposition to scientific research now comes not only from individuals and organizations of specialized kinds of political opinion but appears to have become endemic and diffused throughout our society.

On what do I base these conclusions? My data are the best I could collect; I could find no survey that deals with the subject, but I have talked to more than a hundred social scientists, key figures in government agencies, and officers of scientific organizations, and read everything I could find on the matter. I also posted my research interest on a number of sites on the Internet, thereby reaching a broad (though admittedly nonrandom) sample of social scientists, mostly American, many of whom replied, either offering to tell me their own experiences or directing me to others whose research, they had heard, had been interfered with, obstructed, or even totally halted by politically motivated opponents.[3] The notes to each chapter, acknowledgments, and references cited specify my sources.

* * *

I said above that I have two other warnings to offer, and I issue them now.

One: Ever since my enlightenment in 1948 I have been a political liberal, and I remain one in this era when that label has become for many people a pejorative. I interpret our constitutional guarantee of freedom of speech to include freedom of research, by which I mean freedom to explore any and every aspect of human individual and social behavior, no matter how repugnant or unwelcome the findings might be to one group or another. There is, to be sure, a limit to this freedom: I wholly subscribe to the doctrine set forth in the Nuremberg Code, an outcome of the Nuremberg Trials, that in research with human beings "the voluntary consent of the human subject is absolutely essential." I give a fuller exegesis of my stance in chapter 1 and in the epilogue.

Two: Readers are entitled to know that I have been financially supported in researching and writing this book by a grant from the Pioneer Fund. That fund has been fiercely attacked by some liberals and leftists as racist and supportive of fascist researchers. This is not the place for an appraisal of the charges. Briefly, however: Six decades ago the Pioneer Fund did support some research with racist implications (at that time even such leading social scientists as Henry Goddard and Lewis Terman believed in the inferiority of certain racial groups), and in recent decades it has made grants to several social science researchers interested in the average differences among the major races in intelligence and other traits. Most of its recent grants, however, have gone to scientists interested not in racial differences but in the genetic components of personality and mental abilities, a field now in the respectable mainstream of psychology.[4]

One could spend hundreds of pages on the pros and cons of the case of the Pioneer Fund, but what matters to me—and should matter to my readers—is that I have been totally free to research and write as I chose. I alerted Pioneer to my political views when making the grant proposal for this book but its directors never blinked. Nor did they offer any comment about the fact that my proposal plainly said I would show the harm done to science and American society by conservative opponents of research as well as by politically correct liberals and leftists. Their support has been unquestioning and unqualified; what I say in this book is what I would have said had the grant come from the Ford Foundation.

But I have detained you long enough with these apologies. Let us begin.

Introduction

1

A Clear and Present Danger

Forbidden Fruit

Herewith, three brief stories (to be retold in more detail later) refuting my former naïve belief that no Lysenko-like political purge of research could ever happen here:

• In 1991, David Wasserman, professor of law and public policy at the University of Maryland, had a bright idea: Since knowledge about genetic influences on human behavior was rapidly expanding, it would be useful to gather the latest research findings of the role of genetic factors in crime and explore their implications for the prediction and control of criminal behavior.[1]

Wasserman submitted a proposal for a three-day conference on the subject to the National Institutes of Health (NIH), won a grant of $78,000, gathered a distinguished roster of speakers, and made all arrangements—at which point Dr. Peter Breggin, a leftist Bethesda psychiatrist, launched a vitriolic mail campaign against the conference. He blasted the conference as racist (because it might find genetic components partly responsible for the disproportionate rate of crime by blacks), and stirred up such a wave of protest by black groups and black politicians that Bernadine Healey, the director of NIH, suspended the grant—although it had passed peer review—and later canceled it altogether.[2]

• In the summer of 1991, two well-regarded sociologists at the University of North Carolina, J. Richard Udry and Ronald Rindfuss, were about to launch an $18 million national survey to learn what part families, schools, peer groups, and other social factors play in the shaping of teenagers' sexual behavior. The survey, which had taken years of planning, was funded by the National Institute of Child Health and Human Development (NICHD, a branch of NIH), which needed the information as a basis on which to design programs to decrease teenagers' risks of contracting AIDS and of unplanned pregnancy.

3

Shortly before Udry and Rindfuss's teams were to take to the field, political conservatives undertook to kill the survey: A talk show host attacked it on the Christian Network; William Dannemeyer, a conservative California congressman, sent a letter assailing the survey as a plot against American morals to all members of the House of Representatives; the Christian Coalition and the ultraconservative Family Research Council issued condemnations of it to the media; and the Christian Action Network provoked a blizzard of outraged letters from its listeners to NIH officials and their superiors in the Department of Health and Human Services (HHS). Dr. Louis Sullivan, President Bush's appointee as head of HHS, summarily canceled the program, despite its having been peer-reviewed and approved by the heads of his own agencies, on the ground—for which he had no evidence—that asking teenagers about sexual behavior might encourage casual sex.[3]

• In 1993, Ronald Wood, a psychologist on the faculty of New York University Medical Center, was studying behavioral changes in squirrel monkeys and macaque monkeys caused by the inhalation of crack, a research project he had been conducting for years in an effort to gain deeper understanding of the effects of crack on human beings. A scientist with an admirable track record of findings, publications, grants, and awards, Wood was making good headway when, one dark day in the fall of 1993, he learned that the Office of Protection from Research Risks (OPRR), a federal watchdog agency, had received a complaint from an animal rights organization called In Defense of Animals (IDA), charging him with failure to comply with various animal welfare regulations of the Department of Agriculture and, in effect, implying that he subjected his research animals to barbaric conditions and horrendous tortures. Over the next two years IDA leveled many other charges at Wood in more than a dozen letters, along with private laboratory papers, memos, letters, and minutes of meetings copied and smuggled out by an informant in Wood's laboratory.[4]

During the three years of OPRR's investigation of the charges, the atmosphere at Wood's laboratory was thoroughly poisoned and the pressures on him grew so insufferable that by mid-1996 he decamped to another institution. I spoke to him at that time; he sounded haunted and frenetic, and would say little, fearful that his words could be used against him in a pending lawsuit and might tip off his enemies as to where he hoped to continue his work.[5]

* * *

These stories and many others like them update the biblical myth of the forbidden fruit. Instead of Adam, social scientists are forbidden to eat the fruit of the tree of knowledge; instead of God, colleagues, neighbors, fellow-Americans, and members of Congress try to prevent their eating it; instead of expulsion from Eden for seeking impermissible knowledge, they suffer public castigation, defamation of character, ostracism by fellow-professionals, the cutting off of their funding, and the loss of their academic posts.

In the course of the past decade and a half, especially the past half dozen years, a variety of social science research projects have been impeded, harmed, and in some cases wholly closed down by individuals and groups opposed to them for ideological or political reasons. Freedom of scientific research is, presumably, included in our constitutionally guaranteed freedom of speech—construed as freedom of speech and expression*—since research is an expression of the twin beliefs that truth is valuable and that it can be discovered. The opponents of social science research projects, however, are not deterred by respect for such freedom, and believe it is their right to prevent scientists from conducting any inquiry likely to yield knowledge that might challenge their cherished beliefs. They want to know nothing that would challenge those beliefs; what is far more serious, they want no one else to know any such thing. In the symbolism of the myth of the Fall, they regard social scientists as the serpent enticing humankind to seek knowledge that will damn it.

Some observers of this development see no cause for undue alarm; they admit that the situation is not good, but say that it is no worse today than it has been since 1981, when the Reagan administration began slashing science research budgets. I heard this kind of cold comfort from people in government or government-supported agencies— Wendy Baldwin, deputy director of NIH, Cora Marrett, assistant director for social, behavioral, and economic sciences of the National Science Foundation, and certain officials who preferred not to be named.

Others, however, whose view of political opposition to research is broader and includes not only cutbacks in government funding but interference of every kind from all segments of society, are far more pessimistic. Philip Smith, former executive officer of the National Academy

---

*So construed by Justice Cardozo in *Palko v Connecticut, 302 U.S. 319, 327* [1937], and by Franklin D. Roosevelt in his message to Congress, January 6, 1941.

of Sciences and the National Research Council, said that the sciences, especially the social sciences, are suffering from a recent trend toward "attack politics." Michael McGeary, a political scientist and co-author with Smith of a forthcoming book about science policy, commented, "Today, whatever people don't like, they feel the right to attack." Frederick Goodwin, former head of the National Institute of Mental Health and now a professor at George Washington University, a man of unusual breadth of vision, termed current political opposition to social research "a hugely important and under-realized area, a very dangerous trend." Susan Persons, director of government relations at the American Psychological Society when I interviewed her (and now the public policy liaison officer in the social sciences research office of NIH), was candid and blunt about the deep concern in the endangered disciplines: "Everyone in the social science community and the medical community is very scared."

These and other informants consider the trend socially perilous for two main reasons:

The first: Our society urgently needs the information and insights yielded by social science research; its findings are essential to the design of programs to counter family violence, substance abuse, mental illness, teenage pregnancy, the spread of AIDS, and crime. But research in these areas, unlike most research in the physical and biomedical sciences, impinges on religious, moral, and political beliefs. Moreover, as several social scientists I spoke to commented, many of the issues that social science researchers investigate are aspects of everyday life about which most people feel they have a right to opinions, even though in the past the majority have so often been wrong about such realities. Accordingly, these are the very areas in which the New Know-Nothings most actively attempt to halt studies they see as jeopardizing their beliefs and values.

The second: In earlier decades, opposition to particular programs of social science research came largely from one or another subset of Americans—religious conservatives at one time, student radicals at another, and so on. Today, however, the idea that a group has a moral right to disrupt and halt research its members disapprove of or find offensive has diffused throughout our society; such efforts are no longer the temporary aberrant behavior of some special segment of society but the chronic normal behavior of organizations and bodies of every kind and political persuasion. Social scientists have good reason to be very scared; those who are not, are not so much brave as blind to the situation.

The Repression of Science, Old Style

The ideological suppression of scientific knowledge is nothing new, although the best-known instances of it occurred within the physical and biological sciences long before the social sciences emerged from philosophy.

The most famous case was the Inquisition's fight against the heretical theory that the earth and the planets move about the sun—heretical because Church doctrine, based on biblical cosmology, had long maintained that the earth is the center of the world, a view contradicted in the seventeenth century by accumulating evidence, particularly of the motions of planets, as observed through Galileo's recent invention, the telescope. The high point of the struggle took place in 1633 in a vaulted chamber of the Vatican: At a dais sat a handful of stern-faced, splendidly robed cardinals—officers of the Inquisition—and all around stood a phalanx of Church dignitaries and officials; before the dais, on his knees, a frail elderly man, gaunt and trembling after a long winter journey to Rome, months of imprisonment and trial, and the prospect of being burned at the stake, read from a paper in a quavering voice:

> I, Galileo, son of the late Vincenzio Galilei, Florentine, being in my seventieth year, arraigned personally before this tribunal and on my knees before you, Most eminent and Lord Cardinals Inquisitors General against heretical depravity throughout the entire Christian Commonwealth, having before my eyes and touching with my hands the Holy Gospel...[do] altogether abandon the false opinion that the sun is the center of the world and immobile, and that the earth is not the center of the world and moves....Desiring to remove from the minds of your Eminences, and of all faithful Christians, this vehement suspicion rightly conceived against me, with sincere heart and unpretended faith I abjure, curse, and detest the aforesaid errors and heresies...[6]

For good measure he was obliged to add, also under oath, that he would denounce to the Inquisition any other man of science whom he might discover supporting that heresy. Only then was he allowed to struggle to his feet (whispering to himself, according to a story first told more than a century later and probably apocryphal, "*E pur si muove*"—"Nevertheless, it moves") and make his way to confinement in a secluded house in Arcetri outside Florence; there he lived out his last years, ailing, impoverished, remote from family and friends, deprived of his professorship, and obliged to remain silent in the face of repeated slanders and denunciations by his clerical enemies.[7]

Galileo's recantation was the Church's most signal victory in its effort to stamp out the Copernican (heliocentric) view of the world. In the early centuries of Christianity, the Fathers of the Church had formulated the doctrine, based on the Bible and Ptolemaic cosmology, that the earth was the center of the universe and that the sun, planets, and stars revolved around it. In the course of the following dozen centuries Church theologians elaborated the theory in order to accommodate observations that did not fit it, finally positing a cosmos of nine concentric spheres, each containing various heavenly bodies and rotating about the earth, with heaven enclosing all.

The opposite view—that the earth and planets circled around the sun—had originally suggested by Pythagoras and other Greek philosophers but long more or less lost to view. It was revived in Renaissance times by the Polish mathematician and scholar Nicholas Copernicus, who developed the theory by 1500, but fearing he would be charged with heresy, kept it mostly to himself; not until forty-three years later, when he was nearing death, did he publish it in his book *The Revolutions of the Heavenly Bodies*, and even then carefully said that it was only a hypothesis, not a fact.

The Church ignored the work until 1616, but then, when Galileo declared it to be the truth, condemned it, placed it on the *Index Librorum Prohibitorum*, and forbade anyone to read, teach, or discuss it or any other book affirming that the earth moved. Galileo, for praising Copernicus's book, was summoned before the Inquisition and threatened with imprisonment in the dungeons unless he renounced his view. He did so, though he quietly continued his studies over the years; but unable to keep truth to himself, he spent six years writing *Dialogue on the Two Chief World Systems*, in which the arguments for and against the Ptolemaic and the Copernican systems were debated by three friends, and published it in 1632. The dialogue format was meant to fool the censors as to what Galileo himself believed but did not, and the pope himself ordered Galileo, seriously ailing at the time, to promptly come to Rome, and threatened to bring him by force if he failed to obey. The grand duke of Florence generously provided a litter in which, in the frigid February of 1633, Galileo was carried to Rome; there, on his knees, he saved his life by swearing that the truth was other than he knew it to be.

The heliocentric theory, despite what Galileo was forced to say about it, rationally and parsimoniously explained what astronomers were now seeing with their telescopes, but the Catholic Church—and some Protestant denominations—opposed it so fiercely, punishing any who professed belief in it, that nearly two centuries passed before the theory was generally and openly accepted by scientists and scholars throughout Europe. Not until 1992, more than three and a half centuries after Galileo's trial and recantation, did the Vatican announce to the world that the Inquisition had erred in forcing him to publicly recant his belief in heliocentric theory and affirm the truth of geocentric theory.[8]

Another area in which the Church fought long and hard to halt scientific research was anatomical knowledge acquired through the dissection of human cadavers. From medieval times well into the Renaissance, dissection of any corpse except that of an executed criminal was held to be impious, for the body could not be resurrected at the final trump if it had been disassembled, especially if its only incorruptible bone (never identified but believed to be the nucleus of the resurrectable body) was destroyed. Anatomists and physicians therefore avoided the dissection of human corpses except, on rare occasion, those of criminals put to death (who, it was assumed, were condemned to hell in any case), relying instead for their knowledge of anatomy on what Galen had written in the second century, much of it erroneous.

Early in the seventeenth century the young Dutch anatomist Andreas Vesalius, driven by burning intellectual curiosity to learn how the body was constructed, foraged among the corpses of criminals strung up outside city limits and brought their rotting, reeking parts home, hidden in his clothing, to study. He eventually published the richly illustrated *Structure of the Human Body*, which made him famous and within a few decades became the basis of anatomical teaching in medical schools throughout Europe. But in one of his later revisions of the book Vesalius revealed that he had also obtained specimens from noncriminal sources, and in consequence was sentenced to death by the Inquisition for body-snatching and dissection. The sentence was commuted to an expiatory pilgrimage to Jerusalem; Vesalius made the trip, but on the way home was shipwrecked and died on an island.[9]

* * *

Psychology and sociology, born more than two centuries later, faced no such organized institutional opposition for some time. But in the twentieth century, in the two major totalitarian nations of Europe many social researchers were experiencing repression akin to that suffered by Galileo.

In the Soviet Union, genetic science as understood in the West was half-crippled by Lysenko and his followers in the late 1930s, and from 1948 on was virtually banned and replaced by his bizarre, specious theory. Although Lysenko was primarily interested in agriculture and livestock breeding, the success of his brand of genetics made it impossible for scientists to openly conduct any research on the hereditary components of human mental abilities, personality, and behavior. A few Soviet biologists did, however, carry on genetics research secretly and in camouflaged fashion until 1965. Then, the accumulating evidence that the application of Lysenko's genetic doctrines failed to yield improved crops and strains of livestock led to his downfall and the full-scale resumption of genetic research.[10]

Soviet psychology was strongly influenced by the behaviorist doctrines of Ivan Pavlov and by a political ideology according to which human behavior could be shaped however society wished it to be, an essential tenet of the communist view of the future. Accordingly, although many Soviet psychologists were interested in Freudian psychology in the 1920s and did some research along Freudian lines, by the end of that decade Marxist ideologues had decided that its portrayal of human nature as largely the result of innate drives was reactionary and bourgeois. And when in 1930 Freud himself made critical comments about communism in his *Civilization and Its Discontents*, Stalin ordered an end to psychoanalytic therapy and research, and the exclusion of Freudian writings from bookstores and libraries.[11]

For over six decades no one in the Soviet Union dared to practice psychoanalysis or conduct research based on its tenets, although some Freudian writings were circulated in *samizdat* form and read secretly. Only after the collapse of the Soviet Union—and even then not immediately—did some Russian psychologists openly begin to study and make use of psychoanalytic theory and methodology. Finally, in July, 1996, President Boris Yeltsin signed a decree officially recognizing psychoanalysis as a legitimate form of therapy; with that, it swiftly became part of the curriculum for psychology students and a legitimate basis for therapy and research.[12]

In Nazi Germany, Hitler banned psychoanalysis in 1933 and ordered Freud's books burned in public.[13] Carl Jung, once so close to Freud, sounded the official note in 1933 in the journal of the New German Society of Psychotherapy: "The factual and well-known differences between Germanic and Jewish psychology should no longer be blurred, which can only benefit science," and in the following issue attacked both Freud's theories and the "Jewish theory" of Alfred Adler.[14] From then on throughout the 1930s Jewish psychologists and sociologists were passed over for appointments in universities throughout Germany, harassed in various ways, ousted from their positions, and prevented from carrying on their research projects; the prudent ones fled.

The most serious mistake the Nazis made about scientific research, however, was not in a social science but in physics: they condemned and banned any use of research based on the "Jewish" relativity theory of Einstein, and in consequence lagged so far behind the United States in research on atomic fission that they never developed a feasible design for an atomic bomb. Had they pursued the mass-energy conversion implications of Einsteinian physics and engineered a bomb as soon as or sooner than we, history would surely have followed a very different and horrendous course.

The Repression of Science, New Style

In the United States, no large-scale efforts were made to halt any genre of research until after World War II, and then not by Marxist or Nazi ideologues but by scientists and legislators with decent and humane motives.

For decades, biomedical researchers had been freely testing new drugs and other therapies on patients—sometimes even exposing them to pathogens—without revealing to their subjects what they were doing to them. In the social sciences, similarly, researchers seeking to understand human behavior conducted numerous experiments in the 1920s and 1930s that today would be considered ethically atrocious and could not, under present laws and federal regulations, be funded by any federal agency and probably not by any foundation or university. But in those earlier decades neither the government nor any citizen group objected to them or sought to stop them, and in fact some of these studies yielded important knowledge.

In the winter of 1919–20, for instance, John B. Watson, the founder of behaviorism, and his assistant, Rosalie Raynor, set out to create a conditioned fear response in an eleven-month-old baby boy, Albert B., whose mother was a patient in the Phipps Psychiatric Clinic at Johns Hopkins University, where Watson was a professor. He and Raynor placed a white rat near Albert, who showed no fear and reached out for it, but just as he touched it, they banged a steel bar behind him, startling him, and he fell forward and buried his face in the mattress. On a second trial, Albert still reached for the rat, but again the researchers banged the bar; this time when Albert fell forward he began to whimper. A half-dozen more trials produced a full-fledged conditioned fear response:

At the mere sight of the rat he would begin to cry and crawl away as rapidly as possible, and his fear now extended to other furry things such as a dog, a seal coat, and Watson wearing a Santa Claus beard. Watson and Raynor made no effort to decondition Albert, whose mother left the clinic with him a few days after the final tests. The researchers did say in their published report of the study that they might have tried deconditioning him, had they had the opportunity, but they jested that since they had not, twenty years hence some psychoanalyst might extract from Albert a false memory of having played with his mother's pubic hair and been harshly scolded for it.[15]

A number of equally inhumane experiments were conducted by other researchers in the early decades of the new science. A particularly sadistic one was begun in 1932 by the psychologist Wayne Dennis, then at the University of Virginia, who managed to get an indigent Baltimore woman to turn over to him her five-week-old, nonidentical twin girls, Del and Ray. Dennis and his wife reared them in their home for more than a year, if "reared" is the right word: Because Dennis wanted to find out what forms of behavior would arise spontaneously in infants deprived of all stimulation and learning, he and his wife never smiled or frowned at the infants, never played with them or petted them, gave them no toys, and kept a screen between their cribs so that they could not even see each other.

The girls did develop some normal scraps of behavior—they sometimes laughed, put their toes in their mouths, and cried at unexpected noises—but they lagged far behind normal and normally reared children in crawling, sitting, and standing. Although Dennis gave them a period of training at fourteen months, he fairly soon divested himself of them and they spent the rest of their childhood in institutions and the homes of relatives. He never followed up on them, but a study he later made of orphanage children elsewhere suggests how Del and Ray may have turned out: Dennis found that many orphanage-reared children, neglected and given little individual attention, were mentally retarded in childhood and remained so as adolescents, which is as far as he was able to follow them.[16]

Such psychological and social experiments met with no serious interference until the postwar years, when the world learned of the atrocities committed by Nazi doctors on concentration camp prisoners in the name of scientific research. At the Nuremberg trials evidence was produced of experiments such as floating healthy men in a tank of ice water to see when their various vital processes would fail and when death would ensue; subjecting others to simulated high-altitude conditions in a decompression chamber to find out how long it took, at various altitudes, to bring about collapse and death; forcing subjects to drink sea water (treated to conceal the taste) for up to twelve days to determine how long it took to cause diarrhea, how long convulsions, and how long death; infecting prisoners with malaria, typhus, smallpox, cholera, and other serious diseases in order to investigate the value of various vaccines; administering poisons to POWs in their food and performing autopsies on them to observe the effects on their organs (and, if any failed to die, killing them so that autopsies could be conducted); breaking the bones of inmates' arms and legs, letting them heal, and breaking them again to find out how strong the healed areas had become; and exposing the genitalia of males and females to various doses of x-radiation to learn the amount needed to make the subjects permanently sterile.[17]

Twenty Nazi doctors were convicted of crimes against humanity; of far greater importance, the trials led to the formulation by the Nuremberg Tribunal of a code of ethics governing medical research with human subjects, the fundamental clause of which read: "The voluntary consent of the human subject is absolutely essential….[He or she] should have sufficient knowledge and comprehension…of the subject matter…to make an understanding and enlightened decision."

This soon became known as the doctrine of "informed consent," and from then on world medical opinion held that biomedical researchers were morally obliged to gain the informed consent of their subjects before conducting any research upon them. Nevertheless, many researchers, not yet constrained by laws or regulations, continued to take the far easier course, conducting experiments with subjects unaware of what was being done to them. Sometimes the treatments were beneficial, sometimes did neither good nor ill, and sometimes were harmful. During the 1950s and 1960s a number of these experiments came to light, and public and congressional pressure led the Public Health Service (PHS) to adopt certain regulations, among them the requirement of informed consent, governing the acts of biomedical researchers. The regulations were binding only on researchers supported by PHS grants, but its grants were the support of the great majority of persons doing such work in the United States.

By far the most morally repugnant medical experiment conducted in the United States came to public attention a few years later (1972); the Tuskegee Study, supported by the PHS for several decades beginning in 1932, followed the course of syphilis in some 400 lower-class black men who were deliberately not treated—although they were led to believe otherwise—in order to study the natural history of the disease.*[18]

* * *

A development analogous to the formulation of the Nuremberg Code had, however, already taken place in the United States, where the PHS had developed regulations making informed consent a necessary condition in any biomedical research that it funded. By the late 1960s, the question as to whether informed consent should also be required in social psychological experiments was being much debated in scientific societies and in Congress; the problem was that in many experiments researchers felt that it was essential to deceive subjects as to what was being done to them to ensure that their responses were not influenced by knowing what the researcher was looking for, and that informed consent would make many valuable experiments impossible. But one that was particularly criticized and offered as evidence that control of such research was needed was a study of obedience conducted in 1963 by Stanley Milgram at Yale. Pretending that he was studying an aspect of the learning process, Milgram instructed his naïve (uninformed) volunteers to administer ever-stronger electrical shocks to another volunteer, heard on an intercom, whenever that person made a mistake in memorizing.

As the shocks grew stronger (up to an ostensibly life-threatening level), the unseen learner—actually, the voice was tape-recorded— would grunt, later utter cries of pain, and finally scream in agony and implore the volunteer administering the supposed shocks to stop the experiment. When volunteers administering the shock wanted to stop, Milgram or an assistant would say that the experiment required them to continue. A number of the volunteers, Milgram wrote in his report, "were observed to sweat, tremble, stutter, bite their lips, groan and dig their fingernails into their flesh"—but, for the most part, obeyed the order. Milgram concluded from the experiment that when someone else is in authority, normal and quite decent people will obediently carry

---

*Whether the findings of such grossly unethical research should be cited in technical publications and used by scientists is a moral question of great difficulty. For a penetrating discussion of the issue, see Caplan, 1993.

out brutal acts toward others, a finding that he suggested cast light on the behavior of ordinary Germans during the Nazi regime.[19]

Debate over such research eventually resulted in the creation of controls. In 1971 the Department of Health, Education, and Welfare (HEW) had extended the PHS research regulations to all its other agencies, and in 1974, in accordance with the National Research Act passed that year, greatly toughened its rules, not only construing informed consent very strictly but making it apply to research in social psychology as well as biomedicine. The new rules required nearly all psychological research projects funded by HEW agencies to be approved in advance by an Institutional Review Board (IRB), a watchdog committee set up within every research foundation and university to see that research projects met the spirit and letter of the federal regulations. Any institution failing to comply could lose all its HEW subsidies, a punishment no such institution could survive.[20]

Because the HEW guidelines ruled out all experiments involving deception except for the most minor and innocuous forms, the research efforts of behavioral scientists were seriously impaired. Within a few years more than half of a large sample of behavioral scientists queried by the Survey Research Center of the University of Michigan said that the new regulations were impeding research.[21] Many social psychologists said that because they were able to conduct only experiments requiring little or no deception, the range of behavior they could investigate was greatly restricted, and even a quarter of the sociologists queried, most of whom did no laboratory work, said they had experienced "significant problems" in meeting IRB requirements. Many behavioral scientists stopped conducting experiments and turned to other kinds of research such as observing people in public places or asking subjects how they thought they would react in hypothetical situations; observations in public places, however, are useful only in the study of a limited range of behaviors, and the hypothetical-situation method is of doubtful validity.

As the complaints of the scientific community grew louder, Congress became concerned and created two commissions to study the problem. With the introduction of a new ethical measurement, the "risk-benefit ratio," HHS (the Department of Health and Human Services, successor to HEW) eased the regulations somewhat in 1981, softening the definition of informed consent and allowing IRBs to approve research if the withholding of information from subjects involved minimum risk to them and if the research "could not practicably be carried out otherwise."[22]

Although this freed researchers, within bounds, to conduct experiments on social behavior, most psychologists continued to feel that many legitimate and important kinds of research remained seriously hampered by the regulations and by meddlesome IRBs. As the late Edward E. Jones, an eminent social psychologist at Princeton, remarked some years ago, "The regulations have exerted a profound influence on our thinking. You don't even *consider* experiments that would run into resistance—it just doesn't occur to you to tackle a problem that would require deception of a kind that will create trouble with the IRB. Whole lines of research have been nipped in the bud."[23] John Loehlin, a noted researcher of genetic influences in psychology, has likewise said that federal regulations and IRBs have caused many researchers to censor their own research interests:

> I suspect that the biggest effect of politicization of a research area is not in shutting down ongoing research but in discouraging the undertaking of new projects. Any reasonably creative researcher has ten times as many ideas for possible research projects as he can actually undertake. Why should he commit himself to something that is bound to involve a lot of hassle and grief, such as a study dealing with race differences, when there are a dozen other equally interesting things he might do that are much less likely to blow up in his face?[24]

The sociologist Irving Louis Horowitz cites an example:

> Recently, a colleague of mine who did a study on children's attitudes toward work and the labor process simply discarded all the data he had on race, since attitudes of black children were radically at variance with those of white children. As a result, a study with a perfectly fascinating potential for helping us understand racial differences regarding work became a pedestrian examination of different attitudes among white children. This is unfortunately all too common.[25]

* * *

HHS regulations were the ancestor of recent congressional efforts to restrict and even ban certain kinds of social research, but a very different social development of the 1960s and early 1970s was the source of the present-day obstruction of social research by citizen groups of all shades of political opinion.

In the tranquil 1950s, many scholars believed that the diverse peoples of the United States had learned how to compromise their differences peaceably and to play by the rules; they saw our country's long history of mob violence, citizen uprisings, riots, and other actions by groups that felt they could not achieve their goals by legal and democratic procedures as behind us, part of our past.[26] But the scholars were self-deluded. A number of factors, among them the infuriatingly slow progress made by blacks and women, the widespread sense of betrayal among liberals and the young due to the Vietnam war, the assassinations of three liberal leaders, and the multiple malfeasances of the Nixon administration, widely eroded confidence in traditional values and ways of getting things done and resulted in the emergence of a number of citizen groups with their own interests: Students for Democratic Society, the black power movement, the women's movement, the gay power movement, the consumer movement, and others.[27] These forces all relied on pressure tactics and confrontation to achieve what the existing order had not let them achieve by orderly democratic processes. It was an era of unrelated but concomitant citizen uprisings: black riots, antiwar demonstrations, student and youth rebellions, feminist rallies and political campaigns, gay rights protests, and radical acts of violence against nuclear power installations, computer centers, and selected heads of industry.

Although all these movements presented themselves as fighting for true democracy, they were generally quick to interfere with the freedom of expression of those they opposed, including the freedom of research by scientists, against whom they had a pervasive bias and some of whom in particular—those whose investigations and hypotheses challenged their views on a wide range of issues—they considered enemies who should be silenced and halted in their work by any means necessary, including violence. Ironically and tragically, the activists of that time perceived scientists, long associated with liberalism and democracy, as part of the reactionary and antidemocratic establishment. A recent study by a biologist and a mathematician ascribes this perception to:

> the long tradition of fear and loathing toward the nuclear arsenals of the world and the technocrats who created them. It was greatly intensified by the brutal spectacle of the war in Indochina, where all the technical ingenuity of the most scientifically advanced culture in the world seemed to have been conscripted to inflict butchery on a peasant culture. Finally, the misgivings of the environmental movement toward technology as such became a common currency within the left, thereby widening still further the rift between contemporary radicalism and the Enlightenment tradition of science as the ultimate product of human wisdom and the staunch ally of liberation.[28]

So it was that at the height of 1960s–70s social activism there was a rash of demonstrations and other attacks, on campuses and elsewhere, against researchers investigating the genetic component of IQ, racial differences in scholastic achievement and, indeed, racial differences of any kind, hereditary factors in personality, and many other areas of mental abilities and social behavior.

I offer a trifling but illuminating personal experience illustrating the antiintellectual mind-set among the students and faculty that later came to be known as political correctness. In the early 1970s I was writing an article about the belief, popular among young people at the time, that "you can't trust anyone over thirty." I told a liberal professor I knew that I was conducting an informal survey of students on this notion and asked him to put a few innocuous questions I had formulated to his class. He agreed to do so, but later reported back to me that they voted unanimously not to answer because, as he quoted them, "Questions from a researcher are mind-fucking, and we're not going to be mind-fucked."

Activist demonstrations and violence subsided in the latter 1970s, but it was only a period of dormancy. A generation of students had been radicalized, and from their ranks came the next generation of faculty members; political correctness became pervasive throughout most of academe, and faculty members who dared to research any non-P.C. topic began to be subjected to pressures, applied by their own faculty, including ostracism, poor performance ratings, and denial of tenure, and by a new crop of P.C. students who circulated petitions demanding that the administration fire the professors, mounted noisy and disruptive demonstrations, posted defamatory signs on campus and near the errant professor's home, and on a few occasions resorted to physical attacks.

All of which was bad enough, but in recent years there has been a much more serious development: Activist groups—advocacy groups, as some scholars prefer to call them—have sprung up throughout the political spectrum and been interfering with research they dislike or even detest. The psychologists Diane Halpern, Richard Gilbert, and Stanley Coren, in a thoughtful and troubled essay on the invasion of freedom of research by such groups, write:

> Current academicians are now far more vulnerable to the actions of passionate groups than they are to the constraints imposed by large, social institutions....The proliferation of specific lobbies and identity groups bound together by strongly held beliefs is accelerating in contemporary society....It remains to be seen whether the scientific community can adjust to these contemporary challenges to academic freedom or whether interest-group pressure, in conjunction with an undisciplined press, will produce a long chill in the process of free intellectual inquiry.[29]

On the conservative end and the far right are religious fundamentalist groups that do their best to cripple and destroy all research on human sexuality, impose impossible requirements on surveys of schoolchildren, and even seek to defund all social research, which they regard as intrinsically liberal.

In the middle are groups with many different agendas: They variously assail researchers who use animals in behavioral experiments, whose research suggests that prolonged day care impedes normal child development, whose studies challenge the claims of "recovered memory" therapists, whose field research casts doubt on the value of needle-exchange programs for drug addicts, and others conducting a variety of other seemingly nonpolitical matters.

To the left are groups that feel fully justified in trying to stop researchers from investigating racial differences in IQ, school achievement, crime rates, and parenting practices; gender differences in personality traits and leadership ability; the personality and cognitive similarities of adopted children to their biological parents rather than their adoptive parents; and in general any research exploring the hereditary components of personality, behavior, and cognitive development.

The diffusion of antiresearch attitudes and behavior throughout the body politic should deeply disturb all those who believe that science, rather than religious, political, or philosophic doctrines, offers the best hope of understanding the world and human nature. It is easy to see why extremists have no concern about the right to freedom of thought and expression of those whose ideas they oppose, but less easy to see why that is now also true now of so many more moderate groups. Thoughtful people I have talked to in the sciences and in government agencies, and others whose analyses I have read, have offered a number of answers—and perhaps all their answers are correct; perhaps the phenomenon is overdetermined.

One reason, mentioned earlier, is that the methods and justifications of antiwar, black power, and feminist and gay liberation groups in the 1960s and early 1970s were seen by others to achieve some success. The tactics of confrontation and disruption were effective: They included, according to Neil Hamilton, a law professor and expert on the decline of academic freedom, ridicule, rudeness, inflammatory false accusations, and other forms of abusive language intended to degrade and silence others.[30] These and other aggressive methods, along with the ethos that justifies them—the view that it is legitimate and good to interfere with the work of anyone whose research is antithetical to the beliefs of one's own group—have become been disseminated throughout the culture and adopted by all sorts of advocacy groups.

A second reason, allied to the first: A loss of consensus and faith in the democratic system, evidenced by the steadily declining percent of citizens who bother to vote, has led to the rise of what various scholars call "identity politics," "special interest politics," "attack politics," "advocacy group politics," and so on.[31] The activist groups of the 1960s were primarily liberal and leftist in orientation, but by the late 1980s and the 1990s this phenomenon had metamorphosed into a society-wide plethora of special-interest, advocacy, and activist groups—a disintegration and loss of consensus that has been called the "balkanization of American society."[32] The special interest groups march under a multitude of parochial banners and use whatever means they can, often borrowed from the 1960s radicals, to advance their own cause by militating against, interfering with, and trying to silence those whose interests run counter to their own. Hugh Heclo, professor of public affairs at George Mason University, sums it up neatly: "Post-modern policy-making is rights-based group conflict."[33] When the values and interests of advocacy groups are opposed to those of research scientists, as is often the case, the advocacy groups intemperately attack the researchers, calling them variously torturers of animals, racists, reactionaries, dangerous radicals, destroyers of morals and the family, and so on and on.

A third reason: Nuclear power, genetic engineering, and global warming are among the products of modern science that many people find frightening; as for current scientific theory, most of it is incomprehensible to them. The result is a growing distrust and fear of science, and a readiness to believe that the social costs of its applications now outweigh its benefits; that in many ways it is bringing humankind to the brink of self-destruction (it is probably no coincidence that in 1996 in the Unabomber suspect's cabin writings were found to the effect that scientific inquiry and technological advances are ruining the world); that researchers waste vast amounts of public money on absurd projects; and that many scientists commit outright fraud, "cooking the books" (falsifying their data) in order to advance their careers. (In one recent survey, half of a sample of faculty and graduate students from four academic disciplines said they had direct knowledge of at least one case of scientific misconduct, ranging from outright fraud to sloppy record-keeping, and an article in the *New York Times*, based on the survey, was headlined "Misconduct in Science Is Not Rare, a Survey Finds"; in actual fact, the survey reported that scientific fraud had been observed by only 8 percent of the people surveyed.[34]) Finally, one other reason for public loss of faith in science is that it often fails to live up to its promises. In fields ranging from biomedicine to rehabilitation of criminals, from artificial intelligence to weather prediction, the public's great expectations of science have been deflated time and again, partly because the media have raised hopes too high, but partly because scientists themselves, caught up by their own enthusiasm, have overstated what they soon will be able to accomplish.

As a result of the widespread disaffection with science, many relatively unlearned and unsophisticated people prefer to put their faith in simpler explanations of the world such as astrology, miracles, and various brands of religious fundamentalism. And many well-read and supposedly thoughtful people, equally alarmed and baffled by modern science, subscribe to the view currently popular among the antiscience intelligentsia that scientific theories and findings are "social constructions"—that scientific objectivity is only a fiction, concealing the social values and preconceptions of scientists and science, and that, as antiscience intellectuals sometimes put it, "All knowledge is political."*[35]

Lastly, a fourth reason: With the Republican domination of both Houses of Congress in 1994, arch-conservatives had to be taken seriously when they proposed legislation that previously would have seemed an outlandish imposition on the freedom of researchers but now were piously presented as protective of the American family. One such, to be discussed later, is the Family Privacy Protection Act, passed by both House and Senate (although not yet fully in effect), which will require any federally funded researchers conducting a survey of minor children to submit their questionnaire to at least one parent of every child and get that person's written approval. Patrick O'Malley, head of Monitoring the Future survey (conducted by NORC, the National Opinion Research Corporation, which has been tracking the changing views and behavior of young people for over two decades), told me that if that proviso were strictly construed by the regulations that will eventually be formulated, "We would lose completely any ability to compare new data with former data because procedures and methods and sampling would be different, and we wouldn't know what's happening. We'd be

---

*A 1995 survey conducted by the National Science Board for the National Science Foundation found that only a minority of Americans actually hold (or at least admit to) such attitudes. But the survey also found that only 41 percent have confidence in the leaders of science and that roughly four out of every ten people feel that nuclear power, genetic engineering, and space exploration have done more harm than good (National Science Board, 1996: 7–17 through 7–19).

completely unable to mark progress or change or regress in terms of a lot of the social problems we're talking about."

So there you have four reasons for the rise of political opposition to behavioral and social research—four, though quite possibly there are others. But since this book is primarily a work of reportage, I will leave it to social analysts to tease out the other reasons from the tangled skein of social process.

The Boundaries of Freedom of Research: First Thoughts

Granted, research that harms innocent people or does things to them without informed consent should be banned, but how should we feel about research that invades no one's rights and does nothing to anyone without having his or her informed consent but is highly offensive to some group on ideological grounds? Has the researcher a right to conduct it—and is it licit for the offended group to try to suppress it?

These questions are derivatives of a larger one: Should there be any limit to free speech and expression? Justice Oliver Wendell Holmes long ago gave a classic and often-quoted answer: "The most stringent protection of free speech would not protect a man in falsely shouting fire in a theatre and causing a panic."[36] That guideline sensibly denies protection of the freedom of speech to any communication that would cause serious harm to society or any segment of it and has no legitimate purpose—note Justice Holmes' "falsely"—that outweighs the harm it would do.

That standard applies equally to freedom of scientific research. Quite apart from the protection of individual human rights embodied in the requirement of informed consent—which prevents the likes of Nazi barbarities and the Tuskegee study—no scientist should be free to conduct any project that is certain to do significant harm to society or to any group within it. But "certain" is the key word. Some of the most vociferous and even violent opponents of research on racial differences assert that all such studies demean minorities and will cause major social disorder. Black activists, civil rights advocates, and liberal and leftist whites see all research on racial differences, whatever the researcher's motives, as blatantly racist and certain to worsen racial animosity and increase conflict.

But is all scientific research on average differences between races racist and socially disruptive? Is it racist and disruptive to study the greater incidence of sickle-cell anemia in blacks than in whites? Or the difference in testis size between white males and Chinese males? (Danish males' testes average more than twice the size of those of Chinese males.[37]) Or the superiority of black athletes to white ones? (Some black activists charge that this labels the black as physically superior but mentally inferior.) Such group differences, attributable not to differences in life-chances and social advantages but to genetic determinants, do not denigrate any race or seem likely to foment social disorder. The gathering of such data may in some or even many cases have no useful purpose, but scientific research with no useful goal in mind has proven time and again to be the source of significant improvements in the general level of human health and well-being.

Since we so often fail to foresee the practical value of various research projects, we are likely to be wrong when we claim to foresee the evil social effects of research that offends us or challenges our values. This may be why people of undoubtedly high principles can make extraordinarily obscurantist judgments. The distinguished psycholinguist Noam Chomsky, for instance, has argued that some research questions ought not be investigated because it is evident that the data gathered will have ill social effects, but he never says how anyone can be certain of those effects. Some years ago, in the course of an attack on Richard Herrnstein's studies of racial differences in IQ, Chomsky wrote that every scientist "is responsible for the effects of what he does, insofar as they can be clearly foreseen. If the likely consequences of his 'scientific work' are [socially harmful] he has the responsibility to take this into account." He added, for good measure, that any objection that this implies that "society is best left in ignorance" deserves to be met with "justifiable contempt."[38]

Even a highly respected academic publisher can take a similar position. The sociologist Erich Goode offers an illuminating story:

> Anastasia Karakasidou, an anthropologist, conducted a study of ethnicity in Greece; she wrote a 300-page manuscript, entitled *Fields of Wheat, Hills of Blood,* and submitted it to the Cambridge University Press. The expert review panel whose members read the book praised it and urged publication. In December 1995, Dr. Karakasidou received some surprising news: Cambridge University Press had rejected the manuscript for publication. The reasons? The book was too controversial. It argued that many residents of Macedonia, a province of the former Republic of Yugoslavia, a region which some nationalistic Greeks consider part of Greece, speak a Slavic language and consider themselves culturally and ethnically as Slavs, not Greeks. The book would offend ultra-rightist, nationalist Greeks, and, Cambridge felt, endanger Cambridge's employees in Athens.*[39]

---

*The book was, however, published in 1997 by the University of Chicago Press. Professor Goode gives the title as *Fields of Wheat, Rivers of Blood*, but I have emended it in the above quotation to the title under which it was published.

Halpern, Gilbert, and Coren see "the frightening possibility" that,

> a field will adopt a more utilitarian position, in which researchers, as citizens of the broader society in which they work, will be asked to address the costs and benefits of dissemination of the results they obtain before releasing them. In this latter scenario, the researcher becomes a censor of scientific information.[40]

But how can the researcher know with any certainty what effects his or her findings will have? Halpern et al. point out that chlorine can be used for water purification but also as a gas to kill people, dynamite can be used to make wells and tunnels or as part of a bomb, and methods of producing attitude change can be used to encourage giving to support the needy and disadvantaged but also to promote racism and hatred.

Whatever harm a research project might result in, it may well be that greater harm would be done by closing off avenues to knowledge. Research on racial differences may offend members of a race being studied or all those who subscribe to the ethically admirable doctrine that all races are equal and all human beings are siblings under the skin. But to find racial-comparison research offensive and therefore impermissible is to blind oneself to the value of knowledge both as pure understanding and as information that might, unpredictably, lead to betterment of the condition of the offended group.

Right-wing advocacy groups and conservative members of Congress oppose the federal funding of sex surveys on the grounds that the dissemination of information about deviant practices encourages their spread, but sociologist Edward Laumann and his colleagues eloquently defend their recent sex survey (funded by a consortium of foundations):

> We contend that orchestrated ignorance about basic human behavior has never been wise public policy. Anti-intellectualism and fear are not convincing arguments against inquiry and knowledge.... As a democracy [we need] to make judgments and reach agreements about the rules by which we all will live—rules about the treatment of homosexuals, about public nudity, about sexual harassment, rape, and gender discrimination, about contraceptives, about sexually transmitted infections, and on and on. Information is imperative if we are to make wise collective judgments.[41]

Yet the possible usefulness of knowledge is only one sound reason for defending freedom of research. An equally sound reason has nothing to do with utility; it is simply that one of the most valuable of human traits is our chronic curiosity. Beginning in babyhood, we want to find out how things work, what explains what we see, what is the truth about as much of the world as our minds can experience—everything from our own thoughts to the origins of the universe. This trait, and its expression in scientific research, whether aimed at useful knowledge or simply at a deeper understanding of reality, is the mechanism that has produced the world's cultures and humankind's most notable achievements.

And therefore the ultimate rebuttal of the Know-Nothing view is that the offensiveness of a research project is neither a fair nor a sound reason for declaring that it should be stopped. Justice Holmes himself may have found that his own metaphor of shouting fire in a crowded theater could too easily be taken to justify suppression of unpopular views, and ten years later, in another opinion, he offered a wonderfully clarifying comment: "If there is any principle of the Constitution that more imperatively calls for attachment than any other it is the principle of free thought—not free thought for those who agree with us but freedom for the thought that we hate."[42]

Translating that into the realm of science: Freedom of research means freedom not only for research we find worthy, but research—if it respects the rights of the individual and is not certain to yield more harm than good—that we loathe because of what we fear it may reveal.*

---

*We will take a second look at this question at the end of this book.

Part 1

Attacks from the Left

2

The Roots of Illiberal Liberalism

Ancient Debate

A paradox, mentioned above: Science has traditionally been seen as a progressive force, emancipating humankind from beliefs and actions based on ignorance, superstition, and mysticism, and hence allied to liberal and idealistic social forces, yet many of the recent attacks on social science research have been made by liberal and leftist individuals and groups.

Although the paradox is a recent development, it is a manifestation of an intellectual debate that can be traced back to the golden age of Greece, if not even further. The issue at the heart of the debate is most commonly known by the name the British psychologist/anthropologist Francis Galton gave it in 1874—"nature and nurture"—and which he aptly summarized as follows:

> The phrase "nature and nurture" is a convenient jingle of words, for it separates under two distinct heads the innumerable elements of which personality is composed. Nature is all that a man brings with him into the world; nurture is every influence that affects him after his birth. The distinction is clear: the one produces the infant such as it actually is, including its latent faculties of growth and mind; the other affords the environment amid which the growth takes place, by which natural tendencies may be strengthened or thwarted, or wholly new ones implanted.[1]

Galton's "convenient jingle" has generally been construed as "nature *versus* nurture," since the debate has traditionally concerned whether human behavior is determined primarily by nature (heredity) or by nurture (environment and experience), the issue usually being posed in zero-sum terms—that is, on the assumption that the larger the role of one of the two forces, the smaller the other. Of late, however, many scientists have asserted either that the nature-versus-nurture issue has been resolved, or is a naïve and simplistic formulation, or in the light of recent knowledge is no longer relevant, or is obsolete and repugnant (one literary pundit calls it "old, dreary, and indecent, philosophically shabby and politically ugly").[2]

Most of which is wishful thinking. The majority of those who dismiss the controversy like to believe that it no longer has any basis for existing, but in fact it expresses an ongoing conflict between two persistent and contradictory views of human nature. Although some scientists see the question as resolved and obsolete, for many others—plus the great majority of nonscientists—it is a template of current social beliefs and a burning issue. One side or the other of the dispute, or both, are continually presented in media as dissimilar as learned journals and sensationalist tabloids, on occasions as unlike as academic conferences and barroom wrangles, and in forms ranging from formal research reports to soapbox denunciations and rowdy demonstrations. The debate may be shabby and politically ugly but it is very much alive and relevant.

Its origins are lost in the mists of the unrecorded past, but the written record shows traces of it at least as far back as the fifth century B.C. In that century, astrologers maintained (as do their present-day counterparts) that each person's nature and behavior are determined by the configuration of the heavenly bodies, and Socrates and Plato, far more rational but equally deterministic, held that knowledge exists within us from birth and that experience and reasoning merely enable us to rediscover what we already know. In contrast, Democritus, Protagoras, and their followers contended that each person's mind and knowledge are formed by perceptions (and thus, by implication, that behavior is shaped by experience).

In the seventeenth century the two opposing views of human nature began to be allied to political philosophies. The philosopher Thomas Hobbes believed that human beings are by nature selfish, competitive, and brutal, and that in order to overpower these innate biological traits so that they can live in communities, they subscribe to a social contract, giving up many of their rights and powers to a central authority, the stronger the better. Accordingly, he thought ill of democracy, preferred benign despotism, and was himself an extreme Royalist. The philosopher John Locke, on the other hand, argued that the mind of the newborn is a *tabula rasa*, a blank slate devoid of innate ideas or tendencies, on which experience and upbringing write the messages of personality and knowledge. He, too, believed that human beings live together under the terms of a social contract, but with his more optimistic view of the potential of human nature, he saw the ideal social contract as taking the form of a limited, essentially democratic, government that assures equal rights to everyone.

From then on, most of those who subscribed to a psychology of innate ideas or "nativism" were social conservatives; in simplest terms, their doctrine held that the existing social order is the natural outcome of hereditary differences in abilities and traits, and hence is justified. The adherents of associationism or "empiricism," on the other hand, tended to be liberals; they conceived of human nature as the product of experience and upbringing, and hence saw no justification for existing social inequities or inherited political power. (For convenience, from here on I shall often refer to adherents of the two sides as naturists and nurturists.)

The dichotomy is, to be sure, a great oversimplification, as are, too, the usual identifications of Alexander Hamilton and other Federalists with Hobbesian naturist political theory and of Thomas Jefferson and other Republicans with Lockean nurturist political theory, for the Founders, like most human beings, were far from consistent in their thinking. Madison, for instance, made a strong case in *The Federalist* for a conservative republican form of government but explicitly attributed social conflict to the unequal distribution of property rather than to Hobbesian innate brutishness.[3] On the opposite side, the great democrat Jefferson, though he said that no select group of men had been born "booted and spurred, ready to ride [the mass of mankind]," also said that he was grateful for the existence of a "natural aristocracy...of virtue and talent" that counterbalanced the shortcomings of others and whom "Nature has widely provided for the interests of society."[4] Late in life he wrote of blacks, "Nothing is more certainly written in the book of fate [than] that these people are to be free,"[5] yet he felt pessimistically certain that because of "deep rooted prejudices entertained by the whites; ten thousand recollections, by the blacks of the injuries they have sustained; new provocations; the real distinctions which nature has made; and many other circumstances," the two races would never be able to live together peaceably and that social convulsions would "probably never end but in the extermination of the one or the other race."[6]

Nature Ascendant

Almost all peoples believe that children are more or less shaped by the kind of upbringing they receive; at the same time, they also believe that their own group is by nature superior to the members of every other group. Although such ethnocentrism is socially valuable in that it knits the group together, it also produces some of the most detestable acts of human beings toward others, including slavery, warfare, and genocide.

When Galton, in the latter half of the nineteenth century, produced the first scientific evidence of the part nature plays in determining human personality and achievement, he did not use it to justify inhumane behavior toward people outside his country but he did see it as vindicating the class structure of British society. More idealistically, however, he also saw it as the basis of a system of improving the human race by selective breeding—much as farmers have improved livestock over the centuries—which he named "eugenics," the science of good procreation. For some decades, his research and the concept of eugenics distinctly tilted the ancient debate in a naturist direction.

Galton, born in Birmingham in 1822, inherited enough wealth at age twenty-two to spend his life as he chose, and for a while he played the part of an English gentleman of leisure, riding, shooting, attending parties, and traveling. But having a restless and inquisitive mind, he soon abandoned these idle pleasures to make himself into an independently and largely self-trained scientist.[7] In the mid-nineteenth century, it was still possible for a person without formal training in science to do important work in any of the sciences and even in several of them. Galton made important contributions to geography, meteorology (he was the first to develop weather maps from which predictions could be made), fingerprinting technology, statistics, psychology, and anthropology, and invented a number of useful devices, among them a printing telegraph, a rotary steam engine, and, because he himself was very short, a periscope for seeing over taller people in crowded places. Despite his diminutive stature, Galton's penetrating blue eyes, jutting nose, and firm slit of a mouth gave him an air of authority a far larger man might envy, and his reports of his many diverse findings conveyed his certainty that he was right. Time has, indeed, proven him more often right than not.

Of Galton's many interests and achievements, two are relevant to our concern here.

The first is his investigative work on the inheritance of "genius," as he called it, although later he said he should have called it "talent." In 1859 Charles Darwin, Galton's first cousin, had published his epochal *On the Origin of Species*, the central argument of which immensely impressed Galton. Darwin assumed that among the individuals of any species of animal there are small heritable differences (though he had no idea by what mechanism those differences were passed on from parent to offspring) and that evolution takes place by means of the natural selection of the fittest members. Galton applied this concept to human-kind, hypothesizing that the human species evolves by means of the natural selection of those who have higher intelligence and better character, these powers and traits being transmitted to their children.

This accorded with the impression he had had while at Cambridge that most of those who won high honors had honors-winning fathers and brothers. Deciding to put his hypothesis to the test, Galton pains-takingly sought out and compiled the record of all Cambridge students who had achieved top scores in classics and mathematics in the previous forty-one years and found, as he expected, that top honors tended to be won by men in certain families.[8] For the rest of his long life, the hereditary nature of intelligence and character was his major interest; he undertook a number of research projects on the matter and reported his results in four major books tracing familial ties among unusually gifted or successful people and comparing the data to the distribution of such abilities and achievements in the population at large. According to his findings, the closer the relationship between an eminent person and a relative, the greater the likelihood that the relative, too, was eminent. Galton was quite convinced that "a man's natural abilities are derived from inheritance, under exactly the same limitations as are the form and physical features of the whole organic world," and that the truly successful were neither made nor self-made but born that way:[9]

> I have no patience with the hypothesis...that babies are born pretty much alike, and that the sole agencies in creating differences between boy and boy, and man and man, are steady application and moral effort. It is in the most unqualified manner that I object to pretensions of natural equality. The experiences of the nursery, the school, the university, and of professional careers, are a chain of proofs to the contrary.[10]

Galton's findings and the statistical method known as correlation that he and the mathematician Karl Pearson developed to extract the significance of two sets of data—in this case, achievement and familial relationship—strongly tipped the scales in the nature-nurture debate toward the nature side. But because, as we will see, the scales later and for decades tipped very strongly the other way, Galton's name faded from view; today it is virtually unknown to the public and means little even to most contemporary psychologists. Nonetheless, Raymond Fancher, a historian of the discipline, holds that "few men have had greater impact on modern psychology."[11]

The other one of Galton's interests that concerns us is his advocacy of eugenics as the way to improve the average level of mental ability and the character of humankind. From 1869, when he published his first book on hereditary genius, to his death in 1911, he tirelessly promoted the concept that society should encourage the breeding of "superior" people and discourage the breeding of "inferior" ones. In his words: "[Eugenics is] the science of improving stock, which...takes cognisance of all influences that tend in however remote a degree to give to the more suitable races or strains of blood a better chance of prevailing speedily over the less suitable than they otherwise would have had."[12] He even predicted that some day people of inferior ability or character who produced children against society's better interests might be penalized in one way or another: "If these continue to procreate children inferior in moral, intellectual and physical qualities, it is easy to believe that the time may come when such persons would be considered as enemies to the State, and to have forfeited all claims to kindness."[13]

This has an appalling sound to modern ears, but Galton was not advocating imprisonment or euthanasia; he was suggesting only that some day society might deny social support to those inferior people who propagated more of their kind. (He took it for granted—as modern geneticists do not—that people of low ability or poor character can beget only more of their kind.) Galton's intent was to improve the British population by favoring the breeding of the successful, most of whom were middle or upper class; in addition, he opposed the mixing of other races with the British stock since, like most other nineteenth-century Englishmen of his class, he saw many other races as having undesirable hereditary traits:

> The Mongolians, Jews, Negroes, Gipsies, and American Indians severally propagate their kinds; and each kind differs in character and intellect, as well as in colour and shape, from the other four. They, and a vast number of other races, form a class of instances worthy of close investigation, in which peculiarities of character are invariably transmitted from the parents to the offspring.... The Negro has strong impulsive passions, and neither patience, reticence, nor dignity.... He is eminently gregarious, for he is always jabbering, quarreling, tom-tom-ing, or dancing.... [As for Jews] it strikes me that they are specialized for a parasitical existence upon other nations, and that there is need of evidence that they are capable of fulfilling the varied duties of a civilized nation by themselves.[14]

And so on.

Nor could individuals of what he called "low races," adapt to the ways of a better one; he said he knew of many instances where children of a "low race" had been reared by families of a better one, only to revert at some point to the ways and values of their biological parents.

In Galton's time, of course, and well into the twentieth century, the majority of educated Englishmen and Americans, including social scientists, were not only naturists but relied on hereditarian reasoning to justify their racist views. Charles Davenport, the biologist who is credited with bringing eugenics to the United States early in the 1900s, maintained that Poles, Irish, Italians, various other national groups, and "Hebrews" all were biologically different races and that their distinctive characteristics were hereditary. Italians, he asserted, had an innate tendency toward "crimes of personal violence" while "Hebrews" were "intermediate between the slovenly Servians [*sic*] and Greeks and the tidy Swedes, Germans, and Bohemians," and given to "thieving," though rarely to personal violence. Although he said that no race was undesirable as such, and favored a selective immigration policy that would exclude not races but families with poor hereditary history, he also predicted that the influx of immigrants from southeastern Europe would soon cause a rise in "crimes of larceny, kidnapping, assault, murder, rape, and sex-immorality."[15]

In the eleventh edition of the *Encyclopaedia Britannica* (1911), the article on the "Negro," written by Walter Francis Wilcox, a professor of social science at Cornell University, included these statements:

> Mentally, the negro is inferior to the white.... While with the latter the volume of the brain grows with the expansion of the brainpan, in the former the growth of the brain is on the contrary arrested by the premature closing of the cranial sutures and lateral pressure of the frontal bone.... The mental constitution of the negro is very similar to that of a child, normally good-natured and cheerful, but subject to sudden fits of emotion and passion during which he is capable of performing acts of singular atrocity, impressionable, vain, but often exhibiting in the capacity of servant a dog-like fidelity.

Lewis Terman, the psychologist whose 1916 "Stanford-Binet scale" was for many years the standard instrument for measuring IQ, similarly used "racial" to refer to ethnic groups and said that differences in intelligence between such races and American whites were hereditary:

> [Low intelligence] is very, very common among Spanish-Indian and Mexican families of the Southwest and also among negroes. Their dullness seems to be racial, or at least inherent in the family stocks from which they come.... [I predict that] there will be discovered enormous significant racial differences in general intelligence, differences which cannot be wiped out by any scheme of mental culture.[16]

Terman and others with such views found eugenics doctrine attractive; it seemed to them to offer a scientific solution to a multitude of social problems. Terman forecast in 1916 that in the near future, intelligence tests would bring "high-grade defectives" under "social control," and that this would "ultimately result in curtailing the reproduction of feeble-mindedness, and in the elimination of an enormous amount of crime, pauperism, and industrial inefficiency."[17]

By then, other developments were lending strong support to the cause of eugenics. Although Galton had labored for decades to establish such a movement, it had not caught on, probably because an essential piece of the concept was missing: he and Pearson had based their arguments for eugenics on the statistical analysis of traits measured in groups of people, but like Darwin he and Pearson had no idea by what mechanism the traits were passed down from parents to children. In 1900, however, three European botanists rediscovered Gregor Mendel's publications on the principles of genetics, based on the findings of his experiments, that had been published thirty-four years earlier but ignored by biologists. After their rediscovery, however, Mendelian genetic theory was swiftly adopted by biologists, and eugenics, now bolstered by a scientific explanation of how traits were transmitted from generation to generation, rapidly became a major intellectual movement. Eugenics societies were formed in a number of countries, research projects undertaken, and journals launched. In the United States top-level American universities began offering eugenics courses after 1910, and by 1928 some 20,000 students were enrolled in eugenics courses in 376 colleges and universities.[18]

Putting eugenic theory into practice, one state after another enacted laws authorizing sterilization of hereditarily "unfit" persons. In 1927, in the famous case of *Buck* v. *Bell* these laws were validated by the Supreme Court. At age eighteen, Carrie Buck, the feeble-minded daughter of a feeble-minded mother, had an illegitimate child, also rated feeble-minded at seven months of age by the biologist Harry Laughlin, superintendent of the Eugenics Record Office at Cold Spring Harbor, Long Island, a center funded by the Carnegie Institution of Washington. Under Virginia law Carrie Buck was ordered sterilized but appealed, and her case went up through the courts to the Supreme Court. The justices affirmed the state's action; the decision, written by Justice Holmes, acerbically concluded, "It is better for all the world, if instead of waiting to execute degenerate offspring for crime, or to let them starve for their imbecility, society can prevent those who are manifestly unfit from continuing their kind.... Three generations of imbeciles are enough."[19]

With sterilization thus legitimated, by 1931 a total of twenty-seven states had enacted such legislation; by the middle of that decade a total of some twenty thousand mentally and socially "defective" people had been legally sterilized in the United States and over the next two decades many more thousands were subjected to the treatment.[20]

The eugenics movement also lent intellectual support to consideration of a revised immigration bill being considered by Congress from 1922 to 1924. The House Committee on Immigration and Naturalization, dominated by conservatives, welcomed and responded to testimony by various witnesses that many immigrants from the Eastern and Southern European nations were hereditarily undesirable. This bias had gained scientific support in 1917, when Henry Goddard, director of the research laboratory of the Vineland, New Jersey, Training School for Feeble-Minded Boys and Girls, spent a week, at the behest of the United States commissioner of immigration, at Ellis Island in an effort to see whether his translation of the Binet test could identify "high-grade defectives" who should not be admitted. Picking out thirty-five Jewish, twenty-two Hungarian, fifty Italian, and forty-five Russian arriving steerage passengers who, to his eye, were neither obviously feeble-minded nor obviously normal, he tested them through interpreters, and concluded that his Binet test had successfully measured the intelligence of most of those in each group—and that most were, indeed, defective (though he did not claim that this could be generalized to the populations from which they came).[21]

Although neither Goddard nor the other major figures in the testing movement appeared before either the House or the Senate immigration committees, Laughlin presented their general interpretation of the existing testing data, along with other data on racial and ethnic differences in crime and insanity rates, to the House committee. He told the members, among other things, that immigrants from Greece, Italy, the Balkan states, and Mexico had high rates of institutionalization for crime; that "the races of northern and western Europe, more closely than the races of southern and eastern Europe, resemble the main body of the American people"; that "immigration into the United States, in the interests of national welfare, is primarily a biological problem, and secondarily, a problem in economics and charity"; and that while he was "not an advocate for or against any race," the committee "must draw its own conclusions."[22] Other testimony and documents offered to the committee included citations from Professor Carl Brigham's strongly racist book, *A Study of American Intelligence*, which drew heavily on the tests of Army conscripts in World War I and was strongly biased against Southern and Eastern Europeans. All of which amplified the wave of anti-Catholicism, anti-Semitism, and bias against Southern and Eastern Europeans following World War I; the 1924 immigration law did, in fact, reduce quotas for immigrants from those areas of Europe to less than a fifth of those for Northern and Western Europe.*[23]

* * *

It is easy to pile up such evidence showing the association of the naturist school of psychology, and especially eugenics, with bias against the lower classes and with racism.[24] But it would be a serious mistake to view naturist and eugenic theory as no more than a scientific justification for elitism and racism. The genetics of mind and character and its application in eugenics also appealed greatly to a number of liberal and reformist intellectuals who believed that their world would be greatly improved if the propagation of persons with hereditary mental deficiency and other weaknesses were halted. To social reformers and a number of progressive educators, eugenics offered a rational, scientific approach to many of the most serious problems of a complex, multicultural, industrial society.[25] As Daniel Kevles writes in *In the Name of Eugenics*:

> In 1908, the American geneticist Raymond Pearl noted that eugenics was "'catching on' to an extraordinary degree with radical and conservative alike".... In Britain, eugenics united such social radicals as Havelock Ellis, Ottoline Morrell, George Bernard Shaw, Harold Laski, and Beatrice and Sidney Webb with such establishmentarians as Leonard Darwin...and Dean William Inge of St. Paul's Cathedral.... In the United States, the eugenics movement brought together conservatives like Davenport with progressives like Gifford Pinchot, Charles R. Van Hise, Charles W. Eliot, and David Starr Jordan and radicals like Emma Goldman and Hermann J. Muller, a future Nobel laureate for his work in genetics.[26]

Margaret Sanger endorsed eugenics in 1922, though with some reservations: She said that its goal of encouraging superior people to be-

---

*How much influence the testing data and eugenic data had on the passage of the act is open to debate. Gould, 1981, and Kamin, 1974, both of whom are liberals and critics of IQ testing, assign it a major part; Snyderman and Herrnstein, 1983, conservatives and supporters of IQ testing, conclude from an examination of the hearings and the act itself that the data played only a minor role in its passage.

get more children had failed to arouse interest, but that its other goal, halting the procreation of "human beings who never should have been born at all," could be realized through birth control and would be socially of great value.[27] In 1924 the Marxist British biologist J. B. S. Haldane envisioned a utopian society of the future in which eugenic engineers would control all human reproduction to improve the makeup of humankind.[28] In the 1930s he and Muller (at that time also a Marxist), though they criticized the "mainline" eugenicists' elitism and racism, urged the use of eugenics to reduce society's burden of hereditary defects.[29] Julian Huxley, a leading biologist and a social liberal, also actively advocated eugenics in the 1930s; although critical of the conservative position on race—he said that "most so-called racial traits are in point of fact national traits"—he held that "striking and rapid eugenics results" could be achieved by the "virtual elimination of the few lowest and truly degenerate types and a high multiplication-rate of the few highest and truly gifted types.... [Eugenics] is not merely a sane outlet for human altruism, but...of all outlets for altruism that which is most comprehensive and of longest range."[30]

In 1939, Haldane, Muller, Huxley, and a number of other biologists drafted and released "The Geneticists' Manifesto," proclaiming the benefits of eugenics if practiced within a socially egalitarian society and asserting that "there can be no valid basis for estimating and comparing the intrinsic worth of different individuals without economic and social conditions which provide approximately equal opportunities for all members of society instead of stratifying them from birth into classes with widely different privileges." Genetic improvement of the world's population would be possible, the Manifesto declared, only with the abandonment of race prejudices, the legalization of birth control, and the creation of some sort of federation of the world's nations. The Manifesto saw the genetic improvement of humankind as "much more than the prevention of genetic deterioration...[namely,] the raising of the level of the average of the population nearly to that of the highest now existing in isolated individuals."[31]

Nurture Ascendant

But another manifesto, published a quarter of a century earlier, had launched a contrary movement, an extreme version of nurturism that slowly and ineluctably dominated the social sciences and became the prevailing dogma of political liberals and leftists.

The manifesto, titled "Psychology As the Behaviorist Sees It," appeared in *Psychological Review* in 1913 and was the work of John B. Watson (who would later conduct the infamous experiment on little Albert B.). Watson, like the American psychologist Edward Thorndike at Columbia University and the Russian physiologist Ivan Pavlov at St. Petersburg University, had conducted experiments with animals that investigated the phenomenon of "conditioning," the establishing of a learned connection between a given stimulus and a particular response. Of an animal's possible actions in response to the sight or smell of food, a foe, or a potential mate, the one that led to a reward was the one it learned to perform, while it learned not to respond in ways that failed to do so.

Watson, a cocky and egotistical fellow, proposed in the article and subsequent papers a radical new theory of psychology based on the elemental laws of conditioning. Psychology, he asserted, should abandon all efforts to explore the workings of the mind, consciousness, and mental states, all of which he regarded as metaphysical, conjectural, and obsolete; instead, it should study only behavior—the visible, testable connections between stimulus and response. Behaviorist psychology would be "a purely objective experimental branch of natural science" that dealt only with the overt actions of animals and humans.[32] Not only would this put psychology on a footing comparable to that of the natural sciences but it would clear away all worthless speculations about inherent or innate mental tendencies; all behavior could be understood in terms of observable learned connections between stimuli and responses—a theory that, in effect, was Locke's *tabula rasa* revived and remade in experimental terms. A decade later, Watson's sweeping denial of all naturist assertions of innate responses to stimuli led him to make a famous boast about behaviorist psychology:

> Give me a dozen healthy infants, well-formed, and my own specified world to bring them up in and I'll guarantee to take any one at random and train him to become any type of specialist I might select—doctor, lawyer, artist, merchant-chief and, yes, even beggar-man and thief, regardless of his talents, penchants, tendencies, abilities, vocations, and race of his ancestors.[33]

After a slow start, behaviorism gained favor among psychologists, especially in America; by the 1920s it was beginning to pull ahead of naturist theories and by the 1930s had moved into the forefront of academic psychology. Although developers of mental testing, child development psychologists, clinicians, and a few others were still concerned with innate and inherited traits and differences, on most campuses behaviorism was the favored and only philosophically acceptable theory. By mid-century, according to one historian of the subject, it could have cost one's career to publish any research or theoretical material not based on behaviorism or explainable in its terms.[34]

The success of behaviorist psychology was partly due to its focus on objective and observable facts rather than inferred internal mental processes; it seemed to be more genuinely scientific than most of the previous work in the field. But there were also deeper-seated reasons for its appeal to psychologists and to intellectuals in general: It spoke to the prevailing mood and outlook of twentieth-century Americans, with their profound faith that scientific knowledge could be put to practical use to improve life by making human products, human beings, and human society better than they were, and it fit in with the 1930s sympathy of liberals and radicals with socialism and the Soviet experiment, and with the belief that human nature could be remade nearer to the ideal by a more cooperative and humane society than our own.

In other social sciences, comparable nurturist views were becoming popular and eventually dominant in the 1930s. Anthropologists were inclining toward cultural relativism, the view that all cultures were equally valid and valuable; sociologists were increasingly interpreting social behavior as the result of social structure and processes, not inherent human tendencies; and even the sacrosanct behavioral and temperamental differences between the sexes were being portrayed by Margaret Mead and others as culture patterns, not inherent traits, as learned, not instinctive, behavior.

In the 1930s, the Nazi ways of practicing eugenics—forcible sterilization of hundreds of thousands of people with hereditary disorders, euthanasia by shooting or gassing of mentally ill persons, and financial subsidizing of "Aryan" parents who produced third and fourth children—so befouled the name of eugenics that the movement was all but dead in Britain and the United States only a year or two after the publishing of its Manifesto.[35] Its demise, plus the growing dominance of the behaviorist/nurturist view of human nature, caused state legislators to reconsider their eugenics laws; the state programs fell into disfavor, and after the war the laws were repealed in one state after another until by the 1960s the American experiment with eugenics was over.

* * *

During the 1930s, the overt expression of Nazi racist ideas in the form of atrocities against Jews, gypsies, and others began to make racism unacceptable in most Western countries, at least as theory, although many of the elite and most of the *Lumpen* continued to harbor their traditional prejudices and hatreds. During World War II, as word leaked out to the West about the Nazi program of "racial purification" by genocide, racism became increasingly identified with Nazism, and after the war, when the world learned in detail of the horror of the death camps, the notion that people of any race were biologically and hereditarily inferior to any other was so loathsome to most social scientists and the intelligentsia that it became unacceptable to suggest that any differences among the races—even of the most innocuous kind—were of innate origin.

The very concept of race was said by many people to be a fiction, and an unspeakably vile one. In 1950, a UNESCO committee that included the eminent biologists Muller and Julian Huxley, the economist Gunnar Myrdal, and the psychologists Hadley Cantril and Otto Klineberg promulgated a statement that was said to be the most authoritative expression of modern scientific doctrine on the controversial subject of race that had ever been issued.[36] It asserted that while there were three major subdivisions of humanity, the Mongoloid, the Negroid, and the Caucasian, race was not a reality and the term "race" should be dropped and replaced by "ethnic group":

> For all practical social purposes, "race" is not so much a biological phenomenon as a social myth.... Biological differences between ethnic groups should be disregarded from the standpoint of social acceptance and social action. The unity of mankind is the main thing.... According to present knowledge, there is no proof that the groups of mankind differ in their innate mental characteristics, whether in respect to intelligence or temperament. The scientific evidence indicates that the range of mental capacities in all ethnic groups is much the same.[37]

While this may have pleased many people of goodwill toward humankind, it sent social scientists a mixed message about research on racial differences: It approvingly alluded to scientific evidence that there are no mental or temperamental differences among ethnic groups (formerly known as races), yet implied that further such research would be worthless and should be disregarded.

Many biologists and social scientists, though they approved the moral sentiments of the statement, were distressed and angered by its disregard for evidence that contradicted its viewpoint and for its hostility to any further scientific inquiry into racial differences. There was ample evidence that differences among specified human populations did exist—not only the obvious physical traits we see, which are easily confounded by and confused with ethnic differences and have always been the basis of prejudice and race hatred, but more specific biological traits that have nothing to do with ethnicity and bolster no prejudice. Many biologists, for instance, viewed the differing percentages of populations with various forms of the Rh blood group gene as a valid basis of categorizing them as races: one form of the Rh gene is possessed by 53 percent of Basques but 0 percent of Javanese, another form by 76 percent of southern Chinese but only 4.7 percent of Bantus, and so on.[38] The eminent biologist Theodosius Dobzhansky, a thorough egalitarian and liberal, made the case for the reality of race as well as anyone could in his 1973 book *Diversity and Human Equality*:

> The population of our species is complexly subdivided into a variety of subordinate Mendelian breeding populations. In each of these, the probability of marriage within is greater than between populations.... Mendelian breeding populations within a species are more often than not overlapping, which does not make them unreal. The population of New York City has WASPs, Jews, Catholics, and blacks; wealthy, moderately well-off, poor, and destitute; educated and ignorant; people of English, Irish, Italian, Greek, and other ethnic groups, partly preserving their cultural backgrounds....
>
> All these subdivisions are not only social and economic but also biological— a fact which may not be pleasing to social scientists who would like to make their field entirely autonomous from biology. But in man sociological and biological factors are almost always intertwined.... Gene variants which control some traits, from blood groups to intelligence, may be species wide in distribution, and yet be found more frequently in some subpopulations than in others. This is not a biological technicality but a fact of cardinal ethical and political importance. [Still,] every person must be rated according to his individual qualities, regardless of the subpopulation from which his genes came.[39]

But such reasoned argument and evidence was of no avail: Race had become a forbidden topic in most of academia and in the intellectual life of the nation, and courses on race and human variability disappeared from the curricula in most colleges and universities.[40] The animus against the subject of race was so widespread and powerful by the 1970s and 1980s that, according to Sandra Scarr, a well-known research psychologist and herself a thorough liberal, scientists whose research unexpectedly turned up evidence of racial differences in any trait were likely to "try to hide such variation under the general rubric of research on children or social class or parenting practices...[even though] good psychologists are aware of the enormous research literature on race differences on nearly every behavioral measure."[41]

To this day, the thinking of many nurturists and liberals is epitomized by the assertion of one writer in the *New York Times*: "Among the ideas that have harmed mankind, one of the most durable and destructive is that the human species is divided into biological units called races and that some races are innately superior to others."[42] That statement deliberately compounds two distinct ideas—that there are such things as races, and that some races are innately superior to others—although the first does not automatically entail the second. Like that writer, in the postwar era many people so loathe the abominable acts committed because of racial hatred that they convince themselves that race is a false concept. And yet our national program of affirmative action and our complex rules of political districting, both meant to insure fairness, assume that race is a reality and put that assumption to work; with extraordinary illogicality, it is reckoned proper to use race as a determinant in social policy but improper and detestable for scientists to investigate racial traits.

A datum that nurturists find particularly appealing, since it seems to show that race must be a fiction, is that all people around the globe have well over 99 percent of the same genes. Most of those who cite this statistic are unaware that *Homo sapiens* and *Anthropopithecus troglodytes* (the chimpanzee) also have over 99 percent of genes in common, from which it should be obvious that it takes very few differences in the total complement of genes in the fertilized egg to make for significant differences in what that egg turns into.[43]

* * *

Race has been the most taboo of all subjects in the scientific domain for nearly half a century, but it is only one of a number of subjects that have been impermissible in academia and intellectual circles in this era. Almost every research topic that links any form of normal behavior to genetic propensity has been labeled hereditarian, elitist, and reactionary by nurturists; most liberal and leftist people simply feel in their bowels that such topics are wrong and evil, and are unwilling even to consider the evidence. "It's the atmosphere of our time," says the psychologist Irving Gottesman, "it's the *Zeitgeist*. It's true throughout the many facets of a university professor's life—publishing, meetings, committees, and within-department business."

From the mid-1960s on, it was distinctly risky for a scientist to do any research on the influence of biological or genetic factors in human behavior. Among the proscribed and dangerous topics were racial differences in mental abilities, the development of job ability tests (which might show racial differences), research on differences in temperament or behavior between the sexes, adoption studies that showed the extent to which adopted children reflect their biological inheritance rather than the influence of their adoptive families, and research on genetic influences on mental illness and homosexuality.

In the eyes of the nurturist majority of academics and intellectuals, all of these naturist studies were not only basically wrongheaded but harmful to society. Evan Balaban, a biologist at Harvard, told John Horgan, a senior writer at *Scientific American*, that the possible dangers of such research outweigh any benefits; as an example, he said that studies linking genes to a slightly higher risk of schizophrenia than normal were more likely to lead to discrimination by insurance companies and employers than to therapeutic benefits.[44] Richard Lewontin, another Harvard biologist, writing in the influential *New York Review of Books*, saw even greater danger in such research; he said that the claim that genetic defects lie at the basis of heart disease, schizophrenia, alcoholism, drug dependence, violent behavior, unconventional sex, and shoplifting shifts the blame for these and all sorts of other social ills and inequities from society and its power elite to the powerless and misused; ergo, such research is inherently bad.[45]

In 1984, Lewontin and two colleagues, in a book attacking "biological determinist" research, *Not in Our Genes*, were quite candid about the political nature of their hostility to it:

> We share a commitment to the prospect of the creation of a more socially just a socialist society. And we recognize that a critical science is an integral part of the struggle to create that society, just as we also believe that the social function of much of today's science is to hinder the creation of that society by acting to preserve the interests of the dominant class, gender, and race.[46]

Although the fiery demonstrations of the 1960s and early 1970s, some of them aimed at researchers inquiring into the forbidden topics, have for the most part died down, the hostility of blacks, feminists, liberals, and radicals toward research on the biological and genetic influences on human behavior has not. The faculties of today's educational institutions are largely drawn from the ranks of the impassioned students of that turbulent era; political correctness, a major force on many if not most campuses to this day and the embodiment of nurturism at its extreme, carries on the warfare, as later chapters of this book will show.

One small recent episode will exemplify the level of antipathy toward research on the taboo topics. In June, 1995, at the annual meeting of the Behavior Genetics Association (BGA), its outgoing president, Glayde Whitney of Florida State University, delivered his presidential address, "Ideology and Censorship in Behavior Genetics." In it he reviewed the history of what he referred to, unwisely and unfairly, as "Left-Liberal Marxist dogma of environmental determinism" (unfairly, because few liberals and only some leftists are Marxists). Challenging the notion that race is necessarily an elitist concept and devoid of scientific merit, he presented a series of statistical comparisons of murder rates for blacks and whites which showed the black rate to be several times that of the white rate. From the data, he concluded, "Like it or not, it is a reasonable scientific hypothesis that some, perhaps much, of the race difference in murder rate is caused by genetic differences in contributory variables such as low intelligence, lack of empathy, aggressive acting out, and impulsive lack of foresight."[47]

In the middle of Whitney's talk, Jim Wilson, the president-elect, walked out; afterward and for the rest of the conference Whitney was shunned by many colleagues and scolded by others. The Executive Committee of BGA issued an official denunciation of his talk, the editor of its journal, *Behavior Genetics*, refused, contrary to custom, to publish it, a number of BGA's officers and members condemned Whitney on BGA's electronic bulletin board, and quite a few others called for his resignation. None of this involved scientific rebuttal; it was all a purely political response to politically repellent research data. Whether or not Whitney's data and suggestions have any scientific merit is beside the point; the important issue is that the presentation of research data and inferences from them that conflict with the nurturist position on race was seen by the majority of members of BGA—the very scientists one would suppose able to dispassionately appraise such data—as unacceptable and requiring his condemnation and ostracism.

Nature Redivivus

From the 1960s on, however, a quiet undercurrent of research on the biological and genetic determinants of behavior was being swelled by a series of discoveries and breakthroughs and by the 1980s it had become a torrent.

Some of the discoveries linked specific ailments or behavioral tendencies to physiological rather than psychological causes. A few examples:

• Tourette syndrome, a behavioral disorder characterized by tics, grunting and barking, echolalia and coprolalia (the compulsive repetition of dirty words), had long been interpreted as a psychological malady of anal-sadistic and perhaps erotic origin, yet no form of psychotherapy was of any avail. By the 1970s, however, physiologists discovered EEG abnormalities and other organic indications of an organic, and probably hereditary, source of the syndrome, and indeed the condition proved to be remarkably improved in 90 percent of Tourette cases by the administration of haloperidol, a strong dopamine blocker, suggesting that the brain neurons of Tourette sufferers were hereditarily predisposed toward abnormal dopamine uptake.[48]

• A series of studies, also conducted in the 1970s, found that alcohol causes a pronounced flush in American Indians but not in American Caucasians and that the former metabolize alcohol considerably more slowly than the latter. This suggested that the social inequities that Amerindians suffer were not the sole cause of their high rate of alcoholism, but that the stresses of their lives interact with their special physiological vulnerability to the effects of alcohol.[49]

• Aggression had long been understood in psychodynamic terms as the result of frustration, anger, inadequate socialization, and so on, but in the 1960s and 1970s animal experiments found that the administration of testosterone induced aggressive behavior; from these data it was inferred that animals or humans whose genotype favored high testosterone levels were likely to be particularly aggressive.[50]

• Overeating had been conceptualized by psychotherapists almost entirely in terms of psychological motivation—a self-comforting response to feelings of deprivation, loneliness, and low self-esteem. But by the 1970s, biologists had discovered that certain opioid peptides produced by the brain, most notably cholecystokinin (CCK), were the chemical mechanism governing the motivation, and that the administration of CCK to animals and humans alleviated hunger and suppressed feeding. It appeared, therefore, that in at least some overeaters, the behavior might be due to a genetically or developmentally inadequate production of CCK.[51]

These exemplify the many small, special findings of biochemical research that were beginning to offer physiological and genetic explanations of forms of behavior that had been previously accounted for solely as the result of life experiences. As a review article put it in 1984: "A renewed interest in sensory control and hedonics...indicates that we are viewing motivational processes in a broader perspective. We now see an increased awareness, at least in some areas, that genotype is an important variable...[and note] a rapid growth of interest in the biochemistry of behavior."[52]

In the 1980s, a very different kind of research, begun by Galton more than a century earlier, began to provide remarkable new evidence of the extent of genetic influences on behavior and abilities. This was the study of twins, in particular, identical twins reared apart; if their upbringing was notably or even somewhat different, they should develop differently—unless genetic identity caused them to develop personalities and abilities as alike as their looks. In the 1870s Galton, writing to a wide circle of acquaintances, was able to locate ninety-four sets of twins, thirty-five pairs of whom looked very much alike. At the time, lacking any knowledge of Mendelian genetics, he could not accurately discriminate between identicals, who have exactly the same set of genes, and fraternals, who have half their genes in common; he did, however, pose the question in terms close to those it would take in more modern research:

> It occurred to me that the after-history of those twins who had been closely alike as children, and were afterwards parted, or who had been originally unlike and afterwards reared together, would supply much of what was wanted.... The evidence was overwhelming that the power of Nature was far stronger than that of Nurture, when the Nurture of the persons compared were not exceedingly different.[53]

In this century, a number of small studies of identical twins reared apart—genetic knowledge now makes it possible to be precise about the kind of twins being studied—have replicated and greatly refined Galton's conclusions; such twin studies are an important source of data in the contemporary field known as behavior genetics. Of the numerous twin studies carried out in recent decades, one of the largest and most productive in findings has been conducted at the Minnesota Center for Twin and Adoption Research at the University of Minnesota. Since 1979, when its director, the psychologist Thomas J. Bouchard, Jr., began the project, he and his associates have collected detailed data on thousands of twins and studied most closely seventy-eight pairs of identicals reared apart, fifty-six pairs of fraternals reared apart, and for comparison, several hundred identicals reared together and several hundred fraternals reared together.* All twins underwent about fifty hours

---

*"Several hundred": The total number of identical and fraternal twins reared together varies by test; the data have been gathered by mail and the number of valid replies received varies. On the Multidimensional Personality Questionnaire, the Center has 553 monozygotic (MZ) and 459 dizygotic (DZ) twins reared together, while on a vocational interest questionnaire it has 512 MZ and 390 DZ twins reared together. Personal communication from Dr. Bouchard.

of intensive tests and interviews, and the same procedures were carried out with a number of identical and fraternal pairs reared together. One can hardly conceive of a more ideal natural experiment for appraising the relative influence of heredity and of environment.

Bouchard and his team found that most pairs of identical twins who had been separated at or soon after birth and reared under different circumstances not only looked strikingly alike in adulthood and even old age,* but, far more interestingly, were also astonishingly alike as to IQ, traits of personality, tastes, and even habits—far more so than fraternal twins reared together. Bouchard's very first case, indeed, has often been cited in popular accounts of his work because of the almost incredible similarities of the two brothers involved. The "Jim twins," as they came to be known, were identicals who had been separated at birth and met only thirty-nine years later; at that time they not only looked almost identical, but both had been married twice, first to a woman named Linda, then to one named Betty; named their firstborn child James; gone on vacations to the same Florida beach, worked part-time in law enforcement; and shared a taste for the same brands of beer and cigarettes.[54]

Such stories make for entertaining pop-science writing, and although Bouchard and his colleagues prefer to avoid such anecdotal tidbits in their journal articles, they have occasionally reported some believe it or-not similarities. In a recent paper, they cite one pair of reared-apart male twins both of whom were gifted raconteurs of amusing stories; another pair both of whom resolutely avoided expressing opinions on controversial topics; a female pair who were habitual gigglers, though there were no gigglers in the families they were reared in; a male pair both of whom used Vademecum toothpaste, Canoe after-shave, Vitalis hair tonic, and Lucky Strike cigarettes; and a female pair both of whom refused to enter an acoustically shielded chamber in Bouchard's laboratory unless the door was wired open, and at the beach entered the water backwards and only up to their knees.[†55]

Relating such curiosities is not the business of Bouchard et al.; their goal is to establish the correlations of abilities and traits in their twin

---

*Identicals can, however, differ slightly in some physical traits, including fingerprint patterns and susceptibility to multifactorial diseases (Shattuck 1996: 214).

†A rare exception—not part of the Minnesota study—is the case of Claude Steele and Shelby Steele, identical black twins and both successful academics; Claude, a psychologist, is a liberal, Shelby, an English professor, is a conservative, and the two do not speak to each other.

pairs and, by means of the differences in the correlations of identicals reared apart and together, and of fraternals reared apart and together, to derive a measure of the genetic influence on intelligence and on five clusters of traits of personality: extraversion, neuroticism, conscientiousness, agreeableness, and openness. Their findings are in good accord with the findings of a number of other researchers using twin pairs in comparable research.[56]

The crucial datum resulting from their measurements and statistical analyses is the percent of variance in personality traits that can be ascribed to genetic influence. Variance means the range of differences in any measured particular: If individuals in a given sample range from, say, extremely neurotic to totally healthy, and if the width of that dispersion or spread is due half to genetic influence rather than to upbringing and other environmental influences, the variance due to heredity is said to be 50 percent. Bouchard recently summed up the Minnesota data in a brief report in *Science* as follows:

> The most parsimonious fit to the Minnesota data is a simple additive genetic model for all five traits with an estimate of genetic influence of 46%.... [and] of shared environmental influence [of] 7%. Of the remaining variance, about half is due to nonshared environmental influences, and half to error of measurement. Thus, about two-thirds of the reliable variance in measured personality traits is due to genetic influence.[57]

Bouchard and others who conduct behavior-genetics twin studies have come under repeated and severe attacks by liberals and leftists. In the early years of his project, Bouchard was attacked by SDS activists on campus; they labeled him a racist in their handouts, linked his name with "German fascism," spray-painted slogans calling him a Nazi on campus walls, and demanded that he be fired.[58] Bouchard, who apparently has a cast-iron stomach and who had the university administration's support, stood fast and survived the attacks, which eventually died out. But liberal scholars have continued to assail his work at forums and in print. In one such article, Barry Mehler, a professor at Ferris State University in Michigan, set the tone by mentioning that Dr. Josef Mengele conducted experiments with twins at Auschwitz and going on to say that Bouchard "rehabilitated this line of research," that he had never released his data and methods for objective scrutiny (an outright lie; Bouchard and colleagues have published numerous papers in peer-reviewed journals), and that "Bouchard has cautiously refrained from making public statements that might be construed as racist," the implication being that Bouchard is a closet racist.[59] Bouchard, who is proud that he went to prison for a day in the 1960s as a participant in the Berkeley Free Speech Movement and says he would do so again today, considers the political correctness movement, epitomized by Mehler's attack, to be "antithetical to the Free Speech Movement and...a very serious threat to the entire intellectual enterprise."[60]

The reared-apart twin studies are, obviously, adoption studies, since at least one twin, and often both, were brought up in families other than those of their biological parents. But other kinds of adoption studies—the adoption of non-twins into homes of a different class, ethnic background, or even race than that of the biological parents—were also proving to be a fertile source of data on the relative influences of genetics and environment on mental abilities and personality. Such studies can cast more light on the similarities of children to those who rear them than studies of children reared by their own biological parents, since in the latter the influences of genetics and environment are confounded. Adoption-study design, according to psychologist/geneticist Robert Plomin and social ecologist Denise Daniels, "powerfully cleaves these two sources of family resemblance."[61] And indeed adoption studies have furnished some startling findings: A historic early one (1949) found no correlation between the IQs of adoptees and their adoptive parents but a correlation of .38 with their biological mothers, and four others conducted in the 1970s and 1980s yielded a very low average correlation (.05) in personality traits of adoptees and their adoptive parents but a considerably higher correlation (.15) with their biological parents.[62]

A particularly interesting but politically controversial subspecies of adoption studies has involved transracial adoption. A datum deeply troubling to most social researchers but established beyond question by many studies in the 1960s and 1970s was that black children reared by their own families averaged 15 points lower in average IQ scores than white children reared by their own families.[63] Naturally, there were two clashing explanations of this, the naturist and the nurturist. Since any useful remedy of the low black IQ and its effects on school achievement and eventual employment would have to be based on the correct explanation, Sandra Scarr and Richard Weinberg conducted a study of 101 white Minnesota families into which 130 black children had been adopted. Scarr and Weinberg, whose 1950s and 1960s education had been thoroughly environmentalist, knew that in investigating this matter they were treading dangerous ground; as Scarr later wrote:

> For those of us who have incorporated race into research designs, there is great danger in the outcome. If one deliberately sets out to investigate racial or gender

differences that have unfavorable possibilities for the underdog, one is in danger of ostracism and worse from one's well-intentioned colleagues. The messenger with the bad news seems to be blamed for having invented the message.[64]

She even told her friends that if the results showed a substantial relationship between black ancestry and low intellectual skills, she was prepared to emigrate rather than endure what Arthur Jensen had experienced at the hands of his colleagues.*[65]

The findings of the Scarr and Weinberg study actually furnished support for both sides of the question. On the one hand, being brought up in middle-class white homes had a distinctly beneficial effect on the IQs of black children; on the other, the adopted children never reached parity with their white adoptive parents or their white adoptive siblings. Here are the findings, in brief:[66]

• The average IQ of adopted children, 106, was 15 points higher than the national average for black children reared in their own homes in that region, and higher than the IQs of their biological parents.

• The adopted children's average IQ was distinctly lower than that of their adoptive parents (119) and the biological children of those parents (117).

• The adopted children's school achievement was comparable to their IQ scores.

Because the social background of the biological mothers of the adopted children influenced how early and by whom the children were adopted, and because some of the children were of mixed parentage (one white and one black parent), the study was not a clear-cut demonstration of the influence of genetics and environment on IQ; it did, however, indicate that both influences were at work—and that neither had a merely trivial effect, a conclusion that remained true in a ten-year follow-up study of the same children.[67] But Scarr and another colleague summed up one crucial finding of the 1976 and similar studies quite plainly: "Adopted children on the average have IQ scores above those of their biological parents, yet the *correlations* of adopted children are higher with their biological than adoptive parents."[68]

A curious and counter-intuitive finding of later studies by Scarr and Weinberg and other researchers was that in terms of personality measurements, transracial adoptees came to resemble their adoptive parents *less*, not more, by their adolescence than during their childhood;

---

*Jensen's story appears in chapter 3.

this suggested that genetics plays an increasingly large role in the course of personality development.[69] Similarly, personality tests of children at various ages show that siblings become more and more dissimilar in middle and later childhood; some of this divergence may be due to "nonshared" experiences within and outside the home, but some, perhaps much, is likely to be the expression of innate, unfolding personality traits.[70]

Scarr and Weinberg interpreted their 1976 data cautiously, saying that the roles played by the social and biological variables could not be clearly or precisely compared, but in the eyes of a number of liberal colleagues they had done a bad thing. One critique in a leading journal called their study scientifically slovenly, reactionary in its interpretation, and derogatory to blacks in that it suggested they would do better by their children to raise them according to white standards.[71] Another admitted that Scarr was a "centrist, a moderate, and a liberal" in the IQ debate but faulted the study on data-analytic grounds and found it socially and scientifically valueless, and politically reactionary:

> Though in other contexts Scarr has recognized that social rewards need not, and perhaps ought not, to be contingent on "heritable" differences, it seems to me that the basic social function of research in IQ heritability is…to attribute the inequitable distribution of worldly goods to "genetic" causes…[and so] to legitimize it.[72]

* * *

A quite different genre of research that investigates the influence of innate personality tendencies is the longitudinal study of human development. A major study, conducted by a team at the University of California's Institute of Human Development at Berkeley, tracked 200 children from infancy to age thirty; at the outset, the researchers predicted that the children in troubled homes would become troubled adults, those in happy, secure homes would become happy, secure adults, but a generation later, two-thirds of the predictions proved to be wrong. As psychologist Jean Macfarlane reported, many children who had had "easy and confidence-inducing lives" became "brittle, discontented, and puzzled adults," while many others who had had "severely troubled and confusing childhoods and adolescences" became "mature and competent adults."[73] A reasonable interpretation was that the child's own innate strengths or weaknesses played a far larger part in the end result than anyone had realized.

Another longitudinal study was focused on "temperament"—the built-in tendency, either genetic or acquired during development in the womb, or both, for a child to react in a characteristic way to stimuli and new situations. Two psychiatrists, Drs. Alexander Thomas and Stella Chess of New York University Medical Center, began observing the behavior of newborns in the 1940s and followed them over the years. They found that about two-thirds of newborns exhibit a characteristic temperament early in infancy: Some are more active than others; some have regular rhythms of eating, sleeping, and defecating while others are irregular; some like new food while others do not; some are happy most of the time and others unhappy; and so on. Summing up, Thomas and Chess reported that four out of ten are "easy" (placid and adaptable), one out of ten is "difficult" (irritable and hard to pacify), and one out of six is "slow to warm up" (moderately fussy or apprehensive but able to get used to things and people).[74]

These differences are deep-seated and lasting: Thomas and Chess, tracking the individuals over the years, noted that in general they continued to behave in their own temperamental styles throughout childhood and adolescence. Not in all cases, to be sure; some or much of a child's basic temperament could be modified by a major event (a serious accident or illness, death of a parent, a dramatic alteration in family finances). But when there were no such events in a child's life or changes in the environment, the temperamental style of the first days of life was apt to be the temperamental style of the grown person.[75]

* * *

In the mid-1950s, the use of psychotropic drugs to control psychotic symptoms and behavior had revolutionized the treatment of the mentally ill, but psychiatrists had no idea how the drugs did what they did. By the 1970s, however, neurophysiologists had begun spelling out the precise actions of neurotransmitter molecules in the normal brain; it became clear that in all sorts of mental processes and emotional states, specific neurotransmitter molecules conveyed the appropriate messages across the synaptic gaps between brain neurons. It also became clear that in emotional and mental disorders, something was amiss in neurotransmission: A particular neurotransmitter might be produced in too great or too little quantity, the dendritic receptors toward which the neurotransmitter molecules were drawn might be plugged up by some other brain-produced chemical, and so on. With this, researchers began to understand and spell out how the various psychotropic drugs worked: Sometimes they would increase the production of a needed neurotransmitter that was in short supply, sometimes absorb molecules of a neurotransmitter in oversupply or occupy some of the receptors to which it gravitated, and so on. Distortions of thought and mood were beginning to be understood in terms of the physiological processes that underlay them.

Even more basic research on the biological sources of human behavior became possible after 1953, when Francis Crick and James Watson reported their discovery of the molecular structure of DNA, and after the 1960s, when others cracked the genetic code and showed that the sequence in which the nucleotide bases making up each gene are strung together determines the production of amino acids, the basic building blocks of the body's proteins and enzymes. Since then, by identifying particular "markers"—DNA fragments of a recognizable size and makeup—microbiologists have been able to identify the particular genes responsible for certain single-gene diseases such as cystic fibrosis and Duchenne muscular dystrophy.[76]

For a time, molecular geneticists hoped to be able to identify the genes responsible for specific personality traits or kinds of human behavior. It turned out to be a simplistic hope. Genetic studies (of hereditary patterns) and DNA analysis have shown that most human traits are complexly determined by the linked action of a number of genes and, in most cases, the simultaneous and interacting influence of environment. It seems most likely, as of now, that in each individual, many genes make small contributions that add up to the individual's predisposition or tendency toward specific traits and behavioral tendencies.[77] Despite the high hopes of many molecular genetics researchers, most complex human behaviors such as the traits of temperament and intelligence, and complex disorders such as bipolar disorder (manic depression) and alcoholism, have not been tied to any individual genes; yet there are strong indications in twin and familial studies that they are often, though not always, genetically based. In some people, the genetic influence is strong enough that it takes no great environmental stress to elicit the trait or behavior, in others, it appears only under considerable environmental influence.[78]

But as molecular genetic research advances, it is almost certain to target and identify the polygenic linkages responsible for traits and disorders that are of genetic predisposition, and for the interplay of those linked genetic influences with experience and environment. Given the speed of current advances in molecular genetics research, Plomin writes,

> the safest bet is that at the turn of the century, researchers will be investigating multiple-gene influences for complex dimensions and disorders.... [and] DNA

markers will be found that are associated with behavioral traits.... [Molecular genetics] will revolutionize behavioral genetics...investigating multivariate and longitudinal genetic issues, the links between the normal and abnormal, and interactions between genotype and environment.[79]

Resolutions

In one sense, a resolution to the nature-nurture debate has emerged in recent years, at least among many of the most knowledgeable. Daniel Koshland, the editor of *Science,* the most influential peer-reviewed journal in the U.S., said in a recent editorial that the nature-nurture debate is basically over.[80]

But the resolution has not been the result of the victory of one side or the other; Plomin, himself both psychologist and geneticist, writes:

Is there a single scientist today who truly believes in either the hereditarian or environmentalist extreme? A century of research in the field of behavioral genetics has shown that genetic influence is significant and substantial for most areas of behavioral development...[and that] for some traits such as cognitive abilities, genetic differences among individuals can account for about half of the variance in test scores.... Nonetheless, if genetic differences account for half of the variance, this means that genetic differences do not account for the other half.... I would argue that behavioral genetic research has provided the best available evidence for the importance of the environment.[81]

The flood of new behavioral-genetic findings has not swept away environmentalist psychology, nor have the many recent advances in developmental psychology and cognitive science overwhelmed hereditarian explanations of behavior. Instead, a number of researchers trained both in mainstream psychology and behavior genetics have been developing a new and sophisticated form of interactionist theory.

Interaction, in its early naïve form—the zero-sum view mentioned earlier—held that genetics and other biological factors comprised some of the influences on the development of the human mind and personality, experience and environment the rest; how much each contributed depended on the biases and methodology of the researcher. The new concept of interaction is radically different; based on a wealth of recent empirical findings, it sees genes and environment as interacting in a multitude of ways, with the relative roles of genes and environment, and their combinations, varying widely. and the interaction changing in character as the organism develops.

Any home gardener knows that a particular variety of tomato plant will grow tall and produce large, delicious tomatoes, provided sun, water, and nutrients are in good supply, while if they are not, the plant will be either leggy or stunted and produce only smallish and relatively flavorless fruit. Another hardier variety, however, that yields only small and bland tomatoes, may have a much narrower range of variation across differing conditions.

With human beings, the interaction of genetics and environment is analogous, though vastly more complex. A simplistic example of one way the interaction works is that an "easy" infant (in Thomas and Chess's terms) is apt to elicit different parental behavior than a "difficult" infant; the two infants' differing experiences of parental behavior—induced by their own genetic propensities—are significant environmental influences shaping the further development of their personalities. Similarly, at the adult level people create their own environments by the way they behave, then respond to the impacts of those created environments. There is, in other words, a feedback mechanism in the new view of interaction: Genetic tendencies are causes of effects in the environment, but those effects become causes of changes or development in the individual's innate capabilities.[82]

Another way interaction works is that genetic tendencies cause different individuals to seek out those aspects of the environment with which they are comfortable, live in them, and react to the environment they have chosen for themselves. Bouchard and colleagues put it succinctly several years ago: "The proximal cause of most psychological variance probably involves learning through experience, just as radical environmentalists have always believed. The effective experiences, however, to an important extent are self-selected, and that selection is guided by the steady pressure of the genome."[83] More recently Bouchard has epitomized the process in a striking epigram: "The term nature vs. nurture should perhaps be replaced by the term nurture via nature."[84]

But Plomin provides a note of caution: "People *to some extent* choose their environments; the environments chosen are *influenced by*, not 'determined by,' the genotypes of those who choose. Moreover, many environments are not chosen as much as imposed."[85]

This is one of three kinds of genotype-environment interaction that have been spelled out as hypotheses, and to some extent tested empirically, over the past two decades by Plomin, Scarr, Bouchard, and others. Scarr and McCartney summed them up in 1983 as follows:

> The process by which children develop is best described by three types of genotype → environment effects: a *passive* kind, whereby the genetically related parents provide a rearing environment that is correlated with the genotype of the

child (sometimes positively and sometimes negatively); an *evocative* kind, whereby the child receives responses from others that are influenced by his genotype; and an *active* kind that represents the child's selective attention to and learning from aspects of his environment that are influenced by his genotype and indirectly correlated with those of his biological relatives.[86]

That paradigm has been refined, expanded, and applied to adult behavior in a seven-hypothesis theory by Plomin.[87] The details are beyond the scope of this book, but the core concept is still the same: Genetic tendencies and environment interact in a number of feedback patterns such that no simple additive theory of heredity and environment, each contributing a part of the final effect, is adequate; rather, in a step-by-step process, individual development follows a course, as does individual behavior, that is the unique product of each individual's unfolding responses to his or her interactions with his or her environment.

All of which is neatly exemplified in this hypothetical graphic representation of the various combinations of genotype and environment in the development of IQ:

FIGURE 2.1

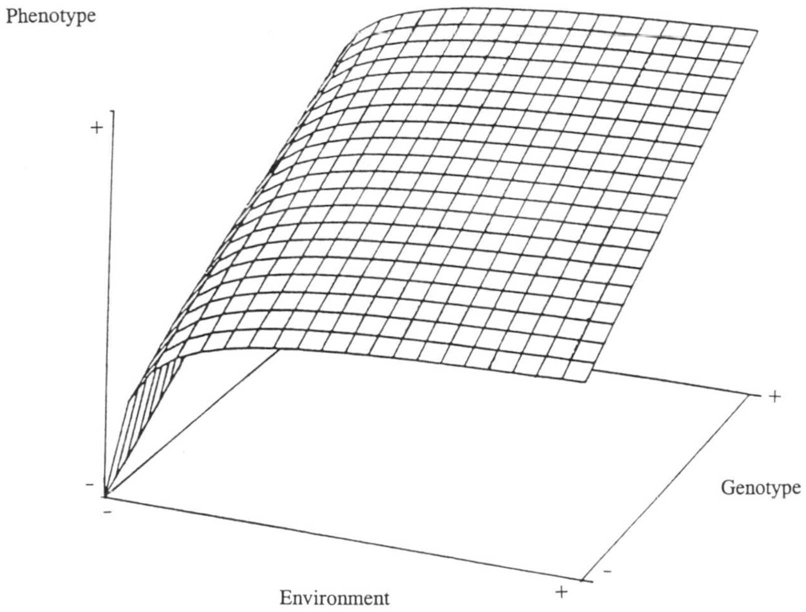

Hypothetical reaction surface for intelligence, showing a positive linear slope along the genetic axis and sharp decline in the range of very poor environments.

Source: Figure 1 from Turkheimer and Gottesman, 1991, p. 108, by permission.

The above figure suggests the possibilities when various genotypes exist within different environments. From front to back, genotypes range from poor to very good; from left to right, these develop within environments ranging from poor to very good. The curve nearest the viewer represents the low order of development of a poor genotype, reaching only a slightly higher level of development in the best environment than in the worst one. In contrast, a very good genotype, though it achieves only a low development in the poorest environment (the low end of the curve is hidden from view but easily imagined), reaches a very high level under good to excellent environmental conditions.*[88]

One other note of resolution: Eugenics, under a dark cloud for many years, has revived in a new and more socially acceptable form. Both geneticists and physicians are in general agreement with the view of eugenicists of the prewar era that modern medicine, in prolonging the life of many people with serious hereditary illnesses, is nullifying the process of natural selection and producing an ever-increasing "genetic load" (Muller's term) that society must bear. But instead of advocating the eugenics measures of the past such as sterilization, voluntary abstention from procreation, and euthanasia, today the modus operandi is genetic counseling. Through family histories, biochemical tests, and DNA analysis, genetic counselors can tell a couple who suspect they harbor recessive genes for such grave hereditary disorders as Tay Sachs disease, sickle cell anemia, and cystic fibrosis what the chances are that a child they would conceive might inherit such genes from both of them and so fall prey to the disease. But the couple, when so advised, are still free to decide for themselves whether to take the risk or not (some ethicists, however, argue that this pays too little attention to communal and social welfare).[89] In consonance with the new functions of eugenics, the word eugenics disappeared years ago from the names of organizations, publications, and university departments and was replaced by inoffensive terms such as "human genetics," and in 1972 the American Eugenics Society renamed itself the Society for the Study of Social Biology.

* * *

This section began with the statement: "In one sense, a resolution to the nature-nurture debate has emerged in recent years," and has sketched

---

*The assertive cognitive scientist Steven Pinker of MIT says that interaction is so bad an idea it can't even be said to be wrong, but he is in a distinct minority, perhaps even a minority of one.

out the terms of that resolution. But in a different sense of the word, the resolution of hardliners in both camps has remained firm.

Many deeply committed behavior geneticists talk as if much or most of human behavior—sexual preferences, child-rearing practices, problem-solving ability, mental disorders and addictions, prosocial behavior, and all forms of antisocial and criminal behavior—is very largely gene-directed. Significant segments of the American population are not only convinced hereditarians but rely on this orientation to justify their biases against blacks, Orientals, Hispanics, Jews, and others, and reactionary policies toward women and gays. Not only the extremist militias and other radical rightists but even some professors at major universities consider some races distinctly inferior to the white race and see affirmative action and uncontrolled immigration as causes of an impending and disastrous decline of American society.[90]

On the opposite side, many liberal and leftist environmentalists continue to regard the findings of behavior genetics as implausible, elitist, racist, sexist, unscientific, and socially destructive. Dorothy Nelkin, a sociology professor at New York University, and her co-author, Susan Lindee, in a 1995 polemic called *The DNA Mystique*, write:

> The idea of genetic predisposition encourages a passive attitude toward social injustice, an apathy about continuing social problems, and a reason to preserve the status quo.... Biological narratives...attributing social differences to genetic differences, are especially problematic in a society that tends to overstate the powers of the gene.[91]

After Nelkin attended a conference on genetics and crime (to be described in chapter 5), she wrote, in a *New York Times* op-ed piece, that behavior genetics is ammunition for reactionaries: "By making social factors irrelevant, genetic explanations of crime provide convenient excuses for those seeking to dismantle the welfare state."[92]

Richard Lewontin, the Harvard biologist cited earlier as co-author of *Not in Our Genes*, a wholesale attack on behavior genetics, sees his role and that of others who fiercely oppose hereditarianism as heroic:

> There has been, since Lombroso,* a major intellectual industry tracing the [innate] causes of social inequality between classes, races, and the sexes. A vast literature has been created and, in reaction, a smaller group of debunking critics of biological determinism has emerged in what those of us involved liken to the

---

*Cesare Lombroso (1836–1909), the Italian founder of the science of criminology; see also chapter 5.

work of a volunteer fire department. No sooner has one blaze set by intellectual incendiaries been doused by the cool stream of critical reason, then [*sic*] another springs up down the street.[93]

The great debate may be resolved in the minds of many researchers and others who are deeply conversant with current knowledge and theory, but it is not resolved elsewhere in academe or in the thinking segment of the American population, and surely not in the far larger unthinking segment. The debate goes on, and on.

Debate, in itself, is not an ill. One might wish there were a tranquil end to the heated charges and countercharges but heated words have always been part of the scene in the marketplace of ideas. What is an ill, however, is the effort by partisans of any position in the debate to stifle or prevent the expression of opinions by the other side and particularly to block or forbid the efforts of researchers whose possible findings they view with fear or revulsion.

Scientists, Bouchard has recently written,

> must be free of ideology, we must be free from but not disrespectful of cultural conventions, and we must stand in doubt of all conventional wisdom. This process is like a long and difficult journey. If we take it we will at times face great difficulties. Its demands will, on occasion, isolate us from friends and loved ones. It won't necessarily make us happy, it is unlikely to lead us to riches, but it will make us free. We will own our own mind and our own soul. It is a worthwhile journey, it is the journey of scholarship and science as opposed to the journey of ideology.[94]

Some years ago Sandra Scarr defended, in words that deserve to live, the right of researchers to go where their intellectual curiosity leads them. Replying to Leon Kamin, a passionately antihereditarian psychologist at Princeton who believes that knowledge about genetic differences in behavior poses a grave danger to society, she wrote:

> In my view, there is no danger so great as the suppression of knowledge. There is nothing we could learn about ourselves that would justify abridgment of scientific inquiry. There are methods of investigation that pose unconscionable threats to the participants in research. Methods should be subject to regulation. But there should be no regulation of scientists' rights to think, propose, and conduct ethical investigations on any question, however distasteful it might be to others.[95]

Since that expresses as well as any words I can think of what I believe and what is the central message of this book, it is time to conclude this review of the great nature-nurture debate and turn to our case histories of the efforts of the new Know-Nothings to stamp out research that they see as dangerous to their beliefs and ways.

3

The IQ Wars

Swamp

When I mentioned to a leading social scientist and friend that I was doing research for this chapter, he said, "Stay away from it. The genetics of intelligence is bound to drag you into race differences in intelligence, and that's a swamp in which you can sink and perish."

Swamp? Perhaps a better metaphor is long-term war. Ever since Alfred Binet's intelligence tests were brought to this country, the enthusiastic proponents and vitriolic opponents of such testing—there are few neutrals on the matter—have been fiercely embroiled with each other. Of the various issues they have fought about, the most hotly contested has always been whether IQ tests measure hereditary ability or acquired competency, and a correlate of that issue has been the hate-engendering one of whether racial differences in IQ are of genetic origin. From the start, one side has regarded intelligence research and testing as scientific and socially valuable, the other as pseudoscientific and worthless—or, rather, pernicious because of the conservative social views of many of those who believe in it.

The earliest conflict, during the 1910s, concerned the use of Terman's Stanford-Binet test in schools, but this was mere skirmishing. As it became clear that the United States would become embroiled in World War I, the Army, facing the huge problem of how best to utilize two million conscripts, enlisted the aid of a team of psychologists who hastily constructed two tests, to the use of which there was no resistance, perhaps because objections would have been deemed unpatriotic.

Many an objection, however, was voiced after the war, when the Army tests set off an explosive expansion of intelligence testing in civilian life. The two tests, the Alpha (verbal) and Beta (pictorial, for illiterates), had been given to nearly all the conscripts, and on the basis of the results many thousands of low-scoring soldiers had been assigned to menial duties in labor battalions and the like, while some 200,000 who did well had become commissioned officers. The psychologists who designed the Alpha and Beta, and other advocates of testing, regarded these outcomes as legitimate and socially beneficial, but postwar critics charged that the tests had been culturally biased and the outcomes unfair. The Alpha, they said, measured not native intelligence but certain kinds of knowledge possessed by men with schooling and a modicum of sophistication. It included, for instance, such questions as:

> The Knight engine is used in the:
> Packard
> Stearns
> Lozier
> Pierce Arrow,

and

> The cause of echoes is:
> the reflection of sound waves
> the presence of electricity in the air
> the presence of moisture in the air,

along with questions that dealt in values, such as:

> It is better to fight than to run, because:
> cowards are shot
> it is more honorable
> if you run you may get shot in the back.

In the Beta, illiterates had to complete a number of incomplete pictures such as a face without a mouth; that was fair enough, but other drawings, such as a light bulb without a filament and a tennis court without a net, made many lower-class men and new immigrants from other cultures seem stupid.[1]

And, indeed, the data of the Army tests and the Stanford-Binet led conservatives, elitists, and some eugenicists to assert that immigrants from Eastern and Southern Europe were innately inferior in mental abilities to those from England and Western Europe, and that efforts to improve the education of low-scoring children were useless. These views, which strengthened the hand of isolationist and conservative elements, were voiced not only in Congress and the news media but in scare-mongering books such as Lothrop Stoddard's *The Rising Tide of Color Against White World-Supremacy* and *The Revolt Against Civili-*

zation, Madison Grant's *The Passing of the Great Race*, and Carl Brigham's *A Study of American Intelligence*.

A broad counterattack by liberals against intelligence testing and its applications was headed by the esteemed pundit Walter Lippmann, who wrote popular articles charging that IQ testing in the schools would lead to what he termed the "contemptible" and "crazy" abuse of classifying and differentially educating children on the basis of "a set of puzzles" and the child's capacities on the particular day and at the particular time of testing. He called IQ testing in the schools a "revival of predestination" and said that it had "no more scientific foundation than a hundred other fads—vitamins and glands and amateur psychoanalysis and correspondence courses...palmistry and characterology...[etc.]."[2]

Although Lippmann's views carried weight with many among the intelligentsia, a great many other people thought that testing was not only scientific but socially progressive; widespread public approval led to the creation of many new tests and the rapid spread of testing throughout the nation's school systems and employment offices.[3] At the same time, as we heard earlier, data compiled from the Army Alpha, Army Beta, and other tests lent respectability to proposals in Congress to drastically restrict immigration except from England and the nations of Northern and Western Europe and to the passage of the xenophobic 1924 immigration law.[4]

With that, the testing battle was more or less decided; apart from minor intermittent scuffling, the victorious pro-testing forces remained dominant until 1969. Then an earnest, dogged researcher, a forty-six-year-old educational psychologist with a respectable record of studies of learning and basically liberal political views set off an explosion, much to his own surprise, that precipitated an intellectual Thirty Years War between opponents and proponents of intelligence testing that still shows no signs of abating.

Mild-Mannered Troublemaker

A stranger unaware of who he is would never take this tall, soft-spoken man, whose broad face and plain features convey placid earnestness, to be the fomenter of social strife and the dangerous demagogue his enemies say he is. One would not imagine this grey-templed emeritus professor who reacts to the severest attacks on him in a tone more of regret than outrage, scholarly bemusement than fury, to be a wellspring of poisonous material used by reactionaries and racists, as his opponents have characterized him. One would not suppose that this "sweet and gentle man," as one colleague describes him, who even at seventy-five looks unmarked by stress, has endured decades of philippics against him in scholarly journals, popular magazines, and student pamphlets, physical threats, hate mail, near-riots, and police escorts.

Nor would one imagine, seeing this unremarkable-looking man, who could pass unnoticed in a crowd, that his name spawned a new word in our language in 1969: Arthur Jensen, emeritus professor of psychology at the University of California, is the progenitor (though not originator) of the noun "jensenism," referring to the hypotheses that made him the center of the long-lasting intellectual conflict, namely, that differences in individual IQ are very largely of genetic origin, as is the well-established difference in average IQ between whites and blacks.

Jensen is not proud that his name has thus entered the English language, since jensenism is used as a pejorative to signify a racist and elitist explanation of the poor average IQ scores of blacks. Such has been, and still is, the interpretation of his research and conclusions by the politically correct, although his findings have been quietly accepted by most of his colleagues. *Quietly accepted*: very few have openly defended his work because of the serious political risk of doing so, but in the safety of a recent anonymous survey of 661 psychologists, the great majority indicated that they believe that genetic endowment does play an important part in individual differences in IQ and that one or more existing sources of data—kinship correlations, twin studies, and so on—provide reasonable evidence of the heritability of IQ, a concept central to Jensen's work and for which he has time and again been verbally flayed.[5] (Heritability will be discussed shortly.)

Jensen's paternal grandparents came from Scandinavia, his maternal grandparents from Germany; whether his stolid responses to stress are a cultural or a genetic inheritance from the Scandinavian side is a question he has never researched.[6] He was born in San Diego in 1923, where his father owned a building supplies business and made a comfortable living. As a child, Jensen took piano and clarinet lessons, and in his teens aspired to be an orchestral conductor. But at seventeen, when he played for a season as a clarinetist with the San Diego Symphony and at the same time read books about the great conductors, he realized that they had been true prodigies, that he himself was not, and that he could never become an important conductor, an insight that foreshadowed his later research investigations on hereditary abilities.

By a roundabout route, via the University of California-Berkeley and Columbia University, Jensen found his calling in psychology. Like most other young psychologists in the 1950s, his orientation was behaviorist and environmental; he was, moreover, a political liberal who opposed the Vietnam War, was a member of the American Civil Liberties Union, and harbored a deep wish to serve his fellow human beings. He has never changed his basic social outlook, but his psychological perspective began to broaden when he read a book by the fast-rising English psychologist H. J. Eysenck, secured a National Institute of Mental Health (NIMH) fellowship to work as a postdoctoral fellow in Eysenck's laboratory at the University of London's Institute of Psychiatry, and spent two years in close contact with him.

Eysenck, whose psychological views ranged across most boundaries, was deeply interested in twin studies and had done some work in that area. Jensen's exposure to the striking evidence such studies provided of the influence of heredity should have jolted him out of his allegiance to total environmentalism but did not; however, it probably planted in his unconscious mind the seeds of interactionism that germinated a decade later. In 1968, by which time he held a research post in the educational psychology department at Berkeley (where he soon rose to professor), he was planning a book that would account, in environmentalist terms, for the difficulties that many minority group children experience in school. As part of his preparation he read widely in the burgeoning literature of behavior genetics in order to be able to dismiss genetic factors as a source of the children's problems, but was disconcerted by what he learned. His recollection:

> As I read up on it, I found it was not dismissable. It wasn't pleasant for me to find that, and I knew that if I attributed the minority-group children's school difficulties even in part to genetic factors I'd elicit a lot of disagreement and criticism from other people. But it seemed to me this was something that had to be pulled out from under the rug and considered properly.

Almost by accident, Jensen was lured into conducting research of his own devising on this very issue. One of his graduate students, a school psychologist, asked Jensen if he knew of any good culture-free intelligence tests that might solve a puzzle she had encountered: In her school district there were many low-SES (socioeconomic status) Mexican-American children, and although an unusually large number of them tested below IQ 75, which in California classified them as "educationally mentally retarded" (EMR), she had observed them in the playground and been surprised to see that their physical and social behavior seemed normal compared with the more general ineptness of middle-class white children in the same EMR range. "This convinced my student," Jensen later wrote, "that the IQ tests were somehow unfair to the minority pupils, even when they were administered in Spanish and even if scores were based upon non-verbal tests which ruled out language handicap per se."[7]

His curiosity piqued, Jensen decided to investigate; he created several new tests to determine how fast the children could learn something new, so that he could sidestep their cultural disadvantage in IQ tests, most of which draw in considerable part on previous learning. One of his new tests, for instance, consisted of the recall of a list of anywhere from twelve to twenty familiar objects (book, pencil, doll, and so on), named either in English or Spanish. To his and his student's surprise, the EMR Mexican-American children did much better on this learning test than middle-class EMR children of the same low IQ; many, indeed, performed as well as children of average IQ, and some did as well as children at the gifted level. This led Jensen to wonder whether the low-SES children, despite their low IQ scores, were as intelligent in some sense as high SES children. His concern that the disadvantaged children were being rated unfairly by standard IQ tests led him, paradoxically, to the very work that would cause him to be accused of racism.

The results Jensen got with the learning tests, plus the reading he had done in behavior genetics, convinced him of the validity of two concepts concerning intelligence, both of which were regarded as benighted and reactionary by environmentalist psychologists.

The first is g (it stands for "general intelligence"), a factor so named by the British psychologist and statistician Charles Spearman early in the century. Spearman had found that many mental abilities are correlated—that, for instance, a person who does well in vocabulary tests is likely also to do well at solving puzzles, constructing block designs, and repeating series of numbers. Spearman concluded that people possess a general mental facility or g that determines how well they do on intelligence tests.[8] For many years prior to Jensen's interest in the matter, g had been accepted by most psychologists as a reality—a general mental ability influenced by both environmental and genetic factors. But the civil rights movement of the 1960s had brought about a radical reconsideration of the matter: In the view of the new egalitarians, who granted not one inch to hereditarian influence, g was a mere statistical artifact, differences in IQ were wholly due to differences in SES and experience, and tests measuring IQ were essentially a device for keeping the downtrodden, especially people of minority groups, in their place.

Jensen, however, had by now come to believe not only that *g* was a reality but, after plowing through the voluminous research literature on it, that heredity played a larger role than environment in differences in intelligence.[9] (These days Jensen avoids the term "intelligence," preferring such more specific terms as *g*, IQ, musical aptitude, and the like.) The central datum relating to *g* that concerned Jensen was its heritability, a concept that had long been accepted but in the 1960s had also come into disfavor among egalitarians, since it is a measure of the extent to which any trait is hereditary.

Heritability is that fraction of the total range of differences in a trait, within a given population, that can be attributed to heredity; it thus applies to group data, not to any individual's score. A particular population may have eye colors ranging from pale blue to dark brown, but since eye color depends entirely on the dominant and recessive eye-color genes of the parents, environment exerting no influence, the heritability of eye color is 100 percent. In contrast, the spectrum of languages spoken by human beings is very wide—humankind speaks some 6,500 tongues that cover a wide range of grammatical, semantic, and phonetic types—but the language spoken by any particular people is governed entirely by learning and owes nothing to genes; its heritability is zero.

The heritability of IQ, however, is far more complicated. Here, as in many other traits, any given genome—the total complement of an individual's genes—will interact with one environment to produce a result different from that of its interaction with another environment. It is obviously unethical to inflict a suboptimal environment on any infant for the sake of experiment, but certain natural experiments that are relevant do exist: When identical twins are reared together, we witness the outcomes of identical genomes in the same environment; when fraternal twins are reared together, the outcomes of genomes that are 50 percent alike in the same environment; when identicals are reared apart, identical genomes in different environments; and so on. From the data of such studies plus the correlations of the IQs of relatives of various degrees of nearness, a number of researchers had already arrived at estimates—varied but all substantial—of the heritability of IQ. By the mid-1960s, just when heredity was turning into a dirty word in psychology, it was becoming well established among knowledgeable researchers that genetics played a significant part in the differences in IQ scores within any given population. As the distinguished biologist Theodosius Dobzhansky would sum up the matter several years later:

> Researchers have...securely established that *individual* differences in scores are genetically as well as environmentally conditioned. The evidence comes from more than 50 independent studies in eight different countries. But how much of this variation is due to genetics, or heritability as scientists call it, is unknown. The best estimates come from studies on twins and other close relatives reared together and apart.[10]

Dobzhansky had italicized "individual" to emphasize that he was not saying genetic influence accounted for between-group differences—as Jensen did—although he allowed that this might be the case. But in admitting this possibility, he stressed that even if the heritability of IQ were quite high, it would not mean that genes alone determined the resulting IQs: "The same gene constellation can result in a higher or lower score in different circumstances. Genes determine the intelligence (or stature or weight) of a person only in his particular environment."

This interactionist view, however, although accepted by biologists and by biologically knowledgeable psychologists, was strenuously rejected by the great majority of social scientists and others sympathetic toward, and concerned about the welfare of, poor and minority groups. Jensen became sharply aware of the extent of that rejection during his immersion in the research literature on the disadvantaged and his testing of the EMR Mexican-American children. As he later recalled:

> What struck me as most peculiar as I worked through the vast bulk of literature on the disadvantaged was the almost complete lack of any mention of the possible role of genetic factors in individual differences in intelligence and scholastic performance. In the few instances where genetics was mentioned, it was usually to dismiss the issue as outmoded, irrelevant, or unimportant, or to denigrate the genetic study of human differences and to proclaim the all-importance of the social and cultural environment as the only source of individual and group differences in the mental abilities relevant to scholastic importance.[11]

Intrigued, he now wrote several articles about genetic research on intelligence and its relevance to problems in the education of the disadvantaged. The articles brought him an invitation from the editors of *Harvard Educational Review* to summarize his views on the topic for their journal. Jensen accepted, intending to write a relatively brief piece, but his own dogged thoroughness, plus a request from the editors asking for broader treatment after they read his first draft, led to his producing a manuscript that took up 123 pages of the Winter 1969 issue of the journal, the longest article it had ever run.

The article bore the unthreatening title, "How Much Can We Boost IQ and Scholastic Achievement?" and dealt mostly with controversial but by no means incendiary topics: the apparent (to Jensen and many others) failure of large-scale compensatory education programs, the evidence for a large genetic component in individual differences, and a theory of Jensen's, based on his work with the EMR Mexican-American children, that there are two distinct levels of mental abilities, one having to do with rote learning and memory, the other with reasoning, essentially the *g* of IQ tests.

But in a ten-page segment of the article Jensen went beyond the issue of the genetic component in individual differences (those *within* any group) to discuss the highly controversial matter of the genetic component of group differences (the differences *between* groups). This was intellectual dynamite, since it raised the question—which Jensen had not originally had in mind but came to seem significant to him in the course of his research—whether the average IQ score of blacks, well known to be fifteen points lower than that of whites, was partly due to genetic causes rather than solely to the severe disadvantages of being black in the United States. The *Harvard Educational Review* had asked Jensen to cover this subject; he expected his views to be unpopular (though he underestimated how unpopular) but felt that to duck the matter would be contrived and dishonest, so he came at it head-on.

First, he reviewed the abundant evidence of the difference in average IQ between whites and blacks. Next, he mentioned some obvious and well-accepted genetic differences between racial groups (skin color, hair types, physique, and so on), and said that there was no reason to suppose the brain should be exempt from such differences. But, he asked, would genetic differences in the brains of the races result in behavioral differences such as the blacks' lower average performance on IQ tests or was this due entirely to their socioeconomic disadvantage? He then cited research data showing that when blacks are compared with whites at the same socioeconomic level, presumably eliminating the factor of socioeconomic disadvantage, the average fifteen-point difference diminishes—but only to eleven points.* This, plus certain other findings of a

---

*Some later studies support Jensen's finding, others contradict it. For the former, see E. Hunt 1995: 26–27, discussing a study by the Educational Testing Service showing that only half of the difference in literacy scores between whites and blacks whites was eliminated when groups with the same educational level were compared. For a contra-Jensen finding, see Brooks-Gunn and Klebanov 1996, a report of a study of five-year-

statistically sophisticated nature, led him to the following conclusion, in which he sought to sound moderate and reasonable but which he says caused the violent reactions that ensued:

> It seems not unreasonable, in view of the fact that intelligence variation has a large genetic component, to hypothesize that genetic factors may play a part in [the racial difference in IQ].... Such an hypothesis is anathema to many social scientists...but it has been neither contradicted nor discredited by evidence.
>
> The fact that a reasonable hypothesis has not been rigorously proved does not mean that it should be summarily dismissed. It only means that we need more appropriate research for putting it to the test. I believe such definitive evidence is entirely possible but has not yet been done. So all we are left with is various lines of evidence, no one of which is definitive alone, but which, all viewed together, make it a not unreasonable hypothesis that genetic factors are strongly implicated in the average Negro-white intelligence difference. The preponderance of evidence is, in my opinion, less consistent with a strictly environmental hypothesis than with a genetic hypothesis, which, of course, does not exclude the influence of environment or its interaction with genetic factors.[12]

The timing of Jensen's article could hardly have been worse. With the civil rights movement nearing its zenith, almost any statement running counter to a totally environmentalist explanation of individual or group differences in IQ or in social achievement was sure to be assailed by liberals, leftists, minority activist groups, and in general by people opposed to racism, elitism, class barriers, and ethnocentrism.

It was a year when the eminent British novelist and scientist Sir Charles Snow—himself a liberal—brought down wrath upon his head for ingenuously commenting that the astonishing disproportion of Jews among Nobel Laureates and other outstandingly intelligent groups suggested that "something in the Jewish gene-pool...produces talent on quite a different scale from, say, the Anglo-Saxon gene pool." The remark, though clearly admiring, touched off a barrage of criticism from non-Jews—and Jews, many of them liberals—including charges that his view was "benign racism" and a "mirror image" of Nazi racist theory.[13]

It was a year in which black militants, activist groups of other minorities, and whites who sympathized with the struggles of minorities for equal treatment generated such pressure against IQ testing in the schools that a number of large cities, including New York, Washington, D.C., and Los Angeles, banned such testing in their grade schools on the grounds that it was inherently unfair.[14]

---

old white and black children in which half the IQ difference disappears when SES is held constant, but when the degree of learning stimulation provided in the home is also held constant, about half of the remaining IQ difference is eliminated.

It was the year following the assassinations of Robert Kennedy and Martin Luther King, a year when the Black Panthers were gaining strength and making themselves felt, when student opposition to the Vietnam War was at its height, and when the Chicago conspiracy trial took place; a year, in short, in which nonviolent dispute was giving way to physical confrontation and violence.

It was a year when campus protests and demonstrations against anyone and anything construed as unfair to minorities were endemic, coercive, and sometimes riotous, a year in which an impartial study of the reasons for campus protests conducted for the NIMH was publicly denounced by a confederation of radical professors as "an intelligence operation designed to ferret out 'disruptive' elements on campus," with the result that on several campuses masses of completed questionnaires were burned and on others faculty members, some sympathetic with the radicals but others merely fearful, refused to cooperate with the study.[15]

It was therefore a year in which Jensen's article, despite its hedging and caution, elicited an extraordinary outpouring of hostility, both verbal and physical, among academics, in the media, and on the part of student groups.

On the academic level, the article was criticized in the same issue of *Harvard Educational Review* by seven professors and in later issues by twenty-four others—the beginning of a torrent of responses and rebuttals that continued for many years—most of them far more vituperative than is usual in scientific critiques. Some, to be sure, were thoughtful examinations and legitimate challenges of Jensen's methods and inferences, but others were largely billingsgate.

Richard Lewontin likened jensenism—the word had been coined by a writer for the *Wall Street Journal*—to Jansenism, which he identified as a theology condemned by Pope Innocent X as a "pernicious heresy" that espoused "total depravity, predestination, and limited atonement"; he added that "Jensen has made it fairly clear to me what sort of society he wants" (the implication: one dominated by whites).[16]

Two organizations of psychologists called for Jensen's expulsion from the American Psychological Association; the Society for the Psychological Study of Social Issues, a division of that association, denounced him vehemently in *American Psychologist*; and the American Anthropological Association, at its 1969 convention, passed a resolution condemning Jensen's position on racial differences.[17]

Jerry Hirsch, a psychologist at the University of Illinois-Champaign, said in addresses and various articles that Jensen's "avowed goals" were "as heinously barbaric as were Hitler's and the anti-abolitionists," another psychologist accused him of preparing for "a holy war against 'environmentalists,'" and a political scientist later labeled Jensen's work a "perversion of science."[18] Two philosophers said straight out, in the journal *Philosophy and Public Affairs*, what many other critics had hinted at, namely, that such research simply should not be done, specifying that if the media are biased and inaccurate; if the research has methodological problems and is open to a wide range of interpretations; if those in power can find data in it to rationalize their political and social programs; and "if one believes that the likely benefits [of such research] are minimal and the likely harms grave, then one has a responsibility to cease such investigations while the above circumstances obtain."[19]

Such criticisms of Jensen's science as the product of retrograde political views were an ominous departure from the traditional ethos of science, one feature of which is that the validity of any piece of scientific work is not dependent on, or to be disparaged because of, the researcher's political or religious beliefs. As this doctrine was summed up many years ago by the sociologist Robert K. Merton: "The acceptance or rejection of claims entering the lists of science is not to depend on the personal or social attributes of their protagonist; his race, nationality, religion, class, and personal qualities are as such irrelevant."[20]

An attack on Jensen's work unusually violative of normal academic proprieties was made by Professor Martin Deutsch, director of the Institute for Developmental Studies at New York University, who alleged in *Harvard Educational Review* that he had "found 17 errors in a casual perusal" of Jensen's article, and later, at a professional conference, greatly expanded that claim, saying, "Certain of my associates and myself have spent the last eight weeks going through every single one of Arthur Jensen's references and we found fifty-three major errors or misinterpretations, all of them unidimensional and all of them anti-black." That statement was widely repeated and circulated throughout the psychological community, but when the editor of *Psychology Today* asked Deutsch about the list, Deutsch denied having made it. Jensen, however, had been given a tape-recording of Deutsch's comments by a friend and sent a copy to *Psychology Today*; Deutsch, confronted by this evidence, said that his statement had been only an impromptu answer to a question from the audience. Meanwhile, Jensen had had a lawyer write to Deutsch asking for a list of the errors; Deutsch refused to answer, but at the lawyer's suggestion Jensen wrote to the ethics committee of the American Psychological Association, which directed Deutsch either to furnish the list or retract publicly. After a year he finally produced a list, but Jensen wrote a painstaking rebuttal of all but one—a typographical flaw of no importance—and publicized his rebuttals in *Cognition*, essentially concluding the affair.[21]

Far less virulent and widespread criticism than this by fellow academics has often been enough to choke off a researchers' interest in a troublemaking topic and cause him or her turn to safer research subjects. In science, more than in business, ill repute and ostracism by one's peers are harder to live with than many can endure; Jensen has said that in some circles the person who is critical of a totally environmentalist explanation of human differences "is viewed as a moral pariah."[22] Characteristically, he views those who condemn him with a measure of charity:

> With the exception of such radical political groups as the Students for a Democratic Society...I believe that those who have most strongly opposed me on essentially non-scientific grounds have done so out of noble but mistaken sentiments.... We all feel some uneasiness and discomfort at the notion of differences in traits that we especially value, such as mental abilities, which have obviously important educational, occupational, and social correlates....It seems to us so intrinsically unjust that some socially defined groups, through no fault of their own, should be disadvantaged with respects to traits which all persons value that we are easily inclined to deny such differences or at least attribute them to relatively superficial external causes and appearances.[23]

Media criticism, too, has driven researchers away from taboo topics; a bad press is less immediately threatening to one's career than professional criticism, but it is humiliating and frightening to see oneself depicted in national and local newspapers as a person of evil intent and despicable biases. As soon as Jensen's article was in print, he and his ideas became the subjects of scorching headlines and articles in national newspapers and magazines, campus publications, and broadcast media. The syndicated columnist Carl Rowan, a black, wrote an article headlined "Racist Attempts to Revive IQ Myth"; the *New York Times Magazine*, though it ran a well-balanced article on the controversy, then published fifteen letters in response, fourteen of them condemnatory; and for weeks *The Daily Californian*, the student newspaper at Berkeley, ran articles with headlines such as "Teachers State Jensen's Theories Are 'Frightening, Damaging'" and "Education Caucus Supports SDS in Jensen Firing" and letters demanding that he be fired and urging students to boycott his classes. (Some articles and letters did, however, defend his academic rights.)[24]

The most directly harrowing of Jensen's experiences were the protest actions of various student groups, especially Students for a Democratic Society. The Berkeley campus police kept track of planned activities of the student groups and, when they could, warned Jensen in advance of demonstrations to be held at his classes. Sometimes he had to conduct graduate seminars secretly in other parts of the building, but at other times, when he could not, his classes were filled with hecklers whose shouting prevented him from being heard. Handbills distributed on campus demanded that the administration fire him, students marched in the courtyard under his office window chanting, "Fire Jensen!", a sound truck circled the campus blasting "Fight racism! Fire Jensen!", and pamphlets were distributed bearing his picture and headlined, "HITLER IS ALIVE AND WELL AND SPREADING RACIST PROPAGANDA AT BERKELEY! Come and help fight in the struggle against racism at Jensen's class!"[25]

These disturbances went on month after month, but the administration at Berkeley refused to heed the academic, media, or student demands for Jensen's ouster or muffling. As he himself noted in 1990, "All but one of the members of my department, and the dean, and the higher university administration fully supported me right from the first blast of public controversy up to the present day.... I not only continued to receive my regular promotions, but even got accelerated promotions as well, and have made it to the very highest level of professorship."[26]

After three years Jensen thought that the worst was over; as he hopefully wrote in 1972 in the preface to his *Genetics and Education*, "The storm of ideologically, often politically, motivated protests, misinterpretations, and vilifications prompted by this article has by now fortunately subsided.... The heat and smoke have largely abated."[27] He was wrong; in a recent letter to me he said, "Many other fantastic things have happened to me over the years since that preface was written, at which time I had no premonition of some of the 'horrors' that were still awaiting me and my family." A few examples of what awaited him in the 1970s and 1980s: [28]

• Jensen was invited to speak about twin research at the Salk Institute in La Jolla, but nearly 100 demonstrators in the lecture hall kept up a deafening racket of shouts and chants, and he never was able to say a word. When the furor escalated and it looked as if the demonstrators were about to mount a charge, Salk officials smuggled him out by a back exit and sent him on his way.

• When Jensen was scheduled to address 700 scholars at the annual convention of the American Educational Research Association in Chicago, AERA officials learned that the Progressive Labor Party was planning a massive demonstration and disruption. The AERA officials contacted the PLP and offered to allow them five minutes to make their case before Jensen's address. The PLP leaders agreed, but when their spokesman was introduced by the chairman of the event and came to the dais, he seized Jensen's notes, tore them up, and threw them in his face. The PLP spokesman then delivered a lengthy harangue, after which Jensen was introduced—and was met by a din of mechanical noise-makers and the hoots and yells of the cadre of demonstrators. Unable to be heard, Jensen tried to hand out copies of his talk, but the demonstrators rushed the stage to stop him and Jensen was whisked away by a tactical squad of Chicago police, who took him out via a back exit and freight elevator.

• Jensen was invited to speak at a synagogue in Berkeley, but a bomb threat phoned in just before he was to go on caused the event to be canceled. When he tried to go home, he found that for good measure his opponents had slashed his tires.

• Jensen was invited to address graduate students of the Institute of Child Development at the University of Minnesota on bias in mental testing. Sandra Scarr was to introduce him, when she and he walked toward the hall, they found a phalanx of radical and black students lining the walk, and as they made their way through them, Jensen was spat upon. Revolted and shaken, Scarr and Jensen continued into the hall, where as soon as he began his address, he was drowned out by catcalls and shouts, fist-fights broke out in the audience, and the campus police, fearing a full-scale riot, hurried him out the back way and down a fire escape, drove him to the office of Willard Hartup, the director of the institute, and left him in Hartup's care. As soon as the police were gone, a group of demonstrators appeared and pushed into the office; Hartup, fearing for Jensen, shoved him into a storage closet and locked the door, and aided by several graduate students stood toe to toe with the shouting demonstrators until the police, summoned by his secretary, returned.

• Jensen met much the same treatment at various events in England and Canada. In Australia, he and Eysenck were to lecture at eight universities, but at Melbourne University, the first of the eight, a well-prepared crowd of demonstrators banged on garbage cans, blew whistles constantly, and chanted "What do we want? Jensen! How do we want him? Dead!" University officials guided Jensen out and to a studio in the basement, from which he began to deliver his speech to the lecture hall by closed-circuit television; seeing this, the mob charged down to the basement, broke through police ranks, and began pounding on the studio door until police reinforcements arrived and took Jensen back to his quarters. At Sydney University, demonstrators improved on the tactics used at Melbourne: In addition to chanting and blowing whistles, they threw water bombs and a smoke bomb. In view of these disturbances, three of the eight universities canceled the engagements.

• In 1980, after Jensen published a book on mental testing that amplified his views on the genetic component of intelligence, he began receiving phone calls at home that threatened injury or worse to him and his family, including his daughter, who was in school at the time and had to walk to and from a bus stop. Jensen notified the police, who arranged to have calls to the Jensen home routed to headquarters so that they could listen in; when they did so, they told Jensen they thought the calls were not the work of a prankster but someone serious, and advised that the Jensens leave home for at least a few days and hide out, which they did.

In all, over a period of two decades Jensen experienced about two dozen major assaults or disruptions at Berkeley, close to a dozen in other countries, and many lesser incidents of which he has kept no record. (There have been no serious incidents in the 1990s, although he has continued to suffer "disinvitations" to important events at which he has been scheduled to be a keynote speaker until protests poured in.) None of these obstructions and harassments halted his pursuit of what he saw as a worthy goal, the deeper understanding of racial differences in mental abilities. With what can be seen either as principled courage or remarkable bullheadedness, he has neither backed down from his expressed views nor thought of turning to other research areas. "People suggested that I give it up," he says, "but I never considered it. I couldn't see any good reason for not persisting. It just didn't seem the right thing to do." From the onset of his tribulations he readily granted interviews in person and on the phone to reporters, patiently composed detailed replies to journal articles attacking him, and continued his research on the heritability of IQ and on racial differences (his C.V. shows no let-up in his output after the appearance of the 1969 *Harvard Educational Review* article). Remarkably, he never suffered from insomnia, digestive disorders, or other symptoms of stress; one of his colleagues has said that Jensen has a skin a rhinoceros would envy.

After several years as the target of academic, media, and student attacks, Jensen wrote, "I am frequently asked whether the agitation following my article has had any adverse effect on my own research activities. Although this is difficult to judge from my own standpoint, it seems to me the answer in general is no."[29] He did, however, suffer one early and considerable cut in his research: The Berkeley Board of Education had appointed him research director of a large study of the scholastic effects of racial desegregation in the schools, but when the controversy over his 1969 article flared up, the school authorities asked him to give up his directorship and become a more or less invisible research consultant; he agreed, but shortly the Board voted to halt the project altogether.[30]

* * *

Why has Jensen held fast to this course? Is his constancy due to stubbornness and a desire to triumph over his opponents? He has his own much nobler-sounding explanation:

> Some research questions are undeniably disturbing and painful to any thoughtful person, and we would prefer that they not have to be raised. Yet when we come face to face with the really hard problems, we cannot gain by shying away. The researcher who ventures into this territory of differential psychology which deals with group differences...hopefully to increase our understanding of the nature of population differences in psychological characteristics, treads a most difficult, not to say dangerous, path.... Fortunately, quite aside from whatever practical or social implications one's research might have, such work has an engrossing fascination of its own, much like the game of chess and working a puzzle. It is mainly this intrinsic aspect of research activity that keeps up one's enthusiasm day to day.[31]

And indeed many other researchers, particularly as behavior genetics has become a hot area in recent years, have been exploring the issues of the patterns of interaction between heredity and environment in the development of mental abilities and the resultant heritability of g within groups and between groups.

But is there any practical or social value to such work—in particular, Jensen's work? If blacks do have an average g less than that of whites, or some tendency to have lesser mental abilities on average than whites, does that suggest that black children should be shunted into different schools or onto different educational "tracks" than white children? Jensen is clear enough on this point: In 1970 he wrote, "I have always advocated dealing with persons as individuals, each in terms of his own merits and characteristics, and I am opposed to according treatment to persons solely on the basis of their race,"[32] and he has reiterated that stand many times since. I asked him if he still considers himself a liberal; he said, with a chuckle, "Yes. I might even be a radical by now." Then, rethinking his answer, he said, "These days I'm a social libertarian and a fiscal conservative."

What, then, are the practical implications of his 1969 article, and of his three subsequent decades of refinements and expansions of its central ideas? About that he is less clear. On the last pages of the 1969 article he suggested that more diverse and specialized educational programs, suited to the varied mental ability patterns of individual children, would benefit them:

> If the theories that I have briefly outlined here become fully substantiated, the next step will be to develop the techniques by which school learning can be most effectively achieved in accordance with different patterns of ability.... There can be little doubt that certain educational and occupational attainments depend more on *g* than upon any other single ability. But schools must also be able to find ways of utilizing other strengths in children whose major strength is not of the cognitive variety.... Schools and society must provide a range and diversity of educational methods, programs, and goals, and of occupational opportunities, just as wide as the range of human abilities.[33]

He is still saying the same thing; in a recent interview he commented, "I believe it is necessary that the aims and methods of education be made sufficiently and appropriately diverse to accommodate the wide range of variation of mental ability in the entire school population, and much the same can be said about employment opportunities."[34]

But since *g* and other mental abilities of most whites and blacks lie within the same boundaries—the averages of the groups differ but the two curves of distribution largely overlap—and if, as Jensen believes, opportunities should be tailored to each child's abilities, not determined by his race, what is the use or good of research on racial differences? His answer to me:

> The good of it is so that we know what's causing these group differences, because only on the basis of that knowledge can we take any really constructive action and not go on with some kind of mythology about them. You get a whole mythology in the social sciences if you don't know the true causes of a phenomenon, and that leads to a lot of misguided social action. I believe strongly that each person should be treated as an individual in his or her own right, and on his or her own merits, but treating groups of people on the basis of mythology, an ideological but incorrect explanation of the causes of a problem, as in affirmative action programs, is all wrong.

Jensen does not see himself as a technician looking for specific educational methods that will benefit disadvantaged children; his primary goal, his basic motivation, is that of most serious researchers in every science: the desire for explanations, the hunger for knowledge itself.

What use, if any, society makes of that knowledge is another issue and the business of other people; educators may find ways to make good use of Jensen's findings, racists may find ways to make evil use of it. As the sociologist Bernard Barber has said, "Knowledge is the power to do good and evil alike, but we cannot throw away the power. We have faced the same dilemma in the consequences of the natural sciences, and we have chosen as we have had to choose, for the partial control that it gives us."[35]

Researching the Impermissible, Reporting the Unspeakable

As is evident, the most conflictual genre of research in the social sciences is that on racial differences; the psychologist Irving Gottesman, an involuntary combatant, has written that by 1974 it had become an ideological fight of such animus that it was immune to salvation by science.[36] White egalitarians, civil rights advocates, and minority-group activists see virtually all such research, whatever the researcher's motives, as blatantly racist, even if the difference under study is a health risk that might be lessened by treatment based on knowledge, even if the difference is an excess of a trait that is valued and admired (as noted earlier, it is not politically correct to say that blacks have unusual athletic abilities). All the more reason, then, that a researcher who finds that one race possesses less, on average, of a valued trait than another, as Jensen did, is seen by members of the devalued race, egalitarians, and most of those who believe in the brotherhood of humankind as a vicious bigot, an enemy of democratic society, and a threat to social order.

Such has been the case with J. Philippe Rushton, a professor of psychology at the University of Western Ontario (UWO) in London, Ontario, whose racial-differences research goes much farther into taboo territory than Jensen's and who, accordingly, has been subjected to even severer forms of harassment and obstruction. His experiences of political opposition, although they took place in Canada, are comparable to those of many researchers in the United States with one exception: Canada's federal code has a provision making it a criminal offense to "willfully promote hatred against any identifiable group," and Ontario's Human Rights Code includes a ban on the dissemination of hate propaganda, in particular allegations that any specific group is racially inferior.[37] In the United States there is no such federal or state law; hate speech is constitutionally protected, as long as it does not create a clear and present danger of disorder, although according to a recent survey thirty percent of American universities have enacted their own speech codes, some of which include restrictions on hate speech.[38] (The university codes are on shaky legal ground; not long ago a federal court struck down that of the University of Michigan as a violation of the First Amendment.[39])

In 1987, when I was writing a book about human altruism, I interviewed Rushton by phone about that subject, on which he had done much noteworthy work. At the end of our conversation he mentioned casually that his interest had recently changed and that he was now gathering and analyzing data on average differences among the three major races as to brain size, intelligence, sexual behavior, temperament, social behavior, and other traits. A pattern appearing in all these data, he said, indicated that of the three major races Orientals are the most highly evolved, whites less so, and blacks the least. He would shortly present his data and conclusions at a major scientific meeting. It seemed an alarming prospect, and to learn about the outcome of that presentation, I kept in touch with him by means of phone calls, letters, faxes, E-mails, and, after some years, a two-day visit in Canada.

I had felt somewhat uneasy when writing to Rushton or talking with him; although he sounded reasonable, civil, and apparently motivated by a pure desire to know the facts, I found his subject and conclusions repugnant and suspect. But when I visited him in 1993, my uneasiness swiftly dissipated; he proved to be a trim, well-dressed, clean-featured man nearing fifty who spoke softly, learnedly, and logically in a pleasantly English-accented speech, never used derogatory terms about blacks (or, indeed, any group), and earnestly said of his purposes, "I'm genuinely interested in searching for knowledge, in knowing the truth. I think that knowledge is valuable, and that knowledge about the human species is invaluable. In this case, I admit, the truth is discomforting, but I believe that the truth will make us free—will free us from making wrong choices, both individually and as a society."

Rushton did not take up research in this area to justify any personal prejudice; on the contrary, it was the research that changed his views, which formerly were thoroughly egalitarian. Born in Hampshire, England, he was educated at the University of London, where he absorbed the prevalent view that human nature is the product of "social learning," not innate tendencies. For a decade, as a "slightly left of center liberal"—his self-description—he researched altruism from this viewpoint. But he kept coming across studies of altruism in animals and in human twins reared together and reared apart, and the findings, particularly of the human twins studies, shook his belief in an unequivocally environmentalist explanation of human personality; for the first time, he began to think that altruism in human beings must be in part, perhaps large part, genetically determined. But if that were so, why not other personality traits? For months Rushton read up on behavior genetics and evolutionary theory. "It was as though blinkers had been taken away from my eyes," he told me. "I couldn't believe how narrow a trough I had been plowing."

With Eysenck—his mentor at the Institute of Psychiatry, University of London—and several other colleagues, he took part in a massive twin study of altruism, the major finding of which was that about half of the variance in altruism is due to genetic influences, half to environmental ones.[40] That led Rushton to begin collecting existing research data on the role of heredity in many other traits, beginning with intelligence, where he found considerable evidence, including Jensen's, of a strong genetic component.

"But I pondered long and hard whether or not to pursue the subject," he recalls. He had had a taste of what it could involve: He had been present at a conference at the University of London when Eysenck, there to talk about the role of heredity in intelligence, was mobbed by rioting leftist students whose shouted slogan of the day was, "Fascists have no right to speak!" Rushton was one of several people who struggled to keep the students from reaching Eysenck but in vain; Eysenck was roughed up and his glasses smashed before the students were repelled. "But even having seen that," Rushton says, "I had no idea how entrenched political correctness was in the establishment and I underestimated the ferocity of the reaction I would encounter," and he went ahead with his research. Some people who know Rushton say that he did so because he is stubborn and has a taste for controversy; he denies this, saying with a chuckle, "I'd much prefer everybody to say I'm right."

For a while he encountered no opposition in England or, later, at the University of Western Ontario, although some colleagues grew cool when they learned what he was working on. But his department at the University of Western Ontario rated his research as excellent, in 1987 he won a faculty contest for a research award, and in 1988 he received a Guggenheim Fellowship to take a sabbatical to concentrate on his research. Neither his department head nor other superiors at the university realized that he was assembling a mass of dangerously combustible materials.

In San Francisco on January 19th, 1989, a fateful day in Rushton's life, he read a brief paper at a symposium on evolution and the social sciences at the annual meeting of the American Association for the Advancement of Science (AAAS).[41] In the paper he summarized a mass of data he had gathered on racial differences in various physical and behavioral characteristics, among them average cranial capacity ("Mongoloids," to use his term rather than the now-preferred "Orientals," 1448 cc.; "Caucasoids"—whites—1408 cc.; and "Negroids"—blacks—1334 cc.), average speed of maturation (Oriental babies are slowest to crawl or walk, whites quicker, blacks quickest), twinning frequency (four twins per 1,000 births for Orientals, eight for whites, sixteen or more for blacks), plus comparisons of the average size of the three races' sexual organs, frequency of copulation, aggressiveness, law abidingness, marital stability, impulsivity, aggressiveness, and other personality traits.[42]

In offering these data Rushton piled faggots at his own feet and tied himself to the stake; in suggesting a hypothesis to coherently explain them, he put the torch to the pile. Why he felt compelled to do so is a matter for conjecture; to hear him tell it, he seems to have felt, like Luther, that he could do no other. All the racial differences he had compiled, he said, could be accounted for in terms of "*r/K*" theory, a concept he borrowed from the biologist Edward O. Wilson, according to which living creatures employ one or the other of two reproductive strategies, or some trade-off between them: Strategy *r* is to produce as many eggs as possible, strategy *K* to take care of the infant.[43] Oysters, an extreme case of strategy *r*, produce 500 million eggs a year but provide no parental care; the great apes, an extreme case of strategy *K*, produce one infant every five or six years and provide a great deal of parental care.

Rushton said the differences he had compiled showed that of the three major races Mongoloids were the most inclined to use the *K* strategy, Negroids the most inclined to use the *r* strategy, Caucasoids in between. What was the source of these differences? His answer: Evolution, as measured by genetic distance. Genetic distance data—the number of differences in the DNA of the three races—indicated, he said, citing sources for his data, that Negroids split off from the ancestral hominid line 200,000 years ago, Caucasoids 110,000 years ago, and Mongoloids 41,000 years ago.[44] Assuming, he said, that the earlier

the split-off, the earlier a race's stage of development, Negroids appear
to be an earlier and less evolved form of *Homo sapiens* than Caucasoids, Caucasoids less highly evolved than Mongoloids.[45] He added,
however—and has often repeated since then—that racial averages im-
ply nothing about any one person and that each human being deserves
to be judged and treated as an individual.

Even before Rushton delivered the talk, the press, reading advance
copies, had swarmed over him and AAAS officials, and by the time he
got back to Canada, newspapers in London (Ontario) and Toronto were
denouncing him almost daily. The *Toronto Star*, under the headline
"Theory 'Racist': Prof Has Scholars Boiling," labeled him a fraud and
caricatured him wearing a KKK hood. Another newspaper had him talking on the phone to a pleased-looking Adolf Hitler. The *London Free
Press* bannered a story "Race Issue: Alliance Demands 'Full Force of
Law'; Ontario's Attorney General Has Been Asked to Silence Philippe
Rushton and His Race Theory." ("Alliance" was the Urban Alliance on
Race Relations; the request to the attorney general came from a special
committee formed by the Mayor of London.) The premier of Ontario,
David Peterson, told a *Star* reporter, "I would fire him if I could," and
phoned the president of the university to urge Rushton's dismissal.

Responding to mounting student agitation, Greg Moran, chairman
of the department of psychology, asked Rushton to engage in a public
debate that would give the agitators a spokesperson. The event, held in
Alumni Hall and televised across Canada, pitted Rushton against David
Suzuki, a geneticist and popular broadcaster with the Canadian Broad-
casting Company. The audience of 2,300 hissed and booed many of
Rushton's comments but cheered wildly when Suzuki, calling Rushton's
work unconscionable and demeaning to black people, said, "There will
always be Rushtons and we must always be prepared to root them out
and not hide behind academic freedom." Moran had hoped the debate
would provide catharsis, relieving the tension on campus, but it seemed
only to heighten it.

The president of the university, K. George Pedersen, reluctantly
making a public statement in response to mounting demands to halt
Rushton's research, said that the principle of academic freedom protected Rushton and his work. He was frank about his lack of enthusiasm at having to take this stance; as he told a student activist group, "I
have no choice but to defend Professor Rushton."[46] Emöke Szathmary,
the dean of social sciences, assailed Rushton, whose professorship lay
within her domain, saying to a reporter from the *Star*, "This man has no

scientific credibility left, at least not in this area. And his inter-racial stuff has been under heavy criticism."[47]

At this point, Rushton was invited to appear on the Geraldo Rivera show and asked for a meeting with Pedersen to inquire whether the university would provide legal expenses if the need arose. At the meeting, to which Pedersen had invited administration allies—Provost Thomas J. Collins, Moran, and several other officials—Pedersen and the others told Rushton that the show was not an appropriate forum and pressed him to decline the invitation.[48] Rushton refused, and two days later received an ominous letter from Collins suggesting that by going on the show he would overstep the bounds of protected academic freedom: "In our view, talk-show appearances and participation in similar events in the popular media are not consistent with the responsible use of your academic freedom.... The right to academic freedom carries with it the duty to use that freedom in a responsible way."[49]

The warning did no good; Rushton appeared on the Geraldo show, considerably intensifying the conflict. Anti-Rushton articles and angry letters by faculty members appeared in campus, local, and national papers, forty-five faculty members signed a petition asking the administration to fire him, a CBC national science program devoted an hour to attacking his work, campus activist groups held sit-ins and demonstrations, and an increasing number of attacks on him by academics appeared in scientific journals, some disputing his facts and interpretations, others assailing him for researching questions that they said should not be asked.[50]

Deliverance for the university appeared possible in March 1989 when the Ontario Provincial Police launched an investigation to determine whether Rushton had violated the federal criminal code of Canada by willfully promoting hatred against an identifiable group, a crime for which, if convicted, he could be imprisoned for up to two years.[51] The Attorney General of Ontario, Ian Scott, assigned a team of investigators to the case, but after half a year of work they turned in a hundred-page report that gave Scott no grounds for proceeding. He called a press conference at which he announced that Rushton's ideas were "loony but not criminal" and that he would therefore not be prosecuted.[52]

While Scott's decision was in the making, the academic mill was grinding out another possible solution. In July 1989 the departmental committee that annually rates faculty performance notified Rushton that it found his scholarship "borderline" and rated the rest of his performance and his overall merit index "unsatisfactory." This was a remarkable change from the preceding years, during which he had been doing research of the same kind, when his overall rating had been either "good" or "excellent" and when Pedersen and others considered him an outstanding member of the Social Science Faculty.[53] The unsatisfactory rating denied Rushton not only merit pay but the usual salary increase; far worse, if it were followed by unsatisfactory ratings the next two years, he could be dismissed despite tenure.[54]

Both Szathmary and Moran, when I asked them what had been unsatisfactory about Rushton's performance, declined to answer on the grounds that the work of the committee is confidential. No scientific ground for the committee's rating is on public record; its letter to Rushton said only, "Your unacceptable scholarly performance in race differences outweighed your obvious productivity and the commendable character [of your other work]."[55]

Many another scientist would, at that point, have switched to a research area the committee could approve; Rushton was determined to fight it out. He explains:

> Maybe this reflects badly on me. I did think about trying to steer clear of the problems this research produces by downplaying my public appearances and wedging more qualifications into my writing. But I felt it was outrageous that lies about the human condition were being told and maintained—lies about the total similarity of all human beings, incorrect analyses of the human condition that prevent us from having a truthful biosocial perspective on who and what we are. I also felt it was outrageous to call me a racist just because I reported the facts about the average brain size of the races and other racial differences.

Fortunately for him, nature or nurture or both had constructed his personality in such fashion that this prolonged trial by fire did not break his spirit. He says that he isn't physically brave and admits to being quite nervous when he has to fly, particularly in a small plane, but the manifold attacks on him for his research made him angry and combative rather than fearful.

Determined not to back down, Rushton continued to produce studies amplifying his 1989 paper and amassing data on a wide variety of racial differences culled from many sources, most of them papers published in refereed journals or government collated technical reports and thus scientifically credible.[56] Though Rushton's opponents could rarely fault the data themselves, most of them were highly critical of the inferences he drew from them, many saying that his analyses of the data were bad science and some specifically linking his ideas with the worst use of racism in recent history, as did a psychologist named Richard Lerner, who wrote that Rushton's thinking was "redolent of Nazi-era political and scientific pronouncements about advances in cures of genetic disease."[57]

Since Rushton's poor department rating was an even graver threat to his livelihood than such criticism, he doggedly protested it over the course of a year through four successive levels of appeal and grievance. Twice defeated, he won at the third level, when a grievance committee found fault with the departmental committee's rating and returned it for their reconsideration. The departmental committee then filed its own appeal to the fourth and highest level, but lost. The committee thereupon had a remarkable change of heart and decided that Rushton's overall performance had, after all, been satisfactory in 1989 and good in 1990.[58]

Other forces, however, kept trying to silence Rushton, who, anything but silent, kept advertising his position via scientific journals, symposia, and newspapers. On the UWO campus, students and bussed-in sympathizers held a rally in March, 1990, at which they demanded that Rushton be removed; afterwards, a contingent of them stormed through the psychology department building, banging on walls and doors, bellowing slogans through bull horns, spray-painting swastikas on the walls, and writing on Rushton's door "RACISTS PIG LIVE HERE" (*sic*).[59]

Moran and Szathmary, concerned that demonstrations might become violent, ordered Rushton to cease teaching his classes in person and to videotape his lectures; students who wished to take his course would have to view the videotapes. Rushton, of course, filed grievances against this order, and after half a year of delivering lectures via videotape succeeded in gaining permission in January, 1991 to resume teaching in person. Demonstrators promptly met this challenge by massing outside his classroom and shouting slogans so loudly and continuously that the first scheduled class had to be canceled and on three subsequent occasions jammed the doorway to the classroom, preventing Rushton's students from entering. Provost Collins then notified five of the demonstrators that further disruption of classes would lead to suspension and legal action, and the shouting and doorway-jamming stopped.

The demonstrators then came up with a different and potentially far more decisive stratagem: In late May 1991, eighteen current and former UWO students filed a complaint with the Ontario Human Rights Commission (OHRC) charging that Rushton's research and publications violated the Ontario Human Rights Code by "causing or permitting the promotion of racism in the academic learning environment at the University of Western Ontario."[60] For good measure, the complaint charged

Pedersen and Collins with permitting Rushton to propagate racism and with taking reprisals against students who protested his doing so. The complainants asked that Rushton be fired and that the teaching of racist academic theories at UWO be prohibited.[61]

The complaint was no empty threat; the OHRC had the power to dismiss Rushton from his professorship, which, since that action would mean it had found the charge true, might well have ended his academic career. Rushton filed his reply and Pedersen and Collins theirs later that year, but the matter remained undecided, hanging over Rushton's head month after month, year after year. Not until November 1995, more than four years after the OHRC inaugurated its case against Rushton, was the matter resolved when the commission closed it, not because of a lack of merit but because all the student complainants had left the scene and either could not be found or made no reply to letters from the OHRC.[62] This outcome, though a great relief for Rushton, was hardly the "small victory for academic freedom" that he proudly called it.

By subtler means his voice has been somewhat muffled in certain scientific quarters ever since 1989. He had been scheduled to be guest editor of a special issue of a leading journal but the project mysteriously fell through; the important British scientific journal *Nature* rejected an article of his and instead published a full-page editorial criticizing his work; the publisher of a textbook he had co authored paid him to permit them to drop his name from a new edition of it; and a book contracted for by a major university press, in which he assembled all his work on individual and group differences, was turned down when the press "changed its mind."

On campus, however, things gradually quieted down, student demonstrations ceased, and colleagues who used to ostentatiously cross the street when they saw Rushton coming or move away if he sat near them in a seminar grew subtler about avoiding him. Rushton comments:

> I'm a known quantity now, and by and large I'm no longer subjected to sudden fits of strange behavior. People who don't care for me tend to avoid making eye contact or standing or sitting next to me, and I do the same. We just get on with it.
> But what's still disturbing is when I go to a scientific conference and there's some overt demonstration against me, as there still occasionally is. In February 1996, for instance, at an AAAS convention in Baltimore, I had a poster booth where I was going to display a poster on brain sizes of the races.* A group called

---

*At many scientific meetings, presentations of findings that have not been scheduled as talks are granted the lesser status of poster displays; the posters present data and findings in abbreviated form.

INCAR—International Committee Against Racism—also had a booth in collaboration with the Progressive Labor Party, and about ten of their people—all white, by the way—came to a big AAAS reception the day before my presentation and when they spotted me started screaming, right in the midst of the reception, "There he is, there's Rushton the racist!" and pointing at me, and kept it up until after about five minutes I left because I was terribly embarrassed. And the next day, even though I had several policemen guarding me at my booth, they came up and started chanting and carrying on in front of the booth, and one of them took my picture and said, "This is for a 'Wanted: Dead or Alive' poster—you won't be living much longer," and they kept it up until I took down my poster and went away.

In 1993, four years after Rushton's ordeal began, he told me that his career and credibility had been very seriously harmed by the bad press and academic attacks, but by 1997 he said that he felt he had regained some of the lost ground. Ever since his successful fight against his bad evaluations, he has been receiving much better ones—not the "outstanding" ratings of formerly but "good" or "very good," which is as far as the committee is willing to go. Many liberal social scientists continue to consider him essentially a racist, but others, particularly behavior geneticists and psychologists interested in the genetic components of behavior, accept him as a serious researcher and quite a few tell him privately that they agree with him about most of the racial difference correlations he has computed.[63] Some of the latter, however, feel that he has been insensitive in his presentations of work that can only seem degrading to blacks,[64] and even a sympathetic reviewer of *Race, Evolution, and Behavior*—the book about which the prestigious university press changed its mind, and which was later published by Transaction Publishers—calls it:

dynamite [that Rushton] fails to handle with sufficient care.... Rushton has written his own epitaph...[to wit:] "The evolutionary psychology of race differences has become the most politically incorrect topic in the world today." Mr. Rushton's work may be ignored by the fearful, damned by the liberals, and misused by the racists. It is unlikely to be truly understood by anyone.[65]

Rushton finds it ironic that white academics who find his views about blacks insensitive or offensive never seem to be affronted by his statements that whites are less evolved and, on average, less smart than Asians.

More often than not, his book has been trashed by reviewers who find his views loathsome and therefore say his science is faulty; typically, the anthropologist Susan Sperling, in the *Nation*, called the book "racist trash" and said that it deals in "ignored data, twisted teleologies and naïve evolutionary reductionism...[and] drags the whole dusty display of nineteenth-century race libels down from the colonial ethno-graphic museum shelf."[66]

* * *

Does Rushton's work merit defense in the name of free speech and freedom of scientific inquiry? Even if one regards his data and inter-pretations as morally repugnant, does his work lie within the bounds that should be protected by academic freedom? Or does the social dam-age it might do so outweigh its possible contribution to human knowl-edge and the betterment of the human condition as to make it akin to that false cry of "Fire!" in a crowded theater? Reaching a rational judg-ment on the matter is a most difficult exercise and one that few people can do with total impartiality. Scores of eminent scientists, among them Lewontin, Leon Kamin, and David Suzuki, have condemned Rushton's work not only as bad science but as damaging to blacks and to the society they live in; scores of others, among them Eysenck, Bouchard, and Irenäus Eibl-Eibesfeldt, have written letters defending his scien-tific work and his right to pursue his inquiries, and the principle of freedom of research.

Many others, perhaps the majority, are ambivalent, recognizing the paramount importance of preserving freedom of research but detesting Rushton's message and wishing it could simply be ignored. Just such ambivalence was expressed by the administrators at UWO most closely involved in the Rushton affair when it was at its hottest. In 1993, Emöke Szathmary (who now is the president of the University of Manitoba) agreed with the department committee's unsatisfactory rating of Rushton's work but added, "It is quite possible that some researchable questions would have some direct and difficult social results, but I can't conceive of any research where I would not feel obliged to defend the freedom of the researcher conducting it." Greg Moran (now provost of UWO), who chaired the committee that found Rushton's work unsatis-factory, said, when I asked him if research that violates social taboos should be halted, "It is impossible and ill-advised to decide to stop work we think might be used by mean-spirited and antisocial types to serve their ends." K. George Pedersen (then president of UWO and now retired) took a somewhat ambiguous position: "Rushton's work has created a fair amount of discomfort, but the raison d'être of a uni-versity is to provide academic freedom and the right to pursue ques-tions that are controversial. The only conclusion I have been able to come to is that the parameters of what is acceptable or not acceptable are defined by the law of the land"—clearly implying that had the OHRC decided to silence Rushton, he would have accepted and acted upon its decision.

Rushton's case is an acid test of one's devotion to freedom of research. His findings and his interpretations of them, though welcome to some people and unwillingly accepted by others, are so offensive to people of goodwill and egalitarian ideals that some believe his work should be halted by one means or other. But the history of ideological opposition to research makes it plain that offensiveness should not be the determining factor; what the Inquisitors found insufferable in Galileo's views was not only the truth but a truth that did, indeed, make us all freer than we had been.

Does Rushton's work free us? He believes so, but shies away from specifying the policy changes that should follow from his findings. As he says in *Race, Evolution, and Behavior*, "There are no necessary policies that flow from race research. The findings are compatible with a wide range of recommendation: from social segregation, through laissez-faire, to programs for the disadvantaged."[67] But Irving Louis Horowitz, a conservative sociologist and the president emeritus of Transaction Publishers, says that although Rushton is on record as vigorously opposing racial genocide and eugenics, theories like his can be and have been misused for the most horrendous ends: "Some forms of totalitarianism have historically adopted racial doctrines to justify everything from medical experimentation on human beings to mass murder ostensibly for the greater goal of the improvement of human species."[68]

When Rushton is asked what value data on racial differences can have if each person should be treated on his or her individual merits, he tends to answer in lofty and rather vague terms:

As Enrico Fermi remarked, "Whatever Nature has in store for mankind, unpleasant as it may be, men must accept, for ignorance is never better than knowledge." What we need is a correct genetic, biosocial perspective on the human condition so that we can come to grips with what we are as individuals and as a species. That would be potentially beneficial in so many ways that I hardly know where to begin. People are so afraid of finding race differences that they don't even want to find genetic differences in individuals. That outlook has distorted the entire edifice of social science, and of our policies on racial questions. When I was younger, the prevalent view was that we were so malleable that you could become anything you wanted to be, and we know now that that's just not true and is potentially very harmful, because it guides you away from what you really are and can be. If this is true for individuals, it's true for the species as a whole.

That answer will strike many people as socially divisive and as unfair to blacks. But those who think Rushton a racist and his scientific work dangerously wrong need not, and should not, try to halt his work and suppress his message by political means. A more legitimate and constructive alternative exists: They can and should attack him by means of research that contradicts or disproves his findings and his theories; that is the path of salvation for science in a democracy. It is an onerous and demanding answer, but as Spinoza so eloquently said at the conclusion of his mighty *Ethics*, "If salvation lay ready to hand and could be discovered without great labor, how could it be possible that it would be neglected by almost everybody? But all noble things are as difficult as they are rare."

Sundry Battles on the IQ Front

The Jensen and Rushton affairs are only two of the many cases in which research on racial differences, particularly as to IQ and cognitive abilities, has met with opposition by individuals or groups convinced that all inquiries into such differences are motivated by racism and are intended to do them damage. Many studies of the effects of the Head Start program, for instance, found that the gains in IQ and achievement that it produced in poverty-level black children were impermanent, but the researchers who delivered this unwanted message were often accused of political and racial bias.

Based on what I have heard from a number of sources, I suspect that virtually all researchers whose work yields evidence of racial differences in IQ and other cognitive abilities, except those who have not yet made their findings known, have met with coldness and hostility on the part of many colleagues, condemnation and vilification in journals and in the media, efforts to downgrade their ratings or even to oust them from their professorships, protest demonstrations by students, mob interference with lectures and conferences, hate sloganeering, hate mail, and threats to the individual and his or her family.

Herewith some generalized comments about the techniques and movements by which political opponents of research on intergroup differences in cognitive abilities attempt to halt it and the applications of its findings in schools and employment offices.

Streetfighter Tactics

We have seen some examples of the tactics of student protesters bent on disrupting or preventing lectures and conference presentations of research that they hate. The tactics, to recapitulate, include obstruction of doorways, preemptive possession of the seats in an auditorium, shouting, banging of lids, chanting, blowing whistles, throwing eggs and tomatoes, rushing the stage and tearing up displays and lecture notes, spitting at speakers, and roughing them up, to say nothing of spray-painting slogans and epithets, bullhorn ranting, hate mail, and threats of violence and murder. Scarr, Eysenck, Raymond Cattell, and Richard Herrnstein are only a few of the many scientists who have experienced these stratagems.

We have seen enough of this in relation to IQ research; let us pass on. I will, however, have to mention the topic again in later chapters.

The Antitesting Movement

In the 1960s, as already noted, militant minority groups and their white sympathizers succeeded in getting the boards of education in several major cities to stop IQ testing in the public schools. Public demonstrations and mass protests by activist groups died down by the late 1970s, but efforts to stop IQ testing continued by means of court cases and pressures on state legislators.

And with considerable success. By the 1990s, in schools throughout California, and in many school systems in other states, laws had been passed that forebade giving standardized tests of intelligence and academic aptitude to minority black and Hispanic children who had scholastic problems.[69] In other cases school administrators who were not legally forbidden to do such testing avoided it in response to the wishes of parents, since testing, though strongly favored in the 1950s and early 1960s, had fallen into general disfavor with the literate public a generation later.[70] By the 1980s, between a third and a half of all public school districts administered no group intelligence or aptitude tests to students at any time between kindergarten and twelfth grade, and of those that did do testing, about half, according to a 1982 survey of fourteen western states, seldom or never made any use of the results to tailor programs of study to children's abilities. As a result, most children lost the benefits of a proper use of their scores in individualizing instruction.[71]

Typical of the antitesting propaganda aimed at parents by school administrators in the 1980s and to this day, undoubtedly influencing their views of testing, are statements such as that repeatedly made by Rudy Crew, chancellor of the New York school system: "IQ tests are illegitimate.... Smart is not something you are. Smart is something you get."[72] In 1996 Jeff Howard, a black educator and the organizer of the Efficacy Institute, a teacher-training group, was quoted in an education article in the *New York Post* as saying, "The Efficacy Institute believes that all children are equally capable of learning, regardless of race, economic background, gender, or any other factor."[73] The editors of *The Bell Curve Debate*, a best-selling anthology of articles highly critical of the eponymous book, concluded their introduction by approvingly quoting, as if it were a profound insight, the comment of a black high school basketball player: "I used to think there were smart people and dumb people, but that's not true. Everybody's got the same brain."[74]

A number of legal challenges have been made to the use of job tests, the results of which are usually highly correlated with the results of IQ tests, and some of the challenges have succeeded in getting tests banned on which blacks averaged considerably lower scores than whites. An example: In 1984 the Golden Rule Insurance Company of Indianapolis acquiesced to a legal settlement binding it to not use tests in which blacks average scores are more than 10 percent lower than those of whites.[75] In 1985 the state of Alabama reached a settlement under which it agreed not to use teacher certification tests that produced differences greater than 5 to 10 percent between black and white candidates.[76] In other cases, the solution has been to make tests so easy that everyone passes. Texas recently gave a teacher examination that nearly 97 percent of candidates passed.[77] Another approach is to rely less on test scores and more on other factors: In a recent review article on politics in testing, David W. Murray, a social anthropologist, reported that the SAT (now known only by those initials, its former names—Scholastic Aptitude Test, and later Scholastic Assessment Test—no longer being considered politically appropriate), which measures verbal and mathematical skills but requires a foundation of general intelligence, particularly in the mathematics portion, is being given less weight than other criteria or even dropped altogether by many college admissions officers on the grounds that it is culturally and gender biased.[78]

The Test-Adjustment Movement

A quite different and widely effective attack on testing takes the form of adjustments to make tests fair to minority test-takers.

In one such approach, the administrators of tests "correct the bias" against minority candidates for college entrance or for jobs by raising their scores by some factor, a procedure some critics liken to the type of science fraud known informally as "cooking the books." David W. Murray reports that adjustments of this type are made by some college admissions officers to SAT scores, and the Educational Testing Service, publisher of the SAT, has recently decided to "recenter" SAT scores, adding points to the average score until it resides at 500, which somewhat pulls up the scores of low-scorers and lowers those of high-scorers.[79] Ironically, while these adjustments benefit some minority groups, they hurt others: Asian-American students, who on average outperform native whites in mathematics, end up having their scores adjusted somewhat downwards.[80]

Many employment tests measure specific learnings and acquired skills rather than IQ, but as is true of the SAT, the scores are strongly influenced by the test-takers' general intelligence. In the era of civil rights and affirmative action, the use of such tests to place people in jobs was called unfair because it resulted in disproportionately low shares of jobs going to minority groups. In line with the effort of affirmative action to make up for the severe disadvantages historically suffered by blacks, the Equal Employment Opportunities Commission invented a solution, put into effect in 1981 by the United States Employment Service, that was known as "race-norming" or "within-group norming": Test-takers were rated according to where they placed within their own group, not where they placed in relation to all applicants.[81] A black who scored in, say, the 85th percentile of blacks would be on an equal employment footing with a white who scored in the 85th percentile of whites, even though the black's score was considerably lower than the white's.[82]

Advocates of affirmative action argued that this procedure compensated for the social disadvantages of being black in America and harmed neither employers nor society, since, they claimed, intelligence as measured by tests has little value as a predictor of success in the workplace, where other traits and training count for more.[83] Opponents of race-norming countered with the argument that race-norming was unfair to whites, since it obviously counted their scores as worth less than equal or even lower scores of blacks. In political circles, a critic of the fairness or the social value of race-norming could speak freely with no fear of consequences, but in academia a researcher who dared to do research on the relation between measured intelligence and job performance could be in serious trouble, as a professor named Linda Gottfredson found out.

Gottfredson, a sociologist in the department of educational studies at the University of Delaware, thought that this topic deserved to be investigated and set out to do so. In her mid-thirties at the time (the mid-1980s), Gottfredson, an affable, attractive woman, termed herself an old-style liberal, and had, in fact, taught in ghetto schools and served in the Peace Corps in Malaysia. At the University of Delaware her work in vocational counseling led her to take an interest in the relation between intelligence, as measured by standard tests, and performance in the workplace, her impression being that intelligence was a good predictor of successful job performance, and she decided to conduct research on the matter.[84]

She needed funding for a research assistant and other expenses, and applied to various major foundations, but without success, and concluded that none of them would back research linking human cognitive abilities to genetic endowment. She then applied to the Pioneer Fund, which did give her a substantial grant; as is customary, the money would go to the university, which would then disburse it to her. After many months of analyzing a large mass of sociological, psychological, and employment data, Gottfredson concluded that tested intelligence does indeed correlate strongly with job performance and that the higher the level of the job, the stronger the relationship between intelligence and job performance.[85] She reported these findings in two research papers along with her conclusion that within-group norming, though meant to serve a worthy goal, actually hurts those blacks it places at levels of employment where they cannot perform well, and thereby also hurts society "That I reject preferential treatment by race," she wrote, "reflects my judgment that it will do great harm in the long run to the nation and to the favored groups themselves."[86]

Although her articles had passed peer review and were published in the respectable *Journal of Vocational Behavior*, as soon as they appeared a number of her colleagues and superiors began attacking her research and seeking to halt it. Events in her case started out like those in Rushton's: A departmental committee that had rated her work outstanding in 1988 rated it unsatisfactory in 1989, and the Promotion and Tenure Committee and her department chairman, Victor Martuza, denied her an expected promotion. Next, another form of political attack, a formidable one that had not been used against Rushton, was launched by William Frawley, a linguistics professor, who wrote to the university's president, E. A. Trabant, that the Pioneer Fund was racist and that the university should not accept grants from it. Trabant ordered the Faculty

Senate Committee on Research to study the matter, and in May, 1990, the committee recommended that the university refuse grants from Pioneer on the grounds that its aims and Gottfredson's research were incompatible with the university's commitment to racial and cultural diversity.* Trabant promptly halted further acceptance by the university of Pioneer money, cutting off support for Gottfredson and Jan Blits, a political scientist with whom she had begun to collaborate.[87]

Additional pressure was brought to bear on Gottfredson and Blits by the University of Delaware African American Coalition, a student group that sent out a press release identifying Gottfredson as one of those who "preach hatred, call it research, and then claim academic freedom."[88] She became something of a social outcast on campus; a number of colleagues overtly shunned her and black students held demonstrations against her and sometimes blocked entrance to her classes.

She and Blits chose to fight. They filed a grievance with a faculty welfare committee, which upheld their complaint of interference with academic freedom; when the acting provost rejected the decision, they appealed to the local chapter of the American Association of University Professors, which, after studying their case, filed a complaint with the American Arbitration Association, saying that in cutting off Gottfredson's and Blits's funding, the university had violated their academic freedom. The arbitration procedure, which required the filing of detailed briefs and a lengthy hearing, dragged on over sixteen arduous months, but in the end the arbitrator found the university in the wrong and the funding was restored.

Having scored a victory, Gottfredson and Blits then threatened the university with a lawsuit on the grounds of other forms of harassment, including the denial of Gottfredson's promotion and the departmental rating committee's reclassification of some of her and Blits's research as "non-research" in order to lower their yearly evaluations. In April 1992 the university settled out of court; it gave Gottfredson and Blits a paid year's leave of absence, reclassified the "non-research" as research, and yielded on certain other terms that remain confidential.[89] The students also gave up, and there have been no further student demonstrations.

Gottfredson's research continues without interference, but she remains somewhat isolated. As she said some time ago, "The colleagues who used to think of me as a fringe character who ought not be on

---

*See comment on Pioneer in the preface, and rebuttal of charges against Pioneer in Weyher 1997.

campus now think of me as a legitimate scholar but one whose views are unpopular."[90] Although she and Blits won their fight, she is not sanguine about academe's defense of academic freedom; as she said in a recent article reviewing their case:

> Faculty are now being punished, not on the basis of their extramural utterances and activities, but for the content of their research or teaching within the institution.... Our central administration was simply reactive—at first, in appeasing certain politically powerful coalitions on campus and later in resolutely rebuffing all claims that our rights were being violated. We survived largely by getting support from outside academe.[91]

The practice of within-group norming by state offices of the U.S. Employment Service was hotly debated by Congress in 1992 and abolished by it in that year, but the goals of test-score adjusting are being met to some degree by other methods. The Nassau County, New York, Police Department, for instance, commissioned experts a few years ago to create a new test for police force candidates that would have no "adverse impact upon blacks, Hispanics and females." The experts achieved that goal by omitting from the test all questions that require intelligence and substituting components that measure reading skills and judgment—but only questions that had been pretested and shown to produce no average between-group differences in scores.[92]

Refusal to Publish

The editors of general publishing houses have every right to choose what they wish to publish and to reject what they do not; they are in business, and are entitled to decide what will sell and what will not.

In the domain of science publishing, however, the goals and methods of appraisal are somewhat different. Manuscripts submitted to publishers of scientific works are judged less by their potential sales than by their scientific merit as judged by peer reviewers. This is intended to insure the publication and availability to scientists of new discoveries and findings of merit, and their transmission to the general public through media reportage of these publications. When the methodology, findings, or interpretations of the authors seem flawed to scientist readers, they voice their criticisms in the form of book reviews or critiques submitted to journals in the field, thereby realizing the democratic ideal of a free exchange of new findings and of differing interpretations of them.

Of late, however, this system appears to have become vulnerable to political pressure in the case of research reports and books by competent scientists interpreting ethnic and racial differences in average IQ scores from a genetic viewpoint. The following three cases have been reported in the press; how many others have gone unreported is unknown.

• Jensen, whose books had previously been published by Columbia University Press, the U.S. Office of Education, Methuen, and the Free Press, spent years writing his magnum opus, an 800-page manuscript summing up his life's work and titled *The g Factor*. None of the top university presses he approached would publish it. Finally, he contacted Wiley & Sons, a solid publisher with an important science division, and was invited to show it to them. Wiley's psychology editor read and approved the manuscript, which received favorable reviews from independent referees to whom Wiley sent it, one even writing that "it could be the definitive study on general intelligence for years to come."[93] But after ten months—an unconscionably long time to hold a manuscript—Wiley sent it back to Jensen with a brief letter stating simply that they had decided not to publish it. When asked by a reporter why not, Susan Spilka, Wiley's manager of corporate communications, said, "I have no idea and we'll probably never know. Chances are it wasn't a quality factor." Then she added, letting the cat out of the bag, that the rejection was a "very deliberate decision" and that Wiley does "not want to publish in this field."[94] (In early 1997 Jensen's manuscript was finally accepted for publication by Prager.)

• Rushton wrote a book, *Race, Evolution, and Behavior*, in which he presented all his research data and hypotheses about the evolution of individual and group differences in intelligence, sexual behavior, parenting behavior, and a great deal more, but as we have seen, the prestigious publisher who had planned to bring it out changed its mind after Rushton became notorious. As already mentioned, however, it was accepted and published in 1995 by Transaction Publishers, a medium-sized academic house that often issues works of a conservative cast.

• Christopher Brand, a professor of psychology at Edinburgh University, wrote a book with the same title as Jensen's, *The g Factor*, a study of *g* and of the evidence that heredity plays a part in it. Wiley's English branch, apparently unconcerned about its American branch's rejection of Jensen's book, planned to publish Brand's book in February 1996 and processed the manuscript through the several phases of editing and production. Nothing in the book went beyond the bounds of the kinds of evidence gathered by Jensen and many other workers in the intelligence field, and Wiley had no misgivings about it, viewing it as "a scientific monograph intended for a very limited audience."[95] They got as far as sending out prepublication review copies and shipping books to book stores when Brand, doing advance publicity for the book, made some honest but brash and imprudent remarks to reporters that caused Wiley to take a different view of what it was publishing: Brand was not only forthright about his belief that genes play a role in average IQ differences between races but, when asked if he were a racist, denied that he was—and then added that he might be called a "scientific racist" and that "I do think not only that there's a link between race and psychology, in particular between race and IQ, but of course I think and have the honesty to tell you—other people wouldn't—that the link is, shall I call it, deep-seated."[96] Having put his foot in it, he put in the other one, terming feminism a "menace" and suggesting that single mothers ought to mate with males of a higher IQ.[97] The furor was instant, fierce, and widespread, and three days later Wiley's New York office took remarkable action and issued this statement:

> After careful consideration of the statements made recently by author Christopher Brand (as reported in the British press), as well as some of the views presented in his work, *The g Factor*, we have decided to withdraw the book from publication.... [Wiley] does not want to support these views by disseminating them or be associated with a book that makes assertions that we find repellent.[98]

Books were withdrawn from stores and plans for U.S. publication were canceled. Brand hoped to find another publisher, but as of this writing had not been successful.

In an article in *National Review* Kevin Lamb, a library assistant at *Newsweek*, suggests that these three cases are not isolated ones.[99] But since more stories of the same kind would become repetitive, we move on.

Ad Hominem Attacks

A number of the instances already cited have included incidental denigration of the character and motives of the researcher, but in other cases this has been the primary method of attack. The pervasive incivility of the present era seems to have seeped into the domain of science and badly eroded its former collegial decency; defamation has become an accepted weapon of scientific debate. Since reputation is of paramount importance in the sciences, damage to one's good name is a far more devastating and long-lasting injury than the physical traumas sometimes inflicted on researchers by protesters at public appearances and more serious even than the emotional harm of physical assaults.

The cases of Jensen, Rushton, and Gottfredson all bear witness to that. Although with the passage of time there has been some recognition among social scientists that research on the genetics of, and racial differences in, intelligence merits attention and that rebuttals should take the form of contradictory evidence, not character defamation, their names continue to have dark connotations in the minds of many colleagues and their students. Their repute is somewhat like that of a high government official accused of corrupt practices of which a long investigation could find no evidence; although formally cleared, his name continues to conjure up such thoughts as "Isn't that the guy who took payoffs from industry...or so it was said...or wasn't that ever proved? ...well, I guess where there's smoke, there's fire."

It would be possible to compile a long list of other researchers who have been similarly defamed in order to negate their findings and dishearten them to the point of giving up their research. But one more case, that of the late Richard Herrnstein and Charles Murray, co-authors of *The Bell Curve*, can stand for the many.

The Bell Curve, as most readers know, was the 1994 best-seller by Herrnstein, a Harvard psychologist who died in 1994, and Murray, a conservative social policy analyst. In the book, a weighty tome some 800 pages long, Herrnstein and Murray exhaustively reviewed and analyzed a mass of existing research data on cognitive differences among people and groups in America, discussed the differences in intelligence test scores and the evidence that part of those differences is the result of hereditary factors, and drew politically conservative conclusions as to the policies these realities should dictate.

It is, of course, entirely legitimate and appropriate for social scientists and reporters to differ with Herrnstein and Murray's research, selection of data, analyses of those data, and conclusions, and many have done so, some dispassionately and effectively. What is neither legitimate nor appropriate—what is, indeed, seriously damaging to the mores of the scientific community—is to defame and vilify the authors, sometimes in the form of direct personal invective, more often in the form of characterizations of their work as the product of abominable motives and intentions. Murray, interviewed on National Public Radio on October 28, 1994, shortly after the book was published, said, "I have been appalled by the last couple of weeks, and a friend of mine said to my wife when she made this point, 'Well, what is it? You sound like somebody who got into

World War II and is surprised that they're firing real bullets.' So I guess I shouldn't be surprised in some ways, but I am." Some time later he wrote, "The book was said to be the flimsiest kind of pseudoscience. A racist screed. Designed to promote a radical political agenda. An angry book. Tainted by the work of neo-Nazis."[100]

Some examples of the ad hominem attacks on Herrnstein and Murray:

- "corrupt" (Leon Kamin in *Commentary*, August 1995);
- "Their description of these data goes beyond dubious analysis, beyond irresponsibly selective choice of evidence, to become outright misrepresentation" (Richard Nisbett in *Commentary*, August 1995);
- "[Stephen Jay] Gould made him [Murray] out to be an intellectual lackey... of the far Right...In Gould's view, Mr. Murray's scholarship was...flimsy, based on discredited psychometrics, the antediluvian g, and the outmoded IQ concept.... Gould left little doubt as to the charlatanry of the authors...." (W. H. Ryan, describing a lecture by Gould at Harvard in *Commentary*, August 1995);
- "a work of...presumptuous single-minded wisdom...profound fatalism and austere elitism...." (Steven Fraser, in Fraser, 1995: 2–3);
- "the work of a controversialist and popularizer [referring to Murray] from the fringes of the academy" (Jeffrey Rosen and Charles Lane, in Fraser, 1995: 61);
- "intellectual brown shirts...a vile, disingenuously vicious book by two truly odious men" (Adolph Reed, Jr., "Intellectual Brown Shirts," *Progressive*, December 1994).
- "a scabrous piece of racial pornography masquerading as serious scholarship.... a genteel way of calling somebody a nigger" (Bob Herbert, "Throwing a Curve," *New York Times*, October 27, 1994.

These comments illustrate the recent abandonment by many scientists and science writers of another component of the classic scientific ethos, namely that disagreement over research findings and their interpretation, however intense, be governed by the principles of civility and mutual respect. In recent years the climate of intellectual discourse in the social and behavioral sciences has been coming to resemble the climate of political discourse in our Congress and even at times the spirit of sanctioned savagery of the newest form of spectator sport, "extreme fighting." A development more destructive of the behavioral and social sciences is hard to imagine. One might even see this phenomenon as a symptom of the insidious evolution of our society—a downward evolution, a Spenglerian decline of the West.

4

Anatomy Is Destiny

Male and Female Created He Them

So God created man in his own image, in the image of God created he him; male and female created he them.—Genesis 1: 27

The Judaic myth of creation portrays God as a sexual egalitarian, at least on day six, when, according to Genesis, he made both male and female in his own image. But the profoundly paternalistic men of primitive Hebrew society saw woman as a different and lesser form of human being, inferior to man in mind, judgment, and character, and their myths of the events subsequent to the creation of Adam and Eve supported this view and justified the way they treated their women. The crucial event is, of course, the first and worst sin: Eve, poor in judgment, is easily beguiled by the serpent into eating the forbidden fruit of the tree of knowledge of good and evil; deficient in virtue, she tempts Adam to do likewise. Her poor judgment and weakness of character lead Adam to sin, resulting in God's expelling both of them from Eden and condemning woman forever to suffer in childbirth and to live as a lesser person, governed by her husband:

Unto the woman he said, I will greatly multiply thy sorrow and thy conception: in sorrow thou shalt bring forth children: and thy desire shall be to thy husband, and he shall rule over thee.—Genesis 3:16

Down the centuries of Hebrew history, woman is often portrayed in the Old Testament as a good mother, sometimes as a sexual delight, and occasionally as a heroine, but always as distinctly inferior to man in mind, character, and status in society. In the Christian era, Saint Paul, the architect and evangelist of the new faith, established as official doctrine an even lowlier image of woman for unknowable reasons of his own.

The head of every man is Christ; and the head of the woman is the man; and the head of Christ is God.... The man is not of the woman: but the woman of the man. Neither was the man created for the woman; but the woman for the man.... Let your women keep silence in the churches: for it is not permitted unto them to speak; but they are commanded to be under obedience, as also saith the law. And if they will learn any thing, let them ask their husbands at home... (I Corinthians, 11. 3, 8–9, 34–35)

This view of woman (which would become even more jaundiced when Church theologians officially declared the Original Sin to be the work of Eve, the sexual temptress) was augmented by attitudes and beliefs of the Greco-Roman culture in which Christianity developed. Although the Greeks had never thought of woman as the temptress who led man into sin (an idea foreign to them), they did see her as a lesser form of human being whose functions were to serve and please the higher form, man. Four centuries before Paul's time, Plato said that woman possessed all the same "gifts of nature" as man, "but in all of them a woman is inferior to a man."[1] Aristotle later went even farther, declaring, "We must look upon the female character as being a sort of natural deficiency."[2] Upper-class Greek men of the Golden Era and succeeding centuries saw their wives as housekeepers and childbearers but not as equals entitled to take part in the world outside the home, and not even as companions with whom to share evenings of intellectual discourse, a favorite pastime described by Plato and others that was a strictly male affair.

In the *Economist*, a dialogue giving practical advice on home and farm management, the historian Xenophon tells us how a typical well-to-do Athenian man at the end of the fifth century B.C. perceived and treated his wife. It opens with Socrates asking Ischomachus, a rather smug and self-confident young husband, whether his wife came to him well prepared for her role. "My dear Socrates," says Ischomachus, "how could she have had sufficient knowledge when I took her, since she came to my house when she was not fifteen years old and had spent the preceding part of her life under the strictest restraint in order that she might see as little, hear as little, and ask as few questions as possible?" He himself, he says, educated her, instructing her in caring for children, watching over the servants, and seeing to household tasks, but taught her nothing of reasoning, learning, philosophy, science, or decision making, since females were innately incapable of such matters.

The *Economist* and many other documents portray the upper-class Athenian female as living largely in seclusion—less so than women in Oriental harems but not free to come and go as she pleased; indeed, not even entrusted with shopping, a task carried out for her by trained slaves. And not as her husband's confidante; he went out into the world in the morning and spent his days in public places engaging in serious pursuits, but when he came home at night had no interest in sharing with a naïve and ignorant wife the intellectual experiences of the day or the intricacies of current politics. In a famous court oration Demosthenes summed up the limited capacities and several functions of woman: "Mistresses we keep for pleasure, concubines for daily attendance upon our persons, and wives to bear us legitimate children and be our housekeepers."[3]

The blend of Greco-Roman culture and Christianity determined the image and social status of woman in the West down the centuries. One can, of course, rummage around in history and find the occasional great empress, female philosopher, or other outstanding woman, but they are rarities. For every Aspasia, the beautiful courtesan who taught Socrates rhetoric and wrote orations for Pericles (whose mistress and political advisor she was), there have been countless courtesans and mistresses who taught men nothing but salon gallantry and bedroom skills; for every Elizabeth I, deftly running a nation, there have been hundreds of queens who bore their husbands' children and whom we remember only because we remember the kings they were married to; for every Marie Curie or Florence Nightingale there have been millions of women who, if they had somehow acquired learning, wisely followed the advice tossed off in a Jane Austen novel, "A woman, if she have the misfortune to know anything, should conceal it as well as she can," or, having been brought up to know very little, regarded themselves as half ministering angel, half entrancing fool, who had to play the part described in 1748 by Lord Chesterfield:

> Women are only children of a larger growth; they have an entertaining tattle, and sometimes wit; but for solid, reasoning good sense, I never in my life knew one that had it.... A man of sense only trifles with them, plays with them, humors them, and flatters them, as he does with a sprightly, forward child; but he neither consults them about, nor trusts them with, serious matters, though he often makes them believe that he does both.[4]

Or, in the sentimental Victorian era, the sweeter and sappier role idealized by Tennyson:

> For him she plays, to him she sings
>   Of early faith and plighted vows;
>   She knows but matters of the house,
> And he, he knows a thousand things.

> Her faith is fixt and cannot move,
>   She darkly feels him great and wise,
>   She dwells on him with faithful eyes,
> "I cannot understand; I love."
> —*In Memoriam*, 97

So it went until there came the first tiny breezes, premonitions of future storms, in the form of the first women's college in 1839, the Women's Rights Convention in 1846, the handful of radical feminists who dared to wear pants, smoke cigars, extol free love and socialism, and the many discontented housewives who listened and cheered (silently, for the most part) when feminist Victoria Woodhull proclaimed, "We mean treason, we mean secession, and on a thousand times greater scale than was that of the South. We are plotting revolution."[5]

By the latter half of the nineteenth century women were beginning to inch their way into men's world of education and work, though not of governance. But even as they won a few battles and mounted a long-term campaign for the vote (which they won in America in 1920), Sigmund Freud, who was having so powerful an impact on the thinking of the intelligentsia, pronounced woman's fate in three words: "Anatomy is destiny." His exegesis of the apothegm: Woman is doomed by the construction of her body to be inferior to man, for the female child's discovery that she lacks a penis causes her to develop traits of personality and mental abilities different from and less desirable than those of the male child: "After a woman has become aware of the wound to her narcissism, she develops, like a scar, a sense of inferiority...[and] begins to share the contempt felt by men for a sex which is the lesser in so important a respect."[6] Believing herself to be an inferior human being, she behaves like one: She is prone to jealousy, develops a weaker sense of ethics and of justice than the male, is sexually passive, and is influenced in her judgment by feelings of affection or hostility rather than rationality.

How could any sensible person disagree?—was it not obvious that very few of history's most eminent people (3 percent by one authority's reckoning[7]) were women? Where were the great women statesmen, scientists, explorers, inventors, lawgivers, empire-builders, philosophers, composers, dramatists? One or two, here or there; no more. The only area in which a respectable number of women achieved some eminence, when women had achieved a degree of emancipation in the nineteenth and early twentieth century, was belles lettres—although, ironically, George Eliot and George Sand felt obliged to hide behind men's names.

Most men, if they ever thought about why there had been so few women of achievement, assumed that it was because their mental equipment simply was not up to it. Not until the liberation of women in recent decades was it recognized—and then mostly by thoughtful and reasonably well-educated people—that there might be another and concurrent cause: Society had always determined the appropriate sex roles for each sex and made it all but impossible for women to receive the training and take part in the activities that might lead to achievement.*[8] When Sir Thomas More, lord chancellor to Henry VIII, found one of his daughters in tears one day over a difficult Latin text she was trying to read, he considered it his duty as a loving father to shepherd her back into the safe path of approved female behavior by gently taking the book away and telling her that such difficult mental work was not for women.[9] The Puritan governor of Massachusetts, John Winthrop, musing in 1645 about the insanity of Goodie Hopkins, the wife of Connecticut's governor, ascribed it to her exertions at reading and writing: "If she had attended her household affairs and such things as belong to women," he wrote, "and not gone out of her way and calling to meddle in such things as are proper for men, whose minds are stronger, etc., she had kept her wits."[10]

In Freud's time, two and a half centuries later, most men still had much the same view of things. Emancipation, to be sure, proceeded steadily though slowly during the twentieth century, with increasing numbers of women going to college, working outside the home, making their way in substantial numbers into teaching and the care-giving professions, token numbers into medicine, law, and other bastions of male privilege, and considerable numbers during World War II into assembly lines and managerial positions. But despite woman's struggling free of a number of long-standing social and legal limitations, she could shake off little of the great weight of cultural tradition that shaped her as she grew up into a creature who only half-believed that she was the equal of man. The easier, more acceptable, and less alarming route was to work a bit after

---

*Some social scientists and feminists now use the terms "sex roles" and "sex differences" to refer to *biological* distinctions between males and females, "gender roles" and "gender differences" to refer to *psychological* and *social* distinctions. But as Diane Halpern points out, biology and psychosocial influences are so interwoven that it is often difficult to decide whether a distinction is due to a biological difference or to its psychosocial concomitants (Halpern 1992: 18). Like Halpern, therefore, I use "sex roles" and "sex differences" to refer to differences of either kind or both.

completing one's education, flirt and date around a little, and then marry a man for whom she would tend the home and bear children while he earned the family income and made its major decisions about how to spend or invest its income and even how to vote.

With so much having opened up for women, why could they not see themselves as the equals of men and live accordingly? Was it that men kept the gates barred? Yes, in part; but in part it was their own belief that men were right to see them as persons of weaker and lesser abilities and character. That was the message they got from their mothers and fathers, their teachers, the society around them, and from that society's new cultural priesthood, the psychoanalysts. Wilhelm Stekel, for instance, told them that woman's greatest pleasure derives from the "will to self-subjection," and Helene Deutsch said, "The theory I have long supported—according to which femininity is largely associated with passivity and masochism—has been confirmed in the course of years by clinical experience.... I venture to say that the fundamental identities 'feminine passive' and 'masculine active' assert themselves in all known cultures and races."[11] Much the same message was passed on to them again and again by the acolytes of that priesthood, the mass-media popularizers of psychology; a typical article in *Good Housekeeping* said that a truly feminine woman would accept her altruistic and "womb-centered" nature, eschew pseudo-masculine aims, and put her husband and children "way before self."[12] And tell herself, as her Victorian grandmother had, that in so doing she was exerting mighty influence over events outside: "The hand that rocks the cradle/ Is the hand that rules the world."

* * *

But then in 1963 came the second wave of feminism, the women's liberation movement, and genuine change. Along with all the activist tactics of marches, demonstrations, letter-writing campaigns, petitions, delegations calling upon legislators, and boycotts of the products of companies deemed unfair to women, the movement introduced a new view of woman as man's equal in all things—a person for whom a man curbed his impulse to open a door lest he be sneered at as a male chauvinist, and whom he silently allowed to split the check for dinner, since his paying it alone might look like a favor for which he expected a sexual favor in return.

In the early intoxicating years of the movement, many women eagerly accepted the new doctrine that almost all the well-known differences between the sexes were not the dictates of anatomy but social constructions. In addition to the major (but ill-fated) national drive to pass the Equal Rights Amendment, they asserted their equality in many simpler and more mundane ways: They burned their bras, wore flat-heeled shoes and pants, cut their hair short, did without makeup, pushed for the use of "Ms.," kept their maiden name when they married or linked it, hyphenated, to their husband's, met in study groups to stare in hand-mirrors at their own genitalia and strive to admire them, strenuously objected to the use of "girls" to refer to any female beyond puberty and of "man" and "he" to refer generically to human beings, seriously debated whether the love of other women might not be better than the love of men (and, in some cases tried it and preferred it), fought for unisex gymnasiums, cheered what they saw as a significant victory when Billy Jean King beat Bobby Riggs in a male-female singles tennis match, and tried to rewrite history and mythology to stress the reigns of queens and the ancient long-lost roles of goddesses.

Some of these new folkways caught on and became part of the culture; some, like the linking of last names in marriage, proved a nuisance and withered away; and many gross inequities and certain sex differences stubbornly survived all efforts to uproot them. By the end of the 1980s, after two and half decades of women's liberation:

- Women still earned only two-thirds as much as men doing the same kind of work; less than two percent of the top executives of Fortune 500 companies were women; and more than 60 percent of adults living below the poverty level were women.[13]
- Despite all the feminists' efforts to liberate females' anger and free them to be more aggressive, not one woman was a player at the major league level in baseball, basketball, or soccer.[14]
- Female students continued to suffer math anxiety and to score appreciably lower in the math section of the SAT than male students, did better in some components of the verbal section, and responded somewhat differently to some parts of nearly all personality inventory tests.[15]
- Women comprise only 9 percent of U.S. engineers, perhaps 5 percent of airline pilots, about 10 percent of the seats in the House and the Senate, 13 percent of members of boards of major corporations, and 13 percent of members of the New York Stock Exchange.[16]

Even in the 1990s, sex-determined roles and behavior were more the rule than the exception. As Diane Halpern, an expert in sexual differences in cognition, writes:

If anyone doubts that women and men still tend to live sex-segregated lives in contemporary American society, a casual visit to a PTA meeting, or the restaurant in a large department store midweek, or a trade union hall, or a corporate engineering department will attest to the fact that while changes in the societal roles of women and men are occurring, there are still considerable differences in men's and women's experiences. High school cheerleaders are still virtually all female while shop classes remain virtually all male. Few girls play in the now "coed" little league games (especially in the high school leagues), and few boys elect to take home economics classes. Despite all of the efforts of those associated with the "women's movement," de facto sex-related life differences are alive and well.[17]

* * *

To what extent were sex-role differences, both those of the past and those that remained in the 1990s, direct results of biological differences, whether genetic, hormonal, or neuroanatomical? To what extent were they the psychological results of perceiving one's biological differences (as in Freud's psychology)? And to what extent were they the results of socialization by the family and society? A vast mass of research on sex differences conducted prior to the women's movement had measured cognitive and personality differences without seeking to determine whence they arose: females' greater fear of spiders, lesser mathematical ability, greater verbal ability, lesser aggressiveness, stronger altruistic impulses, lesser visual-spatial abilities, greater tendency to conform to group opinion when being observed, and many others.[18] But from the mid-1960s on, with the growth of psychobiology and behavioral genetics, research on sex differences has increasingly sought to determine whether they are caused in part or even wholly by genetic, hormonal, and other biological influences—whether there is, for instance, a causal relationship between male-female differences in the XX and XY chromosomes and differences in cognitive abilities, between male-female differences in brain lateralization and cognitive abilities, and even between sex hormone monthly fluctuations in women, seasonal fluctuations in men, and variations in cognitive functions.[19] Increasingly, researchers of male-female differences are taking a holistic view in which genetic and other biological influences are seen as interacting with parental and societal influences; the answers to the questions are complex, different for each ability or trait, and only beginning to be spelled out in interactionist terms.

Clearly, such information would be of considerable value to those educators, legislators, justices, parents, and others who seek to rear the nation's children and to treat its adults rationally and fairly. But many feminist activists and their sympathizers (both female and male) have held, and hold today, that the questions need no research; they maintain that aside from the indisputable facts that woman is on average smaller than man and has certain obviously different sex characteristics, there are no substantial mental and emotional differences between the sexes, and, anyway, if there are any, they have been foisted on woman by male-dominated, traditionalist society.[20] As Cynthia Epstein, a feminist sociologist, has written:

> The expectation that a class of people is destined to play out their lives according to a given sequence because of the traits they inherit or the situations they encounter in their early years is essentially conservative in perspective. If it were based on clearly established truths, then we would, as a society, have to learn to live with it. But the evidence is highly questionable.... Men probably will never be able to have babies, but they may be able to mother or teach young children as well as women do. Women may never win a weight-lifting contest competing with men matched for weight and training, but they are fast catching up in marathon running and solving mathematics problems. It seems clear that intellectual capacity and emotional qualities are distributed throughout humanity without restrictions of sex any more than race or nationality.[21]

Most feminists are therefore hostile to research on sex differences, particularly any effort to link them to biological influences, on the grounds that it is prejudiced, sexist, and unscientific. Those scientists who do research seeking to measure the extent of biological influences on sex-role behavior, and those who use the findings of such research to explain male-female differences they have measured, are, in feminist eyes, either avowed opponents of the women's movement or witless providers of ammunition to the enemy. Even if their motives are the best, feminists say, their research is inherently biased by their cultural preconceptions about the subject and about themselves as males; these preconceptions warp the way they look at the problem, design their investigations, and interpret their findings, and therefore by far the greater part of the vast mass of scientific research ostensibly demonstrating the biological determinants of sex differences is flawed and valueless.[22]

What, then, is to be done about sex-differences research? asks Anne Fausto-Sterling, a feminist biologist, and answers:

> We could call for a ban on all research into sex differences. But that would leave questions of genuine social and scientific interest unanswered. We could claim an agnostic position—that all research is good for its own sake—but no one really believes that.... We ought, therefore, neither to impose research bans nor to claim agnosticism. Instead, we ought to expect that individual researchers will articulate—both to themselves and publicly—exactly where they stand, what they think,

and, most importantly, what they *feel* deep down in their guts about the complex of personal and social issues that relate to their area of research.[23]

But even if those who do research on the biological influences on sex differences were to confess their innermost feelings in the introduction to their research reports—about as likely as presidential candidates' freely revealing every detail of their sexual, emotional, and financial lives—their work would still be either dangerous or damaging to women, since it could be misunderstood by the public and misused by male chauvinists. As Diane Halpern states the problem:

> It is frightening, and perhaps even un-American, to consider the possibility that even a small portion of the sex differences in cognitive abilities may be attributed to biological factors.... What such a conclusion does...is create the potential for misquotation, misuse, and misinterpretation, in an attempt to justify discrimination based on sex. Perhaps the very publication of such research results create a considerable risk.[24]

Halpern then candidly poses the question this implies—the very issue to which this book is addressed—and, although a feminist, answers it as an advocate of academic freedom: "The question that is being raised is whether there should be censorship in science, even self-imposed censorship, when results are likely to be misused. However, the danger inherent in censorship is far greater than the danger in publishing results that could be used for undesirable purposes."[25] Even though sex-differences research may contribute to what she calls "the media circus" and its "simplistic analyses," she defends such work:

> Empirical research doesn't create stereotyping, as its critics imply; the systematic study of sex differences using scientific rules of evidence is the only way to dispel stereotypes and to understand legitimate differences.... The insistence that we study only similarities creates a false dichotomy because research on similarities is not separable from the study of differences.[26]

Many a feminist takes a very different view of the matter. In an article in *American Psychologist* euphemistically titled "Issues to Consider in Conducting Nonsexist Research: A Guide for Researchers," one team argued that sex differences should be reported only under limited circumstances, or better yet, not at all, and a male feminist psychologist, writing in the same important journal, took the unequivocal stance that researchers should stop reporting any between-sex comparisons.[27] Still others, though seemingly less severely censorious, achieve much the same end by asserting that much or most sex-difference research is a waste of time and effort; Fausto-Sterling herself, after reviewing a broad range of biologically based research on sex differences, concludes:

> I do *not*...believe that *all* of the research areas covered in this book warrant further investment of time, money, and talent. We need to learn more about menstruation and menopause...[but] further research into sex differences in cognition or brain laterality seems to me uncalled for.... Similarly, it is not worthwhile to continue to do research on animal aggression in highly artificial settings.... As exemplified by the work on rape, to take even very extensive animal research, define it according to uniquely human behaviors, and then to use it to analyze human behavior is both logically flawed and politically dangerous.[28]

Such feminist hostility toward biologically based research on sex differences rarely takes the form of disruptions of meetings and physical assaults such as we saw in the cases of Jensen and Rushton; nevertheless, says Halpern, the political climate regarding such research has been combative since the onset of the women's movement and "few areas of study engender as much controversy and acrimony."[29] Edward O. Wilson, the Harvard naturalist who initiated the sociobiology revolution (to be discussed later in this chapter), says that the biology of gender differences is still taboo and that although the overwhelming evidence of recent research has lessened the power of that taboo, "it's still dangerous for a researcher to push strongly for biologically based differences."

Even an interactionist stance, recognizing that both innate and environmental factors are involved, is often seen by feminist activists as biased and unacceptable, and taking that stance can be personally and professionally costly. To see what that means, let us look now at the experiences of two leading researchers of male-female differences in mathematical ability.

Why Aren't Girls Better at Math? Don't Ask, Don't Tell

Neither Professor Julian Stanley nor his co-author, Camilla Benbow, a graduate student, anticipated that they would be fiercely attacked by feminists or, indeed, by anyone when their brief report "Sex Differences in Mathematical Ability: Fact or Artifact?" was accepted by the journal *Science* and published in its December 12, 1980 issue. Failing to anticipate the ferocity and volume of the response it would engender, they were in for a most unpleasant surprise.

It had long been widely known and documented by many studies that girls did less well than boys in math in junior high school and still less well in senior high school, some studies finding the differences to be minor, many others substantial.[30] What made Stanley and Benbow's report incendiary was not their data showing that there were many more boys than girls among the mathematically gifted but their conclusion as to the cause of that difference.

Stanley, a tall, slender man then of middle age, courtly of manner and with a mellifluous Southern accent, had for years been doing rather abstract work on the statistical analysis of test results, but the more concrete subject of mathematical talent had intrigued him since his thirties when, for several years, he had been a high school math teacher in Atlanta and had seen, as had everyone in that profession, that like those few musicians with absolute pitch, some students possessed a seemingly native and remarkable facility at mathematics.

In 1968 a teacher of a summer computer science program sought Stanley's advice about what to do with Joe Bates, a thirteen-year-old boy in her program who was extraordinarily gifted at mathematics. "I was somewhat hesitant and perhaps even reluctant at first to get involved," Stanley has written, "but I did, and my life and career were never to be the same again." With little specific knowledge to draw on, he relied on his expertise in measurement and gave Joe Bates the Scholastic Aptitude Test in math and several College Board achievement tests, all usually given to sixteen- and seventeen-year-olds, and was delighted that the boy did well enough on them to qualify for college courses. Stanley thereupon got him accepted at Johns Hopkins to study calculus, computer science, and physics; Joe Bates thrived in all three, earned a Master's in computer science at seventeen, and today is a leading researcher at Carnegie Mellon University.[31]

Stanley's experiences with Joe Bates spurred him to start on a new line of scientific inquiry. In 1971, with support from a private foundation, he launched a project of his own devising, the Study of Mathematically Precocious Youth (SMPY), to learn whatever he could about the cognitive skills, early educational background, and other factors that might account for exceptional math ability in young people, and how to make the most of it.

A side issue that later became a leading issue was that girls, by and large, did distinctly less well in math than boys at the high school level. Why this was so had never been established, but two major possibilities had been suggested: the less favored one, that boys were, for some genetic or other biological reason, innately better at mathematical reasoning; the more favored one, that for psychosocial reasons—the views of girls' parents about what girls were and were not good at, girls' own self-image, and their perception of what boys would think of them if they were good at math—girls felt that math was not a feminine accomplishment, had therefore taken fewer math courses in the earlier grades of school, and so had a poorer preparation for junior and senior high school math.

Camilla Benbow, in her mid-twenties in 1980, was, like many another graduate student, drawn toward the subject her mentor was most interested in. Although she was carrying a full load of graduate studies, she was intrigued by some of Stanley's SMPY data showing that boys gifted at math had higher scores, on average, than girls gifted at math, and that more boys got top grades than would be the case if the scores of both boys and girls were normally distributed.

What could account for the boys' higher average scores and for the excess of top-scoring boys? It occurred to Benbow that perhaps the data of all six SMPY searches could be combined and used to test the hypothesis that top-scoring boys had taken more math courses in their early grades than top-scoring girls. She suggested this to Stanley, who thought it an excellent idea, urged her to go ahead with the project, and conferred with her from time to time as she laboriously collected and verified the data, some of which was on computer tapes, some on punched cards (this was 1980), and some on paper. Neither she nor Stanley had any preconception or preference as to what they would find; as Stanley said, "Let's just do the science."

After several months of work, Benbow had produced a table summarizing the scores of 9,937 students, all of whom had tested in the upper 2 to 5 percent (the percent varied by the year of search) in math ability for students at their grade level as determined by a standardized math achievement test, and, as participants in the SMPY, had taken both the Scholastic Aptitude Test-Verbal (SAT-V) and Mathematical (SAT-M), and whose earlier training in math was on record.

Benbow brought the compiled data to Stanley, and together they analyzed it statistically to see what the figures meant. There was no average difference between boys and girls on the verbal test but there was, as expected, a large average difference on the math test: Boys scored, on average, about one-half standard deviation higher than girls, meaning that a boy who had an average score for boys did better than about two-thirds of the girls. That would lead one to expect higher scores for the upper 2 to 5 percent of boys than for the upper 2 to 5 percent of girls, and this was the case; but more importantly, there were more such high-scoring boys than one would predict from curves of normal distribution—there were, it seemed clear, many more math-talented boys than girls.

This was a puzzle, though no surprise, to Stanley; he'd seen such results in all six surveys over the years. He had, though, been surprised years earlier when he first saw such results; as he told me, "I'd had no experiences with sex differences until 1972, when the SMPY did the first talent search, and it was amazing to my student assistants and me how much worse females scored than males. Especially at the high end—26 percent of the boys scored higher than any girl! Even though there had been many reports by others that on average boys were somewhat better at math, we hadn't anticipated anything like such an enormous difference between the most talented boys and the most talented girls."

In 1974, Stanley and two of his graduate students, Daniel Keating and Lynn Fox, in a book of reports on the SMPY findings that they co-edited, sided with the familiar nurturist hypothesis as to the cause of the sex difference: Girls had for one reason or another taken fewer basic math courses such as algebra before tackling junior and senior high school math, and therefore were less skilled than boys in mathematical reasoning.

But the hypothesis had been untested and unproved. Now Benbow's compilation of the data from the six SMPY's enabled her and Stanley to put it to the test, which they did with a result that surprised them and that they felt would surprise others in the field. Together they drafted a brief report for the journal *Science*, introducing the subject as follows:

> Huge sex differences have been reported in mathematical aptitude and achievement. In junior high school, this sex difference is quite obvious: girls excel in computation, while boys excel on tasks requiring mathematical reasoning ability. Some investigators believe that differential course-taking gives rise to the apparently inferior mathematical reasoning ability of girls. One alternative, however, could be that less well-developed mathematical reasoning ability contributes to girls' taking fewer mathematics courses and achieving less than boys.[32]

But their findings contradicted the differential course-taking hypothesis and supported the less well-developed math reasoning ability hypothesis: The nearly 10,000 math-gifted boys and girls in the six SMPY's had had essentially the same amount of formal training in mathematics prior to the seventh grade, yet even by then boys averaged forty points higher (out of a possible 800) than girls on the SAT-M, and although there was little difference in the number of math courses the boys and girls took through eleventh grade, the difference in their average scores increased, reaching fifty points by the time of graduation from high school.

Benbow and Stanley summed up, "Our data contradict the hypothesis that differential course-taking accounts for observed sex differences in mathematical ability." As to whether other environmental influences might have played a part, they were cautious, saying that it was hard to "dissect out" the influences of societal expectations and attitudes on mathematical reasoning ability; they did, however, point out that a liking for math and an expectation of its importance in future careers—matters about which every student in the talent searches had been asked—appeared to have no relation to their SAT-M scores. Their final conclusion was that differences in innate ability accounted for the results, although they allowed that environmental factors might also have played a part:

> We favor the hypothesis that sex differences in achievement in and attitude toward mathematics result from superior male mathematical ability, which may in turn be related to greater male ability in spatial tasks. This male superiority is probably an expression of both endogenous and exogenous variables.* We recognize, however, that our data are consistent with numerous alternative hypotheses. Nonetheless, the hypothesis of differential course-taking was not supported. It also seems likely that putting one's faith in boy-versus-girl socialization processes as the only permissible explanation of the sex difference in mathematics is premature.

Stanley and Benbow knew that feminists were closely allied to and supported by the liberal-left political correctness (P.C.) movement, and that it was not P.C. to suggest that females were inferior in any way to males either by nature or upbringing. They therefore expected some adverse criticism, but were taken aback by the heat and extent of it. Their report, only two pages long, was like a lighted match tossed into dry underbrush during a windstorm; it touched off a fast-spreading conflagration of articles and letters in the media throughout the country and in scientific journals. In the same issue of *Science* as their report, staff writer Gina Kolata wrote a pro-and-con piece saying that "by sticking their necks out" in their conclusion, "Benbow and Stanley seem to be asking for an attack," which she then produced by interviewing researchers who scathingly dismissed the Benbow and Stanley findings: Mary Gray, a mathematician, said she could not see on what basis they

---

*That is, internal (biological) and external (psychosocial) factors.

drew their conclusions; Elizabeth Fennema, a researcher of cognitive abilities, said, "I think they are on darned shaky ground when they draw conclusions about genetic differences"; and Patricia Casserly of Educational Testing Service, publisher of the SAT's, flatly denied that the Stanley and Benbow results meant high school girls could not score as well in math achievement as boys.

Articles and letters in the *Washington Post*, the *New York Times*, *Time* magazine, many other magazines and newspapers, and many scientific publications, reported Benbow and Stanley's finding, in most cases stressing its inflammatory nature. Some popular articles distorted the message in ways bound to enrage the public and scientists: *Newsweek*'s article was headlined "Do Males Have a Math Gene?" (Benbow and Stanley never mentioned the word "gene"). An Associated Press special was headlined, "Hopkins Study Called 'Ridiculous'" and quoted the public statement of a feminist contingent at an annual meeting of the American Mathematical Society in San Francisco, "It is virtually impossible to undo the damage of the publicity surrounding the report," and two female math professors said substantially the same thing in a *Science* editorial denouncing the Benbow and Stanley report. Curiously, the editors neither advised Stanley and Benbow of the editorial in advance nor, as is customary, invited them to respond. [33]

All this was only words, but contrary to the nursery-school saying, words can harm scientists' reputations and research funding opportunities. Stanley, speaking about the controversy in his characteristically calm and judicious manner, says that it's hard to know how much damage it did. His post at Johns Hopkins was secure; he had been a full professor since 1957 and, he says, "I'm almost impervious to any kind of direct attack. But I found it harder to get grants after that. I'd been getting support from a major foundation for many years and suddenly they said, in effect, 'Well, we've given you enough.' But I had a telephone conversation with the president of the foundation, and he told me that my work on gender differences was embarrassing to them. From then on I could get no funding from them, nor could anybody associated with me. I've also been turned down by the National Science Foundation, and while I can't be sure that that's because of my gender-difference work, I did get two NSF grants back in the 1970s without any trouble and was turned down when I applied after the 1980 paper."

How had the controversy affected his standing with his fellow academics? "One of my male friends said to me back in the early 1980s, 'You're one of the men most hated by women in the country.' I think that's probably true. One reason is that our work threatened the effort of Senator Kennedy and others to plow huge amounts of money into work on training women in math and science."

Despite Stanley's unruffled demeanor, he admits to having been distressed that so much was made of the very little that was controversial in what he and Benbow wrote: "It was a sentence or two in our conclusion speculating about the causes of the differences that got us into trouble. But the rest of the paragraph—which nobody ever quoted—qualified that speculation and left room for other interpretations."

He also laments the fact that research on sex differences has tended ever since to steer away from the risky and keep to the safe ground:

> At the last convention of the American Education Association, for instance, there were a lot of papers on gender differences but hardly any that dealt with abilities. Most were about how men and women *feel* about this or that. And none of the current Harvard School of Education dissertation proposals on gender differences have anything to do with ability. The whole field is out, even though it's so important to know what the differences are. People have been saying that the differences are small and getting smaller, but there are quite big differences in some places, and they're not going away, for the most part. We need to know what the situation is in order to decide what to do about it, what are the causes of it, and in what ways we can ameliorate it.

Camilla Benbow, who now is a full professor of psychology at Iowa State University and dean of its College of Education, says, looking back,

> I guess I was totally naïve—I was really shocked by the response to our *Science* article, I wasn't prepared for it. I could only think, "Well, these are the data—they're *important* data—and if you don't know that there are these differences or if you're pursuing the wrong explanation of them, you're not going to help the people you should be helping."

The opposition, she says, was less organized than that experienced by either Jensen or Rushton, but alarming nonetheless. "No one came and protested outside my office, but there were a lot of very angry letters and articles. And I heard rumors that there were investigations and there was a possibility that our grants would be taken away from us." Many responses were demeaning, one in particular:

> I won the best paper of the year award for research in human development of the American Educational Research Association, and Anne Petersen, who's now a deputy director of the National Science Foundation, was the vice president of that division of AERA at the time, and when I picked up the award, she hadn't signed it. I sent it back and asked for her signature on the certificate, and got a very nasty

letter from her saying that she refused to sign it because of my work. Eventually the AERA had to issue me a new certificate without her name on it because she still refused to sign it.

That bit of petty malevolence hurt, but what hurt worse was the general politically biased reaction to Stanley and Benbow's work:

All the recent reviews of the literature show quite sizable gender differences in abilities, and almost everybody today says that the differences are caused by a combination of biology and environment working together—exactly what we said in 1980, but at that time we were fiercely criticized for it. Right after our article was published, an American Women in Science convention canceled a whole afternoon of sessions just to make time to attack our work. People were very cold to me. I went to an APA [American Psychological Association] convention in 1983 to give an invited talk, and all sorts of people stood up and attacked me, not for what I said there but for what they said I stood for. And I've been turned down for certain awards because of outright bias against me; in one case that I know of, a woman on an awards committee gave me the lowest possible rating even though I have a much better vita than many other people who have received awards. And Julian and I had a hard time getting some of our subsequent papers published.

It is some measure of Benbow's merits as a scientist that, despite these obstacles, she has published over seventy papers, four books, and several dozen chapters in edited books, all within seventeen years.

Eight years after the 1980 paper, when Benbow published a study of sex differences in mathematical reasoning ability based on the SAT scores of the several hundred thousand talented twelve- to thirteen-year-olds who had been tested by the SMPY up to that time, her paper, appearing in *Behavioral and Brain Sciences*, produced an onslaught of hundreds of pages of criticism from every conceivable standpoint.[34] In her reply Benbow said, "After my initial despair…it became apparent that my commentators had outlined a research program for my next 40 professional years. (Now all I need is a grant for half the national debt and 124 hours per day!)"[35]

Had the hostile criticism of her work ever made her consider turning to a less contentious kind of research?

No, but I've tried to play it down. If I turn in a proposal presenting gender differences in a way that isn't politically correct, I get turned down. I put in for grants where I don't even mention gender differences. But in my work with gifted kids, the gender differences appear anyway, and I get attacked for it. The gender differences thing has made it very hard for me to get external grants; it's been a very arduous process, working with review panels, and it has made me put some of that work on the back burner. My last grant proposal to the NSF was vehemently attacked for reasons that had nothing to do with the proposal at all; they were all outside issues. That was the most discouraging thing that's happened lately.

But I haven't abandoned my work on gender differences. In fact, I'm now collecting data for a twenty-year-afterward assessment of what has happened to kids in the original study. It's going to be a major study. I was able to get foundation support, but I can't name the foundation; they insist on anonymity. I think the twenty-year follow-up is going to show that gender differences in abilities are small compared to gender differences in actual achievement. Gifted women mostly prefer a different career path than gifted men—they try to balance family, friends, and spirituality with career, where men mostly concentrate on career. Not that those are hard and fast distinctions—there's a lot of overlap—but those are the major tendencies I'm finding. I'm sure this is going to be a bombshell when it comes out, and I'm not shying away from it.

Which suggests that a researcher, though once burned, may have what Freudians call a repetition compulsion and go back to try the fire again.

A final affirmative note: A task force appointed by APA to produce a report on knowns and unknowns about intelligence summed up a brief discussion of "spatial and quantitative abilities" as follows: "Females have a clear advantage on quantitative tasks in the early years of school...but this reverses sometime before puberty; males then maintain their superior performance into old age."[36] Among the authorities whose data were cited as evidence: Camilla Benbow and Julian Stanley.

Feminist Thou-Shalt-Nots

Militant feminists and even many moderate supporters of the women's movement oppose and seek to demolish the credibility of various other research projects on biological influences on sex differences and sex-linked behavior that they claim are sexist and designed to keep woman in a subordinate place in society. We need not examine them in detail or exhaustively; a glance at several will serve.

PMS (Premenstrual Syndrome)

Feminists opposing research they consider sexist have neither the kind of political influence that might persuade Congress to block federal funding nor the temperament to mount disruptive or riotous demonstrations. Instead, they rely on severe and even vitriolic criticism of the research, accusations of sexist and misogynistic motives on the part of the researchers, and publicly displayed ostracism. This excerpt from a recent polemic attacking research on PMS is typical:

The popularity of the idea of PMS rests upon invidious ideological assumptions about the nature of woman.... This bias is best characterized as masculinist, where "masculinism" is defined as an ideological perspective in which gender differences are depicted as binary oppositions, negatively weighted in favor of males and used to justify male domination over women.[37]

When researchers have reason to believe they will be accused by many of their colleagues of such biases and purposes, they are likely to rethink their interest in PMS and its effects on cognition and behavior, and to drop the subject or suppress relevant data that has unexpectedly appeared in their findings. Such self-censorship is a subtler infringement of freedom of research than censorship by others but equally serious. Researchers less academically secure than Julian Stanley and less committed to their subject than he and Camilla Benbow might well abandon a line of inquiry that caused them to be denounced and maligned as Stanley and Benbow were. A number of scientists who have been attacked for investigating biological influences on sex differences in cognition and behavior told me that some, perhaps many, graduate students have turned away from research in these areas when they saw it would engender hostility by many colleagues and blistering criticism by professional associations and advocacy groups, and might well turn their career path into a rocky road leading nowhere.

To be sure, the situation is changing on certain campuses and in some professional circles. With the recent resurgence of interest in biological contributions to human behavior, some researchers have been able to dig deeply into PMS phenomena without experiencing much opposition. Doreen Kimura and various colleagues at the University of Western Ontario have conducted a number of studies of changes taking place in woman's cognitive and motor abilities throughout the menstrual cycle, but Kimura says that although this work has been much criticized in journals and in the media, she has not encountered opposition serious enough to hamper her research.[38]

Many other researchers doing similar work, however, still find themselves subject to intense and pervasive disapproval by their colleagues and superiors that threatens to harm or even abort their careers. Half a dozen years ago, Carol Lewis, a graduate student at the University of Texas, Austin did a study for her master's thesis showing that identical female twins are more alike in their premenstrual feelings than fraternal female twins and that the physical changes of the premenstrual period play an important part in mood changes.[39] Many doctoral candidates go on to pursue the topic of their master's thesis more deeply for the doctoral dissertation but, says Lewis's mentor and co-author Professor Joseph Horn,

After her study appeared in print, she told me she didn't want to do her doctoral dissertation in this area because of the general feeling of academics on this campus, which is that you simply don't publish research that could be interpreted negatively as far as women's attributes and achievement are concerned. As one female colleague said to me, the reason there's so much interest in PMS is that it's a plot by psychologists to hold women back politically, it's a way of saying that people who have PMS shouldn't be trusted with political positions.

Brain Size and Structure

In recent years there has been a good deal of controversy over whether or not anatomical differences exist between the male and female brain, and if so, whether these account in any degree for sex differences in cognition and behavior. Some researchers claim that the greater average size of the male brain—about 100 grams, on average—may account for males' greater mathematical ability; others say this is unproved and absurd. Some maintain that because females' corpus callosum, the band of neural fibers connecting the right and left cerebral hemispheres, is thicker than that of males, their brains are less "lateralized" or specialized and hence mathematically less apt but verbally more so; others say there's no good evidence of this. Some have done research that they claim demonstrates that left-handedness, more common in males than females, is associated with males' greater incidence of reading disabilities and stuttering but also with their higher incidence of mathematical precocity and verbal precocity (females score moderately higher, on average, on verbal abilities but are less likely to be verbally precocious).[40]

Our concern is not with which of these views is better supported by the weight of evidence—the verdict, in fact, is not yet in—but with the widespread and inhibiting attacks on those conducting research in this area. It is understandable that feminists, and indeed most women, find research objectionable that suggests that their slightly smaller and less lateralized brains are less competent in any way than the brains of males. A common type of feminist response is that made a few years ago by Judy Rebick, a Canadian feminist leader, when David Ankney, a psychologist at the University of Western Ontario, published a study linking brain size differences to differences in mathematical proficiency: "I think it's very dangerous," she said, "I think it belongs in the same garbage bin as Philippe Rushton's research. It's just a sophisticated form of prejudice against women."[41]

Diane Halpern, a feminist herself but admirably evenhanded, sums up the evidence favoring differences in brain lateralization and its troubling implications:

Despite the importance of environmental influences, there is no reason to believe that sex role pressures or other environmental pressures are different for right- and left-handed individuals.... The only plausible explanation of the sex by hand-edness interactions...is that they are reflective of underlying neurological differ-ences. This is obviously an incendiary topic, and the possibility that these conclusions will be misused poses a serious concern to anyone who is concerned with prejudice and discrimination.[42]

Calm, reasonable words. But elsewhere Halpern and two colleagues, in an article quoted earlier, document and forcefully object to the bias and savagery of the attacks on her and Stanley Coren's research on this subject. Many fellow academics, they say, publicly attacked the re-search not on the basis of a careful reading of it but what they had learned of it from sensational media stories. Some did so in print, some in person, and some in front of audiences at conferences, where, Halpern told me,: "I've had run-ins with people screaming, 'You must not pub-lish this stuff! You must not say these things!'" A number of journals that had previously published handedness studies by Halpern and oth-ers reacted to the press and academic attacks on their work by refusing to publish or even review their follow-up studies. One journal editor, in a letter to Coren, incautiously revealed the reason: "It now appears the whole issue of handedness is surrounded in [sic] controversy. It is not our intention to deal with such controversial matters in the journal lest they call into question the credibility of other works published here." Another journal editor, after citing the negative reactions in the media and in the scientific community, said that their findings were ipso facto proof of their work's methodological inadequacy; Halpern and her co-authors say of this comment, "A journal's decision that a research pa-per will not be reviewed for possible publication because of the results obtained is obviously incompatible with the spirit and principles of academic inquiry. This is censorship at its worst and is openly commit-ted by the editors of leading scientific journals."[43]

Tomboys, Female Body Fat, Breasts

Nearly three decades ago the psychologists Anke Ehrhardt and John Money studied a handful of girls who as fetuses had been exposed to high levels of androgens and, in consequence, were born with genitalia resembling those of males more than females. All but one underwent corrective surgery, but although this made them genitally female, Ehrhardt and Money reported that they exhibited a higher level of "tomboyism" than a control group of normal girls, preferred athletics and boy playmates, had little interest in dolls, and so on. Ehrhardt and Money interpreted the tomboyism as reflecting masculinity and measuring aggressiveness,[44] and many other researchers have similarly used tomboyism as a measure in studies of aggressiveness and sex-role identification. In a related genre of research, Doreen Kimura and J.A.Y. Hall recently studied the differences between heterosexuals and homosexuals of both sexes by means of two motor skills in which males and females typically differ, namely, hitting a target by throwing a ball, and plugging small pegs into a pegboard; they found that males threw better than females, females did better at the pegboard task, and homosexuals of both sexes performed at levels intermediate between those of heterosexuals of both sexes.[45] Other studies have suggested that there are minor structural differences between the brains of heterosexual men, heterosexual women, and homosexual men that may in part account for their differences in cognitive functioning and other behavior.[46]

Research in this area has been sharply criticized by feminists, one of whom labeled the ascribing of tomboyish behavior to androgen effects on the fetal brain or the developing brain of the child "[an] anachronistic, nineteenth-century, white EuroAmerican value judgment" masquerading as science. Such research, she said, uses, as ostensibly objective indices of masculinity, traits that are actually culture-created and "places the stamp of science on a set of unexamined social values and judgments concerning gender."[47] Although studies linking tomboyism and sex-typical physical abilities to brain lateralization have not produced physical confrontations and riotous assaults, it takes a thick-skinned and relatively fearless researcher to undertake work almost certain to produce carping criticism, rejections by journal editors, disapproval by and alienation from colleagues, and extensive antagonism and denigration on the part of feminists, homosexuals, and those who sympathize with them.

Another kind of sex-role research feminists assail as male-chauvinistic concerns the appeal to males of various female body shapes. Half a dozen years ago, Devendra Singh, a young biopsychologist at the University of Texas-Austin, became interested in this subject; he conducted one study that he honestly but undiplomatically titled "Body Fat Distribution and Perception of Desirable Female Body Shape by Young Black Men and Women," and another about how the waist-to-hip ratio and symmetry or asymmetry of the breasts are taken by men as indications of the woman's willingness to develop romantic relationships.

Singh's work has not inspired hate mail, disruptions of his classes, or physical assaults, but when he speaks in public he is often irascibly challenged by feminists who point out his masculine bias. "Why only the female body?" they ask. "Why don't you ask what's appealing or not appealing about the male body?" His colleagues often take another critical tack: "What particularly gets me in trouble with them," he says, "is when I say why a beautiful body gives so much satisfaction biologically. They keep asking me, 'Why are you using this biological approach? Why are you using evolution as an explanation?' I have to keep defending things that ought not need defense."

Rather more serious than these nagging objections is the difficulty Singh has had getting his reports accepted by prestigious journals. The body-fat distribution study was turned down a number of times and finally accepted by the *International Journal of Eating Disorders*, not exactly a leading psychology publication. Singh did have better luck with a later paper on the influence of the waist-to-hip ratio in mate selection, which appeared in the *Journal of Personality and Social Psychology*, but his findings were as cantankerously received by his critics as his body-fat and breast-symmetry work.

Edward Miller, a somewhat curmudgeonly professor of economics at the University of New Orleans, has published scores of articles in his own field but in recent years has become interested in the biological determinants of human behavior; drawing on his wide and thorough reading, he has written several research articles that have gotten him in hot water with campus P.C. stalwarts and feminists. Like Rushton, he has published data on the lower average IQ of blacks and on the smaller average size of black and female crania, which he links to smaller brains and lower IQs. Among the numerous enemies this work has made him are some of the powers at his university, including the vice chancellor for Research and Special Programs, Shirley Laska, who in a recent issue of a newsletter published by her office raised the question of whether academic freedom should extend to Miller's studies and came up with a rather equivocal answer:

A faculty member has been conducting research peripheral to his discipline specialty on a topic which is very controversial and harmful to persons of African descent. The research is also by extension harmful to ethnic minorities and women because it implies that differences in accomplishment between the dominant group and minorities are due to innate physical qualities....

It is very important that we guard our rights, protect our freedoms, make independent decisions about what research is important to do...but not by putting the community at risk, and not at the risk of being seen as irrelevant or irresponsible. If we are viewed this way...the best outcome we can hope for will be to be seen as not mattering to society, the worst as being problematic for society.[48]

Whether that means that the university should try to stop Miller from further such work, or merely stand aside if others do so, is unclear; what does seem clear is that the vice chancellor is less than wholeheartedly committed to Miller's freedom of research.

Miller has trangressed in yet another way, to his own cost. He researched and wrote a paper titled "Breasts: Their Evolutionary Origins as a Deceptive Signal of Need for Provisioning and Temporary Infertility," which he presented at a meeting of the Human Behavior and Evolution Society and mentioned in the university's faculty newsletter. He tells the sequel:

> When I asked my department head to nominate me for the University Research Award—a very reasonable request—he gave me a lecture about how someone high up (whom he would not identify) disliked the subject of my research and he declined to nominate me and picked someone with perhaps a third as many published papers as my hundred plus.

Miller feels that this is probably an indication of how his career will fare from here on.

(A minor additional note: Miller's reputation among feminists and blacks as a bad person has been worsened by word circulating on campus that he has done research linking large breasts to low intelligence, a rumor that offended both large-breasted and high-IQ women. Miller suspects the rumor started when an assistant asked him if it was true that he did research on noneconomic topics such as breasts and intelligence, to which, having done papers on each, he said simply yes. "Alas," says Miller, "he apparently meant by the question the *relationship* of intelligence to breasts." There is no feasible way to scotch the rumor, which is now part of Miller's unofficial C.V. The assistant, incidentally, once said that he thought an article Miller asked him to locate on the breeding of great tits—the British bird—had a vulgar title.)

Male-Biased Science

The characterization of research on tomboyism quoted above—that it is an anachronistic, nineteenth-century, white EuroAmerican value judgment masquerading as science—exemplifies the radical feminist view not only of research on sex differences but of almost all research on biological influences on male and female behavior, especially if carried out by males. From this perspective, male-conducted research, though supposedly objective and truth-seeking, is neither and should be appraised accordingly; so says, among others, Sondra Farganis, a social scientist at the New School for Social Research:

> What positivists call science is a particular form of knowledge (technical) satisfy-
> ing a particular kind of interest, control of the environment and of other humans....
> Science as practiced is claimed to simplify cause-and-effect relationships: first, it
> looks at bodies as masculine; and second, it makes arbitrary distinctions between
> subject and object, nature and nurture, biology and environment, individual and
> community, ignoring the dialectical interaction of each pair. Feminists have lo-
> cated these false dualities...in the western male-gendered tradition. In the last ten
> years or so, an oppositionary paradigm to these dualisms has emerged.... Women
> have developed an epistemology that builds on the gendered social and psycho-
> logical experiences of women. [49]

Objectivity, the keystone element in the ethos of Western science since its emergence in the sixteenth century, supports and justifies the ruthless male domination of females and animals; so says Lori Gruen, philosopher at the University of Colorado:

> Objective scientists rely on an epistemology that requires detachment and dis-
> tance. This detachment serves as justification for the division between active pur-
> suer of knowledge and passive object of investigation, and establishes the power
> of the former over the latter. By devaluing subjective experience, reducing living,
> spontaneous beings to machines to be studied, and establishing an epistemic privi-
> lege based on detached reason, the mechanistic/scientific mindset firmly dis-
> tinguish[es] man from nature, woman, and animals.
>
> The above-mentioned theoretical frameworks may be seen behind contempo-
> rary practices that involve, to varying degrees, the oppression and exploitation of
> women and animals. [50]

Objective scientists, especially males, not only see reality from a distorted viewpoint but by virtue of that viewpoint are inhuman and incapable of fellow-feeling towards others, women in particular; so says Lynda Birke, a biologist at the University of Warwick:

> Objectivity is part of the stereotypic masculinity of scientific practice...and re-
> quires what Ruth Hubbard has called "context stripping." Feminist critics, on the
> contrary, emphasize the inseparability of subjectivity and objectivity in how we
> know the world.
>
> A corollary of that ideology of objectivity is that it denies feelings, including
> the possibility of feelings of sympathy toward the object(s) of study—be they
> nonhumans, the environment generally, or women. [51]

Science is, in fact, not at all the pure search for truth that scientists themselves claim it is but a biased thought-structure created by the ruling elite who reward scientists for sharing and supporting their biases; so says Carolyn Merchant, a radical environmentalist and feminist: "Science is not a process of discovering the ultimate truths of nature, but a social construction that changes over time. The assumptions accepted by its practitioners are value-laden and reflect their places in both history and society, as well as the research priorities and funding sources of those in power."[52]

Lest these quotations give the impression that the assault on male-biased science comes only from female feminists, here is a snippet of the same kind of thing from a male, Harvard's Richard Lewontin, biologist, Marxist, and tireless assailant of research on the biological sources of human behavior: "Much of the work of the critical science movement in general (and of Science for the People in particular*) is devoted to educating people about science and society. Our goal is to counteract ideology and politics masquerading as 'objective' science."[53]

Is all this to be dismissed with a weary wave of the hand or an indulgent chuckle as mere snarling and growling, and of no consequence? Paul Gross and Norman Levitt say otherwise in their searching and troubling study, *Higher Superstition: The Academic Left and Its Quarrels with Science*:

> That the outpouring of feminist science criticism, a part of the larger genre of "science studies," is revolutionary and of fundamental importance is a given for the academic and intellectual left. Such works as Harding's *The Science Question in Feminism* have already attained the stature of classics; likewise, their writers are widely acclaimed as members of a new wave in scientific epistemology.[54]

Since the percentage of women in the behavioral and social sciences has been steadily rising—in psychology, women have been earning more than three out of five doctorates in recent years—and since it is likely that some older and many younger women social scientists are at least sympathetic with feminist ideas and doctrines, it is reasonable to suppose that feminist attacks on scientific research in general and sex difference research in particular represent a genuine threat to the status of researchers and to the acceptance of their findings.

One might, of course, argue that toppling the male-biased structure of social science would be a good thing—if the feminists had a specific

---

*Science for the People, an organization of radical scientists created to combat psychobiological research and explanations of human behavior, is discussed further in the next section of this chapter.

methodology to replace it, and evidence that their methodology would indeed enable researchers to come closer to the truth. But they have no such methodology or evidence; like many other revolutionaries, they are ready and eager to demolish the city of their enemy but have neither blueprints nor materials with which to rebuild it closer to their heart's desire.

Of Ants and Us

By "anatomy is destiny," Freud did not mean that physiology directly influences attitudes and behavior but that the young girl's realization that she lacks a penis causes her psychological development to take a different course from that of the young boy. But later researchers, as we have seen, made a more direct linkage between anatomy and destiny, spelling out the relationship between circulating hormone levels and behavior, the effects of hormone levels on fetal brain development, and genetic influences on mental abilities and traits of personality.

In 1975, Edward O. Wilson, a Harvard entomologist, made a still more direct, indeed maximal, interpretation of "anatomy is destiny." Having since his teens had a "near obsession" with ants, whose well-ordered social life is directed by the specific biochemical instructions contained in their genes, it occurred to Wilson when he was a young instructor in biology at Harvard to look for comparable influences in the social patterns of other creatures. [55] This became a labor of two decades, during which he formulated the doctrine that the behavior of all social animals is genetically determined and that the genetic instructions as to social behavior are the result of evolutionary processes that produce functional animal and human societies. This doctrine was the organizing principle of a new scientific discipline that had been forming within biology and other natural sciences, and that Wilson popularized in 1975 with his book *Sociobiology*, the work that made the new science known to the public by that name and which, though massive, expensive, and filled with scientific arcana, became an immediate best-seller.

Sociobiology was the realization of Wilson's long-time scientific dream of integrating the natural and social sciences. Although he regards himself as something of a liberal and perhaps somewhat to the left of center politically, he did not mean the work to have any political implications and never imagined that his "new synthesis" of the sciences would result in his being castigated by some of his colleagues at

Harvard and by others throughout academe as a reactionary and the promulgator of a pseudoscience intended to promote racism and sexism, and to justify the evils and injustices of existing social orders.

Even if Wilson, a slender, soft-spoken, and somewhat shy man, had foreseen that he would be seen as a political villain and embroiled in a vicious, long-running intellectual slugfest, he probably would have followed the same route. In 1994, looking back at nearly twenty years of abuse and controversy, he wrote, concerning *Sociobiology*:

> Perhaps I should have stopped at chimpanzees when I wrote the book. Many biologists wish that I had. Even several of the critics said that *Sociobiology* would have been a great book if I had not added the final chapter, the one on human beings.... Still I did not hesitate to include *Homo sapiens*, because not to have done so would have been to omit a major part of biology. By reverse extension, I believed that biology must someday serve as part of the foundation of the social sciences.[56]

Like Alfred Kinsey, the expert on wasps who became an authority on human sexual behavior half a century ago, Wilson was an expert on ants who became a theoretician of human social behavior. He attributes his fascination with tiny things to a boyhood accident that cost him the sight of his right eye; his left eye, however, was uncommonly acute at close range and thus ideal for studying little things. That interest, plus a very good mind, made a biologist and a specialist in insects of him; as a graduate student at Harvard, he did work of such merit in this field as to gain him a post on the biology faculty along with his doctorate.

He might have spent his life conducting special studies of ants and other social insects had it not been for an epiphany he experienced during a two-day visit in 1956 to Cayo Santiago, a small island off the coast of Puerto Rico. Wilson, at that time a young Harvard instructor, went there at the invitation of his first graduate student, Stuart Altmann, to observe troops of macaque monkeys, and what he saw in those two days was, he has written, "a stunning revelation and an intellectual turning point":

> When I first stepped ashore I knew almost nothing about macaque societies.... I was riveted by the sophisticated and often brutal world of dominance orders, alliances, kinship bonds, territorial disputes, threats and displays, and unnerving intrigues. I learned how to read the rank of a male from the way he walked, how to gauge magnitudes of fear, submission, and hostility from facial expression and body posture....
>
> In the evenings Altmann talked primates and I talked ants, and we came to muse over the possibility of a synthesis of all the available information on social animals. A general theory, we agreed, might take form under the name of sociobi-

ology. Stuart was already using that word to describe his studies; he had picked it up from the Section on Animal Behavior and Sociobiology, a working group of the Ecological Society of America.[57]

For nearly two decades Wilson sought to spell out that fantasized unifying theory. It would be based on "population biology," the study of the ways in which genetics and ecology interact in evolutionary fashion to produce each of the social species and its particular forms of social behavior.[58] In ant colonies, for example, evolution favored genetic factors that make some individuals caretakers, others soldiers, and others procreators, provide chemical signals (danger alerts, pathways to food), and so on; in sum, the basis of a successful social life for ants. Each species of social vertebrates, similarly, has its own patterns of dominance, mating, care of the young, defense against outside threats, and the like. It was clear to Wilson that he ought to be able to show that the social life of each species must have a similar evolutionary explanation—that its social behavior was the result of the natural selection of genetically directed behaviors that would make for a stable and successful society.[59]

There was, however, one major problem: If the strongest motive in any creature's behavior is to preserve its own life, how could evolution select such altruistic behavior as that of the warrior defenders of the ant or bee colony who sacrifice their own lives for the benefit of the others? He found the answer to the puzzle of altruism in a theory of kinship behavior proposed by the biologist William Hamilton: If the genes causing the altruistic act are shared by two organisms because of common descent, and if an act performed by one of them results in the greater contribution of these genes to the next generation, the tendency to altruism will increase in the gene pool, even though the altruistic actor loses its life.[60]

In pursuit of his ambitious goal, Wilson read thousands of studies of many species—everything from neurological studies of the role of various neurotransmitter molecules in producing behavior to ethological studies of the mating, dominance, territorial, and aggressive behavior patterns of animals living under natural conditions—searching in each case for insights as to how the specific genetic information had evolved that made each species' patterns of social behavior meet its needs and serve to perpetuate it. And while he was well aware that human beings, unlike other animals, have very varied ways of communicating, mating, organizing themselves into societies, and so on, he felt that much of human behavior must be directed, at least in a general sense, by genetic forces, as evidenced by the findings of twin studies, IQ heritability research, studies of temperament in infants, and other biosocial research. Accordingly, he felt that the ultimate goal of sociobiology was to synthesize the biological sciences with the social sciences, particularly sociology, which up to then had totally ignored the biological influences on human behavior.

And so, at the end of a vast manuscript codifying the concepts of sociobiology by means of illustrative details of the social behavior of a wide range of animal species, Wilson added a final and speculative chapter showing how the same concepts might be applied to human social behavior, a hypothesis he proffered diffidently:

> Sociobiology is defined as the systematic study of the biological basis of all social behavior. For the present it focuses on animal societies, their population structure, castes, and communication, together with all of the physiology underlying the social adaptations. But the discipline is also concerned with the social behavior of early man and the adaptive features of organization in the more primitive contemporary human societies.
>
> Sociology...attempts to explain human behavior primarily by empirical description of the outermost phenotypes and by unaided intuition, without reference to evolutionary explanation in the true genetic sense.... [In] neo-Darwinist evolutionary theory...each phenomenon [of animal behavior] is weighed for its adaptive significance and then related to the basic principles of population genetics. It may not be too much to say that sociology and the other social sciences, as well as the humanities, are the last branches of biology waiting to be included in the Modern Synthesis. One of the functions of sociobiology, then, is to reformulate the foundations of the social sciences in a way that draws these subjects into the Modern Synthesis. Whether the social sciences can be truly biologicized in this fashion remains to be seen.[61]

He claimed only that the broad outlines, not the specific details, of human behavior are determined by genetics, and has described his 1975 position in these terms:

> Human beings inherit a propensity to acquire behavior and social structures, a propensity that is shared by enough people to be called human nature. The defining traits include division of labor between the sexes, bonding between parents and children, heightened altruism toward closest kin, incest avoidance, other forms of ethical behavior, suspicion of strangers, tribalism, dominance orders within groups, male dominance overall, and territorial aggression over limiting resources. Although people have free will and the choice to turn in many directions, the channels of their psychological development are nevertheless—however much we might wish otherwise—cut more deeply by the genes in certain directions than in others.[62]

* * *

Despite all these caveats and qualifications, Wilson admits that "mine was an exceptionally strong hereditarian position for the 1970s. It helped to revive the long-standing nature-nurture debate at a time when nurture had seemingly won."[63] And therefore, despite the esteem in which Wilson was held in his field and the astonishing success of *Sociobiology*—the subject of a front-page article in the *New York Times* announcing the book's "revolutionary" implications, and of many laudatory book reviews[64]—he was denounced by a group of his own colleagues at Harvard and by many others elsewhere as the proponent of a politically reactionary pseudoscience.

The Harvard colleagues were the members of a specially convened committee called the Sociobiology Study Group, an affiliate of Science for the People, an organization of radical activists formed in the 1960s to expose and condemn research they considered politically regressive. The Sociobiology Study Group, dominated by Marxist and leftist scholars, consisted of thirty-five scientists, teachers, and students who got together after the publication of *Sociobiology* to demolish its credibility and reveal what they saw as its regressive political aims. (Wilson says, "It never occurred to me that sociobiology serves such aims, and it doesn't.") They made no plans for overt physical disruptions of sociobiology research, but if their campaign succeeded, the resulting peer pressure and difficulty in getting funding would curtail it. The group met regularly in Lewontin's office, directly under Wilson's (though he was unaware of this); Lewontin, chairman of the department of biology, is a brilliant researcher and thinker whom Wilson, to his future pain, had helped bring to Harvard some years earlier.[65]

The study of sociobiology promised by the group's title was, actually, the study of ways in which to attack the ideas put forth in Wilson's book and to damage his reputation. Under the leadership of the dynamic Lewontin and of Stephen Jay Gould (also a Harvard colleague of Wilson's), the group fired off its first shot a few months after the publication of *Sociobiology*, a long letter published in the November 13, 1975 issue of the *New York Review of Books*. It accused Wilson of numerous gross scientific errors—a legitimate act of scientific discourse—but went beyond the normal bounds of such discourse by adroitly and unfairly linking his work and name to reactionary political movements, racism, and Nazism, asserting that hypotheses as to the biological basis of social behavior:

> tend to provide a genetic justification of the *status quo* and of existing privileges for certain groups according to class, race or sex. Historically, powerful countries or ruling groups within them have drawn support for the maintenance or extension of their power from these products of the scientific community.... [Such]

theories provided an important basis for the enactment of sterilization laws by the United States between 1910 and 1930 and also for the eugenics policies which led to the establishment of gas chambers in Nazi Germany.... Wilson joins the long parade of biological determinists whose work has served to buttress the institutions of their society by exonerating them from responsibility for social problems.[66]

As for its criticisms of Wilson's science, the letter was replete with examples, but many of them, as a later analysis in the journal *Science* showed, misrepresented what he had written. The group portrayed Wilson, for instance, as a thorough determinist and extreme hereditarian, although in fact he had said that "the genes have given away most of their sovereignty [to human culture]."[67] An even worse distortion of his views concerned the question of the adaptiveness of social behavior, that is, whether specific forms of behavior were valuable from an evolutionary standpoint; on this issue, the group wrote, "For Wilson, what exists is adaptive, what is adaptive is good.... This approach allows Wilson to confirm selectively certain contemporary behavior as adaptive and 'natural' and thereby justify the present social order." But Wilson had actually said, "One of the key questions...is to what extent the [human] biogram represents an adaptation to modern cultural life and to what extent it is a phylogenetic vestige. Our civilization was jerrybuilt around the biogram."[68]

Word of the letter (but not of its distortions) spread rapidly at Harvard and throughout academe. Although a number of early reviews of *Sociobiology* by biologists and by social scientists doing biology-oriented research had been highly favorable, after the Sociobiology Study Group's position became public knowledge and national news few Harvard colleagues rallied to Wilson's support. Many agreed with Wilson's scientific views but hesitated to publicly oppose the noble-sounding and politically correct Sociobiology Study Group. The silence of Wilson's colleagues and the flood of harshly critical letters and reviews that began to appear shook his confidence in his work. "Because of my respect for the members of the Sociobiology Study Group I knew personally," Wilson wrote many years later, "I was at first struck by self-doubt. Had I taken a fatal misstep by crossing the line into human behavior?.... I faced the risk, I thought, of becoming a pariah—viewed as a poor scientist and a social blunderer to boot."[69] He undertook a review and reconsideration of his own evidence; he concluded that it was sound after all, his anxiety gave way to anger, and he wrote a strong, though polite, rebuttal to the *New York Review*. From then on he stood his ground and vigorously (but always civilly) defended himself.

And needed to. The *New York Review* letter from the Sociobiology Study Group was only the first salvo of what turned out to be a heavy continuing barrage by its members and others. A longer attack by the group in the important journal *BioScience* implied that Wilson's science was a projection of his own social biases ("determinist theories all describe a particular model of society which corresponds to the socioeconomic prejudices of the writer"); asserted that all such theories "operate as powerful forms of legitimization of past and present social institutions such as aggression, competition, domination of women by men, [etc.]"; disputed and ridiculed his arguments for the genetic influence on altruism, homosexuality, friendship, and other behavior patterns; and again associated genetic determinism with its horrendous past misuses, quoting a 1940 statement by the German ethologist Konrad Lorenz calling for the "extermination" of the defective elements in society.[70]

Having played a leading part in trashing Wilson's science and his character, Lewontin, though formerly a cordial if argumentative colleague, made statements implying that research like Wilson's ought not be conducted at all. In 1973 he had signed a petition published as an ad in the *New York Times* calling for a halt to all "racist" research, and although he said in an interview in the *Harvard Crimson* that sociobiology was not a racist doctrine, he added that it could easily be ammunition for racists: "Any kind of genetic determinism can and does feed other kinds, including the belief that some races are superior to others."[71] In an interview in the *Harvard Gazette*, he said, apropos of *Sociobiology*, "Any investigation into the genetic control of human behaviors is bound to produce a pseudo-science that will inevitably be misused."[72] And more generally, in 1974 he called for an end to research relying on the analysis of variance, in particular heritability research.[73]

Such criticisms and innuendoes were repeated by others until many sociologists and anthropologists, and liberals and leftists unversed in genetics and population biology, came to regard Wilson as a scientific mountebank and bigot. In November, 1976, the American Anthropological Association, meeting in Washington, hotly debated a motion to formally censure sociobiology and to ban two scheduled symposia on it; the motion was defeated, but only by a narrow margin.[74] The anthropologist Ashley Montagu later asserted that Wilson's "biases and prejudices are especially evident in his application of sociobiology to humankind,"[75] and an English social scientist, Mary Midgley, calling Wilson's sociobiology "a real menace," said that although in *Sociobiology* Wilson was Dr. Jekyll most of the time, in the sections on human behavior he was Hyde.[76] At a Midwestern anthropology conference, an anthropologist publicly warned graduate students not to get involved in sociobiological research because, he said, the anthropology panels of national grant-making agencies simply would not fund studies in that area.[77]

The high (or perhaps low) point of the campaign against Wilson and sociobiology came in 1978, when he was scheduled to speak at a large sociobiology symposium during the annual meeting of the AAAS. Although the violent student protests of the 1960s had largely died away, AAAS officials had learned that a demonstration of some sort was being planned by the International Committee Against Racism (INCAR), a group with a reputation for violence. The AAAS officials decided to avoid a physical clash by granting INCAR representatives two minutes at the microphones if they demanded time to speak. As soon as the chairperson introduced Wilson, who was going to deliver his talk from his chair because his right ankle, broken in a fall, was in a cast, a small band of men and women rushed onto the stage, stood behind the speakers, and one of them came forward, seized the microphone, and began to harangue the audience. As he did so, the young woman standing behind Wilson picked up a pitcher of water and poured it on his head while the demonstrators, by prearrangement, chanted, "Wilson, you're all wet!" Wilson, the other speakers on stage, and the audience were stunned and unable to react.

When the INCAR group shortly left the stage, members of the panel did rise to condemn the caper, and from the audience Stephen Jay Gould, though an ardent opponent of sociobiology, spoke up, deploring the incident and calling it "infantile." Wilson, wet and chilled, remained calm (at least outwardly), mopped himself off as best he could, delivered his lecture, and received a standing ovation. One could regard the episode as silly and of no significance, but such events are among the reasons that some graduate students and young academics have turned away from research that might cause them to be humiliated and abused when presenting findings to an audience of their peers.

From 1975 to the early 1990s, sociobiology was assailed in one way or another by a variety of individuals and groups who considered its tenets politically and ideologically hateful. Among the most incensed were feminists; as one analysis of their reactions to sociobiology sums up:

> Sociobiologists, the feminist critics say, portray females as naturally passive, coy, and choosy, while portraying males as fickle and promiscuous.... Not only do

these critics say that sociobiology reduces women to their biological functions, they maintain that sociobiology is deterministic, presenting male and female reproductive behavior as fixed and impossible to change...[and serving] to keep women in their "proper place."[78]

Feminists were particularly infuriated by those sociobiologists who, more Hyde-like than Wilson, viewed the copulation of many birds and other animals in which the male forces himself on the female as genetically appropriate rape, and therefore viewed human rape, though a problem, as "one of a number of co-equal reproductive strategies to have evolved through the millennia."[79] William Irons, an anthropologist and sociobiologist at Northwestern University, says that in front of about forty students, a female faculty member announced that if he put a sociobiological interpretation on date rape, she would punch him in the nose.[80] In feminist eyes, sociobiology, at least as far as it concerns sex roles, was male-chauvinistic and injurious to women, as these comments by a team of three feminists (all men, as it happens) exemplify:

> The implications of this theory are striking. The important traits that have been selected for in evolutionary history are male traits. Only males need compete; therefore selection operates on the genetic variability in males....Females are thus the passive carriers of the selected male genes.... Sociobiological arguments concerning innate sex-role differences clearly have relevance to the debates on [the role of women in society].... Considering the history of the use of biologically determinist ideas, there is good reason to fear that the development of sociobiological theories in the present social context will have pernicious social consequences.[81]

* * *

Wilson, though he stoutly defended himself from attack, was open-minded enough to recognize legitimate criticisms and respond to them. He recognized that in his analysis of social behavior he had dealt only with the influences of the genes and ignored the influence of culture. With a young collaborator gifted in mathematical analysis, Charles Lumsden, he set out to rectify this shortcoming. Together, in the course of a year and a half, they developed a detailed model of a sociobiology specific to human beings. They admitted that the principles of genetic control of behavior described throughout *Sociobiology* were not an adequate explanation, when applied to humans:

> For mankind at least, these postulates are radically incorrect. Behavior is not explicit in the genes, and mind cannot be treated as a mere replica of behavioral traits. In this book we propose a very different view in which the genes prescribe a set of biological processes, which we call epigenetic rules, that direct the assem-

bly of the mind.... Culture is the translation of the epigenetic rules into mass patterns of mental activity and behavior.... Genes are indeed linked to culture, but in a deep and subtle manner.[82]

Genetic influence and culture, they said, interact to produce the individual's behavior, and although changes in human social behavior come about through evolution, it is not merely genetic evolution but a more complex kind that Wilson has explained briefly in his 1994 autobiography, *Naturalist*:

Human social behavior is transmitted by culture, but culture is a product of the brain.... The brain in turn is a highly structured organ and a product of genetic evolution. It possesses a host of biases programmed through sensory reception and the propensity to learn certain things and not others.... In the reverse direction, the genetic evolution of the most distinctive properties of the brain occurred in an environment dominated by culture. Changes in culture therefore must have affected those properties.... We were looking for the basic process that directed the evolution of the human mind. We concluded that it is a particular form of interaction between genes and culture. This "gene-culture coevolution," as we called it, is an eternal circle of change in heredity and culture.[83]

If Wilson hoped that this enriched and, as one might say, cultured version of sociobiology would be better received by his opponents than the first version, he was in for a disappointment. Although *Genes, Mind, and Culture*, the 1981 book in which Lumsden and he set forth the new schema, was reviewed enthusiastically in some places, it was blasted in many others, among them in *Nature* by the anthropologist Edmund Leach; in the *New York Review of Books* by the biologist Peter Medawar; and in *The Sciences* by Lewontin. By and large, most social scientists, feminists, liberals, and leftists continued to oppose Wilson's work and all the many variants of human sociobiological research and theory that had already sprung up (the sociobiology of animals was, however, well accepted), and to regard them as scientifically bad and ideologically worse; for many years the battle lines remained drawn much as they were to start with.

Even though Wilson and most of the other biologists and social scientists who were beginning to do human sociobiological research did not prescribe any specific social policies on the basis of their work, their work continued to be assailed as ammunition for right-wing political activists. As one political scientist wrote in 1989, "Politically, it is increasingly drawn upon by movements of the radical right...to justify extremist social policies."[84] In 1991 Stephen Jay Gould repeated the charge that although sociobiological theory was not motivated by a political agenda, "[political] consequences flow from ultra-Darwinian commitment to the hegemony of adaptation; they are logical entailments of a biological theory."[85] More recently two Dutch political scientists partial to sociobiology epitomized the continuing political hostility to it as follows:

> The political accusation that sociobiology is inevitably leading to conservative and even reactionary social views of the world, or supporting these, must be taken seriously, however incorrect the accusation may be. Of course, sociobiology can be used to support political value judgments. Sociobiology, used in a very particular way, could provide the existing inequality between the sexes or Apartheid* with a legitimation which *looks* scientific, especially for those who are not familiar with the generally accepted rules of the game called science.... [But] admitting that sociobiology can be abused politically is something very different from stating that inclusive-fitness theory, the essence of sociobiology, is a pseudo-scientific, reactionary political cover-up.[86]

By now the conflict has simmered down to a kind of stalemate like that of warring forces maintaining a watch at their dug-in battle lines and intermittently taking potshots at each other. But the metaphor is inexact; sociobiology is actually winning out over the political forces that sought to destroy it. Wilson says that it is now generally accepted, and is being taught and research based on it pursued, on many campuses, although on others political hostility to it has kept it away. While Wilson had hoped that it would synthesize the natural and social sciences, for the most part it is offered and researched within biology departments and only to a limited extent in social science departments. Even within the realm of biology, however, it often goes by other names, the campaign against it having made the original one odious.[87] As William Irons says, "Sociobiology is to many people an evil word. A lot of us try not to use that label any more. We call ourselves behavioral ecologists or evolutionary ecologists or evolutionary psychologists. But the word 'sociobiology' has stuck to me like glue and hurt me and some of my graduate students."

Sociobiology has begun infiltrating sociology and psychology departments to some degree, but its adherents in those disciplines are even more wary than the biologists of identifying themselves as practitioners of sociobiology. Elliott White, a political scientist at Temple University, says that "the best-kept secret within the social sciences is the growing maturity of behavioral genetics"—a central component of

---

*The comment was written in 1990, when apartheid still existed.

sociobiology—"as a field of study and the increasing relevance of its theory and research to the study of social and political life."[88]

As for Wilson, although he continues to be interested in and to use sociobiological theory in his work, in recent years he has become an environmental activist and the author of an ambitious effort to integrate scientific and other forms of knowledge (*Consilience: The Unity of Knowledge,* published by Random House in 1998). As challenging and rewarding as he found the development and defense of sociobiology, looking back from the serene and lucid altitude of his later years he sees that the study of tiny forms of life, so important to him long ago, still is so, although now, if time allowed, he would turn to far smaller ones than ants:

> If I could do it all over again, and relive my vision in the twenty-first century, I would be a microbial ecologist. Ten billion bacteria live in a gram of ordinary soil, a mere pinch held between thumb and forefinger. They represent thousands of species, almost none of which are known to science. Into that world I would go with the aid of modern microscopy and molecular analysis. I would cut my way through clonal forests sprawled across grains of sand, travel in an imagined submarine through drops of water proportionately the size of lakes, and track predators and prey in order to discover new life ways and alien food webs. All this, and I need venture no farther than ten paces outside my laboratory building.[89]

What if he had followed that route and never proposed sociobiology as the synthesis of the natural and social sciences? It is very likely that someone else would have; many scientists were laying the groundwork of such a synthesis from the 1940s on, and in the past two decades a number of lines of research have converged to present a far more complex and complete view of human social behavior than ever existed before. Wilson was the Columbus, but Vespuccis and Magellans were ready to hoist sail.

5

Unmapped Country:*
Genetic Influences on Behavior

Two Views of Everyman

A particularly puzzling paradox of human nature: Every society teaches its young that violence towards others, murderous violence in particular, is forbidden, yet no known society is free of acts of violence and murder.

If we rear our young to be nonviolent, where does violence come from? One answer is that it is part of our nature, it is inherent in us; as America's first psychologist, the great William James, put it, "Man, *biologically considered*, and whatever else he may be into the bargain, is the most formidable of all beasts of prey, and, indeed, the only one that preys systematically on its own species."[1] But there is another and contrary answer: Infants arrive in this world innocent of violent impulses and would grow up nonviolent but for the corrupting pressures and inequities of civilized, and especially urban, life. Human violence is thus another phenomenon explained in apparently opposite and irreconcilable ways by those who hold a naturist and those who hold a nurturist view of human behavior.

* * *

The naturist explanation of violence has ancient roots. Galen, the originator of the humoral theory of temperament, believed that an excess of yellow bile (one of the four "humors" or basic body fluids, according to Empedocles and Hippocrates) causes a person to be choleric, and the more choleric one is, the more likely it is that he or she will act violently. Caesar, like many other Romans and the Greeks be-

---

*"There is a great deal of unmapped country within us"—George Eliot, *Daniel Deronda*, bk. iii, ch. 24.

fore them, believed that a built-in tendency toward violence goes with certain body and personality types: "I am not much in fear of these fat, sleek fellows," he said, "but rather of those pale, thin ones." (Shakespeare much improved the comment; his Julius Caesar says, "Let me have men about me that are fat;/ Sleek-headed men and such as sleep o' nights;/ Yond Cassius hath a lean and hungry look;/ He thinks too much: such men are dangerous.") The seventeenth-century minor poet Sir John Denham said, as a thousand others had said before him, that man is a "savage beast" who "delights to prey upon his kind," and we have heard the dour philosopher Hobbes declare that "the condition of man...is a condition of war of everyone against everyone" and theorize that in order to survive, men had to agree to live together and to have their society control their natural savage instincts.

When psychology emerged from philosophy in the nineteenth century, it brought with it the baggage of the ancient belief in physiognomy—the notion that the shape of the head and details of the facial features denote related personality traits—plus the Galenic theory about the proportions of the humors in the body and their effects on character. The growth of physiological knowledge during that century disposed of the humoral theory, but physiognomy, rather than fading away, seemed to attain scientific stature in 1875 when the Italian criminologist Cesare Lombroso published his findings that criminal behavior is linked to physical anomalies. He theorized that criminality is the result either of degeneration or of a reversion to an earlier evolutionary stage, his evidence being the measurements he had made of criminals, which showed that they have certain primitive physical characteristics, among them large jaws, high cheekbones, sloping foreheads, and prominent brow ridges. But Lombroso had measured only criminals; later, when others compared his data to measurements of noncriminals, it turned out there were no overall differences.

Nonetheless, and despite the increasing attention psychologists were giving to the unconscious as a source of traits of personality—Freud was far from the first to do so—most of them still believed that personality was primarily determined by biology, as witness William James's statement above and Galton's studies of the inheritance of intellect and character. The naturist explanation of behavior gained further credibility in 1921, when the German psychiatrist Ernst Kretschmer reported that he had measured the physiques of patients in several mental hospitals and found that their body shapes bore a relationship to their personalities and mental conditions: Short-limbed, thickset, round-faced patients tended to have mood swings and to be either elated or depressed; long-limbed, slender, thin-faced patients tended to be introverted, shy, and schizophrenic. Kretschmer hypothesized that the differences in their body types and related personality types were the results of differences in hormone secretions.[2]

Although Kretschmer did not directly address the issue of violence, and although other scientists soon found serious flaws in his sampling and data, the body-type theory remained intuitively appealing; we all tend to ascribe traits of personality to facial appearances and body types. New evidence supporting the theory and suggesting a biological basis of violence appeared in the 1930s and 1940s in studies conducted by William Sheldon, a Harvard psychologist, who photographed thousands of nude college students, gave them personality tests, and found relationships between their somatotypes (body types) and personalities. According to his data, there are three basic somatotypes—the endomorph (soft, rounded, and plump), the mesomorph (hard, square, and muscular), and the ectomorph (tall, thin, and large of skull)—each having a distinctive related personality pattern: The endomorph is social, relaxed, and sybaritic, the mesomorph energetic, assertive, and courageous, and the ectomorph introverted, shy, and unsociable. Sheldon maintained that the genes determine which somatotype prevails as the fetus develops and thus which personality pattern is dominant in each individual. (More precisely, he estimated the extent to which each of the three somatotypes and personality patterns was present in each individual.[3]) Somatotype theory held that delinquents and criminals are most likely to be mesomorphs, and by the 1940s Sheldon's typology and theory had been widely adopted by criminologists.[4] Over a period of time, however, many exceptions and other flaws were found in the scheme and it was gradually abandoned.

* * *

Except for somatatype theory, which was popular and widely accepted for some years, the naturist explanation of violence was largely out of favor during the middle half of the twentieth century; this was the era in which behaviorism, a thoroughly nurturist school of psychology, dominated the science. The behaviorist school's explanation of violence and crime as social deformations of the human character can be traced back to several sources.

One is the theory, already mentioned, of Locke and other seventeenth- and eighteenth-century empiricists that the human being is a blank slate at birth and that the child grows up to be whatever message parents and society write upon it. That general explanation of personality and behavior continued to be held by empiricist philosophers and psychologists in the nineteenth century, particularly those of liberal political outlook. John Stuart Mill, for instance, wrote in 1869:

> I have long felt that the prevailing tendency to regard all the marked distinctions of human character as innate, and in the main indelible, and to ignore the irresistible proofs that by far the greater part of those differences...are such as not only might but naturally would be produced by differences in circumstances, is one of the chief hindrances to the rational treatment of great social questions.[5]

A second source is the doctrine advanced by Rousseau and other romantics of the late eighteenth and early nineteenth centuries that human beings are naturally good (or, as Rousseau himself thought, born neither good nor bad), and that it is the conflict-ridden environment of civilized society, particularly urban society, that sets men against each other, generates frustrations in them, and begets discord, violence, and crime.[6]

A third source is Freudian psychology and its many psychodynamic offshoots, which have churned out a vast mass of research on the development of the individual's personality and patterns of behavior. Despite the great differences among the many schools of psychodynamic psychology, they all assume that traits of personality are developed by the interplay of the individual's natural instinctual desires and their fulfillment, redirection, or frustration by parents and society.

A fourth source is experimental laboratory research in animal learning, spearheaded by the work of Ivan Pavlov, Edward Thorndike, and others early in the century, which established the laws of association between stimulus and response. On the basis of these laws, John B. Watson proposed a system of psychology that attributed all forms of animal and human behavior to the rewards or lack of rewards of specific actions: Rewarded acts become part of the creature's behavior pattern, unrewarded or penalized acts do not. Mice could be taught to run a complex maze for the food at its end, hens to peck at a lever that delivered a morsel of feed, circus dogs to jump through flaming hoops, and human beings to play any role within the human repertoire; as we heard earlier, Watson claimed that, given a dozen healthy infants and freedom to bring them up as he wished, he could train them to be anything from a doctor or artist to a beggar-man or thief (or, he could have added, a murderer).

A fifth source is the large body of studies of developmental psychology that trace out the unfolding and shaping of personality in terms of the interactions between the child's growing mind and all its experiences of objects, parents, and other people: studies, for instance, of the effects on the child of being read to or talked to, parental care as a model for the development of altruistic behavior, physical punishment as a model for violent expression of frustration, the socializing influences of peer groups and schools, and a great many others.

Finally, a sixth source is the social idealism variously embodied in the socialist and communist movements in this country, the social reformism of the New Deal era, and the radical movements of the 1960s. Despite the considerable differences among them, they shared the assumptions that antisocial and pathological behavior of all sorts were the products of social inequities, deprivations, and frustrations, and that in a more equitably constructed society such behavior would diminish and eventually disappear.

Rooted in the complex soil of all the above ideologies and social trends was modern criminology; its goal was to treat and rehabilitate criminals, in the belief that their behavior was a result of their experiences rather than a biological compulsion and that their antisocial personalities could be reconstructed and made prosocial. But despite decades of efforts, the success rate of rehabilitation proved to be low; a 1992 meta-analysis of 443 studies of rehabilitative programs found that the average effect was a 10 percent reduction in recidivism,[7] and while that may be worthwhile, the persisting 90 percent means that most delinquent behavior is not amenable to rehabilitation, suggesting that much of it may have causes other than experiential ones—perhaps biological ones.

Yet most social scientists who do research on violence and crime are still firmly in the Lockean-Watsonian-social-reformist camp and either ignore biological influences on crime or find them of minor interest. Some examples:

• A 1996 book by the National Research Council's Panel on Research on Violence Against Women, in reviewing research on that subject, devoted three and a half pages to evolutionary and physiological causes but twenty-three pages to psychological and social causes, concluding that while biological factors may "set the stage for learning," environmental factors play the major part in the actual outcomes.[8]

• The brochure of the National Consortium on Violence Research, located at Carnegie-Mellon University and funded by the National Science Foundation and two other government agencies, says that it is "devoted to advanced study of the factors contributing to interpersonal violence" and names the major factors—without so much as mentioning biology or genetics. (Its director, Alfred Blumstein, writes me, however, "We do intend to address biological issues.... As we move into biological issues, and bring in biological expertise, we will be in a better position to assess the payoff of going down that road [that is, considering genetic causes].")

• A 1996 publication of the American Sociological Association is described as "a guide and resource for those interested in producing knowledge that can answer the basic question: What causes violence in U.S. society?" In answering that question, it offers a thorough review of research on social causes but says nothing about research on biological influences.[9]

All of which is understandable, since it is easier to envision social programs to counteract environmental causes of violence than physiological methods of counteracting genetic and biological causes of violence. But how can we know what solutions biological research might yield if we never consider it?

* * *

Biological influences on violence and crime have, however, again become an important area of research as part of the growth of interest, during the past three decades, in genetic, hormonal, and neuroanatomical influences on human personality and behavior. Today biologically based psychology has become part of mainstream psychology and is edging its way into other social sciences, as discussed in chapter 2. A brief recapitulation of some of the more important findings:

• Twin studies have found far greater similarity of traits of personality in identical twins than in fraternal twins, and great similarity in identical twins separated at birth and reared in different environments.

• Adoption studies have shown greater similarity of traits of personality between adopted children and their biological parents than between the children and their adoptive parents.

• Adoption studies have also shown that by their teens adopted children are *less* like their adoptive parents in personality than they were when younger; apparently, genetic influences tend to overcome upbringing.

• Studies of newborns have found that even in their first days about two-thirds exhibit one of three characteristic temperaments ("easy," "difficult," or "slow to warm up"), and that these temperamental styles more or less persist throughout life.

• The explosively developing fields of neurophysiology and psychopharmacology have linked a number of cognitive, emotional, and behavioral disorders to a lack of, or an excess of, specific neurotransmitter chemicals in the brain, or to either an insufficient or excessive reuptake of these molecules by the transmitting axon; these abnormalities can be caused by drugs or diseases but also by genetic or other biological anomalies.

• In the field of behavior genetics, recombinant DNA research has identified a number of genes involved in specific physical and mental diseases and in traits of personality. The research has not identified anything like a "violence gene" or, for that matter, any single gene responsible for any complex aspect of behavior, but it seems certain that polygenic influences are involved in some personality traits and personality disorders.

• Sociobiology has persuasively pointed to the evolutionary processes by which social creatures, ranging from ants to human beings, have developed genetic propensities toward forms of social behavior that result in stable and successful societies.

• Analyses of the heritability of IQ indicate that when social and economic variables are factored out, genetic differences account in considerable part for IQ differences.

• Analyses of children and teenagers with exceptional mathematical talent show that the greater proportion of males among the mathematically exceptionally talented is not the result of better grounding in math by boys in the lower grades but is a sex-connected difference, probably related in part to the well-documented innate superiority of males at spatial visualization.

• Recent brain research has discovered a minor, but possibly significant, difference between the brains of heterosexual and homosexual males; in the latter, one area of the hypothalamus is smaller than in the former.[10] (It remains to be proven, however, that this region of the hypothalamus is directly concerned with sexual preference.)

Two specific examples may be more persuasive than all these generalizations.

The first: People suffering from Obsessive-Compulsive Disorder (OCD) may feel compelled to wash their hands scores of times a day even though they see they are clean, or, when leaving the house, may have to go back twenty or thirty times to make sure they have turned off the gas. Double-checking or repeating a protective act is apparently a useful, built-in, mental process that is normally controlled by the evidence of the senses, but not in OCD victims; though they can see that it is not necessary to repeat the act, they cannot stop themselves from doing so. The disorder does not have a psychodynamic basis and is not easily ameliorated by counseling and psychotherapy. It does, however, yield to certain new drugs, namely, clomiprimine, fluvoxamine, and fluoxetine, among others. PET scans indicate that the OCD victim has abnormal levels of activity in certain brain areas, and psychopharmacological studies show that in these areas the uptake of the neurotransmitter serotonin is excessive. The anti-OCD drugs block the reuptake of serotonin, reduce the activity to normal, and so permit the sensory evidence to control unnecessary repetitions.[11]

The second example: In 1963 the penis of an infant boy was irreparably damaged by a botched circumcision; his parents sought advice from gender-identity experts at Johns Hopkins Medical School and decided that the best course of action was to rear him as a female. Surgeons castrated the child and constructed a sort of vagina out of the remaining tissue, and the parents renamed the child and raised her as a girl. Her case became famous in the annals of sex research when the sexologist Dr. John Money reported, in 1973, that the former boy was growing up quite successfully as girl, a triumph for the environmental view of sexual identity. But in 1997 Drs. Milton Diamond, a professor of anatomy, and Keith Sigmundson, a psychiatrist, updated the case and revealed that the "girl" never really adjusted to her assigned gender, had always been stubbornly tomboyish, hated frilly dresses, preferred playing with boys and with typical boys' toys, and considered herself a freak. Gradually she came to think she was a he; at fourteen she finally learned the truth from her father, and for the first time things made sense to her—or, rather, him. The youth underwent further surgery to reconstruct a sort of penis, assumed his original sexual identity, and today, in his thirties, is married and reasonably well-adjusted.[12]

These two examples, plus the foregoing evidence, make it clear that total environmentalism is no longer defensible. Increasingly, scientists who have been trained in both conventional psychology and in behavior genetics believe in interactionist theory. There are, however, at least three differing schools of interactionist thought. One: The genes possess a wide repertoire of specific potential behaviors, and environmental influences select which of those genetically programmed behaviors best fit the individual's situation. Two: The genes establish general tendencies or capabilities, and environment teaches the organism—assembles within its nervous system—the behaviors possible within its general tendencies that best suit each situation. Three: Each of the foregoing is true for some genes and behaviors, but still other genes create or provoke environmental reactions such as the responses of parents or others to the individual's innate temperament, and these gene-generated environmental influences then select or call forth other genetically directed behaviors.[13]

Without attempting to apply interaction theory with all its complexities, what can one say in summary form about environmental and genetic influences on violence and crime?

As to environmental influences, it is substantially documented that a wide range of psychological and social factors, among them poverty, overcrowding, parental violence, peer group models and pressures, and so on, are correlated with, and most of them are causal contributors to, violence and crime. These factors are well enough known that we need not review them here.

But what is the evidence for the fiercely disputed and politically incorrect theory that genetic and other biological influences play a significant part in violence and crime? Here is a sampling:

• Many animal studies have shown that the higher the level of circulating testosterone, the more aggressive the creature. In human beings, early studies of this phenomenon were inconsistent and inconclusive, but a recent one found that in two sizable samples of university students, men averaged five times as much testosterone in their saliva as women and, as judged by personality tests, were significantly more aggressive and less nurturant (prosocial) than the women.[14]

• Studies of rhesus monkeys show a correlation between the level of concentration of two serotonin metabolites that are primarily under genetic control and severe aggression.[15]

• Male mice bred to lack a gene essential for the production of nitric oxide, a neurotransmitter, are extremely aggressive to fellow males, often to the point of killing them. Although the finding should not be taken to explain extreme aggression in human beings, it does suggest that research on genetic deficiency of nitric oxide in human beings may prove valuable.[16]

• Classical twin studies show that if one twin has committed a crime, the chance that the other has done so is twice as great in identicals as in fraternals. Although there is probably an environmental influence (identicals interact very closely and mimic each other's actions), the data strongly suggest some genetic influence.[17]

• Several studies have found that children adopted in infancy are more likely, as adults, to have criminal convictions if their biological parents have been convicted of a crime than if their adoptive parents have been.[18]

• Two recent studies found a significant correlation between violent crime and genetic variation in the dopamine D_2 receptor gene; researchers think that the variation in the *DRD2* gene leads to lowered receptor density and a structural mutation in the dopaminergic reward system.[19]

• A growing body of clinical data indicates that low serotonin turnover may be related to habitual violence and impulsivity; the low serotonin turnover is associated with a genetic variation that affects the concentration of a principal serotonin metabolite in cerobrospinal fluid.[20]

• A study of a large group of Dutch relatives found that many of them had periodic outbursts of aggression and that many also had a faulty gene in the X chromosome; the gene was identified as the one that controls production of the enzyme monoamine oxidase, which is involved in the breakdown of serotonin and several other neurotransmitters. (It seems unlikely, however, that such a single-gene identification will prove to be the predisposing or actual causative factor in most violent behavior; all indications are that in most cases the predisposition toward violence and violent crime is influenced by a number of genes working together.)[21]

How these biological predispositions interact with experience and environmental influences is a most promising direction for violence and crime research. But two major efforts to bring together and exchange the findings of genetic research at a conference, in order to see more clearly what specific issues future research should investigate, met with intense political opposition that totally blocked the first effort and considerably diluted the scientific value of the second one, as we will now hear.

An Aborted Research Conference

Until the summer of 1992, research scholar David Wasserman of the University of Maryland would have thought it impossible for anyone to accuse him of being a racist, an intellectual Nazi, and an advocate of atrocious eugenic designs against black children. An earnest, youthful-looking man (he was then thirty-nine) whose heavy-framed glasses and dark beard gave him a scholarly appearance, Wasserman had always considered himself a political liberal and an egalitarian, and had lived the part.[22] He had grown up in a liberal home, majored in philosophy at

Yale, and earned a law degree at the University of Michigan and a master's degree in social psychology at the University of North Carolina. This blend of interests led him to spend five years working for the Legal Aid Society as an appellate public defender for poor and for the most part black young men convicted of crimes.

But being of scholarly bent and wanting to do research, Wasserman eventually left for a research position at the Institute for Philosophy and Public Policy of the University of Maryland, where, among other projects, he sought to study the impact on the justice system of the new biological explanations of behavior that defense lawyers were beginning to introduce as exculpatory evidence.

To obtain better grounding in this area, Wasserman applied for and obtained an NSF fellowship to study genetic typing and criminal justice; he used it to take courses in the Human Genetics Division of his university and to attend several meetings sponsored by the Human Genome Project (HGP) of the NIH. At the meetings, he and other participants discussed the potential value of behavior genetic research for the prediction and control of crime, and the problems such research might create, including invasion of privacy, stigmatization, discrimination in employment, and use or misuse as defense in criminal cases. From these discussions Wasserman got the idea that the time was right for a conference on genetics and crime to round up existing research evidence on genetic predispositions to impulsivity, violence, and criminal behavior, and to consider the implications, both positive and negative, that the research data might have for the legal system and for programs aimed at reducing crime.

Early in 1991, Wasserman, filled with enthusiasm, began to draft a proposal to NIH seeking funding for such a conference, and to compile a list of potential conferees, including such proponents of behavior genetics research as the criminologist James Wilson and the psychologist Richard Herrnstein, and such vigorous opponents of it as the biologists Garland Allan and Jon Beckwith, and the sociologist Troy Duster. The proposal read in part:

> The Institute for Philosophy and Public Policy proposes to hold a conference on the role of genetic research and technology in predicting, explaining and controlling criminal behavior. The conference will provide a forum for presenting the major research programs in this area, comparing their strategies and findings, and debating their application to the criminal justice system....The purpose of the conference will be to clarify the methodological, legal, and ethical issues raised by the development and use of techniques for identifying and treating criminal predispositions.[23]

Genetic research, Wasserman wrote, was "gaining impetus from the apparent failure of environmental approaches to crime—deterrence, diversion, and rehabilitation—to affect the dramatic increases in crime, especially violent crime, that this country has suffered over the past 30 years." He named family, twin, and adoption studies as major sources of scientific findings on the subject, but warned that scientists and policymakers might overlook the "enormous complexities in any genetic contribution to criminal behavior" and pointed out that very similar phenotypes are often produced by different genotypes interacting with environment, while the same genotypes often produce different phenotypes.* Moreover, criminal conduct "is not only socially elicited, but socially constructed: defined by legislatures and courts, and detected by arrests, convictions, and self-reports." After adding a number of other caveats, he admitted that such research might create serious problems, among them the controversy that "will almost certainly surround the diagnosis and treatment of genetic predispositions to crime" and the "strong opposition to using even the most benign drugs and therapies to treat criminal dispositions."

The one major problem Wasserman never mentioned—apparently because it never occurred to him—was that his conference might be seen by blacks and politically correct activists as a racist assault on blacks, since persons arrested for violent crimes are disproportionately black: 55 percent of all persons arrested in the U.S. for murder and manslaughter, and 61 percent of those arrested for robbery, are black, although blacks make up only 12 percent of the U.S. population; thus, in each category the black crime rate is roughly five times the white crime rate.[24] Of course, the disproportion might have a purely social explanation; this was an important issue the conference would undoubtedly take up.

Conceivably, Wasserman's conference might not have come under black attack except for an event unrelated to it, a tactless remark made by the highest-ranking psychiatrist in the government, Dr. Frederick Goodwin, then head of the Alcohol, Drug Abuse, and Mental Health Administration (ADAMHA), a large agency within the NIH. At a meeting in February, 1992, Goodwin announced that the top priority of ADAMHA in 1994 would be the Violence Initiative, a set of studies

---

*A genotype is the total genetic makeup of an organism; a phenotype is the actual individual as produced by the interaction of its genotype with the environment around it.

and programs seeking to control the rising rate of violent crime. The Violence Initiative had been designed in large part by Dr. Louis Sullivan, the black secretary of HHS, of which NIH is a part. Goodwin, a white, said that a central effort of the Violence Initiative would be to identify, early, those children, primarily inner-city youths, likely to become violent, and to seek ways to intervene and head off the development of violent behavior in them. Then, being a man of broad philosophic and scientific interests, Goodwin commented that violence is natural in primates but controlled among humans by civilized restraints; compared to male rhesus monkeys living in the wild who attack each other, he said, only half of whom survive to adulthood, human beings do very well. Had he said no more on the matter, all might have been well, but he added a candid and impolitic thought: "Some of the loss of social structure in this society, and particularly within high impact inner city areas, has removed some of the civilizing evolutionary things that we have built up....Maybe it isn't just a careless use of the word when people call certain areas of certain cities jungles."[25]

The protests were immediate, furious, and overwhelming: Goodwin was accused of having likened inner-city blacks to monkeys. The Congressional Black Caucus, with twenty-six members, met with Secretary Sullivan and told him in no uncertain terms that Goodwin was unfit to serve as head of ADAMHA; various other groups called for his dismissal; and newspaper headlines throughout the country blasted him and generated fury, particularly in black communities. Goodwin apologized publicly three days later, but Sullivan demoted him to head NIMH, one of ADAMHA's three component agencies, where his involvement with the Violence Initiative would be minimal. That more or less concluded the "jungles" foofaraw, but blacks remained up in arms against the Violence Initiative and convinced that any part of it—including, some came to believe, Wasserman's conference—was a scheme by the government to portray young black men as potential criminals in order to justify a major effort to drug and subdue them.

Two of the key leaders in the protests against Goodwin and the Violence Initiative were Ronald Walters, a black political scientist and head of his department at Howard University, and, as mentioned earlier, Dr. Peter Breggin of Bethesda, Maryland, a white psychiatrist who is, by his own avowal, "a nonmainstreamer" of American psychiatry.[26] Breggin's dissent from the mainstream was both professional and political: For two decades he had vigorously opposed all biological treatments of mental illness, considering all treatment by electroshock, psychosurgery, and—most important—psychotropic drugs not only medically but socially wrong and a deliberate evasion of what he said were the right approaches, namely, the use of psychotherapy and the fundamental correction of social conditions that generate mental illness. His stance was thus a combination of therapeutic conservatism and social radicalism. Goodwin's proposed intervention with youngsters who were identified as likely to become violent, Breggin said, would obviously involve treatment with drugs, since that was what Goodwin had always promoted. "I don't think *any* psychiatric condition is suitably treated with drugs," Breggin said, "they are not the answer to human problems."[27]

Wasserman, meanwhile, had received good news: An NIH peer review panel that included three blacks among its fourteen members had found his proposal a "superb job," said that it "addresses one of the areas of greatest concern about uses of information that come from the study of the human genome," and rated it "overall an excellent grant application for a conference on a timely and important topic."[28] The panel's report never mentioned race in connection with the conference. The report's warm recommendation ensured the NIH administration's decision, and on May 1 Wasserman was notified that his proposal had been officially approved and he was awarded a grant of $78,000.

Congratulated by his colleagues at the Institute for Philosophy and Public Policy, he got busy working out the logistics of the conference, notifying speakers, and attending to innumerable details. The conference, to be held at the Center for Adult Education on the campus of the University of Maryland in College Park, Maryland, would last for three days (October 9 through 11, 1992) and would present the research on the genetics of crime and the varied opinions and recommendations of more than forty scientists and scholars, including psychologists, geneticists, legal scholars, and philosophers, as to how to use it.

One of Wasserman's many preparatory labors was publicizing the conference, including the preparation and distribution of a brochure. Breggin, when a copy somehow reached him, reacted like a fireman hearing the alarm bell. On May 26 he got out an emergency mailing to the several hundred members of the Center for the Study of Psychiatry; a political-activist organization he and his wife had founded some years earlier. The letter, sounding his usual themes, read in part:

> We have now obtained an announcement of National Institute of Health's latest activity, which is a conference titled: "Genetic Factors in Crime: Findings, Uses

& Implications." There are no known genetic factors in crime, but merely raising the issue arouses racial prejudices and distracts us from the true causes of the high crime rate within the inner city, including poverty, unemployment, racism, dangerous and inadequate schools, drug abuse, family dysfunction, and a variety of other social and economic factors.

A skilled propagandist, Breggin had managed in a single sentence—the second one above—to arouse the fears and inflame the passions of black activists, liberals, leftists, psychotherapists who feared their livelihoods were threatened by the biological treatment of mental disorders, teachers, and all persons who, on whatever grounds, held nurturist views of human behavior.

The letter was only the first step in Breggin's campaign to wreck the conference. Appearing on radio talk shows and on Black Entertainment Television, he linked the conference to the Violence Initiative and charged that biological research in criminality would lead to the use of therapeutic drugs to control the behavior of inner-city children. "It is the most terrifying, most racist, most hideous thing imaginable," he said, "it's the kind of plan one would associate with Nazi Germany."[29] Wasserman, honeymooning in Europe at the time, was telephoned by an associate who told him about Breggin's attacks, but he was unconcerned. Recalling his reaction, he says, "I thought, 'This guy's a crank. The conference is well balanced. We'll be able to disabuse people.'"

Breggin, playing and replaying the Nazi motif, told a reporter for *Time*, "Redefining social problems as public health problems is exactly what was done in Nazi Germany."[30] He repeated the charge, plus his unqualified and patently false assertion that there are no known genetic factors in crime, on radio talk shows, in letters to the editors of leading newspapers, in an article he wrote titled "Plot to Sedate Black Youth" in *News Dimensions* (a black weekly published in Washington), and at a community rally at Howard University led by Ronald Walters.[31]

These efforts, plus similar ones by Walters, generated fury among the members of the Congressional Black Caucus, who made their ire known to Dr. Bernadine Healy, director of the NIH, and produced a flood of protest phone calls and letters to the agency from chapters of the NAACP, the Association of Black Psychologists, a number of scientists and academics of strictly environmentalist views, and others who had heard Breggin's remarks or read his letters in the newspapers.

Wasserman, back from Europe and busy finalizing the conference arrangements, became increasingly concerned by the mounting opposition and, conferring with people at NIH, drafted a revised brochure and press release to address Breggin's claims about the conference and make it appear less threatening. Having done so, he was about to send it to the printer when, on July 20, he got a phone call from his grant manager at NIH telling him that Healy, responding to the furor, had put a temporary freeze on his funding and that the conference could not be held until she unfroze it.[32] Wasserman was thunderstruck and, when he recovered from his initial shock, furious. As a lawyer, he considered Healy's action totally illegal; moreover, as he told reporters, it undermined academic freedom and the peer review process, and was part of an alarming "pattern of bowing to political pressure."[33] (In retrospect, Wasserman says. "I should not have been surprised. Healy had cut or denied funds or overridden funding for many other projects. Her administration was just a nightmare.")

Healy's freeze of the conference was widely reported in the media, but to Wasserman's dismay relatively few friends and professional organizations publicly supported his cause, perhaps because Breggin had tarred the conference with the charge of racism. A spokesman for APA did publicly deplore the freeze, as did the American Association of University Professors; *Science* magazine said editorially that the freeze sent a message to researchers not to propose any research that might offend certain segments of society;[34] a few newspapers ran editorials saying things like, "Dr. Healy has simply given in to political pressures fomented by ideological zealots"[35]; Arthur Caplan, a leading biomedical ethicist then at the University of Minnesota, said that the freeze of the conference funding was a "moral outrage";[36] and Victor Medina, director of sponsored programs at the university, formally and vigorously protested the freeze to Elke Jordan, deputy director of the National Center for Human Genome Research at NIH, demanding that it "state explicitly its reasons for the freeze" and asserting, "We are aware of no rule, law or regulation which would authorize the interruption of this award."[37]

From NIH word came back to the university and Wasserman that the financing might be restored if the conference were reorganized to take into greater account the adverse criticisms of various scholars and of the black community. Wasserman did his best to comply and notified Eric Juengst, his program director at the genome project, that he was willing to convene a panel including representatives of the black community and listen to their suggestions, make changes in the wording of the brochure, and organize additional sessions that would explicitly deal with racial questions.[38] But other word from NIH was distinctly less encouraging: A letter to Medina from John Diggs, Healy's deputy director and official spokesman for the NIH administration, frostily defended Healy's freeze as "proper public stewardship" and dismissed the university's complaints out of hand.

During the rest of the summer, Wasserman continued talking to his contacts at NIH and trying to rough out with them modifications that would answer Healy's objections. He also began working with an advisory committee of three academics who were knowledgeable about genetics but concerned about the social and racial implications of the conference, and with them began patching together an agenda that would allot more time to discussions of the social and racial issues that critics and opponents of the conference had raised.

Breggin and Walters, for their part, kept on issuing charges and accusations against the conference and the Violence Initiative, Breggin taking the high ground in statements such as, "The flier...[raises] fears that the conference will promote biological and psychiatric intrusions upon presumably dangerous people.... As a psychiatrist, I fear that the federal violence initiative will end up blaming innocent children for society's problems."[39] In an address to the Congressional Black Caucus he said, "We're trying to stop another Holocaust."[40] Thanks to his and Walters' efforts, a number of newspapers ran editorials and articles attacking the conference and the Initiative; typically, one in the *San Francisco Weekly* said, "A growing number of genetic researchers are hell-bent on finding a biological basis for criminal behavior. Is this true science, or a politically-fueled revival of the discredited racial theories of eugenics?"[41]

By early September it was evident that even if a revised agenda were found acceptable and the freeze reversed, too little time remained to complete arrangements and hold the conference as planned on October 9 through 11, and in fact there were no signs from above that the freeze might be lifted. University officials therefore reluctantly announced on September 4 that the conference was being indefinitely postponed.[42] Wasserman's comment:

> Healy's press corps made the most of the situation. As I was getting on a plane the next morning, I saw a headline in the *New York Times* saying that the government had canceled the conference, and the accompanying story implied that Healy had done so because the conference had racist overtones. She was very savvy; she had her people make it seem a righteous act.

At the same time, Diggs wrote another letter, this one thoroughly hostile, to the university and released it to the press; in it he said that

Wasserman was to blame for the impasse, since certain statements in his proposal "not only inflamed public opinion but also represent a radical divergence from the topics for which the grant was awarded.... In structuring and certainly in advertising the conference, Mr. Wasserman grotesquely distorted the nature and scope of the meeting that was originally approved through the peer review process."[43] This was simply untrue; the language and content of the brochure were nearly identical to those of the proposal. Wasserman himself doubts that Diggs, although a black, was expressing his own feelings: "Basically, he was a reluctant front man. He might have wished the conference to go away, but the personal enmity in the letter was Healy's. He should have refused to do what he did, it was discreditable, but I doubt that he was a prime mover."

Breggin and Walters, though gratified by their victory over the conference, continued on with their larger aim of halting the entire Violence Initiative. "The battle has hardly begun," Breggin told a reporter from the *Chronicle of Higher Education.* "The conference was simply the most visible and obviously atrocious example of an attempt to blame crime on the brains or the genes of little black children instead of addressing racism and poverty in America."[44]

Although the *Times* had said the conference was canceled, it still existed on paper but with its funding frozen, ostensibly temporarily. Wasserman continued to work with HGP officials on modifications of the conference agenda and to defend it in the media whenever he had the opportunity. In the *Chronicle of Higher Education* and elsewhere he replied, in rational rather than overheated tones, to the charges of the dangers of discussing such research:

> I do not doubt that the charges [of racism] were false. The conference was designed to subject research on genetics and crime to close public scrutiny, and it included some of the foremost critics of that research, as well as leading researchers...
>
> I believe that studies of twins and adopted children have yielded enough evidence of heritability in criminal behavior to warrant serious debate.... The conference would have given the public a framework for assessing the social risks of research on genetics and crime, and it would have heightened public awareness of measures, like the identification and medication of "hyperactive" children, already being directed toward individuals seen as predisposed to antisocial behavior on the basis of behavioral or psychiatric indicators.
>
> Obviously, assertions made at the conference could have been misquoted, quoted selectively or out of context, or misleadingly appropriated in other ways. The risk of such misrepresentation is inherent in any public discussion, and no public discussion of controversial issues could take place if that risk were regarded as fatal. I have, however, a resilient optimism about the self-correcting quality of "the marketplace of ideas."[45]

But in October, the NIH people Wasserman had been talking to about the revised agenda declined to continue discussing it with him; apparently, word from up above had come down that the conference, though not officially dead, was to remain indefinitely in deep freeze. "I was worn out and disgusted," Wasserman says. "I'd had enough of it. As far as I was concerned, it was ended." He notified university officials and, weary and embittered, cleared his desk of conference materials, stowed them where he wouldn't have to see them again, and turned his mind to other matters. Political opposition to research on the genetics of crime, skillfully managed, had won the battle.

Once More Unto the Breach

For the next half year neither Wasserman, the university, nor his NIH contacts did anything further; the genetics and crime conference remained on NIH's books as an approved and funded project in a cryogenic limbo, neither dead nor alive. But NIH could not maintain it in that state; regulations required that it be either reactivated or formally revoked. No legal grounds existed, however, on which to revoke the conference; nothing had taken place that would warrant revocation. NIH therefore tried a reverse stratagem: Diggs notified the Legal Affairs Office of the university in March, 1993, that NIH wanted Wasserman and the university to relinquish the grant; this would formally cancel the project. Wasserman, when he was notified of this by the Legal Affairs Office, felt like doing so—"I had been worn down," he admits—but the university lawyers told him that the acting provost of the university, Jacob Goldhaber, would have none of it. Wasserman comments:

> Goldhaber is a real academic-freedom person, a man of tremendous principle. He was scandalized. His position was that the conference had been through the peer review process and been approved, and absolutely nothing would justify NIH's reversing its commitment. He felt that it would be a terrible precedent, and that NIH was responding to nothing but public controversy. He had the full support of the university's president and legal staff. They wanted me to see it through, and asked me to help draft a letter to be signed by the provost demanding that NIH either give us the grant immediately or terminate it. If they gave us the grant, fine; if they terminated the project—as we expected—we'd then be able to use the appeal process that exists within HHS.

In April NIH formally terminated the grant. The university promptly filed an appeal on the grounds that the cancellation was "arbitrary and capricious" and that there was no legitimate reason for the cancellation. Goldhaber was determined to carry the appeal beyond the NIH level to the level of PHS, of which NIH is a part, and even up to the level of HHS (of which PHS is a part). Wasserman recalls what then happened:

> We never had to go even to the second step. We filed an appeal in August, 1993—by which time Clinton had removed Healy from NIH, which made the situation easier—and in September we won. But we were required to work with NIH to restructure the conference, and we ended up giving even less time to science than in the revised agenda we had worked out, and more to controversial issues and social implications. NIH actually gave us $133,000 this time—more than half again as much as the first time—in order to enable us to spend much more time and attention on such matters as the racial context of contemporary genetic research, and the history of the eugenics movement and its perversion by Nazi Germany.

Despite the university's victory, for a while Wasserman was ambivalent about the reinstated conference and matters proceeded slowly. It took him and his contacts at HGP a year and a half to reshape the conference, compile a list of persons to be invited as panelists and as observers, and work out most of the logistics.

The emphasis of the new conference, in contrast to the canceled one, would be primarily on the controversies concerning the use of the scientific data, and only secondarily on the data themselves. Its title was "The Meaning and Significance of Research on Genetics and Criminal Behavior," and a Q & A paper titled "Frequently asked questions about the upcoming conference" that Wasserman sent out in the spring of 1995 was explicit about its priorities: "The purpose of this conference is to discuss the social, legal, and ethical implications of current research on genetics and criminal behavior. In order to explore those implications, the conference will begin with a critical assessment of the validity, findings, and prospects of that research."[46] (The purpose of the original conference, quoted above, was to "provide a forum for presenting the major research programs in this area, comparing their strategies and findings, and debating their application to the criminal justice system.")

Along with other Q&A's meant to head off opposition, the paper asked, "Does this conference have anything to do with federal research on biology and violence?" and answered:

> No. It is supported by the Program on the Ethical, Legal, and Social Implications of the Human Genome Project, a branch of the National Center for Human Genome Research. It receives no funding at all from agencies conducting or supporting research in genetics and criminal behavior. Its participants include

researchers who receive such support, as well as critics of the research and its funding.

The conference, evidently, had been defanged and declawed. It would still deal with some of the originally planned scientific topics, but the scientific sessions would be surrounded and rendered innocuous by political and ethical criticism, historical background, and discussions of the racial implications of the research, motives of the researchers, and possible social damage of making the research data known to policymakers and the public. Wasserman assured reporters that the 1995 conference would not be what they had thought the 1992 conference would be. "We want to disabuse anyone of the impression that this conference is meant to celebrate human behavior genetics as a panacea of the crime problem," he told Natalie Angier, a science writer for the *New York Times*. "The conference has changed from three years ago. We're placing a greater emphasis on the issue of race and racial tensions."[47] A number of prominent critics of the genetics approach to crime would be on hand, he added, including several blacks, most notably the sociologist Troy Duster, who would have been a participant in the 1992 conference and had played an important part in the shaping of the 1995 conference.

But lining up panelists, blacks in particular, proved to be more difficult than the first time. Some of the minority opponents who had previously agreed to take part declined to do so now because of the acrimony that had surrounded the 1992 conference. For the same reason, so did some of the ardent advocates of behavior genetic research. Adrian Raine, a psychologist at the University of Southern California who espouses genetics research and did agree to come, explained to a reporter why many people doing such work wanted to stay out of the spotlight or even change their research interest: "There are people for whom, if you do biological research on violence, you are *ipso facto* a racist. A lot of people won't touch the work anymore. And that could be a tragedy. If it turns out that biology is a component in violence, if we don't understand it we won't be able to help."[48] In the end, Wasserman lined up thirty-two academics and other experts as panelists and discussants (he'd had forty-five for the first conference, but it would have run longer).

Peter Breggin, to whom Wasserman sent an invitation to attend, chose to shun it for his own reasons. "They didn't ask me to talk," he told a reporter rather testily, "they just sent me a form letter. And I'm still opposed to this conference. Nothing has changed. I couldn't see myself attending a meeting that will only feed the flames of racism."[49] (One knowledgeable participant thinks that the 1995 version, with so much time allocated to criticisms of behavior genetics, seemed to Breggin not worth the time and trouble to attack.)

Wasserman also sent invitations to journalists he considered responsible, to some of the conference's most vociferous academic critics, and to a member of the Coalition to Stop the Violence Initiative, an activist group formed in 1992 after Frederick Goodwin's unfortunate comment about the inner-city "jungle." But he sought to minimize the chances of serious interference and violent demonstrations by holding the conference not at the university's campus just outside Washington but sixty miles away at the secluded Aspen Institute in Queenstown, near Chesapeake Bay. Either for that reason or because of the altered focus of the conference or both, reservation requests came in from only about forty spectators, including some of the invited opponents of the conference.

Wasserman also heard that some uninvited opponents would be coming: He had received e-mail messages from a member of the Support Coalition International, an alliance of "psychiatric survivors" who, like Breggin, were adamantly opposed to any use of psychotropic medication, saying that they would be putting on a protest demonstration. Because the tone of the e-mail messages was rather civil, Wasserman expected the demonstration to be an orderly display of some kind on the campus, outside the building in which the conference was taking place, and he assumed that there was no need to take advance measures against it.

Despite his efforts to keep everything low-key and to emphasize the criticisms and social implications of the research, many newspaper articles in advance of the conference sounded the old alarums. "Talks to Tackle Volatile Crime-Genetics Issue," read the headline in the *Sacramento Bee*.[50] "Disputed Meeting To Ask if Crime Has Genetic Roots" was the title of a *New York Times* article reiterating and stressing the conflicts that wrecked the previously planned conference. "Scholars to Explore Link Between Crime, Genes," read a headline of an article in the *Philadelphia Inquirer* that sought to make the new conference sound intensely controversial:

> Are some children born to be bad? Can there be a "treatment" to block them from murder? The explosive questions are back. The more explosive answer, in some quarters, is yes. And the renewed debate is sending chills down the spines of those who fear it will bring a Brave New World of mind control to the children of America's violent inner cities.[51]

* * *

The conference began tranquilly on Friday afternoon, September 22, 1995 in the pleasantly rural setting of the Aspen center. The keynote address was an overview of current research on genetics and violence presented by the psychologist Irving I. Gottesman of the University of Virginia, an expert on behavior genetics. Gottesman calls himself "definitely middle-of-the-road" politically and a moderate on genetics and violence issues, and says that is why he was chosen as the keynote speaker, adding:

> But I realized, in the discussion session following my talk, that almost nobody else saw me that way because I was speaking favorably—in part—about the role of genetic factors in aggression and antisocial behavior. There were a number of verbal attacks by members of the audience, and one fellow—Jerome Miller, a criminologist who later became part of the D. C. child welfare agency—stood up and said that after listening to my droning on for an hour he realized that I was an apologist for the far Right. I'm always shocked when that happens to me. I thought I went out of my way to show that I was a good guy.

In addition to the keynote session, the agenda included only two other two-hour science sessions—panel discussions of research methods in genetics and crime, their validity, and their findings—but five two-hour sessions on the debates about the causes of crime, the history of the controversy about biogenetic explanations of crime, the media and public perceptions and misperceptions of the subject, the problems of race and ideology raised by the Violence Initiative, and finally a session on the prospects of medical and public health approaches to crime and violence. Science, clearly, sat below the salt at the banquet.

Still, a fair amount of solid research methodology and data was presented in the two scientific sessions and some panelists even cited possible applications of the biological research findings. Gottesman and others said that the twin-study and adoption-study data were good leads toward identifying genetic components that put people at risk of committing crimes, and Diana Fishbein of the U.S. Department of Justice said that if definitive markers for antisocial behavior were found and manifested early, perhaps early intervention would be possible.[52] David Goldman, a neurogeneticist at NIH, said that there was no gene for violence or crime but that alleles would be found that would influence such behavior, and he listed several genetic factors that are unquestionably linked to specific forms of violent behavior such as Lesch-Nyhan syndrome, which often involves self-mutilation, and attention-deficit hyperactivity disorder, which can be a precursor of antisocial behavior.[53] Dr. David Comings of the City of Hope Medical Center reported success in treating children with "conduct disorder"—a precursor to antisocial personality marked by such behavior as starting fights and setting fires—with clonidine, an antihypertensive drug that stimulates certain adreno-receptors in the brain, reducing sympathetic outflow from the central nervous system.[54]

But throughout the two and a half days, especially during the sessions on social and ethical implications of the research and on the history of eugenics, a number of panelists and members of the audience voiced fears about and anger at research on the genetics of violence and crime. The moderate ones said that research on genetics and crime was a long way from having answers to the problem and could have unfair and discriminatory outcomes. The immoderate ones went much further: William Sacks, a Washington physician and member of the audience, said, "Crime is not a biological concept, it's a social concept. Any investigation into the effects of genes on social behavior is invalid"; the criminologist Jerome Miller said that genetic research was "a nice way to avoid dealing with the complexities of social problems" and that it was a bad time to engage in talk of genetics research "when the country is burning with references to race"; and Adrienne Asch, a social psychologist at Wellesley College, was reported by *Science* and various dailies to have said, "Such research has no place in our society." (She denies having said it. "I'm not ready to say there are topics that shouldn't be studied," she told me, "but we *could* solve more social problems and eliminate more human suffering by doing things other than genetic research.")[55]

Howard University economics professor Rodney Green, a white, was the most aggressively vociferous panelist. "This conference is garbage!" he bellowed on the second day of the conference, adding, "We have to consider whether this conference should continue. What we heard this morning was a racist presentation under the guise of genetics. It promotes the legacy of Nazism. Such conferences should not be allowed to be held. This is pseudoscience!" In rebuttal, the geneticist Gregory Carey of the University of Colorado diagnosed Green's and similar attacks as "paranoid delusions," but the diagnosis did nothing to cure the symptom.[56]

During the history and philosophy session, several panelists reviewed the horrendous eugenics practices of Nazi Germany and said their roots were the genetics-based sterilization laws of many states in the U.S.[57] Six panelists drafted a formal protest of the conference and handed it out to reporters; it read, in part, "Scientists as well as historians and sociologists must not allow themselves to be used to provide academic respectability for racist pseudoscience."[58]

One bit of unintended comedy livened the proceedings: An unidentified black man in the audience stood up during one session and denounced Charles Darwin as a racist—this was presumably relevant, since evolutionary theory is the foundation of behavior genetics—and proved his point by reading in sonorous tones the title of Darwin's famous work, *On the Origin of Species by Means of Natural Selection: Or the Preservation of Favoured Races in the Struggle for Life*. Snickers greeted this momentous declaration; most of the academics present knew that by "races" Darwin was referring not to races of humankind but to animal species.[59]

* * *

So it went. But the high point and, to judge by media accounts, the most significant piece of business at the conference was the unscheduled but anticipated demonstration. Unlike many such events, this one involved no physical attacks on speakers, no destruction or defacing of university property, and, though noisy and disruptive, was almost civil; indeed, a few of the "psychiatry survivors," after a shouting match with Wasserman, shook his hand.

"I'd hoped it would be too much trouble for them to come," Wasserman says, but he was wrong. Late in the morning of the second day, in the middle of Panel III, devoted to "Evaluating the research: empirical and conceptual questions," just as some panelists were denying that behavior has a genetic predisposition, there was a commotion at the doors. Bonnie Bluestein, an "independent scholar," opened them—evidently by prearrangement—and hugged one of the raggle-taggle group of about forty people who burst in. They were mostly young and rather hippy-looking, some waving red flags and others carrying placards reading "Genetics Conference is Criminal" and "Jobs Yes, Prozac No," and chanting "Maryland conference, you can't hide, we know you're pushing genocide!" Their banners and signs identified them as members of two organizations, the Support Coalition International, and the Revolutionary Communist Party (confusingly, some of this second group said they were members of the Progressive Labor Party).

Most of the panelists and audience sat in stony-faced silence, although a few cheered the invaders on. Wasserman leaped to his feet and shouted at the protesters, "Leave! Leave! Your views are already represented by conference participants!" It was a statement unlikely to have any effect, and did not. He tried again, though his oratorical style and message were ill suited to the situation: "There are a hell of a lot of people attending this conference who think the dangers of genetic research are as great in the long term as the dangers of atomic energy!" The state police were on hand, but Wasserman asked them to take no action.

In a moment or two, some of the protesters gained the stage and one of them, Robert Cook, a student at Rutgers University, seized a microphone and said, "You might think you have a right to do the research you are doing, but the bottom line is that it will be used to subjugate people."[60] Another, Adam Stevens, a senior at Columbia University, yelled, "You don't see the eugenics in what you are doing! No freedom of speech for racists!" To which Wasserman retorted in his hopelessly reasonable way, stammering in his effort to speak rapidly, "Many of the concerns you legitimately raise we are already giving voice to at this conference. By stopping the proceedings you're denying other protesters their voice."

The demonstration did produce one minor brawl, though it was touched off not by a protester but by a conference loyalist: A member of the audience, infuriated by Ronald Green's shouted remark that the conference was garbage, started punching him in the stomach, and in the scuffle that ensued as others intervened, he accidentally hit Bluestein in the face, bruising her, although in a sense it was not a misdirected punch since she obviously had conspired with the demonstrators.

Back and forth went the shouting, achieving nothing except the ventilation of anger on both sides. Only when Adrienne Asch stood up brandishing a white cane—she is blind—did the tumult die down. "The purpose of having a conference," she said, "is to find out, and to let people say what they have to say. You're not going to solve the problem by closing the conference down—that's anti-democratic." She sat down, and the chanting and shouting resumed.

Another protester, one of the "psychiatric survivors," yelled, "The real violence in this country is committed against psychiatric patients, who are dying, brain-damaged, twitching shells of themselves." Harris Coulter, a political scientist, bellowed at him and the others, "You're a bunch of fascists, that's what you are! Where's your jackboots?"[61] A protester called out, "Once you spend millions of dollars on this research, what you're doing to do here is trying to legitimize it." Wasserman, red-faced, shouted, "We're not trying to legitimize it! We're trying to raise questions about it." He went on to defend the funding of genetic research and to say what he'd have done if he'd been making budgetary decisions for the government, but a young man in blue jeans and Timberland boots broke in to say, "Right! It would include building work camps and concentration camps if you were in charge."[62]

Clearly, the confrontation had reached the silly stage and both sides realized it; the demonstrators at last acceded to the urging of security officers (who had made no effort to eject or arrest anyone) to leave and straggled out, telling reporters they would hold a press conference on the lawn outside. The conferees, after a few minutes of arguing with each other about the charges leveled by the demonstrators, settled down and resumed the late-morning session. The demonstration had interrupted proceedings for forty-five minutes and produced one sore midriff (Ronald Green's) and one bruised chin (Bonnie Bluestein's); this sounds trivial, but the demonstration garnered most of the media attention to the conference and, for all anyone knows, may have discouraged some scientists who had ideas for meetings of their own.

The rest of the program, continuing during the afternoon and on Sunday morning, went as planned, although with more heated disputation and impassioned political rhetoric than is usual in scientific conferences. But this was not exactly a scientific conference. As originally conceived, it had been half scientific conference, half conference on the ethical, legal, and social implications of the findings; now, political opposition had caused it to metamorphose into something else, a politico-socio-ethico—and, only incidentally, scientific—conference. The opposition had also changed Wasserman's own views. In his original proposal to NIH, he had been considerably more optimistic about the possible applications of research on genetics and crime, and less apprehensive about its possible misuses, than after the 1992 conference had been scuttled. Even in advance of the 1995 conference he took a very guarded view of the research:

> While I do not think that research on genetics and crime should receive lower priority simply because it is controversial, I also do not think it should receive higher priority because it is seen to promise solutions to the problems of crime and delinquency.... It is better to frame, and to fund, this research as basic genetic and neurobiological science, judging it more by the contribution it could make to those areas of inquiry, than by its practical value in solving social problems.[63]

The necessary reshaping of the 1995 conference, and the positions taken at it by many participants—and by the intruders—strengthened his awareness of the views of critics of such research, in particular their doubt that it would ever prove useful and their concern about its social impact. In a recent review of the controversy he summed up their position as follows:

> Neurogenetic research focused on individual differences is unlikely to yield genuine insight into the causes of anti-social and violent behavior, but it is likely to discover markers and genes that are loosely associated with that behavior. The discovery will be highly susceptible to abuse by agencies of social control, from schools to parole boards, because those markers and genes will be easy to detect, and tempting to employ in programs of screening and preemptive intervention.[64]

He did, however, point out that researchers were optimistic that further research on the genetics influences on crime would produce greater understanding:

> Researchers expect the sunset of heritability to be followed by the bright dawn of neurogenetic research, which will trace the complex causal pathways through which specific genes influence [crime and delinquency]. That research will place behavioral genetics on a solid biological footing, and, in substituting narrow, testable causal hypotheses for global estimates of heritability, will be less susceptible to misunderstanding and abuse.[65]

As for research on racial differences in genetic predisposition to crime, he said that it seemed unlikely to have useful results and that he "cannot imagine any reason that a fair and humane society would be interested in genetic differences between racial or ethnical groups." Still, as a believer in freedom of research, he said he would not prohibit such research, although he thought it did not deserve any public funding.[66]

* * *

What did the 1995 conference accomplish, from a scientific standpoint? Perhaps the question is unfair, since it had turned into something other than a scientific conference. The day it ended, the exhausted Wasserman was deeply gratified that it had actually taken place but unsure what had been achieved. "I can't confidently say it was a success," he told a reporter. "The media glare had a terribly polarizing effect. I wonder whether the critics of the research and its proponents were really listening to each other or just paying lip service to each other's views." He paused, then rallied and struck a more positive note: "The fact that the conference, riven by cross purposes"—he does talk like that—"was held at all, despite the storm of controversy and opposition, was a triumph in itself."

I asked him whether, seen from the perspective of a year and a half later, the 1995 conference had achieved the goals he had had for the

1992 one. Seasoned litigator that he is, he artfully sidestepped my question:

> There were always conflicting agendas about what to discuss. The critics of the conference felt that you needed a social context into which to put the science even before you discussed it. The scientists did not want that; they didn't want their work to be seen as a sequel to racist eugenics. The conference actually sharpened the differences between the two sides.

What was originally envisioned as a pooling of scientific research accompanied by consideration of its social and legal implications had been converted, by political pressure, into a conference on those implications, accompanied by discussion of the research. A dispassionate account of the conference in the *Chronicle of Higher Education* commented, "Many scholars said they would have liked more of a chance to learn about the actual research."[67] That they did not suggests which side was the victor.

Sinking an Iceberg

In a letter appearing in the *New York Times* of September 18, 1992, Peter Breggin wrote that the failed 1992 genetics and violence conference was "the tip of a much larger and more dangerous iceberg, the Federal 'Violence Initiative.'"[68]

This, as mentioned above, was the ambitious scheme announced by Frederick Goodwin in February, 1992, which, he said, would be the number one funding priority of the federal mental health establishment in 1994. The Violence Initiative was the brainchild of Louis Sullivan, secretary of HHS, who envisioned a giant umbrella program that would involve three major agencies—NIMH, ADAMHA, and CDC (the Centers for Disease Control)—and would combine and coordinate a large number of current and new research studies of the environmental, developmental, and genetic antecedents of violent behavior. Its overall goals would be to determine the causes of youth violence and to devise programs, ranging from family and community support to pharmacological treatment, to prevent the development in young people of violent and criminal behavior.[69]

Although this omnium-gatherum clearly included the study of social and environmental causes of violence, the political forces that had sunk the 1992 genetics and violence conference blasted away at the Violence Initiative with the same charges of eugenics, racism, and Nazism. As Peter Breggin said in his letter to the *Times*, "[It is a] giant new Federal program to identify potentially violent inner-city children based on biological and genetic 'markers'" Success in stopping the genetics and violence conference, he added, "must not distract from the larger need to stop the violence initiative."[70] In a long article in a quarterly journal published by his activist organization, the Center for the Study of Psychiatry, he wrote:

> Under the leadership of [Ginger] Ross-Breggin, the Center for the Study of Psychiatry has made its number one priority the stopping of this racist program. But the violence initiative is already deeply embedded within the federal health establishment and will not be easily eradicated.... The violence initiative...rationalizes social ills in biomedical terms that blame the victim—in this instance the young inner city black man.... [It] represents one of the most threatening mental health activities in the past several decades. It poses a special menace to the black community, but ultimately endangers all Americans. A concerted effort must be made to stop it.[71]

In addition to the efforts of Breggin's Center, an activist group called the Committee to Stop the Violence Initiative, formed by Lorne Love, a Washington radio talk-show host, generated a good deal of publicity on its own, including statements and appearances by Breggin and by Ronald Walters, who had played a part in the opposition to the genetics and crime conference; the two were the Committee's main sources of information and direction.[72] Walters also organized a meeting at Howard University to talk about the Violence Initiative and told the audience, which included a number of reporters, "There is no science which shows one group is more genetically disposed to violence than another. This [the Violence Initiative] is a fishing expedition based on ideological theories, not scientific ones, and it gives this research a wholly political nature."[73]

The escalating campaign against the Violence Initiative was reported in the October 9 issue of *Science*:

> By canceling the proposed Maryland meeting, government officials thought they had succeeded in smoothing the black community's ruffled feathers. But recent events suggest the conference tiff may be nothing more than a warmup bout for a considerably larger and fiercer fight: one over a "violence initiative" being planned by the Department of Health and Human Services (HHS).
>   The violence initiative—brainchild of African-American HHS Secretary Louis Sullivan and now being developed at the Centers for Disease Control (CDC) by CDC Director William L. Roper—is intended mainly to gather together into one package some ongoing research at a variety of federal agencies. It could cost as much as $50 million in taxpayers' money, but that's not what has made it controversial: the Congressional Black Caucus found it no less offensive than the can-

celed Maryland conference, blasting Sullivan at a 25 September meeting of its members provocatively titled "The Bush Administration's Violence Initiative: Is It Racist?" Indeed, one invited guest, psychiatrist Peter Breggin, director of the Center for the Study of Psychiatry in Bethesda, went so far as to say, "We're trying to stop another Holocaust."[74]

Defending the Violence Initiative against the attacks would have been touchy at any time but was particularly so in the final months of an election year. Deborah Barnes, editor of the *Journal of NIH Research*, quoted anonymous informants in HHS as saying things like "It's a very sensitive issue," "Nobody's really decided how to handle the situation," and "We've been told 'from the highest level that we shouldn't say anything."[75] As Barnes wrote, in a furious editorial:

> If a fanatic would like to make the Department of Health and Human Services (HHS), the Public Health Service, NIH, an institute, or even a particular science administrator look bad—no problem. Simply mix a bit of truth with an outrageous amount of fabrication, catalyze the reaction with charges of racism, and stir in public.
> Peter Breggin, a Harvard-trained psychiatrist based in Maryland, has tested the recipe and it works beautifully. Until late September, no one from HHS would counter publicly Breggin's false assertion that the government was funding research aimed toward identifying and drugging inner city black children as young as 5 to control their behavior.[76]

HHS Secretary Sullivan, himself a black, was the logical person to speak out against the attackers, but that fall he was busy campaigning for George Bush much of the time. He did, however, make two TV appearances in late September in which he denied that government-sponsored research on violence was aimed at blacks. In October, he told *Science* that the Violence Initiative was a much-needed effort to identify factors—social and psychological as well as biological—that lead to violence, and that, rumors notwithstanding, he had no plans whatsoever to cancel it,[77] and in a speech at a meeting on child and adolescent psychiatry later that month he described and defended its aims.[78]

But it was too little, too late, and if nothing else had doomed the program, the election did. George Bush, who had appointed Sullivan, was retired by the American electorate; Sullivan, accordingly, was out, and with him went the Violence Initiative. In an election year, no one in Congress had seen fit to propose it in a bill in Congress and it had therefore never been considered by any appropriations committee. After the election, the ambitious plan not only no longer had a top-level advocate in HHS but its foes were gathering strength; they included an organization called the Citizens Commission on Human Rights, the

African American Coalition for Justice in Social Policy, and the Network Against Coercive Psychiatry, all of which kept up a drumfire of charges, in the media and on the Internet, of the racist and Nazi-like intentions of the Violence Initiative.

Not surprisingly, with no political or administrative advocates and so much vitriolic opposition, it simply faded away and disappeared. President Clinton, in his first administration, said that reducing youth violence was one of his priorities, but most of the measures he advocated were not research but applications: efforts to reduce drug use, step up gun control, strengthen antigang laws, and the like. Meanwhile, researchers in many institutions, believing that effective action is based on knowledge, have been continuing to explore the factors, including genetics and biology, contributing to violent and criminal behavior—mostly keeping a low profile to avoid the publicity that undid the Violence Initiative—but the range and depth of their research studies are, presumably, far smaller than would have been the case under the Violence Initiative.[79]

The nation heard good news in mid-1997, when the FBI announced that in 1996 serious crime had decreased for the fifth consecutive year and that for the first time violent crime had dropped below the level it had risen to in the late 1960s and early 1970s. But the news was not as good as it would have been if anyone knew why violent crime had been decreasing and what to do to keep it decreasing. A front-page report in the *New York Times* cited experts as saying that they did not have an adequate theory to explain the five-year decrease in crime; they did, however, speculate that a miscellany of possible factors might be responsible, among them more aggressive police tactics, neighborhood volunteer programs seeking to change juvenile behavior, tougher federal gun control laws, and the aging of the baby boom population.[80]

The existing research data do support the hypothesis that any and perhaps all of these factors played some part in the decline. But other factors may also have played a part—and possibly might play a far larger part if we knew what they were and could design programs based on that knowledge. But as long as political opposition to research limits our knowledge by interfering with government funding of research that offends particular groups, our policy makers and agency heads will be forced to function somewhat as did surgeons before the time of Vesalius, who, forbidden to dissect cadavers and, ignorant of the body's subtle architecture, probably killed as many of their patients as they saved.

Part 2

Attacks from the Right

6

Keeping Sex a Mystery

Decent Obscurity

In 1894 the editors of the *British Medical Journal* had a problem: Should they, or should they not, mention in their journal the just-published English translation of *Psychopathia Sexualis*? This work of sex research, a compilation of case histories of sexual deviations, had been written in German by the noted neuropsychiatrist Richard Krafft-Ebing, but whenever the details were grossly improper by the standards of the time, he shifted into Latin. In an editorial, the editors admitted their unease:

> We have considered at length whether we should notice this book or not, but we deem the importance of the subject and the position of the author make it necessary to refer to it.... We have questioned whether it should have been translated into English at all. Those concerned could have gone to the original. Better if it had been written entirely in Latin and thus veiled in the decent obscurity of a dead language.[1]

Essentially the same attitude toward the publication of sexual research prevailed in the United States at that time and for the first several decades of the twentieth century. The few social scientists who did serious sex research cautiously refrained from publishing their work until much later. When Freud lectured at Clark University in Worcester, Massachusetts, in 1909, one physician who heard him said, infuriated, that he was a "dirty, filthy man," and a college dean declared that Freud seemed to advocate "a relapse into savagery"; since Freud had lectured in German, it is likely that many others were not similarly aggrieved only because they had not fully understood him. Even from the seemingly liberated 1920s through the 1940s, when the Rockefeller Foundation was funding studies in prostitution and marital sexual behavior, only a handful of researchers were willing to openly conduct such studies.[2] Those few, sex researcher Vern Bullough has written, did so at some risk to their professional image, though they often tried to minimize the risk by stating that the subject was admittedly distasteful but that like every other kind of pathology it had to be studied.[3]

A notable exception was the entomologist Alfred Kinsey of Indiana University, who in the 1930s assembled a team and began the thousands of interviews, at an unprecedented level of intimacy, that resulted in the epochal volumes *Sexual Behavior in the Human Male* (1948) and *Sexual Behavior in the Human Female* (1953). In neither volume did he set himself above the activities described by denigrating them; indeed, in both volumes Kinsey frequently says, of mouth-genital contact, homosexual acts, and other historically forbidden sexual practices, that they are part of "basic mammalian behavior" that has been natural in many species for millions of years and therefore is natural in human beings.[4]

As long as Kinsey and his team carried on their work quietly, they ran into no serious opposition; in fact, by 1941 they were being funded by the Committee for Research on Problems of Sex, a group within the National Research Council (NRC), an agency of the National Academy of Sciences (NAS), and within a few years the Rockefeller Foundation was providing the funding, which was channeled through the NRC committee to Kinsey.[5] At some point, however, certain influential people—perhaps congressmen, perhaps Indiana state officials—got wind of Kinsey's activities and, he wrote in the introduction to the male report, he and his team were "repeatedly warned of the dangers involved in the undertaking and were threatened with specific trouble." He added that there had also been efforts to persuade the university's administration to halt the study or prevent publication of the results, or to dismiss him from his university post.

The university stood fast and the warnings and threats came to nothing, but when the "Kinsey Report" on men was published in 1948 and made headlines throughout the nation, many sexually and socially conservative people were shocked and angered by its extremely frank discussion of its findings on masturbation, extramarital sex, oral and anal sexual practices, and homosexuality. The Kinsey Report on women, published in 1953, offended and outraged even more of them. A number of prominent people attacked Kinsey and the Rockefeller Foundation, among them the sociologist A. H. Hobbs; Harry Emerson Fosdick, a leading New York minister; Harold Dodds, the president of Princeton University; Henry P. Van Dusen, president of the Union Theological

Seminary; former congresswoman Clare Booth Luce, the wife of the publisher of *Time*; and others.[6] The gist of their denunciations was that the Kinsey Reports, which portrayed these and other practices as common and natural, were contributing to the depravity of a whole generation and to the spread of juvenile delinquency.[7]

These criticisms fueled a congressional investigation that posed a serious threat to the Rockefeller Foundation. At the time, a number of large foundations were critically examining the activities of the House Un-American Activities Committee, and congressional conservatives struck back by creating a Committee to Investigate Tax Exempt Foundations. The arch-conservative congressman B. Carroll Reece of Tennessee, who headed the committee, cannily took aim at the foundation-supported activity most likely to arouse wide popular indignation, the Rockefeller Foundation's support of Kinsey's research, and suggested that for funding such research the Foundation might lose its tax-exempt status.[8]

"The Reece attack was quite scary to the foundations," says the sociologist Julia Erickson of Temple University, who is writing a history of sex research. "Dean Rusk, who was president of Rockefeller at the time, made a tremendously strong defense of the Kinsey funding and said things like 'We will not be intimidated,' but in fact fairly soon Rockefeller stopped funding Kinsey." At the same time, by what can hardly have been pure coincidence, the Rockefeller Foundation gave a very large grant to the Union Theological Seminary. In announcing that grant and the termination of Kinsey's funding Rusk said, "Some of the projects formerly supported [by the foundation], including that of Dr. Kinsey, are now in a position to obtain support from other sources."[9] But Kinsey had no other source of support except the royalties on the books, and in consequence although his group continued to do some research, much of its data went unpublished for many years; the findings of a survey completed in 1970, for instance, were not published until 1989.[10]

Reece's committee hearings and the threat that the committee report posed to the tax-exempt status of the Rockefeller Foundation may have been the first direct use of a federal governmental mechanism to cut off the funding of sex research.[11] While it did not succeed in halting the Kinsey research, it severely handicapped it and demonstrated that opposition to research conducted at the legislative level—more fitting for conservatives than the rowdy demonstrations of liberal-left activist groups—could be highly effective.

However, with one notable exception, to be cited in a moment, conservatives did not again use legislative methods of opposing sex research for some years. What kept them from doing so was the sexual revolution of the 1960s, which made it imperative for public health officials to know in specific detail how sexual behavior was changing, especially among the young, and how it was affecting fertility. From the mid-1960s through the 1970s hundreds of studies inquiring into these matters, most quite small and limited to one or a few questions, were funded by NIMH, NICHD, and other federal agencies, and by NSF, without encountering serious political opposition. By the 1980s, although the sexual revolution had died down, AIDS was becoming a major health threat and NIH, needing knowledge about how it was transmitted, funded a great many small surveys of the sexual behavior of homosexuals, drug users, prisoners, and other high-risk groups; these surveys sometimes encountered local opposition but they too went unchallenged in Congress.[12]

The one exception was a study headed by the psychologist Harris Rubin of the School of Medicine, Southern Illinois University. In 1973, Rubin, who had been studying the voluntary control of sexual arousal, submitted a research proposal to NIH for a study of the effects of alcohol and marijuana on male sexual arousal. After much uneasy double-checking on his credentials and questioning of his methods, in June, 1975 the National Institute on Drug Abuse (NIDA), a branch of NIH, awarded him a grant of $49,500 for a first year, with $39,500 recommended for a second year.

Both the subject and the methodology of Rubin's study were catnip to the media. Rubin and his colleagues planned to encircle the penis of each volunteer with a strain gauge transducer and then show him erotic pictures; any resultant engorgement of the member would be accurately measured and recorded. By conducting the experiment with two groups, one given either alcohol or marijuana and the other nothing, Rubin would be able to determine whether either drug increased or decreased sexual arousal, and to what extent.[13] On July 18, the Bloomington, Illinois, *Daily Pantagraph*, which had somehow become aware of the study, ran an article about it, and from then on Rubin's project was in trouble. Newspapers in Illinois, St. Louis, Washington, Chicago, and many other cities ran stories about what quickly became known as the "sex-pot study" or "pot-sex study," a topic so interesting that they ran follow-up stories about it for many months. Displaying suitable outrage, the Christian Citizens Lobby, Illinois governor Daniel Walker, a federal prosecutor, and various Illinois state officials all denounced the study, calling it "disgusting," "pornography," "obscene," and "garbage," and threatening to take action against Rubin.

This was mere growling and snapping, but Congress had the teeth wherewith to bite. Senators William Proxmire and Thomas Eagleton, Democrats but sexual conservatives, attacked it, as did Representative Robert Michel, the ranking Republican member of the House Appropriations subcommittee. Although the secretary of HEW and the president's National Advisory Council on Drug Abuse defended and supported the project, Michel sought to prevent NIDA from funding the Rubin study by tucking an amendment to that effect into the $12.7-billion-dollar 1976 Supplemental Appropriations Bill for HEW, and Senators Proxmire and Warren Magnuson inserted a similar provision into the Senate's version of the bill. The funding of HEW was so crucial to the national well-being that both houses passed the bill with the anti-Rubin provision intact. President Ford signed it into law on May 31, 1976, keeping the vast Social Security system, NIH, and other essential endeavors going—and cutting off Rubin's minuscule funding and putting an end to his research.[14] Rubin had already gathered the alcohol data and he eventually published his results,[15] but the marijuana study died a-borning.

The Kinsey and Rubin cases thus demonstrated that by manipulating congressional committee hearings or inserting amendments into major appropriations bills that forbade federal funding of specific projects, conservatives could effectively block sex research that they saw as a danger to American morals. Decades later, members of Congress who represented the far right would make effective use of that knowledge.

The Need to Know vs. the Need to Not Know

By the early 1980s Surgeon General Everett Koop and PHS officials recognized that AIDS was becoming epidemic and might soon reach socially disastrous proportions. At the time, the only way known to limit the spread of the disease was to prevent its transmission, whether by sexual contact, the sharing of drug-injection needles, or a tainted blood supply. Of these, the most problematic was sexual contact, but PHS officials had no reliable information as to how the number of partners was related to transmission or to what degree various sex practices were involved—whether, for instance, AIDS was contracted primarily through homosexual anal intercourse or also by heterosexual penile-vaginal intercourse, or also by oral-genital contact, or perhaps even by kissing, shaking hands, or drinking from the same cup, nor did they have up-to-date figures as to how common and frequent any of the suspect sexual practices were in the various segments of American society. Obviously, to design a preventive program Koop and PHS needed sound information on these matters; Koop therefore asked NAS if it could help, and after studying the matter, NAS reported back that the best existing data were Kinsey's, but that these were based on interviews conducted half a century earlier, and it recommended that new surveys of both teenage and adult sexual behavior be carried out forthwith.[16]

And there was another reason new surveys were needed: Among teenagers, the incidences of AIDS and other sexually transmitted diseases were rising alarmingly but public health officials had only scattered, small, and not very reliable surveys casting light on how and when teenagers formed their attitudes about sexual behavior, at what age they became sexually active, how much they knew about preventive measures against disease and pregnancy, how many sexually active teenagers—and which partner—took precautions, and how regularly and effectively they did so.[17]

As the necessary groundwork, therefore, to devising programs to combat the spread of AIDS and the growing sexual problems of teenagers, in mid-1987 NICHD published a notice in sources regularly scanned by researchers, inviting them to submit contract proposals to design a national survey of adult sexual behavior and a national survey of teenage sexual behavior. In each case the winner would be awarded a contract to design the survey, though not to conduct it; if NICHD approved the designs, it would then issue a call for grant proposals to conduct them and the winner would be awarded a grant.

(The distinction between "contract proposal" and "grant proposal" would be crucial later: A contract to design a survey involves a study the government wants done; the researchers are in effect working for the government, which therefore has a right to have a say in what is done. A grant is "investigator originated" and the investigator is free to ask any questions and set the research parameters without government interference. Actually, in the appropriations and NIH "reauthorization" processes, House and Senate committees can "review" grants as well as contract studies but rarely do so, since this would violate the peer review process.)

Researchers in a number of universities and survey organizations rose to the bait and submitted proposals offering themselves as designers of the studies. At NICHD, peer reviewers read the entries and cast their votes, and in January, 1988 NICHD announced its awards.

The contract for designing the adult study went to a three-man team; two members were from the University of Chicago and its affiliated National Opinion Research Center (NORC), the third from the Stony Brook campus of the State University of New York. The Chicago members were highly competent, dignified, and moderately conservative scholars: the sociologist Edward O. Laumann, and Robert T. Michael, director of NORC (and, later, dean of the university's Harris Graduate School of Public Policy Studies), both of them old hands at the design and conducting of surveys. The Stony Brook member was the sociologist John H. Gagnon, a rumpled, witty maverick who had spent some years at the Kinsey Institute and was a leading sex researcher.

The contract for designing the teenage study went to two quiet, diligent sociologists from the Carolina Population Center at the University of North Carolina at Chapel Hill, Ronald Rindfuss, who had considerable survey experience, and J. Richard Udry, who had conducted a number of small federally funded studies of sexual behavior in the past decade.

* * *

The Laumann-Michael-Gagnon team had a year in which to devise their design for the adult survey. Working separately in their own specialties but meeting as a team from time to time, they developed an ambitious plan and lengthy questionnaire for a large-scale (up to 20,000 interviewees) national sex survey that would be the first rigorously scientific one ever conducted in America. (Kinsey had relied on "convenience samples"—any groups or individuals he could find who were willing to be interviewed—and all other existing sex surveys had been either small and limited or lacking in methodological rigor.) The adult survey would comprehensively report on American sexuality rather than focus narrowly on disease and fertility issues. The technical details— sampling methods, statistical corrections for underrepresentation and other errors, tests of several methods of data collection (face-to-face interviews, telephone interviews, self-administered questionnaires), and so on—were Laumann's and Michael's territory; the questionnaire content and the special problems involved in asking questions about sexual practices were primarily Gagnon's.

Part way through the year, however, the CDC and four other federal agencies, in urgent need of AIDS-related data, asked the team to conduct a relatively small survey as soon as possible, using a modified version of the questionnaire they had been designing for the major survey. This smaller study, using a national sample of 2,300 adults and later named the Survey of Health and AIDS-Related Practices (SHARP), would yield baseline data from which public health officials could measure the spread of the epidemic; it would also serve to pretest the adult survey questionnaire.[18] But from the start it was a source of many a headache. Gagnon explains:

> CDC's mission was much more AIDS-directed than ours. Ours was AIDS in the context of sexuality; for us, sex was the primary interest, AIDS something you could understand if you understood sex. CDC was obsessively concerned with AIDS questions and not interested in random sampling but rather on surveillance of a particular population group. And we had endless debates with the NICHD folks who were under orders to keep out questions on masturbation, on orgasm, and so on and on—matters that didn't pertain directly to AIDS but that we felt we needed to know for a full picture of sexual behavior. We found the NICHD and CDC people almost impervious to instruction. They treated us like servants, they had the typically bureaucratic—autocratic—mentality.
>
> But finally we and they agreed on a questionnaire that we thought would work, and by the end of 1988, shortly after Bush's election, we submitted it to OMB [Office of Management and Budget]. We had to, because under an old regulation dating from World War Two and intended to prevent redundant surveys, every questionnaire to be used under a government contract has to be reviewed and okayed by OMB before it can be administered to American citizens. So ours landed on the desk of Richard Darman, Bush's appointee as head of OMB—and stayed there for months.

The delay was galling: The tight contract schedule for the pretest survey called for the team to send its research assistants into the field with the questionnaire during the winter, code and analyze the data in the summer and fall, and deliver the findings to CDC by the end of 1989.[19] Darman never said why he held up the questionnaire, though some observers suspect that as a Bush appointee, he had conservative misgivings about the subject matter. In any case, other and more powerful conservative forces rallied and launched an orchestrated attack in April.

The attack came shortly after word got out about the survey and its questionnaire. Gagnon thinks that "we and our plans were being tracked by the Right," which, after the 1988 election, was well represented within HHS and other government agencies. It might have been an inside source at OMB that tipped off *Science* that it was reviewing a federally funded sex questionnaire; the magazine ran that news as part of an article on male homosexuality in its January 20, 1989 issue. The article, illustrated by a picture taken from the film *Bob and Carol and Ted and Alice* of two smiling heterosexual couples in a king-sized bed, reported that OMB was reviewing a questionnaire which would be used in a survey of the intimate details of American sexual behavior.[20]

Laumann, Michael, and Gagnon were aggrieved that *Science*, a publication of AAAS, would treat the matter more as entertainment than real science; and not only aggrieved but fearful that serious trouble was brewing. As indeed it was: The politically conservative *Washington Times*, picking up the news from *Science* (and somehow obtaining a copy of the questionnaire), published a steamy article about the survey and the questionnaire, which immediately led to widespread coverage in the media, including a series of attacks in right wing publications.[21]

Conservatives in Congress eagerly seized the opportunity to assail what could only look evil to their constituents. In the House, the most active and vocal opponent of the survey was Representative William Dannemeyer, a far-right Republican from California, who blasted away at the study on the floor, where he said that the survey seemed "more appropriate for the pages of a pornographic magazine than as something to be passed off as a scientific study."[22] He spelled out his objections in a seventeen-page "white paper" that he sent to all members of the House and Senate, selectively quoting some of the questionnaire's most intimate and, taken out of context, shocking questions, and distorting and misrepresenting various aspects of the survey (he wrote, for instance, that the survey would cost U. S. citizens $15 million, although the contract clearly specified $1.7 million). Laumann wrote to HHS Secretary Louis Sullivan, specifying the falsifications in Dannemeyer's paper and asking for his support, but Sullivan neither answered nor took any supportive action.[23]

Dannemeyer's senior staff assistant, Paul Mero, enlisted many other conservatives and right wing organizations in the fight against the survey, including the formidable arch-conservative, Senator Jesse Helms.[24] On the Senate floor, Helms denounced the survey in his typically florid and ferocious style, charging that it was a plot by homosexuals to legitimate the normality of gay and lesbian lifestyles, that it was an unwarranted intrusion by the government into private matters, and that the project staff had an antifamily agenda.[25] He also made snide remarks, Gagnon says, to the effect that Gagnon wasn't quite normal ("His elevator doesn't go all the way to the top; he doesn't have four wheels on the ground") and that he belonged to various unsavory organizations (to which Gagnon did not, in fact, belong).

But Laumann, Michael, and Gagnon could not publicly rebut any of the misstatements made by their foes, for in April, Kay James, HHS undersecretary for Public Affairs—formerly the public affairs officer of the National Right to Life Movement—imposed a gag rule on them, forbidding them to participate in the public debate over SHARP and specifically ordering them not to speak to the media about it. "This undermined whatever Congressional and public support had been available," the Laumann team later wrote, "and left all public initiatives in the hands of those opposed to the survey. Our supporters in Congress* frequently complained of the lack of authoritative and timely briefings and information packets from NICHD with which to respond to the critics."[26]

Also in April, conservatives attacked from another direction: A religious radio broadcast by a station in North Carolina—Helms's turf—gave Darman's phone number and urged listeners to phone in their objections, and as a result OMB received so many phone calls that its office routines were severely disrupted for a week. That ended Darman's inaction: He divested himself of the problem by sending the questionnaire back to HHS for Sullivan's consideration and in a public letter to Sullivan said that apart from any objections to specific matters considered by the survey, there was a larger problem:

> [The survey addresses] the more general subject of sexual mores, preferences and behavior patterns in American society.... While I in no way question the rights of private researchers to explore this subject, I do question the extent to which it may be appropriate for the public sector to subsidize such research. The matter would benefit from a fresh look at the basic purpose of the study—and the extent to which the proposed survey is consistent with what you take to be an appropriate public purpose.... Let me again please urge you to review the questions personally.[27]

Sullivan did not do so; in Gagnon's opinion, this was because "he was a man of absolutely not one ounce of courage. And HHS, after the election, had been turned over to the right; many of the key people below Sullivan belonged to the Christian Coalition or the Right to Life movement." Sullivan freed himself of the problem by handing it over to his assistant secretary, James Mason, who dealt with it by taking no action and holding onto it for further consideration.

Meanwhile, Dannemeyer and Helms intermittently fired further oratorical salvos at SHARP. In August Dannemeyer told a *Los Angeles Times* columnist that he believed the sex survey was the idea of a con-

---

*Senators Kennedy, Moynihan, and Simon, among others.

spiratorial cell of homosexuals inside HHS. Helms, in the Senate, out-did Dannemeyer in oratorical venom: "The real purpose behind the current sex survey proposals"—he was referring to both SHARP and the teens study—"is not to stop the spread of AIDS.... These sex surveys have not—have not—been concerned with scientific inquiry as much as they have been concerned with a blatant attempt to sway public attitudes in order to liberalize opinions and laws regarding homosexuality, pedophilia, anal and oral sex, sex education, teenage pregnancy and all down the line."[28]

In the fall of 1989, a powerful subcommittee of the House Appropriations Committee, following Dannemeyer's and Helms's lead, answered Darman's question as to whether it was appropriate for such research to be federally funded: The subcommittee tried, condemned, and swiftly sentenced SHARP. The events, as related by Laumann, Michael, and Gagnon in a brief history of the adult sex survey:

> At the insistence of Representative William Natcher, chair of the House appropriations subcommittee that oversees NIH, the appropriation bill in the House removed money for such studies from the NIH budget and forbade NIH from going forward with a national survey of sexuality. The Senate was less severe, indicating that while it would not provide money for such a survey at the time, it would like to see the results of the feasibility study [i.e., the pretest, SHARP]. The debate no longer involved OMB approval of our survey questionnaire; it had widened to include the much broader issue of whether NIH could conduct survey research on human sexuality at all, even though it had done so for decades.[29]

SHARP was now in limbo, but Laumann, Michael, and Gagnon still had funding, under their original contract with NICHD, to develop a design for a national sex survey of adults. Although the prospects for congressional approval of such a survey now looked totally dim, for the next two years they kept working on the research problems such a survey would pose, eventually producing a massive report to guide whoever might conduct such a survey, if one were ever conducted. They also continued to plead the cause of the adult survey on Capitol Hill, aided in their lobbying by APA, the Consortium of Social Science Associations (COSSA), and other groups interested in sexual and reproductive research.

With funding of the adult survey and SHARP eliminated from the next NIH reauthorization bill, the team came up with another and seemingly more feasible scheme; they proposed to NICHD that it give them a grant to conduct a small survey of about 2,500 people in two cities with differing ethnic composition; such a study could accomplish at least part of what they had hoped to do with the full-scale adult survey. In June, 1991 their two-city survey proposal received an exceptionally high peer-review rating and they were notified in writing that NICHD would indeed award them a grant to carry it out, though when was uncertain.

But the opponents of sex research, keeping an eye on NIH and, in particular, NICHD, took the next steps in their campaign. In August Representative Dannemeyer introduced a legislative amendment to the NIH reauthorization bill forbidding federal funding of any national sex survey. The amendment was defeated, but another ominous event suggested that federally funded sex research, even if not blocked by Congress, could be killed off administratively: In July, a major grant already awarded to Rindfuss and Udry for a national teenage sex survey—a story we'll come to shortly—was canceled by Secretary Sullivan in an unprecedented intrusion on the peer-review system by which scientific research is authorized. Laumann, Michael, and Gagnon began to fear that their grant for a two-city survey, though not national in scope, might be on shaky ground.

In early September, 1991, however, reassuring word came through; they were told, unofficially, that the two-city grant would become effective on September 28. But at the same time, their larger survey project, SHARP, came under intensified and deadly attack: Senator Helms introduced an amendment to the Senate version of the NIH appropriations bill to transfer $10 million from NICHD, earmarked for SHARP, to the Adolescent Family Life Program (a pregnancy prevention program favored by conservatives). Laumann, Michael, and Gagnon, in their brief history of the adult sex survey, summarize what took place in the Senate:

> In his opening remarks, Helms explained that his opposition to funding surveys of human sexual behavior is based on his conviction that they are intended solely to "legitimize homosexual lifestyles." He argued that this amendment "presents a clear choice...between support for sexual restraint among our young people or, on the other hand, support for homosexuality and sexual decadence."
>
> Helms also cast aspersions on our integrity, and that of NIH officials, claiming that there was a wide conspiracy of "avidly pro-homosexual members of the scientific community." During the speech, he read questions out of context from the teenage survey and the adult survey, and attacked the character of our staff members, using the same charges asserted in the white paper prepared by Dannemeyer in 1989. The Senate voted 66–34 in support of Helms, with only two Republicans opposing the amendment.[30]

The transfer of $10 million funding within NICHD was deleted in conference with the House, but a provision of the Helms amendment that there could be no federal funding of national sex surveys, specifically SHARP and the American Teenage Study (ATS), passed in both houses and became law. The amendment specified the funding of "national" sex surveys, so the two-city survey was still technically in the clear. But in view of the expressed attitude of both houses toward the funding of sex research, NICHD administrators could easily guess what would happen to them if they funded the two-city study, as they had planned to do. The Helms amendment killed off SHARP; the two-city study was killed off by NICHD itself, as Laumann, Michael, and Gagnon relate:

> The following week, Wendy Baldwin, newly appointed deputy director of NICHD, called to inform us that the NICHD staff had made the decision not to fund the approved two-city grant in 1991.... To give a grant to the research group associated with the pretest survey [SHARP] and which had based its design on the pretest would be "political suicide."[31]

Thus, the peer-reviewed SHARP survey was killed by Congress, and the peer-reviewed and approved grant for the two-city survey was canceled by an administrative action not subject to appeal and review.

Laumann, Michael, and Gagnon conclude their history of the adult sex survey with these somber but hopeful reflections:

> Orchestrated ignorance about basic human behavior as salient as sexuality has never resulted in wise public policy.... Ironically, the inappropriate exploitation of sexual anxiety used by Senator Helms to influence votes in the Senate is evidence of the need for scientific inquiry to enhance understanding of sexual behavior. Knowledge might diminish that anxiety and thus reduce the vulnerability to manipulation. We hope our experience was an isolated instance of aberrant behavior rather than a continuing pattern of political harassment against important research.[32]

They made that statement in January of 1994, but the pattern of political harassment against sex research did continue: In that year, although Bill Clinton was president and Democrats controlled Congress, the NIH reauthorization bill for fiscal 1994 again explicitly prohibited funding of SHARP and ATS, and the same was true of the NIH reauthorization bill for fiscal 1996.[33] But the 1994 bill contained a saving grace: An amendment inserted by Senator Paul Simon permitted NIH to conduct a "national longitudinal study of adolescent health," subject to certain guidelines that left the window open—a trifle—for future sex survey research.[34] In the House, the window had also been left open a crack by an amendment introduced by Representative Henry Waxman that would allow sex research that passed peer review and addressed public health needs.[35]

* * *

ATS also was aborted by conservative opposition, but by means of another mechanism, one that social scientists found even more alarming than amendments to reauthorization bills.

Rindfuss and Udry, having been awarded an NICHD contract in 1987 to design a study of teenage sexual attitudes and behavior, spent eighteen months doing so. The design they devised was for a survey in which, with parental permission, a national sample of 24,000 teenagers would be interviewed and administered a questionnaire that would inquire how family, school, peer group, religious institutions, and community had influenced their sexual attitudes and behavior, and would gather detailed information as to their sexual and contraceptive practices. Special subsample studies would enable whoever carried out the study to separate racial differences from social class differences and to avoid mistaking genetic for social causes of behavior. The sophistication of the survey techniques, plus its size, made it expensive; Rindfuss and Udry estimated that it would cost $18 million.[36]

In mid-1988 NICHD called for grant applications to carry out the survey that Rindfuss and Udry had designed. They themselves submitted an application, which was highly rated by the peer reviewers, and their prospects of receiving a sizable grant for a study that promised to be an important contribution to sex research looked excellent. But in mid-1989 they ran aground on an unmarked political shoal: James Mason, assistant secretary of HHS, asked NICHD to send their proposal to him for his review. Udry says that he and Rindfuss failed to realize how serious a threat this was:

> Our expectation had been that because of the AIDS peril, the study would be less sensitive than it would have been a decade earlier. Those of us who had been doing sex research for the past twenty-five years thought that the national publicity about the AIDS epidemic and the well-known fact that it was closely associated with patterns of sexual behavior would have softened political opposition to sex research. But that was rather naïve on our part. We didn't realize that the politics of the epidemic and the politics of abortion had made sex research more inflammable rather than less, and had produced organized political groups with big moral and political stakes in sex.[37]

Mason, as Rindfuss and Udry learned, had been alerted to the possible political hazards of their study when the Secretary of HHS, Louis Sullivan, had received a request from Representative Dannemeyer for a copy of the survey's protocols. They learned, too, that at that same time Mason was also trying to decide what to do about the SHARP questionnaire that OMB had bounced back to Sullivan and that Sullivan had passed on to Mason. The $18 million teenage survey, like SHARP, was temporarily immobilized and possibly in some peril.

The immobilization, ostensibly temporary, turned out to be seemingly endless; days, weeks, months, and more months dragged by with no word from Mason's office as to whether or not he had found fault with their survey. Unable to take on any other major project, Rindfuss and Udry hung on every phone call and leaped at each day's mail, hoping for an end to their wait. This misery lasted from the summer of 1989 to the spring of 1991; then Mason, who had been unable to find reason to interfere with the project, cleared it and sent it back to NIH. Bernadine Healy, the new director of NIH, who had already praised the proposal, promptly sent it on to NICHD, which, acting swiftly, funded the proposal on May 10.

Rindfuss and Udry immediately fell to, working overtime to assemble a staff, hire interviewers, and make myriad arrangements to field the survey throughout the country. On July 19, just as they were about to launch the first wave of interviews, they got a disturbing phone call from their project monitor at NICHD. He said that according to a front-page article in that day's *Washington Times* (a paper that they, in Chapel Hill, did not see), Secretary Sullivan had appeared the previous day on a talk show on the conservative Coalition for America network and had been asked why he was funding such a threat to morality as the teenage study. Sullivan, disconcerted, replied that he knew nothing about it but that he would personally review it. The following day—only hours after Rindfuss and Udry heard about Sullivan's learning about their survey—Sullivan ordered all work halted until he could learn more about it.[38]

That was bad news, but soon there was worse; the talk-show episode had been, it became evident, only part of a planned, multifaceted campaign. One facet: A few days later, Dannemeyer sent a "Dear Colleague" letter to all members of Congress asking if they had a child or grandchild between the ages of thirteen and eighteen, and if so, how they would feel if that child were a boy and were asked "Have you ever had your mouth on someone's penis?" and "Have you ever put your penis in another male's rectum?", and, if a girl, were asked "In what month and year did you most recently have sexual intercourse?" and "Have you ever been given drugs in exchange for having sex?"[39] A press release over Dannemeyer's name sarcastically listed "ten reasons why NIH wants to spend $18 million on a teen sex study," including "to see if young girls have sexual intercourse *before* their first kiss," and "to see which birth control device sells best."[40] Pat Robertson's Christian

Coalition notified the media that it was outraged by the study; the Christian Action Network urged its constituents to petition NIH to cancel it; Gary Bauer, spokesman for Family Research Council, an ultraconservative activist organization primarily interested in policy issues relating to education and family values, told the media that ATS "offends the sensibilities of millions of Americans"[41] and that it was worthless because it was already obvious that American teenagers were beginning sex too early;[42] and Beverly LaHaye, president of Concerned Women for America, another conservative activist group, issued a public statement, "It's outrageous that millions of our tax dollars are going to be spent to ask seventh-graders if they've experienced oral and homosexual sex acts. This is a totally inappropriate use of government funds."[43]

Sullivan got the message. On July 23, less than a week after having been caught unprepared on the television talk show, he summarily canceled the grant—even though it had passed peer review and been approved by the heads of NICHD and NIH and his own assistant secretary. His reason, he told the press (offering no supporting evidence) was that asking teenagers questions about sexual behavior might encourage them to indulge in casual sex.[44]

His action came as a crushing blow to Rindfuss and Udry, who had expected trouble but not such major trouble. Udry, laconic in describing his and Rindfuss's feelings, says only, "It was a tremendous disappointment, and a tremendous waste of our time and energy. We had several years of our lives invested in getting this thing going, and now that was all lost." When he and Rindfuss recovered from their initial shock, they sought legal advice and concluded that the university had at least a chance of successfully contesting Sullivan's action. But the university's legal counsel felt that it would be a protracted and probably losing proposition, and the university decided not to fight. Udry, reflecting, says, "At the time, we thought it was chicken of them. But subsequently we came to believe that it would have been futile to challenge HHS on it."

The cancellation sent shock waves through the scientific establishment and academe; it was unprecedented for a top administrator to single-handedly revoke a grant that had been made through the established and respected system of scientific peer review and to countermand the decisions of his own agency heads as to the research needs of their organizations. Robert Charrow, the legal specialist of the *Journal of NIH Research*, declared in that publication, "Termination of a grant

for 'policy' reasons has, to my knowledge, never occurred before."
Regulations, he said, do allow for termination at any time if the grantee
failed to comply with the terms of the grant—but there was no such
legal cause in this case. But he concluded that, in view of the current
political milieu, "this may be one of those unfortunate situations in
which there is a right, but no meaningful remedy."[45]

A number of major scientific organizations strenuously protested
Sullivan's action. APA's Council of Representatives unanimously condemned the cancellation as an unprecedented challenge to peer-reviewed
research at NIH.[46] The American Sociological Association (ASA) called
Sullivan's act "totally unprecedented and egregious" and "a serious
threat to the integrity of the peer review process and the independence
of scientific thought."[47] Many other scientific organizations spoke out
in similar terms, and NICHD's Advisory Council—whose members
Sullivan himself had appointed—wrote him that his action "raises the
specter of political veto of scientific and public advisory decisions."[48]
A number of leading newspapers throughout the country ran editorials
condemning Sullivan's action.

All to no avail. Conservative political forces, acting through Sullivan,
had killed and buried ATS, and neither science, academe, nor the media
could exhume it and restore it to life.

* * *

I spoke to Udry some months after Sullivan's cancellation of ATS
(in connection with an article I was writing at the time), expecting to
find that he had given up on it and turned his mind to other things, but,
he said, that was not the case:

> We haven't closed the book on this study, but we don't want to set land mines for
> ourselves by advance publicity. Right now the reauthorization bill before the Sen-
> ate contains an amendment—put in there by our very own senator, Jesse Helms—
> specifically forbidding the federal funding of SHARP or ATS. What happens to
> that amendment has a lot to do with what we do next.

The amendment, as already mentioned, did pass—but even that did
not lead Udry and Rindfuss to abandon ATS; they had put too much
time and thought into it to accept the inevitable. In January, 1993, when
I wrote to Udry for an update, he replied, "We have no concrete plans
for trying to fund the study," but again said, "We have not closed the
book on the study and sent it to the Archives. Therefore we would like
to make sure we don't set publicity petards in place that will blow up in
the middle of some future activity in a way we can't anticipate."

Behind this facade, I supposed, something was going on. As indeed it was—as was also the case with Laumann, Michael, and Gagnon, and the defunct SHARP study.

Reincarnation, More or Less

Almost nothing is as tempting to scientists as some route to knowledge that has been barred by political or other ruling powers. As already mentioned, Galileo, having publicly recanted heliocentric theory, privately continued working with it for years, and many Soviet geneticists, when research based on Mendelian theory was officially banned, secretly carried on forbidden work. The sex researchers, similarly, though they could have turned to any one of scores of other areas of inquiry, were driven by intellectual hunger and professional pride to carry on with their work despite formidable opposition by Congress, right wing activist groups, and conservative administrators.

By the fall of 1990 Laumann, Michael, and Gagnon, realizing that SHARP might be in trouble, had begun to explore the other major way of financing a national sex survey, namely, foundation support. Although foundations had long been fearful of backing sex research, the congressional and conservative obstruction of peer-reviewed and approved sex research made them feel that they had to make a serious effort to get foundation support. Michael, in fact, had already gotten a grant of $825,000 from the Robert Wood Johnson Foundation to conduct a modest survey of sexual attitudes (though not behavior) as part of a general national attitude survey routinely conducted by NORC. Gagnon suggested that, instead, they use the Johnson grant as seed money for a small-scale version of the national adult survey of both attitudes and behavior that they had originally planned to do for NICHD, and solicit other foundations to join in. Gagnon's account:

> In Chicago, Bob and Ed started reshaping the SHARP questionnaire back toward the original adult sex survey format, and in New York I spent months going from foundation to foundation hat in hand, and learning to grovel before my inferiors. I went to Mellon, Rockefeller, Kaiser, the New York Community Trust, the American Foundation for AIDS Research. Eventually they got together and formed a consortium, and all of them, plus the MacArthur Foundation and the Ford Foundation, supported us. I think some of the foundations gave us money not because they were interested in sex research but because they were angry about the violation of the peer review process. In the end, we had raised a total of about $2.3 million.

That was, to be sure, only a small fraction of what they would have sought from NICHD for the original adult survey, and instead of a sample of perhaps 20,000 they made do with one of 3,432. A larger one would have enabled them to reduce the margin of error and conduct more finely detailed analysis, but for most purposes a probability sample of several thousand would serve. "As for our sample," Gagnon says, "we had some good luck. Obtaining a probability sampling of households is one of the big costs of a survey, but a Kaiser-funded study had just done a screening of households in connection with another project and they let us use their list." They also had some luck as to the questionnaire for the National Health and Social Life Survey (NHSLS), as they now called it; as they later wrote: "Ironically, our failure to secure government funding freed us to abandon the overly compromised, narrowly targeted instrument [for SHARP] in favor of the much more comprehensive approach that the government had originally contracted with us to provide."[49]

Gagnon summarizes the time frame of NHSLS:

We started interviewing in February, 1991—in its more comprehensive format, each interview took about ninety minutes, on average—and we completed all 3,400 in a year and a half. By the summer of 1992 we started analyzing the data; that took the next nine months. Then the four of us—Stuart Michaels, who had a major role in mapping out the survey, had joined us as co-investigator—divided up the writing; we started it in April, 1993, and completed the job by mid-1994.

The book, couched in terms meant for professional social scientists and health professionals, was published by the University of Chicago Press late that year as *The Social Organization of Sexuality: Sexual Practices in the United States*. A companion book, *Sex in America*, popular in presentation and meant for a general audience, was written by Michael, Gagnon, Laumann, and science writer Gina Kolata, and published the same year by Little, Brown.

I asked Gagnon if there had been congressional or federal agency interference along the way.

No, we were invulnerable to federal obstruction because we had foundation money. If our enemies had mounted a national publicity campaign warning people about the questions we were going to ask, they probably would have hurt us. But once we weren't in the government, all was quiet. And we were able to show that we could do what we said we could do—what many people believed was impossible in a sex survey—we could use a national sample and get an excellent response rate, with people answering even our most sensitive questions.

Gagnon and his colleagues assert in their book that the breadth and scope of their project differentiate it from other recent surveys of sexual behavior: Unlike the others, it is based on a truly scientific probability sample of the national population, and the design and pretesting of its questionnaire and sophisticated statistical analysis of the responses make it a source of information about American sexual behavior far superior to anything that preceded it.

So their saga ends well enough, even though not nearly as well as it would have, had political opposition not killed the far larger survey they had originally planned, with its greater capability of fine-grained analysis of behavioral details and of correlations suggestive of the causes of those behaviors. The project also was far more costly to the researchers in terms of time and stress than it need have been. In understated academic fashion they write: "This has been an exceptionally engrossing project, and our families and friends have put up with too many stories and suffered through our many setbacks as well as our several successes." Gagnon, in person, is more outspoken:

> This project became seven years of slogging, of putting one foot in front of the other. It should have taken only three years from beginning to end. And the mud thrown at me troubled me. I knew the fear it would create in those I would have to go to for money. I was dragged around to all sorts of meetings and had to make many presentations to prove that I didn't have two heads, that I wasn't an advance member of the homosexual revolution.

Had he ever counterattacked?

> No, that would just have given them something to reply to. They'd have said, "Gagnon, the well-known drug user and homosexual activist, now says—and so on—but in fact—and so on." My father, who was a copper miner and an anarchist, died young and gave me very little advice about life, but one thing he did say was, "Never wrestle with a turd, you'll get covered with shit."

Had he felt a deep sense of gratification when the book was finished? The question evoked a weary sigh. "No; no. I didn't feel like celebrating, I didn't have a party, I didn't pop a bottle of champagne. I felt only, 'Well, *that's* done,' I felt I had fulfilled a responsibility, I simply had a sense of a job completed, after all those years, all those difficulties. I felt—relief." He said no more; there was no more to say.

* * *

Like Gagnon and his team, Rindfuss and Udry also sought help from major foundations for ATS, the teenage study, but were unable to raise enough support to make it worthwhile to proceed. In January, 1993, Udry had written me that their plans for ATS were still uncertain, but later that year he told me that he and Rindfuss considered ATS dead.

But as already mentioned, the same 1993 act that made it illegal for any federal agency to fund either SHARP or ATS had also included a paragraph inserted by liberals and passed by both houses ordering NICHD to conduct a "Prospective National Longitudinal Study of Adolescent Health," which it described as follows:

> The Director of the [National Institute of Child Health and Human Development] shall commence a study for the purpose of providing information on the general health and well-being of adolescents in the United States, including, with respect to such adolescents, information on:
>   (1) the behaviors that promote health and the behaviors that are detrimental to health; and
>   (2) the influence on health of factors particular to communities in which adolescents reside.[50]

This directive was so sensible and wholesome that it was approved by solid majorities in both houses, but so broad in its reach as to permit (or, actually, require) the gathering of at least some part of the information about sexual attitudes and behavior that Rindfuss and Udry had planned to gather in ATS. It was a window of opportunity—open only a crack, to be sure, but a crack through which some useful sex research, as part of a larger goal, might be done. Udry tells what happened:

> We were alerted to the existence of this paragraph, so we inquired of NICHD whether they would be willing to accept an unsolicited proposal from us to meet this congressional mandate. They said yes, they'd be willing to accept it. That was important, because if you have a proposal over a certain amount of money— and this study would clearly run into big money—they don't have to accept it. But in fact they got no other proposals for the longitudinal study and they did accept ours.

Why were there no others? Had everyone else been scared off? "I imagine so. Anyway, we got this encouragement from them in June of 1993 and we got to work immediately."

By "we" Udry did not mean the original ATS team; he had told the other three primary investigators on that team that he was going to submit an application and asked if they wanted to join him, but Rindfuss and one other member of the team decided not to because they had taken on other projects. Udry therefore quickly assembled the core of a new team of primary investigators and they got to work on the proposal. During the next several months they had numerous conversations with NICHD officials and worked extremely hard at putting together as fast as possible a detailed proposal for what had to be a large, complex project. Unlike the ATS proposal that Udry and Rindfuss had prepared under contract to NICHD, this one, being unsolicited, was not funded and they had to do it on their own time. Udry recalls how it went:

> By September—after only three months of work—we turned in a 700-page proposal for a $22-million dollar, five-year project to be called "A Prospective National Longitudinal Study of Adolescent Health." We took the title right out of the Act, but later we called it simply "Add Health." While we were writing it, I was also putting together a team of investigators from all over the country who wanted to be part of this very major study of adolescent health if it went through. I sent faxes, e-mails, made phone calls, talked and talked, and before the proposal was completed I had lined up a team of nine primary investigators. Later, we filled out the team with programmers, project managers, doctoral fellows, and graduate students. There were nearly sixty people on the team at UNC and elsewhere, especially at NORC in Chicago, which would be doing a great deal of the work and getting more than three-quarters of the money.

Udry was optimistic that the proposal would be approved, despite its high ticket price, since NICHD was obliged to conduct the study and his team was the only contender. He was right: NICHD moved quickly and by early 1994 approved the proposal and agreed to fund the study for the requested $22 million; later, other things ran it up even higher, to about $25 million. The design of the survey was extremely complex; it employed half a dozen different questionnaires to be used at different stages of the study. One, self-administered in classrooms and taking about forty-five minutes, would be given to about 100,000 teenagers and would deal with all sorts of health-related behaviors, including the use of alcohol and tobacco, general health, disabilities, exercise, demographic family characteristics, and many other matters. Another would be administered as a home interview to a subsample of 20,000 youths and last about an hour and a half. The interviews would include comprehensive coverage of health issues and would cover some of the sexual issues that had been planned for ATS, though in considerably less detail; the sexual questions would comprise less than 10 percent of all the questions any teenager would be asked. Still other questionnaires would include a forty-minute interview of parents and a questionnaire for school administrators. "All in all, a very complicated study," Udry says. "It had all sorts of wrinkles of research design, and wrinkles on its wrinkles."

He had one scare shortly before the interviewers began their field work: In March, 1994, when NICHD issued a quiet public statement announcing Add Health, an observant reporter for *Science* called Udry on the phone and interviewed him for a brief report to be published in that journal. The resulting story ran only one column long but was head-lined, alarmingly, "Teen Sex Survey Back on Track." It said that NICHD had just "unveiled" a national survey of teen health and, "lo and be-hold, it included a sex component." The report stated correctly that the study would cover a variety of health behaviors including diet and smok-ing, that the part of it that dealt with sexual matters would be asked of only a small subsample of the total sample of teens, and that their iden-tities would be "encoded and maintained by a data center [NORC] that is independent of the research staff." But almost as if eager to stir up trouble, the *Science* report continued,

> That doesn't make this study any more palatable now than it was in 1991 to the Family Research Council of Arlington, Virginia.* Robert Knight of the council says such surveys "scandalize children" and "legitimize" undesirable sexual be-havior by talking about it. He says the group may seek to ban such surveys from public schools.[51]

But perhaps because the survey was so broad and dealt with so many issues that even the most conservative representative or senator could only approve of, Udry's apprehension about the *Science* report proved needless; it had no negative sequelae that he could see.

The in-classroom part of the survey began in March, 1994 and took a year; although the school questionnaires contained no "sensitive" questions, parents had been notified and given the opportunity to refuse permission. The home interviews of 20,000, which included both non-sensitive matters and sensitive ones (drugs, violence, sex, and so on) with explicit parental permission, plus interviews of the parents, were conducted from April, 1995 to December, 1996. Not until the end of 1996, when data collection had been completed, did Udry feel that Add Health was "out of the political risk period, when somebody could try to cancel our grant," and that for the first time in three years he could breathe easily. What remained to be done was to analyze the huge vol-ume of data and to write up the results. The writing up of the findings was under way by mid-1997, and several articles based on the early results of analysis were already in press.

The survey has produced a mass of health information that will prove valuable to NICHD, some of it dealing with the sexuality of teenagers. In a sense, science triumphed over antiscience, but only in a sense, for Udry admits that "Add Health doesn't have nearly as much about sexual

---

*The Council later moved to Washington, DC.

behavior as ATS would have had. And it doesn't have the AIDS emphasis of ATS." But he justifies its shortcomings:

> This was deliberate. We were not interested in violating the law, and we knew that the original study was not to be funded. But we covered everything that should be studied in a comprehensive study of adolescent health. It would have been irresponsible to leave sexual behavior out, but sexual behavior should not have received, and didn't receive, more attention than it deserves in the broad spectrum of health-related problems of adolescents.

Which is a politic way of saying that Add Health studied only as much about teenage sexuality as could be squeezed through the crack in the legal window, a metaphor hardly descriptive of freedom of scientific research.

Defenders of the Family

American children used to be able to play outside without their parents worrying about them; now children are in danger of being abducted and sexually molested. Who or what is to blame?

Marriage used to be strong and enduring; now it is fragile. What happened?

Illegitimacy and sexual diseases have been rising for years. Why?

The Family Research Council, and at least thirty-nine members of the House of Representatives think they know one of the major reasons: The cancers eating away at family life and morals are the sex research conducted by Alfred C. Kinsey, the interpretations he made and promulgated of his findings, the subsequent sex studies carried out by the many others who followed in his path, the introduction into grade schools of sex education based on Kinseyan views, and the sweeping changes in American sexual standards and customs, divorce law, and treatment of sex offenders produced by the sexual liberalism expressed in Kinseyan research.

Such is the message of a number of publications of the Family Research Council, and particularly of "The Children of Table 34," a video produced by the Council in 1994 and aired frequently ever since on conservative television channels. The eponymous table, in the 1948 Kinsey Report, is labeled "Pre-Adolescent Experience in Orgasm" and is a compilation of the orgasmic histories of 317 male children ranging in age from two months to fifteen years. The Family Research Council video says that the data were either obtained through criminal molestation of the children or possibly are fraudulent, though the video clearly espouses the first alternative. A companion brochure written by the Council's "director of cultural studies" (research director), Robert H. Knight, says that the Kinsey childhood sexuality data have been used in "countless federally-funded programs despite critical evidence that the Kinsey studies suffered from severe methodological flaws."[52]

As for the thirty-nine members of the House, they were co-sponsors with Representative Steve Stockman of Texas of a bill, H. R. 2749, introduced in December, 1995, titled "Child Protection and Ethics in Education Act of 1995." In the bill, Stockman, an unremitting opponent of gun control and friend of militias whose views of the federal attack on the Branch Dravidians at Waco are comparable to those of Timothy McVeigh, called for a federal inquiry to determine whether the Kinsey reports, and the data of Table 34 in particular, are erroneous by reason of fraud or were wrongfully obtained through systematic abuse of children. The bill specified that if the inquiry found either to be the case, no federal funding could go to any person or institution teaching Kinseyan material or to any "scholar" (read: researcher) whose work is derived from Kinseyan research unless the teacher or researcher indicated "the unethical and tainted nature of the Kinsey reports." (For the researcher, this would be tantamount to saying in a research paper, "The research reported here is based on unethical and fraudulent theories," which obviously would make the paper unpublishable.)

One cannot dismiss the Family Research Council or the thirty-nine cosponsors of H. R. 2749 as unimportant nutcases; they are not nutcases, and definitely not unimportant. The Family Research Council, headed by Gary Bauer, a former policy wonk in the Reagan White House, is a nonprofit activist organization amply financed by conservative foundations, corporations, and wealthy individual donors; it has bright, well-educated people on its staff and the wherewithal to make its voice heard in Congress and the media, and, at times, to have significant impact on legislation. Robert Knight explained to me the Council's consistent and strong support of congressional efforts to halt ATS and other sex research:

We don't need masses of scientific studies of sex. It's no mystery why kids are tempted by sex and where they get the information. There's a surfeit of information given the children, they're drenched with it, they're obsessed with it. The culture is pressing it on them in ads, TV, in the classrooms. I don't believe that sex surveys of children will result in anything good, because we already know what works and what doesn't work. We've had twenty years of experiments with sex education, and it doesn't work, and we know that it doesn't. These surveys are *not* necessary, they only serve to make kids feel they should be doing it, they validate those who are into sexual experimentation.

Knight was voicing a legitimate concern. It is true that interviewers, in order to get people to admit to off-beat behavior, must ask about it in nonjudgmental ways; as Udry himself has written, "The object is to make [the behaviors] sound ordinary and acceptable. However heinous we may think the behavior, we make it sound OK."[53]

But does asking nonjudgmental questions about a particular sex act induce that behavior in interviewees, particularly in children? Wendy Baldwin, deputy director of NIH, thinks not:

> The notion that if you ask an adolescent about some of these sexual acts, they will immediately go out and do it betrays a very limited understanding of what drives complex human behaviors. Sexual behavior is very complex and intimate, and driven by very complex motives—morality, religious belief, situational influences, the right partner, the community one is part of, and so on. If all you had to do was ask questions and sexual behavior would change, our intervention programs to change undesirable sexual behavior would have a far easier go of it.

Although the thirty-nine representatives who co-sponsored H. R. 2749 included some of the most reactionary members of the House, it is also true that some run-of-the-mill conservatives and a number of other members, though not formally listed as co-sponsors, are reported to have been favorably disposed toward the bill.[54] It was referred to the House Economic and Educational Opportunities Committee, but the committee did not report on it to Congress, and H. R. 2749 is apparently dead or at least moribund. But its moment in the sun was a warning: Some of the more conservative members of the House believe that much or most contemporary sex research and sex education embody Kinseyan findings and values, and would almost certainly vote for a bill that banned the federal funding of most or all sex research, if another one were introduced and favorably reported on to Congress by whatever committee it was referred to.

Table 34, a powerful weapon in the hands of anti-sex-research conservatives, was brought to the attention of opponents of sex research by an independent scholar, Dr. Judith Reisman (whose doctorate is in communication, not in one of the social sciences). At the 1981 World Congress of Sexology in Jerusalem, she delivered a paper in which she questioned how the Kinsey team had obtained the data reported in Table 34. Had parents given consent to the use of the information? Were the data the product of criminal molestation? What part had the Kinsey team played in the children's experiences? In 1990 she answered her own questions in a book, co-authored with others, *Kinsey, Sex and Fraud: The Indoctrination of a People*; she had become convinced that the children whose experiences were reported by Kinsey had been sexually abused by adults in the name of science. That theme is heavily stressed in the Family Research Council video, which broadly hints that "experiments" were the source of the data and that they may have been conducted by Kinsey operatives.

John Bancroft, the present director of the Kinsey Institute, dug into Institute files and spoke to former Kinsey director Paul Gebhard, who was on the original team, to ascertain the source of the data in Table 34. His summary of what he learned:

> Kinsey was never involved in sexual experiments on children and never trained anyone to do them. He gives the impression in the book that the data in Table 34 came from histories of nine adult males who had had sexual contacts with younger boys or had observed their sexual activities, but he was being deliberately opaque. The truth is that all the data in the table came from one man, who wasn't a researcher but had engaged in an exceptional amount of sexual behavior and documented it in great detail, sometimes even using a stopwatch, and as a sort of justification would say "I'm doing research." He wasn't part of the Kinsey team, he was one of their interviewees—in fact, he was interviewed for a total of seventeen hours, the longest by far of all Kinsey interviews. I strongly suspect that Kinsey's reason for giving the impression that the data came from a number of men is that he felt if he revealed that one man had been the source and had had sexual contact with all those boys, there might have been a witch-hunt to find him.[55]

H. R. 2749 owes its genesis to the Family Research Council, which, when it became aware of Reisman's charges, called the matter to Stockman's attention. Stockman saw it as a fine opportunity to do something that would reflect well on him in the eyes of his conservative constituents. Although H. R. 2749 has not become the law of the land, it did briefly pose a serious threat to virtually all federally funded sex research, since almost all sex research is obliged to cite significant previous studies and existing knowledge—inevitably, therefore, seeming to follow in Kinsey's footsteps. The Helms and Dannemeyer amendments have more or less served the purpose Stockman had in mind—more or less, because their effect was to rule out federal funding of sex surveys but not of all sex research, and despite the amendments various health-oriented agencies are currently and legally funding a considerable number of medically and biologically focused sex studies.[56]

So we can count as self-appointed defenders of the family Steve Stockman and the co-sponsors of H. R. 2749, Jesse Helms, William Dannemeyer, the Family Research Council, the Christian Coalition, and the like. If Laumann and his colleagues are right that "orchestrated ignorance about basic human behavior as salient as sexuality has never resulted in wise public policy," who will defend the family from its defenders?

The Morality of Opposition to Sex Research

The political opponents of sex research are religious and political conservatives who combat it because, in their view, it is unnecessary (they say they already know all they need to know about sex), damaging to individuals, families, and society (asking sexual questions spreads harmful ideas and practices), and immoral (researchers in the Kinsey tradition label as "normal" acts that the Bible says are sins or abominations). And they have an even more persuasive argument: The government has no business asking people about their sexual practices and sex research ought not be funded by taxpayers' dollars.

(Even when sex research is locally funded—and even if carried on without public funding—religious and other conservatives will often seek to block it because of their belief that it promotes immorality. A typical instance: Nancy Pierce, a social psychologist who had been doing AIDS education work for the Massachusetts Department of Public Health, wanted to do a telephone pilot survey of Massachusetts parents to find out how many of them would like sex education taught in the high schools. With a minuscule grant from a division of APA, she surveyed parents in two small towns, finding strong parental support for sex education in the schools. At that point, fundamentalist church members and their clergy swung into action; although they were a minority, they deluged people in the school administrations with phone calls at home at night, threatening to block the next school budget and to get the school administrators fired. The school administrators hastily backed away from plans to add sex education, the net effect of the pilot survey was zero, and a state-wide survey that Pierce hoped would result was out of the question.[57])

There may, too, be a more salient motive for opposition to sex research than any of those listed above. Julia Erickson, the sociologist who is writing a history of sex research, says that conservatives have told her that attacking sex research is just one way to attack federal funding:

> What they really think is that the federal government shouldn't be in the business of funding research, whether in the natural or social sciences. Robert Knight of the Family Research Council said to me that as far as he is concerned, the funding

of sex research is like the funding of cancer research: He feels that private industry would have a cure for cancer now if the government hadn't got involved, and that it's only because researchers can come back to the federal trough all the time for more funding that they never finish the job. Sex research, for him, just happens to be a convenient place to oppose federal funding of research.

Two powerful motives are thus combined in the conservative opposition to sex research: a puritanical aversion to openness about sexual matters and a states'-rights or even libertarian hostility to centralized government and its costly programs. Both of these motives deserve respect: Citizens and their organizations have every right to their own moral views and to their opinions as to the proper role of government. But the right to hold and express such views does not entitle those who hold them to deprive other Americans, who feel differently about these matters, of *their* freedom of speech and expression. Specifically, the right of conservatives to hold and express their views about sex research does not justify their interfering with and disrupting studies commissioned by the government elected by the majority of the people and meant to serve the common good.

The moral qualms and financial objections of conservatives to the federal funding of sex research are far outweighed by our society's need for knowledge, both in order to better understand human nature and to serve as a basis for practical programs of public health. Laumann and his co-authors persuasively justify the federally funding of sex research that organized conservative opposition deprived them of:

> First, an informed citizenry is essential in a democratic society, and, while sex is essentially private, it has many public aspects as well. These require us as a democracy to make judgments and reach agreements about the rules by which we all will live—rules about the treatment of homosexuals, about the legality and availability of and methods of paying for abortions, about public nudity, about sexual harassment, rape, and gender discrimination. Information is imperative if we are to make wise collective judgments.
>
> Second, even in our private lives we need guidance from counselors who offer medical advice, religious or ethical guidance, or psychological guidance as we confront the complexities and mysteries of our sexual being. As we discussed our survey plans and the content of our inquiry with professional counselors from many walks of life, we have been impressed with how much these men and women wish to have and eagerly seek better information to inform their counsel.... Be it in the formal curricula in schools or in informal discussions among friends, the absence of information, not its availability, should be frightening to us all.[58]

It is an obligation of government to fund the research needed to carry out public health programs, and it is essential that the elected members of the government, when considering such funding, not impose their personal views or those of their constituents on the decisions as to what specific research projects will be supported by agencies under their control. The psychologists William Gardner and Brian L. Wilcox, in a recent thoughtful examination of political intervention in scientific peer review, see two serious dangers in it:

> The first danger is that political decisions about research funding will degrade the quality of science, because selecting the best science requires judgments about appropriate methods by specialists directly concerned with the field. The answers to empirical questions are embedded in complex inferential networks in which every fact depends on many surrounding facts.... A gap in the network of facts, as may result when nonscientific criteria are used to allocate resources for research, weakens the entire structure of inference. This may lead to bad science and policies that endanger public health.
>
> The second danger is that the government will seek to determine the outcome of public policy discussions by channeling the course of scientific research. Just as lawyers seek to influence the outcome of trials by preventing the judicial discovery of evidence, government officials may seek to influence policy debates by steering scientific attention away from sensitive topics.[59]

Or as Udry has written: "Political officials should decide how much money to spend on science, and should set priorities about what we want science to do for society...[but] never make decisions about individual projects.... When politics is allowed to intervene at the level of individual project funding decisions, the scientific enterprise itself is perverted."[60]

Still, considering the travails conservatives made Udry endure, he is remarkably fair-minded about their opposition to sex research:

> We say to conservatives that we will give them information that they can use for their cause as easily as the liberals can use it for theirs. But the conservatives say, thank you very much, but actually we do not need or want that kind of information. We already know enough for our purposes.... We want policies that encourage traditional values and traditional behavior and that roll back the tide of behaviors we disapprove, and...we especially don't want information when the process by which you get the data actually encourages the behavior we want to discourage. Is this a nutty view? I really don't think so.
>
> So I conclude that the battle over sex research is not a battle between the forces of good and evil, or between sensible people and the nuts.... It is a genuine and legitimate political battle between two groups in the population who hold diametrically opposed policy views.[61]

But in that battle, he adds, conservatives are politically organized, have politically powerful spokespersons, and are thus able to impose a minority view on the majority. The problem, he says, is not that the conservatives are playing dirty politics (but omits saying what is obviously true: that they *do* often play dirty politics); the problem is that Congress and science administrators are not able to stand up to the attacks at the project level and researchers are not very good at helping them. He then names a number of ways in which scientists can organize for political action and can seek out and work with sympathizers in Congress. Finally, he says, sex researchers should search their own souls and examine the charges of their opponents:

> We should not let their strident conspiracy theories keep us from taking them seriously. To what extent does our research agenda reflect the influence of our political agendas? Does our research soften up the respondents toward permissive sex? Do the topics we choose to research reflect a political agenda on our part?.... It is easier to marshal other organizations to the defense of sex research when our research is not seen as a part of our own sexual agendas.[62]

Not all sex researchers—perhaps not many—would go that far in questioning their own motives; most, to judge by what they say and write, believe that their motives are the purest. But even if they are sometimes wrong, even if the research they want to do sometimes expresses their personal values, it still remains true that the ethical, democratic, and socially constructive way to oppose their sex research is by producing or backing valid reanalysis of their data, or conducting other research of greater quality than theirs, that disproves their findings.

To use smear tactics, methods of intimidation, and political trickery to achieve what one considers a moral end is to live by the principle that the end justifies the means. In Arthur Koestler's *Darkness at Noon* the magistrate Ivanov says, "The principle that the end justifies the means is and remains the only rule of political ethics"—but Ivanov is a party-line Communist the effect of whose cynical morality is characterized by the title of the book.

7

Just Say No

Family Privacy versus the Common Good

In 1933, when a number of social critics were commenting with alarm about the declining functionality of American families, the President's Research Committee on Social Trends studied the matter and concluded, surprisingly, that families were still serving their traditional purposes— procreational, economic, educational, religious, protective, status-giving, recreational, and companionship-providing. Even though their everyday customs differed greatly from those of their European progenitors, American families were continuing to perform most of their historic functions, especially that of preparing children to live in their society.

But in the course of the next four decades—a period that witnessed the Great Depression, the transformation of government by a social security system, the colossal costs and disruptions of World War II, and the postwar technology explosion—some of those functions were appropriated in large part by society and its agencies, and others so altered that they hardly seemed to be traditional family behavior.

Two of the changes concern us here because they generated powerful political opposition to certain kinds of social research. The first: The ability of parents to instill their own values in their children was considerably whittled away and taken over by the schools, the media, and peer groups. The second: The perceived right of parents to control and punish their children was increasingly constrained by child-protection laws and appropriated by ever-expanding justice and health agencies. The ancient legal proverb *Jura publica favent privata domus* (Public laws protect domestic privacy) was being contravened: Public laws were invading domestic privacy. And from the 1960s on, other social developments—in particular the sexual revolution, the rising divorce rate, the feminist movement, and the multiple programs of the

Great Society—so much further diminished parental and familial roles that many sociologists and social commentators speculated that in the not-too-distant future the family might wither away and disappear.

Many conservatives began to build legal breastworks from behind which to defend the traditional powers—which they consider "rights"— of the head or heads of the family against the intrusions of society. The most vigorously defended of these supposed rights has been that of parents to refuse to permit the government, or researchers working on the government's behalf, to question their children concerning certain beliefs and behaviors that various agencies of the government feel they need to know about in order to carry out their duties. The conflict over this right, which has gone on for a generation and been particularly intense in recent years, pits two classic and major American values against each other: the prerogative of parents to raise their children as they think proper, free from outside interference, and the prerogative of society to insure that children are reared in ways that will make them law-abiding, self-sustaining, productive citizens; in brief, family privacy versus the common good.[1]

The conflict is far more ingrained in American culture than in European cultures. A belief long central to our national mythology, rooted in the early colonists' flight from European religious repression to the open and undeveloped New World, was that one could escape the repressions and intrusions of society by moving away to the frontier, where it was possible to live as one chose. Even when we no longer had a frontier, the adventurous and the discontented could abandon the cities for the privacy of empty plains, remote forests, or uninhabited mountains. A few decades ago, in hundreds of isolated communes idealistic young dissidents sought to create a private way of life free from the encroachments of the larger society, and today the embittered, alienated people who live in secluded militia camps and the members of fanatical religious cults are expressing a similar resistance to the demands of centralized government.

Of those demands, the queries of the Bureau of the Census about the size of the family, the identity and age of its members, their occupations and income, and so on, have always seemed to some Americans an unwarranted and detestable invasion of their privacy. But the collecting of such information has ancient provenance and undeniable social value. As societies grew beyond the level of small, intimate tribes, their rulers could no longer rely on personal observations and the impressionistic reports of their scouts when making decisions of paramount importance to the general welfare, particularly about war and finances.[2] In the thirteenth century B.C., for instance, when Moses, leading the Israelites through perilous and unfamiliar country after the Exodus, needed to know how large an army he could raise against any enemy, he was directed by God to take a census:

> And the Lord spake unto Moses in the wilderness of Sinai...saying,
>   Take ye the sum of all the congregation of the children of Israel, after their families, by the house of their fathers, with the number of their names, every male by their polls;
>   From twenty years old and upward, all that are able to go forth to war in Israel: thou and Aaron shall number them by their armies....
>   Even all they that were numbered were six hundred thousand and three thousand and five hundred and fifty.
>   —Numbers 1:1–3, 46

Years later, another such census enabled Moses, considering war against the Midianites, to determine that he could call up an army of 12,000 (tiny, compared to the earlier figure of 603,550, which scholars say was undoubtedly a gross exaggeration), or enough to overwhelm the enemy, as indeed they did (Numbers 26:1–65; 31: 1–8).

Similarly, in 1085 A.D., William the Conqueror, seeking to create a strong central government after his conquest of England, realized that he needed to know how many men he could call on to serve as soldiers and how much property was available to be taxed for the maintenance of his army and government. He therefore dispatched teams of royal officers to collect manpower figures for every town and to compile a record of every manor's meadows, pastures, fisheries, and other sources of taxable income; the product of this census, the famous Domesday Book, was his guide to policy. The questions asked by William's survey teams were doubtless resented and unwillingly answered by most of those who would be called upon to fight and to pay taxes, even though William would be protecting them from invaders and despoilers.[3]

In subsequent centuries, limited censuses of one sort or another were conducted elsewhere from time to time, when particular crises made gathering information essential. But the first regularly repeated census of a nation was the one established in the United States by the Constitution, and necessarily so: Because of the federal structure of the new nation, a periodic census was needed in order to calculate and adjust the number of representatives allotted to each state and the amount each state had to contribute to the common defense and general welfare.

The first such census, that of 1790, asked only the name of the head of household, the number of persons in it, and the number of males sixteen years old and up who could be called on for military service.[4] No other data, not even on occupations, were collected, because some members of the first Congress thought it would be an invasion of privacy and others that it would a useless expense.[5] But from that exceedingly limited beginning, the U. S. Census grew in scope and depth in response to the growth of the nation and the corresponding increase in its leaders' need for data on which to base decisions about the affairs of state. Time and again, as the government expanded its services to its citizens, federal legislators found themselves unable to make wise choices, or sometimes any choices, for lack of critical information; during the Depression, for instance, Congress started work-relief programs although the only data it had on unemployment were rough estimates that varied by many millions.[6] As Congressman William Poage of Texas said in 1939, when Congress was considering public housing for low-income people, "We do not know what the housing situation is.... We are spending the Government's money in total blindness."[7]

Repeatedly, therefore, Congress extended the scope of the Census—always arousing the resentment of those Americans who felt that they were being forced to reveal details of their private relationships, income, and possessions that were nobody's business but their own. But as members of an organized society, they were wrong; Congress had to have the information for the common good, and federal law legitimately compelled the people of the nation to answer.

That law applies to the decennial census but not to a number of special surveys conducted by the Bureau of the Census. Nor is there any legal requirement to answer the questions posed by surveys performed by commercial firms on behalf of businesses, political candidates, and others. Nor need people answer the queries of other, more important surveys conducted by such firms or by academic researchers for government agencies that need certain kinds of data in order to carry out missions of national importance ranging from the delivery of health services to the control of addictions, and from crime prevention to assistance to the ailing and impaired elderly.[8] Researchers who gather the information essential to carrying out these important functions must rely on the willingness of people they query to answer them. Until about two or three decades ago, nearly all the people called upon in any survey sample would cooperate, but by the 1970s the refusal rate began to climb worrisomely, especially in big cities, the reasons, it has been suggested, including irritation at being bombarded by surveys and market research, resistance to the erosion of privacy, and the changing nature of inner-city populations.[9]

The problem reached serious dimensions about fifteen years ago. In the early 1950s two major ongoing surveys conducted by the University of Michigan's Survey Research Center had refusal rates of 4 or 5 percent; by the late 1970s the rates had tripled, and in recent years has ranged from 13 to 20 percent.[10] Today a first pass at a sample is very likely to get only about a 50 percent response; it is usually possible, but costly and time-consuming, to pull this up a good deal by making second and third calls on the refusers or the not-at-homes.[11] Currently, some well-regarded major surveys are achieving only a 73-to-82 percent response rate (the missing 18 to 27 percent are in large part refusers, in lesser part people who were never reachable.)[12] But even at 80 percent, a survey runs a considerable risk of distortion; unless the characteristics of the missing 20 percent precisely parallel those of the 80 percent who responded or researchers can determine how they differ from the responders, they cannot know how greatly the resulting data distort reality. It is possible by making repeated return calls to pull the response rate up to 95 percent—most refusers aren't radically opposed to the research—but at a very great increase in cost.[13]

With such a level of resistance to research surveys, particularly those conducted for government agencies on issues that conservatives believe are none of the government's business, it was inevitable that some members of Congress would look for an opportunity to strike a blow (or at least a heroic pose) in defense of family privacy and against the intrusion of Big Government liberals. That opportunity appeared in November, 1994, when Republicans took control of Congress for the first time in forty years.

The Attack on School Survey Research: Round One

The Contract With America, drawn up by Newt Gingrich, Dick Armey, and the House Republicans to serve as that party's major weapon in the 1994 campaign, said, among other things:

> This year's election offers the chance, after four decades of one-party control, to bring to the House a new majority that will transform the way Congress works. That historic change would be the end of government that is too big, too intrusive, and too easy with the public's money. It can be the beginning of a Congress that respects the values and shares the faith of the American family.

One of ten bills that the Contract promised to bring to the House floor within the first 100 days of the 104th Congress was called the "Family Reinforcement Act"; it would comprise "child support reinforcement, tax incentives for adoption, strengthening rights of parents in their children's education, stronger child pornography laws, and an elderly dependent care tax credit to reinforce the central role of families in American society."

Two bills written to carry out part of that promise, the "Parental Rights and Responsibilities Act of 1995" and the "Family Reinforcement Act of 1995," were proposed by House Republicans in the first half of 1995 and energetically supported by many conservative political-action groups, among them the Christian Coalition, the Family Research Council, Of the People, and the Parents' Rights Coalition.[14] The bills dealt with a number of matters outside our purview, but the Family Reinforcement Act contained one section—Title IV, "Family Privacy Protection"—that, while intended to protect family privacy, would severely impede and render of little value most survey research of children and adolescents. Applying to federally funded research on minors conducted in schools—and thus to nearly all research on minors—it placed on researchers the heavy burden of obtaining parental consent for their child's participation in any survey that asked questions about such "sensitive" topics as parental political affiliations or beliefs, mental or psychological problems, sexual behavior or attitudes, illegal, antisocial, or self-incriminating behavior, and religious beliefs. Onerous as that requirement would be, a single word in Title IV was crippling to such research: The parental consent had to be *written*. (The legislators may not have been aware that, as a number of studies have shown, only about half of all parents will trouble themselves to return written permission for such activities, with the result that the sample obtained is unrepresentative and its findings untrustworthy.[15])

Title IV was the long-delayed fruition of a conservative effort to protect parental rights by limiting school survey research. A first small step in that direction was taken in 1974, when Republican Congressman Jack Kemp of New York successfully proposed an amendment to GEPA* (a federal education act); it required that parents of pupils taking part in federally assisted research projects in education be shown

---

*General Education Provisions Act, a roundup of existing statutory provisions applying to federal education programs.

the relevant instructional materials if they wished. But the amendment was limited to education studies funded by the Department of Education, and it did not give parents the power to refuse to let their children participate.[16]

In 1978 Senator Orrin Hatch of Utah, already an influential voice of conservativism, added a more powerful amendment to GEPA; it required parental consent—that is, gave parents the right of refusal—to the child's participation in federally funded educational research that dealt with any of seven sensitive topics (essentially the ones that would reappear in Title IV in 1995).[17] But the Hatch Amendment did not require the consent to be written—if the parents did nothing and failed to formally refuse, that would be construed as "passive consent"—and, like the Kemp amendment, it governed only research funded by the Department of Education.[18]

In 1994, with the Democrats still in control of Congress, the Goals 2000 Education Act, an administration-backed Committee bill increasing the federal role in education, was passed in March. During the debate, Senator Charles Grassley, an Iowa Republican, offered an amendment closely modeled on the Hatch Amendment but expanding it to apply to "any survey, analysis, or evaluation as part of any applicable program" covered by Goals 2000; since the amendment seemed only an extension of existing law, the Senate passed it by a 93–0 vote.[19]

The Department of Education would have to write regulations to carry out the Grassley Amendment, but even before it did so some major researchers saw the amendment as posing almost insuperable obstacles to their work. One who felt that way is Professor Leonard Saxe of Brandeis University, the principal investigator of a multimillion-dollar project evaluating Fighting Back (a national demonstration of a community-based approach to preventing and treating substance abuse by minors). Saxe's study was funded by the Robert Wood Johnson Foundation, not the government, and so would not be directly controlled by the Grassley amendment, but its passage signaled, he says, "a belief by a large number of people that parents and schools needed to control the kind of sensitive data collection we had been doing. It was going to become increasingly difficult for outsiders to get access to the schools in a way that would allow them to do high-quality research. The signal had been given at the national level that parents needed to have direct input." Saxe abandoned conducting his own survey research and took to meta-analyzing (combining the results of) small-scale studies conducted by local school boards or contracted for by local communities and state departments of substance abuse. It is the best alternative he could find to doing original research of his own.

* * *

With the Republican victory in November, 1994, Chuck (as he likes to be called) Grassley saw a golden opportunity to attack all survey research conducted in the schools and with far more effective legislative weaponry. A tall, lanky former farmer with severely straight hair and a Grant Wood face, Grassley is a classic conservative; his resumé says that he has "country-bred political smarts," "uses Iowa common sense to challenge Washington nonsense," and "fights for taxpayer rights in the face of an overzealous IRS." In collaboration with various other Republican leaders, he swiftly drafted the two bills to strengthen parents' rights and transformed his amendment to Goals 2000, which had been limited to educational research, into the puissant Title IV, applying to all federally funded research on minors.

Tactically, it seemed best to have the Family Protection Act proposed first in the House, with its influx of radical-right conservatives eager to carry out the promises of the Contract With America. The bill, with over a hundred sponsors, including almost all the ultraconservatives in the House, was introduced there on January 4, 1995 and its various Titles (sections) were referred by the House to three appropriate House committees for their consideration and recommendations.

Title IV went to the on Committee on Government Reform and Oversight, whose chairman, Representative William Clinger, referred it to the Subcommittee on Government Management, Information and Technology, chaired by Representative Stephen Horn of California. Horn, a moderately conservative Republican with impressive educational credentials—a Ph.D. and professorship in political science, and eighteen years as president of California State University at Long Beach—decided to have a hearing, and directed the subcommittee staff to solicit presentations and comments from a number of individuals and agencies.

While they were doing so, his own staff and those of most of the other subcommittee members heard from COSSA (Consortium of Social Science Associations), which had been closely following the progress of Title IV. COSSA, a small, meagerly funded lobbyist group (it has an annual budget of only about $300,000 and a staff of five persons), was formed in 1981 to defend social science from congressional and White House attacks, and is supported by the APA, the ASA, and ten other professional groups, and gets minor contributions from two dozen others and about sixty universities.

When Title IV was referred to Horn's subcommittee, COSSA called together several social science organizations to consider how to oppose or at least work to modify the bill. A handful of congressional liaison people from those organizations met as an informal coalition, planned their approach, and divided up the task of phoning staffers of the subcommittee members (the representatives themselves are usually very hard to get to on short notice) and calling on them to present research evidence showing that the written-consent requirement of Title IV would seriously damage all school survey research being conducted for federal health, drug addiction, education, and other agencies. The goal of the lobbyists was, of course, for the staffers to brief their bosses, alerting them to the effects of the written-consent requirement.

Horn scheduled the subcommittee hearing for the morning of March 16 in room 2154 of the Rayburn House Office Building.[20] A committee or subcommittee hearing to evaluate a proposed bill can be any one of several kinds of event: a media circus, a searching examination of witnesses and written evidence, or a perfunctory formality. The hearing on Title IV met for only two hours, was attended by six of its fourteen members, heard five witnesses, and inserted six written statements into the record—all in all, seemingly short shrift for so important a task as weighing family privacy against the social benefits of survey research. But Horn's opening statement suggested that he, at least, intended to give the matter serious and impartial consideration:

> The legislation attempts to achieve the right balance between government power and individual rights. [It] would emphasize and recognize parents' role in keeping families strong. We must remain sensitive to the difficulty and delicacy of the balance we seek.... For background, we asked a cross-section of educational, health and related professional associations to comment or suggest changes to the bill. We received a wide range of responses, which will be included in the record. Today we will hear from several individuals with an interest in the kinds of issues Title IV would cover.

By no accident, the lead witness was Senator Grassley, who spoke with pride of his own amendment to Goals 2000, praised the intent of Title IV, and took direct aim at what he saw as the enemy of family privacy, the government's own health and justice agencies:

> Title 4 of your bill expands the protection of the Pupil Rights Amendment from solely the Department of Education to any federally funded department or agency. My opinion is that this expansion is needed and welcome....

[In my amendment] I specifically required written parental consent. It is not enough to get implied consent.... [And] we should not place a child in a compulsory atmosphere in the position of having to determine what is private information and if he should reveal it. These are adult decisions to make. That is why the choice in this language is specifically and deliberately placed in the hand of parents....

I am pleased that the committee has decided to make this language apply in all federally funded programs. Many of the offensive surveys come out of the Departments of Health and Human Services, Justice, or the Centers for Disease Control. However, by covering all agencies, your committee will guarantee family private [*sic*] protection.

Another witness, Matthew Hilton, typified the ultraconservative view of the matter. Hilton, a Utah lawyer who termed himself an authority on family privacy issues, started off by relating an incident in a local Utah school district in which seven- and eight-year-old children were asked, without parental notification or permission, such revealing and perhaps upsetting questions as "I cause trouble to my family. Yes or no," "I behave badly at home. Yes or no," "My family is disappointed in me. Yes or no," and "I'm picked on at home. Yes or no." He offered this as evidence of the need for strict control of school survey research, but did not say (and was not asked) whether the offending survey was conducted for any federal agency or was the work of some independent local researcher. Hilton portrayed the Contract With America as an outgrowth of the Declaration of Independence and the Revolution (which had succeeded, he said, because the colonists and God worked together—"God fulfilled his part by divine intervention on behalf of the colonists"). Although he praised the Contract With America, he urged Congress to enact legislation even stronger than Title IV and to give families the power to determine for themselves when and how to protect their rights.

In contrast, three other witnesses presented the point of view of survey researchers. The first, Sally Katzen, administrator of the Office of Information and Regulatory Affairs of the OMB, was very clear about the harm to survey research and the common good that the written-consent provision of Title IV could do:

Written consent works well when the parent or child is highly motivated to participate in an activity. But when a parent has no strong views one way or the other, the consent form is often perceived as mindless paperwork, and may be ignored.... [Researchers] tell us that a shift from passive to written consent will introduce a burden on the individuals that is sufficient to dramatically lower response rates to the point that it may effectively invalidate the research being conducted....

There are several critical research efforts underway now in the area of adolescent high-risk behavior, such as teen pregnancy and drug abuse. Our ability to approach these issues sensibly and to assess appropriate Federal intervention, if any, depends on our understanding of the extent of the problem and the dynamics that underlie teen decisionmaking and conduct.

Valid research is essential to that understanding, and imposing written consent may jeopardize our ability to conduct valid research and, hence, our ability to address these problems.

Much the same message was conveyed by William Butz, an associate director of the Bureau of the Census, who said that Census officials expected the provisions of Title IV to reduce response rates, increase costs, and increase survey bias.

The witness who was granted the most time and made the strongest arguments against written consent was Professor Lloyd Johnston, principal investigator of Monitoring the Future, a continuing survey, conducted by the University of Michigan's Survey Research Center, that had been tracking changes in the behavior and problems of secondary-school pupils and young adults for twenty-one years. Johnston, an eloquent speaker, said that school surveys provided "a unique window of understanding and measurement and insight" into such major current youth problems as violence, delinquency, and alcohol and drug abuse, and that Title IV, as written, would have a significantly adverse impact on this body of research:

> Our own study,...is one that would be affected, and it deals not only with these problems but also provides some of the measures of the national education goals and the national health goals for the year 2000.
>
> There are other major studies like this—CDC's youth risk behavior system, which deals with measuring health threatening behaviors and health protecting behaviors—exercise, diet, drunkenness, drunk driving, seat belt use, accidents and injury, tobacco, alcohol and drug use, and so forth....
>
> I think this proposed legislation, as currently worded, constitutes a threat to this entire corpus of important work. The viability of the work could be undermined by driving the non-response rates so high that the samples are really useless for interpretation, and/or driving the survey costs so high that we couldn't have large samples and the Federal Government would get a lot less product for its investment in research.... Many, many parents simply do not answer their mail. It's not that they object to their child's participation. It's just that they don't answer their mail. We do an active consent procedure on a particular sample of our study population and we know that 55 percent of the parents don't answer the first mail request for their consent. If you have a 45 percent response rate in a survey, it's useless.

Subcommittee member Carolyn Maloney, a New York Democrat, asked Johnston what kinds of surveys fail to allow a child or parent to decline to take part. "I think probably the most egregious examples that one might dredge up," Johnston said, "would come from local surveys maybe done by local colleges or by people in the school system and so forth, who simply don't think about these things, and human subjects' protection isn't even a phrase in their lexicon." Chairman Horn asked if it wasn't the case—as a former professor and university president, he actually knew the answer—that most academic research protocols require a human subjects review (a review by an IRB—Institutional Review Board); Johnston confirmed that that was so, adding that "most academic work goes through so many procedures that children are properly protected." He also pointed out that the great majority of surveys were conducted anonymously and that individuals were not identifiable from their responses; privacy was not invaded.

After some further questions and routine business, the hearing was adjourned. It had been brief and had received a limited amount of testimony by witnesses and in writing. But either that testimony or the educational lobbying of COSSA or both led the subcommittee members to disapprove of the written-consent requirement. Within a week of the hearing, Horn and the subcommittee revised and unanimously adopted a version of Title IV that clarified some of its language and provisions, and deleted the word "written." The revised bill was then handed up to the full Committee on Government Reform and Oversight with the recommendation that it be reported on favorably to the House as a new bill, H.R, 1271, titled "Family Privacy Protection Act of 1995." The committee, after some discussion, voted unanimously to do so, and sent its favorable report to the House on March 29.[21] The COSSA staff and the social scientists who had been active in the matter considered that they had achieved a definite win, since their major objection, the requirement that parental permission be in writing, had been removed.

* * *

On April 4, less than a week later, the Republican leadership, giving high priority to H.R. 1271 as part of the Contract With America, brought the bill onto the floor of the House. The COSSA-led coalition had not had time to make calls on representatives who might be responsive to the evidence or on their staffers but its members confidently expected the House to be guided by the committee report.[22]

The discussion of the bill, however, started off ominously; instead of considering the bill as recommended by the committee, a procedure that had been informally agreed to by committee members of both parties, one of Gingrich's troopers used an arcane maneuver to invoke a rule making the bill open to amendments from the floor. Anthony Beilenson, a California Democrat and a member of Horn's subcommittee, angrily said, "Unfortunately, it appears that the reason we now have a rule [permitting amendments] for the bill, instead of considering it under suspension of the rules, is a last-minute decision by the Republican leadership not to back the committee product, which was so carefully written." Mrs. Cardiss Collins, a feisty Democrat from Illinois, sided with him, accusing the Republicans of "backroom politics" and of following the recommendations of a staff member of a Republican representative; she did not name the representative but he quickly, and combatively, identified himself: He was Stephen Souder of Indiana, another member of Clinger's committee and a hard-line freshman conservative.

After some disagreeable wrangling, the House voted overwhelmingly in favor of the rule to consider amendments to H.R. 1271, and discussion proceeded. Several representatives spoke in favor of H.R. 1271 as it had been "marked up" (revised by the subcommittee and recommended to the House by the full committee), and Stephen Horn, after briefly reviewing the work of the subcommittee, concluded.

> Mr. Chairman, H.R. 1271 will advance the protection of our children's and our families' privacy beyond the 1994 Grassley safeguards, to protection from all surveys or questionnaires administered with any degree of Federal funding support. We have crafted this bill in a way which will do that without unduly hamstringing legitimate public interest activities.

But after a few routine comments by others, Souder got the floor and offered several amendments, the crucial one of which changed the phrase "without the consent" (of at least one parent or guardian) to "without the prior written consent." After paying pious homage to the family, he sneered at the concerns of survey researchers:

> Written consent is essential, not burdensome. The individual dignity of a child and the privacy of a family are paramount to [*sic*] saving an agency time or money.
> Opponents to this amendment in academia, the Clinton administration, and the Census Bureau find it troublesome that we are seeking prior written consent because data for their surveys might not be as accurate as possible. They are really saying science and data are now more important than the family. Is this what we call family values?

For shock effect, Souder read aloud from a school survey in his own district that had included the following questions and, he said, had upset him:

> What age were you when you lost your virginity?
> Have you had sex with more than five people?

Do you have sex more than three times a week?
Do you know what gonorrhea, genital warts, herpes or syphilis are?
Have you ever performed or received oral sex?
Have you ever had a homosexual experience?

"This type of questionnaire is reprehensible!" he declaimed. "I find it particularly reprehensible because it was given to my two children, one of whom is a junior and one of whom is a freshman." Horn asked him if this had been a federally funded study; Souder admitted that it had not been. (It therefore had nothing to do with the control proposed in H.R. 1271.) Mrs. Collins tactfully said that she understood Mr. Souder's outrage and that she had found the questionnaire (which he had distributed to members of the full committee during the markup of H.R. 1271), "absolutely revolting"—but, she pointed out, "It was distributed by students from the school who worked on the school newspaper. That is a matter internal to the local school board, not to the U. S. Congress." Having thus disposed of Souder's reprehensible example, she told the House that at the subcommittee hearing "every expert witness who addressed this issue testified that requiring prior written consent would undercut the effectiveness of critical Federal surveys." To which she added earnestly, but anticipating defeat,

> We should not second-guess the unanimous position of every expert who testified on the issue. We should not second-guess the unanimous decision of the subcommittee and full committee against requiring prior written consent.... We must stand up for what is right, not what some staff [person] thinks is politically correct.... Unfortunately, it is clear that the bipartisan agreement in our committee was not worth the paper it was written on.

Carolyn Maloney, who also spoke against the Souder amendment, offered a daring and insightful conjecture:

> We are told that this amendment is to bring this bill back into line with the Contract, but that is just a smoke-screen. I believe the changes offered in this amendment are designed to block surveys from ever being performed, specifically, surveys of teenage behavior, including the causes of rising teen pregnancy, drug abuse, and suicide.

Paying the customary (though often less than heartfelt) respect to the motives of her opponents, she concluded, "Members of both parties are sincere in their desire to solve these problems, but pretending a problem does not exist will not make it nonexistent. By rendering these surveys worthless or eliminating them altogether, that is what some Members hope to do, that will not work. It has never worked. It is naïve."

But Maloney, Collins, and Horn could have saved themselves the trouble. The Republican majority of the House, having neither listened to the expert witnesses nor read their written statements to the subcommittee (and thus ignorant of the problems the subcommittee had recognized), and still in the first flush of their election victory, were hell-bent to enact the acts promised by the Contract. Their view of the balance between family privacy and survey research was typified by the remarks of Tom Coburn, Republican of Oklahoma, who, after identifying himself as a physician and scientist, said, with memorably tangled syntax,

> I rise to support the Souder amendment because...scientifically I do not buy the fact that if we have a parent's permission we are going to, No. 1, make the cost too great or, No. 2, make the scientific data to where it is not accurate. That is spurious logic.... I would not necessarily say that some of the questions to this survey would not be good information as a physician and one who treats adolescents and had delivered over 2,000 teen-age mothers...but I am not more interested in that information if it means I violate a parent's right to parent.

There were a few more comments pro and con (including the recital of a long list of the professional social science, medical, and educational organizations opposed to the requirement of written consent); then, with the bill having been under discussion less than two hours, the chair called for the vote. The great majority of Republicans voted in favor of the Souder amendment; surprisingly, so did most Democrats, possibly because they, too, wanted to see school survey research strangled or possibly because they wanted to demonstrate that they were something other than liberals. The final tally on the Souder amendment was 379 in favor, 46 opposed; written parental consent was back in H. R. 1271. Later that day the House passed the bill by the overwhelming vote of 418 yeas to 7 nays.

Why had all but forty-six members of the House voted for the Souder amendment? Ed Hatcher, director of the Public Policy Office of the ASA, told me (and I heard much the same thing from several others on the science side of the issue), "It was a politically appealing idea—family, privacy, parents' rights—and we hadn't had time to mount any serious effort to tell them how it would affect things. The subcommittee had heard from us, but the rest of the House had not."

But the House was not only motivated by the political appeal of voting for family, privacy, and parents' rights (the political equivalent of Mom, the flag, and apple pie), it was also expressing an underlying suspicion of, or hostility toward, social science on the part of a considerable number of its members, as became clear when the House voted that same day on several other amendments to H.R. 1271 offered by Robert Dornan. A far-right extremist from California, Dornan, a spirited combatant, announced in an almost jocular manner and with a wicked smile that he was proposing to ban *all* federal funding of *all* survey research:

> Having fenced briefly in my youth, and it is an elegant sport, the one thing I do remember is the gentlemanly or ladylike challenge at the beginning, "En garde," I would say to my friends in the House who want these surveys. This is simply an attempt to end the surveys at the Federal level totally. So I am saying En garde, and I do want to get a vote on this and will proceed.... Now, what my Dornan amendment would do, the three lines are really all dovetailed together, it would prohibit the funding of all these type surveys.... The Federal government has no business subsidizing government social engineers or people who want this detailed information. No one collects numbers unless they are going to do something with those survey numbers. Surveys based on personal and intimate subjects should not end up being the basis for public policy.

The vote on the Dornan amendments was 291 against, 131 for—which provided research scientists with the discomfiting evidence that at least 131 members of the U. S. House of Representatives in the 104 Congress would have liked to see all federally funded surveys of minors banned.

The Attack on School Survey Research: Round Two

On the day H.R. 1271 was passed by the House, the same bill was read on the floor of the Senate and referred to its Committee on Governmental Affairs for consideration and recommendations. Republican leaders would have liked to see it move along swiftly, but for administrative reasons it languished in that committee for seven months. The committee chairman had been Senator William Roth of Delaware, but when Senator Robert Packwood of Oregon, who had chaired the powerful Senate Finance Committee, resigned from the Senate after revelations of his sexual harassment of women on his staff, the Republican leadership in the Senate moved Roth to the chair of the Finance Committee and appointed Senator Ted Stevens of Alaska to take Roth's place as chairman of the Committee on Governmental Affairs.[23] Stevens, though he was an old hand—he had been a senator for nearly thirty years—needed time to familiarize himself with the committee's pending bills before taking any action on them.

The delay was a boon for the social science community, giving it time in which to develop a strategy. After a flurry of phone calls among leading social science organizations, representatives of COSSA, the APA, the American Psychological Society (APS), the ASA, and several other groups met and formed themselves into an ad hoc steering committee to plan action.

One important step they took was to expand the small working group that had worked with the subcommittee members into a new and larger entity, the Research and Privacy Coalition, a temporary umbrella organization for lobbying and publicity purposes, and within weeks they had persuaded thirty-five scientific and medical organizations to become affiliates of it and to lend their assistance to its efforts.

But the best hope for deletion of the requirement of written parental consent, the members of the ad hoc committee agreed, was to present evidence of the harm it would do at a hearing—if there were one—of the Senate Committee on Governmental Affairs. A hearing is held only if a committee chairman chooses to have one; the goal of the ad hoc committee therefore was to persuade Stevens to call a hearing, and the most practicable way to do that was to convince staffers of his Governmental Affairs committee that one was needed and trust them to convey the message to him. The ad hoc steering committee therefore phoned the staff, asked for a meeting, and were invited to come in. Patricia Kobor and Susan Persons, the legislative liaison officers of APA and APS respectively, Felice Levine, the executive officer of ASA, and representatives of several other organizations went to the meeting, where they presented evidence of the harm the written-consent provision would do to research and urged that there be a hearing at which that evidence could be presented to the senators on the Governmental Affairs committee. Not long after the meeting, they learned that they had been successful: Stevens had decided to hold a hearing and had directed the staff to invite appropriate witnesses and to solicit written statements for inclusion in the record.

* * *

The hearing took place on the morning of November 9, 1995 in room SD-342 of the Dirksen Senate Office Building,[24] but from the look of things, it appeared that the lobbyists of the Research and Privacy Coalition had achieved less than they had hoped. In contrast to the House committee hearing on the bill, at which two witnesses spoke in favor of the written consent provision and three offered evidence of the harm it would do to research, the Senate committee hearing had five witnesses on hand to speak in favor of the proviso and three who would be critical of it. Also disheartening to the social science coalition was the fact that of the nine Republicans and seven Democrats on the committee, only one, Senator Stevens, showed up that morning. He offered an explanation: a markup was going on in the Commerce Committee, and a defense conference was scheduled for later that morning, adding that various other problems might interrupt the hearing and asking that witnesses limit themselves to five minutes each.

Horn had started the House committee's hearing with a carefully impartial statement; Stevens, in advance of listening to the testimony to be offered (though he may have read statements submitted beforehand), began the Senate committee's hearing with a partisan statement implying that he strongly favored the bill:

> H.R. 1271 is derived from Title IV of the Contract with America, and the bill has been sent us from the House, obviously, for prompt handling.
>
> Several cases have been brought to the Committee's attention where someone in school, without any knowledge of the parent, has made a decision on behalf of a minor child. No government official, no school official, and no academic can be a surrogate in carrying out the responsibilities of a parent or guardian.
>
> Specifically, this legislation requires prior written consent for surveys or questionnaires. We often hear reference to the fact that many of society's ills are a result of a breakdown in the family unit and the lack of parental participation in our children's lives. If we do not act to protect parental rights, we will see a continuing erosion of parental participation.

The lead witness was Dr. Wade Horn, a child psychologist and director of the National Fatherhood Initiative, a recently formed profamily organization supported by a number of prominent conservatives and some liberals. Horn took the moral high road, asserting that the concerns of researchers were of no significance and that the overriding issue was the ethical requirements of research:

> There are some who maintain that to require written parental consent is too burdensome on the investigator. But that is the point. Requiring investigators to obtain informed consent from research participants is meant to place a burden on the researcher. It is far too easy for the investigator to believe that what they are interested in researching is critically important and, hence, minimize considerations concerning the welfare of the potential participant....
>
> Others are concerned that requiring written informed consent will increase the cost of the surveys and questionnaires. But the cost of the survey or questionnaire is not a concern of the potential participants. It is the concern of the investigator. As such, the cost of conducting the survey or distributing the questionnaire is simply irrelevant to the ethical requirement to fully inform the parent of the potential participant as to the purpose and particulars of the survey or questionnaire.
>
> Finally, some argue that requiring prior written parental consent will result in less representative samples, and, in fact, this may be the case. But, again, such

concerns are irrelevant to the ethical considerations. Researchers are not entitled to use children as research subjects or to override the right of parents to direct the upbringing of their children simply because they think their survey is important.

Researchers need to appreciate that it is parents, and not they or even the government, who are in the best position to determine what is in the best interests of their children.

Stevens thanked Horn, asked no questions of him, and called the next witness, one of his own constituents, Art Mathias, president of the Christian Coalition of Alaska, who spoke very briefly but submitted a sheaf of documents for the record. In his spoken testimony he narrated four cases that exemplified what he regarded as the usurpation of parental rights of Alaskans by agencies of the government. In one case, a mother of a kindergarten student asked the school principal to exclude her daughter from the sex education class, but her request was ignored. In another, "[a] parent called and told me this horror story how her 16-year-old daughter was removed from her home and placed in foster care because premarital sex was not allowed in that home." What these cases had to do with school survey research he did not say, nor did Chairman Stevens ask him. Mathias then spoke of two other cases that were a little closer to the mark: One parent told him of a survey carried out in her son's social studies class which included a question as to whether he was a conservative or liberal, and Mathias's own son had taken part in a survey the goal of which was to determine his strengths and weaknesses in communicating. It was not clear what these examples proved, although Mathias characterized them as "invasive" and "politically correct"; it was also not clear, nor did he clarify the matter, whether or not they were actually instances of the ostensible subject under discussion, namely, federally funded surveys. In conclusion, Mathias said, "If I, as a member of the Anchorage School Board, cannot protect my own son, who can? Please pass this much needed legislation and promulgate the regulations post haste."

Senator Grassley had arrived while Mathias was testifying, and Stevens welcomed him and asked the other witnesses to let him speak next, since he was on his way to another hearing. Grassley covered much the same ground as he had before the House committee, and concluded by rejecting, in strong and righteous language, the researchers' reasons for opposing the written parental consent provision:

I understand that researchers are concerned that having to get written consent could cost a bit more or hurt their samples. While I appreciate these concerns, the real issue is: Whose child is this anyway? A parent should be able to make the decision of whether his child is used for research purposes. Even the most noble of research projects must defer to the parent's right to protect and direct his own child. Any other decision is presumptuous and arrogant and must be resisted. It is arrogant, and I think we ought to resist that attitude....

In the final analysis, if a survey, analysis, evaluation, or questionnaire reveals private information in any federally funded program, the parents must give written consent. Now, let me emphasize, without that specific written consent their child should not participate, and the law ought to say, "cannot participate."

Grassley was followed by Robert Knight (whom we heard from earlier), director of Cultural Studies of the Family Research Council, who described himself as a former journalist and former fellow at two conservative think-tanks, the Hoover Institution and the Heritage Foundation. Knight, a small, neat fellow, was earnest and voluble. Like Mathias, he threw in several items unrelated to H.R. 1271 for their emotional appeal: an anecdote told by Mother Teresa that illustrated parental devotion to the child; the infamous Table 34 of the first Kinsey Report; and some survey questions about suicide, drug usage, and sexual activities which, he said, planted the ideas of those activities as options in the minds of teens who had never thought of them as such. He portrayed research as an often harmful process:

Any research methods, including surveys, that place a barrier between children and their parents should be outlawed. Increasingly, parents have found themselves fighting for their most fundamental rights against hostile educators and government officials who honestly believe that they, not the parents, know what is best for the children. Such officials work overtime to acquaint children with revisionist history, graphic sexual materials, and relativistic notions of morality—all in the name of research and education.

He ended strongly endorsing H.R. 1271 and linking it to the dictates of the Lord:

The Family Research Council supports efforts like H.R. 1271 to safeguard the rights of parents to direct their children's education and welfare, and that includes how, where and when children are included in research. Parents are assigned that task by no less an authority than God Himself. It would be the epitome of hubris to tamper with that bond because some educational experts feel they are smarter than everybody else.

Matthew Hilton, the Utah attorney who had testified at the House subcommittee hearing, spoke next; he briefly restated what he had said at that time, saying again that H.R. 1271 was, if anything, not strict enough and submitting a formal written statement that specified how he thought the bill should be modified to make it more effective.

Stevens then took a few moments to ask questions of the witnesses who had spoken thus far, apparently in an effort to discount in advance the testimony of the anti-H.R. 1271 witnesses who were about to testify. "Dr. Horn," Stevens said, "my staff informs me that we are going to hear testimony that suggests that survey data is of greater [sic] social value for families as a whole and, therefore, that the written consent will have a negative impact on the usefulness of surveys. What is your comment about that?"

"There is no question," Horn replied, "that some surveys and questionnaires do have the potential for having a positive impact on the general well-being of families and children." But, he said, that did not obviate the ethical requirement to decide whether participation was in the individual child's best interests, adding:

> The person most likely to have the child's best interests in mind in making that judgment is the child's parent.... If large numbers of parents fail to give that kind of consent, it would suggest to me that the researchers should examine whether or not what they are intending to ask of the children is contrary to the prevailing community standards or sensibilities.

Stevens next asked Art Mathias if federal officials believed that because they had aid money to distribute, they had the right to ignore state law on parental consent. Mathias answered a different question: The schools, he said, totally ignore a statute of the State of Alaska, and "something needs to change on this."

"Thank you very much," said Chairman Stevens. He then asked Robert Knight whether he went into homes as well as schools in his research. Knight had said nothing about his doing research but took the occasion to say, "Well, they come to us more often than not. We get calls from all over the country from people who are alarmed at this kind of thing happening to their children." Typical calls, he said, had to do with sex surveys in which a child was asked about "Ten different ways to have sex" and questions like "'When did you have same-sex relations, and how did you do it, and what did you do exactly?' I mean, this is outrageous for children to be subjected to this kind of hazing in the form of research." Stevens thanked him, said "We have to move along with this hearing," and called on the first witness critical of H.R. 1271, Sally Katzen of the OMB.

Ms. Katzen presented much the same testimony as she had before the House subcommittee, saying again that "to insist that all consent be written in virtually all circumstances can have a number of negative effects.... Research indicates that as many as 50 percent of the parents will fail to give the written consent when first approached." (In the written statement she also submitted, she cited the RAND Corporation study showing that requiring written parental consent increases per-response costs twenty-five-fold.) Reduced responses, she continued, led to biased responses; as research had demonstrated, the families least likely to respond were those at highest risk:

> Simply stated, the effect of this bill is to impair the validity and the reliability of important research.... It is essential that we focus our resources on those who are most at risk, and to do that we need to have this kind of information.... Those who favor the legislation do so in the name of children, and I applaud that. I, too, am in favor of children, and the administration is in favor of children. It is important to recognize, however, that by being overprotective in the short run, you may do more harm in the long run.

Stevens, by way of comment, harped again on the issue of surveys that did not require parental consent, saying that he had seen his six children through their teen years and saw no reason why anyone should ignore "our [Alaskan] laws and submit questions to our children that we haven't seen." Katzen gamely parried, pointing out that there are viable, low-cost ways of getting informed consent and that the failure of 50 percent of parents to send back written permission was not because they were against the research but because they simply did not respond in writing.

Stevens apologized for having to move ahead swiftly, saying that he would have to leave when the Commerce Committee called him, and summoned the next witness, Felice Levine of ASA, appearing on behalf of the Research and Privacy Coalition. She spoke very briefly but submitted a number of documents for inclusion in the record in the hope that the absent committee members would read them. She said that the organizations that had joined in the Coalition represented parents, researchers, health care providers, educators, child advocates, and community groups, all of whom "strongly support parental involvement and informed parental consent. However, we are deeply concerned about the negative effects of H.R. 1271 on parents, children, and the Nation's ability to monitor and to understand crucial problems among its youth." After stating the evidence about the non-response rate to requests for written permission and its serious effects on research, she, like Katzen, said that the written-consent requirement would harm those most in need of governmental attention:

H.R. 1271 will harm our ability to know how to help minors who engage in high-risk behaviors like smoking, drug abuse, and violence. Research show that children whose parents do not return parental consent forms are at a higher risk for health and social problems. Therefore, we must ask, who is H.R. 1271 likely to hurt? Ultimately it will hurt the children whose pediatricians may not learn of a new drug being abused and even whose parents may not know how to identify the early signs of problem drinking that they might display.... As the Committee deliberates on this bill, we ask you to consider the harmful effects of crippling our Nation's capacity to protect the most vulnerable among us, our children and youth.

Hurrying things along, Stevens called on Lloyd Johnston of the University of Michigan's Survey Research Center, who began to document the harm that the written-consent proviso would do: "A number of people who have used a written consent procedure," he said, "including ourselves in one component of our own study, get response rates from the youngsters that are in the 50 to 60 percent response-rate range, not the usual 95 to 99 percent response-rate range. These really are response rates which are unusable scientifically." As he was saying, "In-school surveys which provide some of the most valid and accurate data on sensitive behaviors like drug use will either be seriously damaged or eliminated, and this will be a major loss—" Stevens interrupted.

"I am sorry to say I have been called to the other committee," he said. "Thank you very much." To Sue Rusche, executive director of National Families in Action, a parent drug-prevention organization, who had been waiting to say that her movement and other antidrug movements would fail in their work if they lost an accurate measure of what was happening to children, he said, "Ms. Rusche, I am sorry. We will have to take your statement for the record. I hope you will accept my apology." With that, he adjourned the hearing, which had lasted a trifle over one hour.

Rusche's written statement, and a number of others critical of the written-consent requirement submitted by the Department of Health and Human Services, the Department of Justice, and several national organizations, including the National PTA and the National Association of School Psychologists, were added to the record, which, when printed, ran to 196 pages, only twenty-two of which are devoted to what was said at the hearing and heard by the one committee member present, Chairman Stevens.

Decision by Indecision

Chairman Stevens did not call for a resumption of the hearing; he apparently felt that the one-hour session had been adequate. The next step would be a committee mark-up session of H.R. 1271, but he did not convene one for over four months, perhaps because of the press of other matters—but perhaps, some members of the Research and Privacy Coalition conjectured, because it was far from certain that his committee would send a positive report on the bill to the Senate.

For one thing, the statements and documents submitted for the record by the witnesses and organizations critical of H.R. 1271 were impressive, and although senators on the committee may not have had time to read them, it was likely that their staffs did so and briefed them on the material.

For another thing, immediately after the aborted hearing the Research and Privacy Coalition made a concerted drive to persuade as many members of the committee as possible to vote against the written-consent stipulation. Their effort, the most common method of lobbyists, consisted of meetings with the staffs of the senators on the committee. This sounds simple but is not; Susan Persons, who at the time was director of Government Relations at APS (she is now with NIH), explains:

> It took endless meetings and endless decisions about strategies and which one of us would make the call to which senator's staff. Having direct access to a senator is not often possible, so primarily we talked to staff and provided them with information we hoped they would include when writing a memo for their senator preparatory to the markup meeting. Staff works so hard on issues that they often know more about an issue than the member, and they're supposed to point out to the member the good and bad points of a bill. We might say something to them like "I'd like you to ask your boss to vote this way, and I realize that it might be difficult for him, but here are the reasons I'd like you to present to him," and we'd present the hard data as to the effects of requiring written consent and give them a list of at least a dozen major national studies essential to the government that would be affected.

Eventually, Stevens did schedule a markup session on H.R. 1271 for April 18, 1996. It was a contentious session, with several Republican senators strongly defending the written-consent proviso and Senator John Glenn and several other Democrats earnestly objecting to it, as did Republican Senator William Cohen. But when Glenn proposed a substitute measure in which informed consent was required but consisted of notifying parents by mail of a survey and giving them the opportunity to refuse their child's participation—no written consent being required—the senators present voted it down on a party-line basis of seven nays (Cohen did not vote) to six yeas.[25]

Next, a motion to report the bill favorably to the Senate was approved, again by a party-line vote of seven yeas to five nays. Cohen joined his fellow Republicans in that vote but asked that the report contain a statement of his views; it expressed his serious concern about the possible bad effects of the written-consent requirement and his hope that the full Senate would work out a better solution. Five Democratic senators joined in submitting a lengthy, thoroughly documented minority dissent from the committee's vote, concluding, "We all want to protect American families and their children, but H.R. 1271 represents exactly the wrong approach."

The Research and Privacy Coalition lobbyists, expecting the bill to reach the Senate floor by summer, now redoubled their lobbying efforts, contacting primarily the staffs of senators they thought might be on the fence. They also asked the public information people in the Coalition's member organizations to generate publicity against H.R. 1271; this resulted in, among other things, a major article in the *New York Times*, another in the *Washington Post*, and a third in the *Chronicle of Higher Education*; a blizzard of press releases and of letters to key senators from state health officials and organizations affiliated with the Coalition; and an Action Alert message forwarded via the Internet to an uncounted number of social scientists on scores of listservs, urging them to contact their Representatives and Senators.[26] The Coalition also wrote to the Office of Public Liaison at the White House, which resulted in a letter from Donna Shalala, secretary of HHS, to Chairman Stevens, and a "Senate Briefing" (a press conference) on H.R. 1271 in the Dirksen Senate Office Building at which representatives of five major organizations spoke against the written consent proviso to the media.

Stevens finally turned in his committee's report on H.R. 1271 to the Senate on August 2, four months after the markup session, but by then the attitude of the Republican leadership toward it seemed to have changed. Not that anyone said anything to that effect, but, significantly, no one said anything about the bill; although technically in the works, it never came to the floor. The weeks and months went by, the 104th Congress completed its term, and when it did, H.R. 1271, like other bills awaiting Senate action, died.

Susan Persons gave me her insider's informed guess as to why the bill never came to the Senate floor:

> It was probably due to a number of factors: our Coalition's lobbying against it, the Administration's opposition to it, and I would like to think that we did at least put a reasonable doubt in the minds of a number of Republicans about the bill's effect—that it could have a number of unintended negative consequences.
>
> In the Governmental Affairs Committee the vote was on a straight party-line basis, but some Republicans might have decided to vote for the bill in committee

for party reasons but not push for a final vote on the floor, or even to work quietly to keep it from coming to the floor. Many members like to have it both ways. In this case, they could tell their constituents and colleagues who were pressuring them for support that they did support it, and yet they did the right thing by not demanding a floor vote. There's no way to say for sure that this is what happened, but that's my best guess.

It is not certain that the story ends here. A cadre from the Research and Privacy Coalition met with Senator Grassley's staff early in 1997, and one member of his staff indicated unofficially that Grassley was still interested in the legislation, meaning that he might reintroduce it later in the year.[27] (Senator Grassley, to whom I send queries about this three times in late 1997, did not reply.) It has fairly often been the case that a bill that expired when a term of Congress ended without action being taken on it was reincarnated in a later Congress and enacted. As Michael Buckley, a staff member of COSSA, told me:

We succeeded in stalling H.R. 1271, and it looks like it won't become law. But if it gets reintroduced, it will still be a tough one to fight, as it was the first time. Each congressman has to consider that he or she could be labeled "Congressman X, who voted to have your children asked questions like—" and so on. It takes a lot of security to vote against a bill like 1271.

The scientific community, especially that part of it concerned with behavioral and social research, is not confident that it has heard the last of the Family Privacy Protection Act. The Research and Privacy Coalition is currently nothing but a number of inactive folders in the file drawers and floppy disks of some dozens of organizations, but it could be and undoubtedly would be revived by swift e-mail networking at the first sign of a renewed attack on school survey research; the handful of members of the ad hoc committee of the Coalition are still, as of this writing, very much on the alert. In the well-known words of the abolitionist Wendell Phillips, who may have been quoting Jefferson or perhaps Patrick Henry, "Eternal vigilance is the price of liberty."

8

The War Against Social Science Research

The Social Scientist as Dr. Frankenstein

Alarmed as social scientists were by the conservative attacks on sex surveys and school survey research, these were only local battles compared to a far broader offensive launched against basic social science research in two congressional committees in 1995.*

The goal of that offensive was at once very narrow and extremely broad: Very narrow, in that it sought either to cancel indefinitely the funding of one particular section of the National Science Foundation (NSF)—the Directorate for Social, Behavioral, and Economic Sciences (SBE)—or to have SBE dropped from the NSF altogether; and extremely broad, in that SBE, though tiny in comparison with the other six directorates in NSF, was the source of 61 percent of all funding of basic research in the social sciences in the United States.[1] (The NSF funding amounted to only one-tenth of all federal funding of social science research; however, most of the other nine-tenths, supplied by twenty-four other agencies, was for applied social science research, the NSF's tenth for basic social science research.[2])

Why on earth would any congressional committee, rather than trying to weed out specific projects its members considered objectionable or worthless, seek to mow down so much of the field? To answer that question, we need to look back briefly at the antecedents of the campaign, which did not spring forth out of nowhere but had a provenance of many centuries' duration.

Its ancestry can be traced back to an ancient hostility toward science by both the learned and the ignorant, who, for their separate reasons,

---

*A reminder: For brevity, I use "social sciences" to signify "social and behavioral sciences" except where it is necessary, for some reason, to use the longer term.

237

found its discoveries threatening and frightening. In the early seventeenth century, as we have seen, the Inquisitors defending the faith of the Catholic Church regarded Galileo's challenge of the biblical geocentric view of the world as intolerable heresy. Similarly, the earlier experiments and discoveries of Paracelsus and various other alchemists and thaumaturges alarmed many clerics and lay people, who feared that these wonders were achieved with the aid of the powers of darkness. Even earlier, in the late fifteenth century the antagonism of Queen Isabella's advisers, most of them ecclesiastics, toward Columbus's view of the shape and size of Earth prevented him for seven years from getting the backing he needed to try to reach the Indies by sailing westward across the Atlantic.

Hostility toward science was, to be sure, accompanied by wonderment and admiration, but often outweighed them. From the dawn of the scientific revolution at the beginning of the sixteenth century, not only ignorant commoners but the educated heads of state and church viewed scientists with both awe and dread, seeing them as capable of working miracles—and of either accidentally or purposely unraveling the God-given order of things. No single work so well epitomizes that ambivalence as the 1818 gothic novel *Frankenstein, or The Modern Prometheus* by Mary Shelley, the story of a daring scientist who intruded on the prerogative of the Giver of Life, only to have his creation turn out to be a murderous monster who, in the end, destroys him, a just retribution for his presumption. Ever since, any number of dramas, novels, and movies have had much the same moral: Scientific experimentation can work wonders, but when it encroaches upon the laws of God (or Nature) can produce disaster.

In our own time, this is reality, not just fiction: Nuclear energy supplies much of the world's power, but even a tiny part of the existing stockpiles of nuclear warheads would, if detonated, render the earth totally uninhabitable; genetic engineering, beginning to control or even cure hereditary diseases, is capable also of creating varieties of microorganisms and plants that could wipe out most existing forms of life; and the products of our ever more sophisticated factories, airplanes, and automobiles threaten to poison our air, water, and land, warm the entire globe via the greenhouse effect, melt the ice-caps and drown the seashores, and make much of the world's presently habitable land impossible to live in.

These and most other familiar reasons to fear scientific research are in the realm of the hard sciences or biomedicine, but the social sciences too have been viewed with ambivalence or hostility ever since the 1920s, when they first began to have some influence on daily life. In 1922 the widely read pundit Walter Lippmann portrayed social science as speculative and dangerous:

> The physical scientist can make an hypothesis, test it, revise the hypothesis hundreds of times, and, if after all that, he is wrong, no one else has to pay the price. But the social scientist cannot begin to offer the assurance of a laboratory test, and if his advice is followed, and he is wrong, the consequences may be incalculable.[3]

Fortunately, in Lippmann's view, the sensible executive or leader of society recognizes this and pays little attention to the social scientist's prescriptions for social betterment:

> The man of affairs, observing that the social scientist knows only from the outside what he [i.e., the man of affairs] knows, in part at least, from the inside, recognizing that the social scientist's hypothesis is not in the nature of things susceptible of laboratory proof, and that verification is possible only in the "real" world, has developed a rather low opinion of social scientists who do not share his views of public policy.[4]

In the 1930s, however, when the nation was in desperate straits, New Deal Democrats, unlike Lippmann's man of affairs, saw social science as the source of knowledge with which they could shape programs to combat the multiple social ills brought about by the Depression. Social scientists were among the most influential members of the circle of advisors around FDR; some of them, in fact, had earlier been advisors to Herbert Hoover, who, although a political conservative, believed that social policies should be based on social science data and findings.[5] But to most conservatives of the New Deal era, the remedies urged by social scientists often looked like socialism in disguise, and they saw the social scientist as the enemy of capitalism and its values. Hostility toward science, said the sociologist Robert K. Merton in a 1937 address to the American Sociological Society—his comments applied with special force to social science—arises from at least two sources: the first, "[the] conclusion that the results or methods of science are inimical to the satisfaction of important values"; the second, "the feeling of incompatibility between the sentiments embodied in the scientific ethos and those found in other institutions."[6] Both were true of conservatives in 1937 and both have been true of them ever since.

* * *

At the time, however, many liberal policymakers and intellectuals considered the social sciences essential to the governance of modern society and therefore the most valuable and interesting of the sciences. But then came the war, and although social scientists carried out a number of useful studies for the Army, the Office of Strategic Services, and the Office of War Information, the value of their research was overshadowed by the massive projects and achievements in the natural sciences and biomedicine of the Office of Scientific Research and Development (OSRD), particularly the development of atomic power and of penicillin.

Toward the war's end, President Roosevelt asked Vannevar Bush, the head of OSRD, for recommendations as to what the federal government should do to maintain scientific research momentum in the postwar period. Bush spent more than half a year—during which time FDR died—preparing a report that he submitted to President Truman; in it he proposed that Congress create a national research foundation to fund research in academia on a major scale.[7] But as an engineer and physicist, he saw no place for social science in that foundation; in his letter of transmittal to Truman he said, "In speaking of science, [President Roosevelt] had in mind the natural sciences, including biology and medicine, and I have so interpreted his questions"—neglecting to mention that Bush himself had drafted Roosevelt's letter to him.[8] Although Truman and some members of Congress, most notably the influential Senator Harley Kilgore, wanted social science included in such a foundation, conservatives were dead set against it; they felt that a national science foundation would be antithetical to free enterprise, and if it incorporated the social sciences, radical and subversive of American values. As one conservative congressman, Clarence J. Brown, said during 1945 hearings on a bill to create such a foundation:

> The average American just does not want some expert running around prying into his life and his personal affairs and deciding for him how he should live, and if the impression becomes prevalent in Congress that this legislation is to establish some sort of organization in which there would be a lot of short-haired women and long-haired men messing into everybody's personal affairs and lives...you are not going to get your legislation.[9]

In a brief history of NSF, David Johnson, executive director of the Federation of Behavioral, Psychological and Cognitive Sciences, sums up the early conflict over social science research:

> [In 1948,] to everyone's (except possibly Truman's) surprise, the Democrats retained the presidency and recaptured the majority in Congress the following year.

That emboldened the Federation of American Scientists to call for specific inclusion of the social sciences in the 81st Congress's [national science] foundation legislation...[as did] the AAAS group.... Unfortunately, fear of communism had grown markedly in the years since the war, and several of the scientists associated with the liberal, or non-Bush, vision of the foundation were branded as communist sympathizers, especially famed astronomer Harlow Shapley, a member of both the Federation of American Scientists and the AAAS group. Indeed, the very idea of a national science foundation became suspect.[10]

Some conservatives actually asserted that the idea of such a foundation was communist-inspired and others believed that social science research supported by the foundation would seek to improve the status of blacks. (Gunnar Myrdal's *An American Dilemma*, published in 1944, had strengthened the apparent connection between social-science research and efforts to counteract racism.) Only by adhering to the Vannevar Bush model and down-playing the status of social science research was the National Science Foundation Act finally passed by Congress in 1950; although the act did not explicitly forbid NSF to fund social science research, such research, says Johnson, gained "only the most tenuous toehold" in the foundation: NSF was permitted, but not mandated, to fund projects in the social sciences, but such projects, if there were any, would be limited to studies of the impact of the other sciences on the general welfare.

That was fine with the National Science Board—the NSB, a twenty-four-member body of presidential appointees, governs NSF—and NSF staffers, most of whom were natural scientists who doubted that the social sciences were really sciences.[11] This parochial view was shared by many members of the National Academy of Sciences (NAS), an organization of some 1,800 distinguished scientists, mostly in the natural sciences, that acts in an advisory capacity to Congress and congressional agencies, and by ranking officials of NIH,[12] who saw to it that behavioral and social science research in their institutes was limited to applied research concerning their other programs, and some of whom shared the conservative view that the social sciences were politically suspect and a danger to American society.

Up and Down the Greasy Pole

For four decades, social science research occupied a continually changing position within NSF, sometimes struggling upward both as to status and funding, sometimes sliding back down in status and suffering a decrease of funding. The long-term trend, however, was upward, although during those decades the social sciences, unlike Disraeli, never reached the top of the greasy pole.*

The ups and downs of social science were in some part the result of conflicting views and bureaucratic infighting at NSB and NSF, but in larger part a reflection of events in American society and of the dissimilar responses to them of liberal-left and conservative political forces. The details need not concern us, since the central concern of this chapter is a recent congressional effort to gut the entire social science program at NSF, but a few highlights will illustrate how social science research at NSF has long been opposed and sometimes seriously set back by political forces antagonistic to it.[13]

• During the red scare of the 1950s, social science research was a very minor part of NSF's operations, consisting mostly of small programs scattered out among the major divisions of NSF. The low esteem in which social science was held by conservatives in Congress accorded with the view of it held by the chairman of NSB, Chester Barnard, who said that NSF should concern itself only with the "hard science core" of the social sciences, funding only studies "convergent with" the natural sciences and limited to examining the impact of those sciences on the general welfare or performing other functions helpful to them.

• As the red scare subsided, and as it became evident to most of Congress that NSF was not a tool of subversive elements, a number of liberal members of Congress, among them Senators Estes Kefauver, Hubert Humphrey, and Wayne Morse, called for an expanded role for the social sciences at NSF. The first move toward that role came in 1957, when the programs of social science research scattered throughout NSF were combined into a single Social Science Research Program separate from the other science departments and the stifling requirement that its studies be convergent with the natural sciences was lifted. But social science still was low on the greasy pole: Its 1958 budget was a meager $600,000, or 1.2 percent of the total NSF budget of $50 million.

• When Sputnik was launched in October, 1957, Congress abruptly revalued NSF and what it could do for America, more than doubled the fiscal 1959 NSF budget, and increased allocations for social science

---

*Benjamin Disraeli, on being made prime minister, said to friends, "I have climbed to the top of the greasy pole."

research proportionately. More important, the status of the social sciences at NSF was reviewed by a four-person committee of NSB, and although one member of the committee called the social sciences "a source of trouble beyond anything released by Pandora," the views of its chairman, the Reverend Theodore Hesburgh, president of the University of Notre Dame and an ardent supporter of the social sciences, prevailed: In 1959 the Social Science Research Program was elevated in status to the Office of Social Sciences, and in 1960 still higher to the Division of Social Sciences, putting it on a level with—though very far from budgetary equality with—the natural sciences.

• In the continuing wake of Sputnik and the social turbulence of the 1960s, with its race riots, assassinations, bombings, mass demonstrations, student takeovers of university buildings, and other disorders, congressional funding of social science research rose rapidly: The total for all government agencies, including NSF, went from $118 million in 1962 to twice that in 1965 and quadruple that by 1978 (in constant dollars). As Senator Mondale succinctly appraised social science research in 1967, "There must be more peaceful and precise ways than riot to measure the state of our social health." At first, little of the increased research money flowed to researchers through NSF, but year by year NSF's share grew; in 1959 the Office of Social Sciences was budgeted at $833,000, but when the Office became a Division in 1960, its budget more than doubled to over $2 million, and thereafter increased year by year to a peak of $52 million in fiscal 1980.

• In 1970, NSF created a new research program within the Division of Social Sciences, the Social Indicators Program; it would develop measures of social change relevant to social policies and point to solutions of social problems. But this seeming advance for social science was a mixed blessing. For one thing, some social scientists opposed making such an important segment of their field directly answerable to policymakers. For another, the Social Indicators Program hardened the animus of conservatives toward government funding of social science research. As David Johnson points out:

> While the [social indicators] experiment was progressive in the eyes of liberals, it seemed to confirm the worst fears of political conservatives about the social sciences...[They felt] that the federal government should not fund social research because doing so could lead only to centralized social engineering, a cardinal sin under the doctrine of conservatism.... [As a result,] the 1970s turned out to be a decade of approach and avoidance for behavioral and social scientists, a decade in which the ideas generated in the 1960s were half tried.[14]

Which means, of course, half *not* tried; despite overall increases in the social sciences budget, congressional advocates of innovative research programs were unable to muster enough support to pass their legislation. Adding insult to injury, in a reorganizational shuffle the Division of Social Sciences was absorbed by a new directorate—the directorates are the major departments within NSF—that included biological sciences, and although social science did not lose research money, it lost some of its hard-won identity and status.

• In the latter part of the 1970s, despite the presidency of Democrat Jimmy Carter, conservatism was gaining strength for a number of reasons, two of which deserve to be named here: the backlash against much of the radicalism and experimentalism of the previous years, and the spreading feeling that the Great Society programs were failing to solve the nation's problems. For both reasons, hostility toward the social sciences rose; they had helped shape the social programs that conservatives thought had not only failed to alleviate the country's ills but was worsening them. (Even some neoconservative social scientists were highly critical of the social science research underlying liberal social programs.[15]) The idea took root among members of the New Right of getting rid of the social programs they saw as harmful by defunding them; their targets included Housing and Urban Development subsidies for low-income housing, the Legal Services Corporation, the population control programs of PHS, and others—plus the social science research programs of NSF and NIMH.

• In the latter 1970s, social science research at NSF was repeatedly attacked in Congress by Representative John Conlan, a Republican from Arizona, and Representative John Ashbrook, a Republican from Ohio.

Conlan, on behalf of religious conservatives who had appealed to him, conducted a vitriolic campaign against a school social studies curriculum called "Man: A Course of Study" that had been developed with funds provided by NSF's Science Education Directorate; he charged that it taught secular rather than Christian values, was communist-inspired (since it espoused cooperation rather than competition), and promoted evolution over other explanations of human development. His allegations drew enough support to produce investigations of the curriculum both by Congress and the General Accounting Office, and for a while, as pressure mounted, not just the education directorate but all of NSF seemed in danger. After lengthy debate, however, Congress settled for cutting out the funding of the "Man" curriculum.

Ashbrook carried out a broader attack: Each year, when the NSF appropriation bill was being debated he would scathingly describe various social science projects as irrelevant, arcane, and a waste of taxpayers' money, and introduce an amendment cutting the social science allocation at NSF. Other representatives, however, defended NSF's social science projects and Ashbrook's amendments were regularly voted down in the House—until 1979, a time when sentiment for general budget reduction had become strong enough to produce an unexpected victory for the Ashbrook amendment. The Senate, however, voted it down, but the message had been delivered loudly and clearly: The House was willing and even eager to prune or even eliminate social science research funding at NSF.[16] To deal a major blow to such research required only that a conservative occupy the White House and appoint fellow conservatives as heads of the major funding agencies and OMB. That, of course, came to pass in 1980.

Major Attack, Major Defense

When Ronald Reagan took office, he made it clear that he would not be bound by either Jimmy Carter's fiscal 1981 budget or his proposed 1982 budget. In charge of Reagan's budget proposals was David Stockman, whom he had appointed as the new head of OMB. Stockman, a conservative congressman from Michigan, had been an outspoken critic of behavioral and social science when he was in the House, and with other conservatives had drafted a model budget, counter to Carter's, that totally eliminated support for what it termed "soft social sciences" at NSF. When Stockman took over at OMB, he moderated this position, but only slightly, recommending a drastic cut of 75 percent for social science research at NSF. He also issued detailed directives aimed at reducing or even eliminating social science research in other agencies; for instance, an OMB directive to the Alcohol, Drug Abuse and Mental Health Administration (ADAMHA) ordered that all social research with implications outside its immediate purview, such as studies of the mental health effects of poor housing, be eliminated.

The official justification for this extreme stance was that social science research was "of relatively lesser importance to the economy than the support of the natural sciences."[17] This was the reason also given for many other Reagan-Stockman proposed cuts in the budget, but Roberta Balstad Miller (who, as we will shortly see, led the social science fight against the administration's proposals) finds it an inadequate explanation and believes that three other factors were probably involved:

> First, many members of the Reagan administration identified social science research with the social policies of former President Lyndon B. Johnson, who built a number of the programs of his Great Society on the findings of social scientists....
>
> A second, related factor...is that many conservatives had long identified social scientists with liberal attitudes and life styles that were out of place in the new administration....
>
> Finally, congressional debates on the value of social science research over the previous several years had demonstrated that there was political capital to be gained from attacks on social science research—at little political cost.[18]

Congress, still under Democratic control, wrestled with the administration over many details of the budget, including the allocation for social science research at NSF, but in the end the national upsurge of conservatism triumphed, and social science at NSF, though not savaged to the extent that Stockman proposed, suffered a far greater reduction than the other sciences. The Carter 1981 budget had allocated $34 million to the Social and Economic Sciences Division; Congress, though it much moderated the Reagan-Stockman 1981 recommendation for a 75 percent slash, cut the Division's allocation by nearly a third to $25 million. (Even so, says Johnson, that severe a cut "devastated" social science research at NSF.) The prospect for 1982 was no better; in fact, the word was already out that the administration would ask for only $10 million for social science research at NSF, all but wiping it out.

* * *

The Reagan administration had operated so swiftly and effectively in its first months that the social science community had been caught unprepared and unable to mount a defense. But it had forewarning and time to do so against the alarming proposal for social science funding for 1982. Although the social science community had no mechanism with which to counterattack, it did have a shadowy entity that could be made into one: From the 1960s on, an informal group of ten societies known as the Consortium of Social Science Associations (COSSA) had existed for the purpose of holding monthly get-togethers to socialize and talk shop. In the winter of 1981, as the Reagan-Stockman budget proposals were being steamrollered through Congress, Ken Prewitt, the head of the Social Science Research Council (SSRC), one of COSSA's constituent groups, asked a handful of social scientists in other organizations belonging to COSSA to meet with him to plan a counterattack; this cadre, after some tug-of-war discussions, agreed to transform COSSA into an active lobbying organization.

A few of the COSSA societies donated enough seed money to hire Roberta Balstad Miller, a historian at SSRC, and Joan Buchanan, a classicist, as COSSA's staff. They moved into an office lent them by APA and got to work on a campaign that was supposed to last three months. Although neither had any lobbying experience, they rapidly learned the rules of the game. They began meeting with staffers of representatives and senators, particularly Republicans (they assumed that most Democrats were already on their side), especially those whose districts included large universities, and presented evidence of the achievements of social science research and the importance of having a strong base for it at NSF. They also contacted other associations of social scientists to enlist their help, and sent word, through the COSSA organizations and others, to thousands of social scientists, asking them to write to their representatives and senators.

It soon became evident that a three-month campaign would not protect social science research from continuing conservative attack during Reagan's four-year and possibly eight-year term of office. The COSSA member organizations decided to keep the activated COSSA going and set it up in its own quarters. Miller took on the nasty chore of calling upon each of the ten-member organizations to ask for financial support, which a guiding committee of the COSSA associations decided should be a pro rata contribution by each association of $2 per social science member. Miller and the committee members also enlarged COSSA's support base by getting a number of other social science associations to sign on as lower-paying affiliates, and a host of universities to become contributors. As the 1982 budget debates neared, Miller and Buchanan arranged appearances by social scientists at hearings, asked sympathetic members of the House if they would make a pro-social science statement during floor debate, wrote statements for those representatives who wanted them to, and held seminars for congressional staffers at which researchers discussed how their work could be put to use in areas of national interest.

The result was that Congress enacted a budget that did far less damage than the Administration had intended: The Reagan-Stockman budget for fiscal 1982 had requested only $10 million for social science research at NSF—two-thirds less than it would have received under the 1981 Carter budget—but Congress appropriated $17.5 million. Social science research at NSF had survived, although on starvation rations; a political base from which to protect such research had been firmly established; and considerable sympathy for social science had been built up within Congress.

All of which was not enough to put social science research on an equal footing with other research at NSF: By the end of the 1980s, although NSF's funding was 30 percent higher (in constant dollars) than at the beginning of the decade, its allocations for the behavioral and social sciences had shrunk by 30 percent.[19] Much the same was true of social science research in other government agencies: During Reagan's eight years in office, the total federal expenditure on all basic science research rose from $4.7 billion to $9.5 billion but for basic social science research had actually shrunk a trifle, from $147.2 million to $146.8 million.[20]

By the beginning of the 1990s, however, the most virulent enemies of social science were gone from the scene: Stockman had long since departed, as had the several representatives and senators who had led the attack on social science research. In 1992, after three years of discussions, reports, task force studies, and conferences about the future of NSF social science, NSF officials decided to create a new Social, Behavioral, and Economic Sciences Directorate, thus giving these sciences status (though not a budget) on a par with the natural sciences. Social science was, finally, at the top of the greasy pole.

The new directorate, since it comprised three fields of science, had a respectable budget of $98 million in fiscal 1994 and $113.8 million in 1995 (three-quarters of which, in each year, was for research), and for 1996 requested $122.9,[21] when, to the astonishment and dismay of social scientists, Robert Walker, chairman of the House Committee on Science and vice chairman of the Committee on the Budget, unexpectedly launched an attack designed to wipe out social- and behavioral science research at NSF.

Crisis

In the first months of 1995, Speaker Newt Gingrich, the commanding general of the victorious Republican forces in the House, installed his choices as chairpersons of congressional committees, urging them to move swiftly to carry out the promises of the Contract With America. John Kasich, chairman of the House Budget Committee, did so by skipping hearings and keeping a meeting of his committee on May 10 going until nearly midnight in order to minimize outside interference while rushing through a report to the House on a budget bill. Under the circumstances, no member of the social science community or its lobbying organizations knew, until the report was a fait accompli, that one of its money-saving recommendations was to eliminate funding for the Social, Behavioral, and Economic Sciences Directorate, thus doing away with research in those disciplines at NSF.[22] The committee's justification of this proposal was that it was part of an effort to focus basic research on what was important to the nation:

> This proposal assumes that while science and technology must contribute to the immediate fiscal reality, they must also provide for the opportunities that must be developed in the future. In order for the technological revolution to continue, a strong, fundamental science is needed. Therefore, the proposal assumes that basic research should be prioritized. For instance, NSF civilian research and related activities with the exclusion of social, behavioral, and economic studies and the critical technologies institute, can be provided at their current levels plus 3% growth.[23]

The syntax of the last sentence is muddy but its message is clear: NSF is to get 3 percent more each year—except for social, behavioral, and economic studies (and the Critical Technologies Institute), which are not to be "provided," that is, not to be funded.

This potentially lethal blow to SBE—potentially, in that a committee report recommends but does not dictate House action—would, if approved by Congress, erase all the gains so slowly made by the social sciences over more than four decades. Naturally, when word of the committee report got out to the social science community, the reaction was one of shock and dismay. Felice Levine, executive director of ASA, characterized it as "our biggest challenge to date," and David Johnson, executive director of the Federation of Behavioral, Psychological and Cognitive Sciences (a coalition of scientific societies, research centers, and graduate departments), said in an emergency e-mail message to all members, "This is the most important crisis these sciences have faced since Ronald Reagan attempted to eliminate the same sciences in the early 1980s."

* * *

The social science community was not only shocked by the proposed defunding of SBE but astonished. One reason for its astonishment was that the proposal had been introduced in the Budget Committee's deliberations by a congressman they considered a friend or, at least, not an enemy, Representative Robert S. Walker. In the new Congress, Walker, a greying and affable but iron-willed man who looks a trifle like Pat Robertson, held two positions critical to NSF funding: vice chairman of the Budget Committee, which recommends budget allocations for science, and chairman of the Committee on Science, which authorizes NSF's annual allocation. A conservative Republican and close colleague of Gingrich, Walker, a member of the Science Committee since his first year in Congress, had always supported basic research in the natural sciences and had not previously exhibited any special animus toward the social sciences. Why, social scientists wondered, was he suddenly its arch-enemy?

A second reason that Howard Silver, director of COSSA, and other social scientists were astonished by the Budget Committee's action was that killing off SBE would save only an inconsequential amount of money. President Clinton's NSF budget request was for $3.26 billion, of which SBE's share was $112.6 million, less than 3½ percent (and less than one percent of all federal funding of basic research).[24] Why aim at so trifling a target?

The answer to both questions, as pieced together by social science lobbyists in the following weeks, was that SBE was a target of opportunity; a proposal to defund it would safely demonstrate Republican seriousness about budget-cutting—safely in that social science research was largely a mystery to the public and had little popular support. But a more fundamental reason was that it was an area of science that conservatives had always regarded as pro-big government and which, in view of their victory in the election, they believed they had popular support to dismantle.[25]

Walker himself had not thought up the proposal about SBE. Important actions by people in Congress are often originated by their staffers, and this was such a case. Chris Wydler, the legislative director of the Science Committee staff, had come across the suggestion to defund SBE in *Budget-Cutting Options for 1995*, a report by the Congressional Budget Office, which named SBE as a good target. (It was, moreover, perhaps the only radical cut at NSF likely to be acceptable to Congress.) Wydler says that the idea was discussed by the staffs at both the Budget and Science Committees, and that he presented it to Walker, who, though not previously actively opposed to social and behavioral science, now decided that SBE's research, so unlike that of the natural sciences, did not fit in with the purposes of NSF and could legitimately be cut.[26] On May 11, the day after the Budget Committee completed its report, Walker held a press conference at which he justified the defunding of SBE:

> In large part, we think that's an area where the National Science Foundation has largely wandered into those areas in recent years, that was a kind of politically correct decision in recent years. And that is a place where the science budgets can be rescoped.* We think that the concentration ought to be in the areas of the physical sciences.[27]

In the byzantine processes of Congress, the Budget Committee's recommendation, to become effective, would require actions by two other committees: the Committee on Science would have to pass a resolution recommending House adoption of a bill "authorizing" the NSF, and the Appropriations Committee would have to pass a resolution recommending passage of a bill appropriating funds for the NSF; each resolution, with each committee's report evaluating the respective bills, would go to the full House. But before either of those committee actions, the Budget Committee's own resolution and report on an overall budget bill had to go to the House, which would vote on the resolution. The first line of defense against the budget report therefore would be an appeal to members of the House to vote no to the resolution.

Howard Silver, who was the first social science lobbyist to hear about the budget report, immediately notified a number of other people—David Johnson of the Federation of Behavioral, Psychological and Cognitive Sciences, Felice Levine of ASA, Alan Kraut of APS, Liz Baldwin of APA, and others—who shortly met to work out a common strategy. Without waiting for that meeting, Johnson decided to issue an "Action Alert" by fax and e-mail to the psychology departments of the top 100 grant-receiving universities in the country rather than start lobbying in the usual fashion. For one thing, there was no time; the bill would be on the House floor within a week. For another, he felt that given the Republican mood and momentum, the usual lobbying methods weren't likely to be effective:

> In the previous months I had been on a number of Hill visits to Republican House offices on other matters and been shocked by what happened. In some cases, offices refused to give appointments. I had never had that experience before. It's bad enough to have people reject your message, but if they reject even your ability to deliver the message, that's *pretty* bad. In offices where I did manage to get in, I was told time and again that we all had to make sacrifices to balance the budget. Basically, I was told to take a hike.

---

*Presumably meaning "redefined as to scope."

Johnson's Action Alert to the 100 top grant-receiving psychology departments produced a swift and predictable flood of responses to Congress. From those departments, which included officers of most of the social science associations in the country, word rapidly spread to those societies and their memberships, producing a far greater volume of messages to legislators. Though Johnson had not thought to suggest that they post the word to web sites, some of them did so, reaching yet other thousands of scientists in the potentially affected disciplines. The results astonished Johnson:

> It was the first time in science lobbying that we made concerted use of electronic communication. We were trying to have that language [about SBE] taken out before the report reached the floor, but there wasn't enough time. But messages began pouring in, and when we went around to the offices of members of the Budget Committee, we learned that they'd been inundated. Thousands came in, literally thousands. Letters came in not just from the U.S. but from all over the world. Word had spread from the departments to which we sent them to what seemed like every social and behavioral scientist on the face of the earth. The letters and phone calls came in like a tidal wave.
>
> But I had committed something of a sin because I didn't warn the other behavioral- and social science lobbyists in town that they might start getting calls—and they got a whole *lot* of calls. They felt they had been blindsided. But after a while a sort of rivalry occurred among the lobbying groups as each one rushed to put its members into e-mail data bases and get information to them. All of us learned that with the electronic tools now available to us, we can in short order create and maintain a massive grassroots movement when the issue is serious enough to warrant it.

But the Republican juggernaut was not to be so easily halted; and on May 18 the House passed a budget resolution, and the report that accompanied it retained the damaging language. Johnson comments:

> The members of Congress at first had no idea what these letters and other messages were referring to. They, after all, hadn't had an opportunity to read the Budget Committee report. The onslaught angered some members of Congress, but it also forced them to take notice. So we actually lost the first round, but we had reason to hope we had made an impression on them.

The hope was that the flood of communications would cause some legislators, particularly those on the other two committees that had some say over NSF matters, to rethink the SBE cut later on. (There was something of a three-way power struggle over NSF appropriations among the Budget Committee, the Science Committee, and the Appropriations Committee; thus there were two fallback positions at which the lobbyists could make a defense.)

Representatives of the major social science lobbying organizations met from time to time, in an informal coalition, to plot a common strategy and divide up the work. Their plan involved visits to the Hill (despite Johnson's recent poor experiences) to talk to staffers and members of both the Science and the Appropriations committees and to various senators (the Senate had remained more amenable to traditional lobbying than the House); visits to AAAS, NAS, NSF itself (where they met with Director Neal Lane, who said he gave his "absolute commitment to SBE"[28]), and the White House Office of Science and Technology Policy; the preparing of background material on the contributions of the affected science for the use of White House staff in speech-writing and briefings; and so on.

* * *

The next battleground would be Walker's Committee on Science, where a bill to authorize NSF could include language defunding or eliminating SBE. Several members of the lobbying coalition who called Walker's office were told by staffers that Walker did not intend to eliminate SBE but to freeze its funding, a distinction hard to make sense of. Before the full Science Committee could consider the bill, its Subcommittee on Basic Research had to do so and render a report to it. The lobbyists had reason to be hopeful. The subcommittee chairman, Steven Schiff, a moderate Republican from New Mexico, had said at a hearing in February that "NSF has nothing but friends in this Subcommittee,"[29] and prior to his subcommittee's meeting in mid-June to consider the NSF authorization bill he told science lobbyists that he did not intend to sacrifice SBE. Keeping his word, he said in his opening remarks at that meeting that he had received many letters on the matter and that his subcommittee would not single out the behavioral and social sciences for extraordinary cuts. The subcommittee, which had heard evidence at earlier hearings of both the fundamental and practical value of SBE research, agreed with the chairman; it voted to recommend NSF authorization without any mention of either defunding or eliminating SBE, though it did say that SBE funding should be cut by the same proportion as that of the other NSF directorates.[*30]

That report went to the full Committee on Science, where it remained to be seen what Walker would do. In early June, in advance of the

---

*Cut in the sense of increased less than requested in the president's budget.

committee's meeting, Neal Lane, director of NSF, Anne Petersen, its deputy director, and Cora Marrett, the assistant director who headed SBE, came to Walker's office at their own request to confer with him in an effort to understand and, they hoped, modify his attitude toward the social and behavioral sciences.[31] Petersen, in an address to APA at its 1996 annual meeting, recalled her impression of Walker's position at that meeting: "He did not know that research supported by NSF in these areas used the same scientific methods as other fields.... Walker also believed that the research questions and conclusions in the social sciences were politically motivated."[32] Marrett got much the same impression; as she recently recalled,

> He had the image of science as the study of nature, and anything that isn't the study of nature isn't science. We had to go over and over that science is the *approach* one uses, not the subject matter itself. After a while he changed his view to say that there wasn't really anything wrong with those areas of science except what he called "drifting"—moving away from fundamental questions to applications to policy, which he didn't see as appropriate for the NSF.

Lane, Petersen, and Marrett, when they left, felt somewhat encouraged, even though it was not clear to them what Walker's intentions now were.

Walker himself does not recall that he changed his views about the social and behavioral sciences as a result of that meeting; he said, when I queried him,

> I never felt that the social and behavioral sciences weren't "real sciences." I'm a social scientist myself! I have a master's in political science, and I have taught it. But I didn't think that there had to be a specific directorate for those sciences in NSF. They should be there, but only in conjunction with other work done at NSF.

His major objection to those sciences, he said, repeating his press conference language, was that "they wandered off into areas that were nonscientific and politically directed." The outcome of the meeting with Lane et al., as he recalls, was that "we arrived at the conclusion that the director should have the flexibility to do the job as he wished," that is, to decide where social/behavioral research should be housed and by whom it should be judged worthy of funding.

David Johnson's recollection of Walker's position is rather different: Based on word relayed to him from a variety of inside sources, he felt that Walker, despite the efforts of the NSF heads, remained unconvinced that the social and behavioral sciences were on a par with the natural sciences:

In his view, the social and behavioral sciences weren't mature enough to take care of themselves; they had to be housed with "real" sciences, where "real" scientists could keep an eye on their research. He hinted that proposals for grants ought to be reviewed by people in the "real" sciences and that people in the behavioral and social sciences weren't able to determine whether proposals were any good or not.

From which it seemed that Walker was moving away from totally defunding social and behavioral research at NSF to some maneuver that would look, though not actually be, less draconian. That maneuver was unveiled when the Science Committee met on June 28 to mark up the authorization bill recommended by the subcommittee: Walker offered an amendment which passed by a party-line vote, requiring the director of NSF to reduce NSF from seven directorates to not more than six. The amendment did not specify which one should be eliminated, but since SBE was by far the smallest and the most recent of the Directorates, it was the only logical candidate for elimination.

Walker, when I questioned him, said flatly, "We never specifically went after SBE. There was no targeting of SBE." He seemed to have forgotten that his committee's report to the House on the authorization bill was quite explicit about its goal:

> In evaluating the NSF organization, it is the view of the Committee that the current Social, Behavioral and Economics (SBE) Directorate should be examined to determine if its current program level reflects sound priorities for overall science funding.... As the newest and smallest Directorate, SBE is the prime candidate for integration into other research Directorates. SBE programs should directly compete for research funds with other disciplines to assure that scarce research dollars are allocated in the national interest.[33]

In other words, SBE's research projects, though not dropped outright, would be dispersed among the other six directorates, where they would be judged worthy or unworthy of funding in comparison to the hard-science projects of those directorates.

The fourteen Democratic members of the Committee wrote a strenuous dissent, included in the printed report, saying, "The Committee's evident intent to eliminate NSF's Social, Behavioral and Economic Sciences (SBE) Directorate is a particularly ill-advised step, taken without the benefit of hearings or opportunities for comment."[34] The dissent, of course, had no effect on the Committee's decision.

* * *

The next step in the tortuous process was the consideration of the actual appropriation for NSF, first by a subcommittee of the House

Appropriations Committee known in brief as VA-HUD (the subcommittee deals with appropriations for the Veterans Administration and a number of other agencies, including NSF), then by the full Committee.

According to Alan Kraut of APS, Walker is thought to have exerted considerable pressure—his status on two committees and his chairmanship of the House Republican Leadership gave him considerable clout—on the chairman of the VA-HUD Subcommittee, Congressman Jerry Lewis, to get language parallel to his SBE amendment included in its appropriations report. But Lewis, a moderate Republican, aware of the torrent of mail protesting the Budget Committee's and Science Committee's attacks on SBE, risked getting in bad with Gingrich by declining to try to include such a provision. In early July the subcommittee sent its report on the appropriations bill to the full Appropriations Committee without recommending or directing a reduction from seven to six NSF directorates,[35] and later that month the full Appropriations Committee marked up the bill, again without including any such recommendation or directive. Its report even included a comment by Democrat Louis Stokes commending NSF for its basic research on violence—a topic Walker had mentioned as an example of problematic SBE research.[36]

The rest is anticlimactic. On July 27 the House debated the VA-HUD appropriations bill and passed it with no proviso to defund or eliminate SBE or its research projects. (Walker did not introduce an amendment to that effect during the House debate because House rules do not allow amendments to appropriations bills to be offered from the floor.) On September 27 the Senate did likewise. A short time later, a House-Senate conference agreed on a final bill, still without such an amendment. The president vetoed the bill (for reasons unrelated to NSF), as he did other Republican budget-cutting appropriations bills in a running conflict with Congress over budget-cutting that caused most of the operations of government to suffer an unprecedented and historic shutdown. By the time Republicans and Democrats found a way to agree to get the government running again, the bill was dead.

* * *

At a hearing on March 22, 1996, the Subcommittee on Basic Science of Walker's Committee on Science, looking ahead toward the next fiscal year's budget, heard testimony by NSF Director Neal Lane and incorporated into the record NSF's 1997 budget request, including $124 million for SBE.[37] Chairman Schiff alluded to earlier discussions of how many

NSF directorates there should be but the subject was not discussed further. He cautioned that "science is included in the discretionary spending portion of the federal budget, and in both Republican and Democratic plans. Increasing pressure is being placed on discretionary spending to balance the budget,"[38] but nothing was said at the hearing or mentioned in the subcommittee report about eliminating SBE or putting its projects under the control of scientists in other Directorates.

When the full Science Committee met in late April, however, Walker renewed his attack, reintroducing the amendment limiting NSF to six assistant directors and therefore to six directorates, and requiring the director to report to Congress by November 15 how he intended to reorganize NSF—that is, which directorate he would scuttle—to achieve this goal.[39] This time, however, although the committee report commented unfavorably on the value of SBE research, it did not suggest that SBE was the directorate that should be eliminated; that decision was left to the Director.

Actually, the social science lobbyists, judging by Walker's statements and activities, got the impression that he was less keenly interested in constraining social and behavioral research than he had been. Perhaps that was because the effort to defund research in those areas had produced such an outcry, or perhaps because he himself was by then a lame duck. He had announced in December that he would not seek reelection in 1996. (He is now the president of the Wexler Group, a Washington consulting firm that advises a number of large corporations as to public affairs and policy, and manages the Science Coalition, a group of science advocacy organizations.).

To the members of the social sciences coalition, Walker's coming retirement from Congress was good news. They hoped, too, that when he left, the new Science Committee chairman might make some changes in staffing; as Alan Kraut candidly put it in a message to his e-mail list, "While it is true that Walker himself was the leading cause of most of our NSF trouble this past year, that trouble was first sparked by staff who may or may not remain with the Committee."[40] And indeed, when Representative Jim Sensenbrenner took over as chairman in late 1996, Chris Wydler left; the informed guess of social science lobbyists is that this was because Sensenbrenner wanted to reduce his committee's conflict with the social science community.

As of this writing, that is where the Forty Years War of conservatives against social and behavioral science research stands. For the moment, all is quiet on the front, but no social science activist I spoke to thinks that the lull means enduring peace. "We've beaten them back as much as we could," says Alan Kraut, "but the danger's not over." The ideological conflict is deeply entrenched, the opposing forces of science and of conservatism are enduring components of American society, and it is not a question of whether but of when conservatives will again mount an attack on the social and behavioral sciences.

Part 3

Attacks from Points in Between

A Prefatory Note

The previous two sections of this book have reported the major recent efforts by groups and individuals on both the far left and the far right to hinder or halt programs of research in the social sciences that threaten their interests or that they find objectionable.

This final section concerns similar efforts by groups and individuals anywhere between the far ends of the political spectrum. There are many such cases; what follows is only a handful of examples of particular interest. Some of them have posed threats to more circumscribed areas of the social sciences than the ones already presented; accordingly, some of the examples presented in this final section are relatively brief.

9

The Assault on Memory Research

Elizabeth Loftus never supposed, when she tried a little experiment on her students in an undergraduate psychology course many years ago, that it would profoundly change her life, steering her onto a track that would lead her to fame and financial success—and on which she would find herself deluged by hate mail, vilified by fellow professionals, and defamed in the media and on the Internet.

It was in the early 1970s that Loftus, a young assistant professor of psychology at the University of Washington, showed some students a brief film of an automobile accident and then asked them "How fast was the car going when it ran the stop sign?" and "How fast was the white sports car going when it passed the barn?" Many of the students remembered seeing the stop sign (actually, it read "YIELD," not "STOP") and the barn (there was no barn).[1] In another experiment she showed students a videotape in which eight demonstrators burst into a classroom to disrupt proceedings; then she asked half of her students "Was the leader of the four demonstrators who entered the classroom a male?" and the other half the same question but substituting "twelve" for "four." A week later, she asked the same students how many demonstrators there had been; the "four" contingent averaged 6.4, the "twelve" contingent nearly 9.[2]

Loftus, who had been interested in memory for some years, had begun to wonder whether experiences are preserved intact in the mind and can be retrieved unchanged, or are subject to additions and distortions when other information or misinformation is fed into memory or other influences, such as mood, modify them. The little experiments with which she began to explore this subject yielded preliminary but striking evidence that our memories of experiences are not permanent recordings but, as she later wrote, "are flexible and superimposable, a panoramic blackboard with an endless supply of chalk and erasers."[3] Other later experiments confirmed and strengthened her hypothesis that memory, once modified, no longer exists in its original form; no pristine copy exists, hidden somewhere, that can be found and retrieved by suggestion, reflection, or hypnosis.[4] This is not to say that all memories are inaccurate; rather, says Loftus, "We have a mechanism for updating memory that sometimes leaves the original memory intact, but sometimes does not."[5]

The brilliant William James, America's first psychologist, had intuited the malleability of memory nearly a century earlier, although he conducted no experiments to test his guess and prove his point. In his classic *Principles of Psychology* he had simply stated as a fact what he felt to be true:

> False memories are by no means rare occurrences in most of us.... The most frequent source of false memory is the accounts we give to others of our experiences. Such accounts we almost always make both more simple and more interesting than the truth.... Ere long the fiction expels the reality from memory and reigns in its stead alone. This is one great source of the fallibility of testimony meant to be quite honest.[6]

Loftus is one of a small group of contemporary experimentalists who have used the methods of empirical science to verify the hypothesis that memories are subject to modification and that, once a memory has been modified, no original remains in the mind. Ever since her first modest experiments, she has been diligently exploring, in the laboratory and in the outside world, why we remember, why we forget—and why we often "remember" what never happened. She has become a leading expert on memory, a prolific author of research papers, one of the best-known and most-often cited psychologists in the country, and the recipient of three honorary doctorates. Because her special knowledge is pertinent to cases of "recovered memory" of childhood sexual molestation and crimes witnessed during childhood, she has been an expert witness, at handsome fees, in more than 200 trials, and unlike many an academic, has a very comfortable life-style.[7]

On the down side, Loftus has made a host of angry, vindictive, and often aggressive enemies who have tried to discredit her findings, besmirch her reputation, and harass her in an effort to force her to abandon her research or, at least, stop lecturing, publishing, and presenting research evidence at recovered-memory lawsuits.

The reason for this enmity is that her research findings contradict the central claim of the many therapists who now specialize in inducing adult patients to recover what are purported to be accurate memories of shocking and vicious sexual molestation in the patients' childhood.

Loftus's findings have also enraged many feminists who feel that the recovered memories truthfully represent what a great many female children suffer at the hands of sadistic and lustful fathers, brothers, uncles, and other adult males.

* * *

Loftus is only one of a number of memory experts who have come under intense fire in recent years, but her case can be taken as typical. Her bitterest enemies are the latest participants in a mania that has recurred a number of times over the centuries, taking various forms but in each case the affected persons, or at least their leaders, have used whatever means they could to overpower or even destroy those who sought to shed the light of reason on the subject.

The most prolonged and destructive episode of the mania, lasting from the fifteenth through much of the sixteenth century, took the form of the belief, widespread in Europe, in witchcraft. Not surprisingly, most common folk believed in it, but so did many of the more educated classes. Indeed, it was literate and well-read clerics who believed in it most strongly and battled witches with greatest fervor. The Church's Inquisitors headed the fight, obtaining detailed admissions of witchcraft and satanic practices, usually by means of torture, from thousands of women. Many of the accused may well have believed by the end of the process that they must have done what their accusers got them to say they did—cast spells on people, made men impotent, turned milk sour, summoned up plagues of locusts, participated in Black Masses (Witches' Sabbaths), and copulated with the Devil himself. Confession and contrition did not save the torturers' victims; in the middle of the sixteenth century, one officer of the Inquisition estimated that the Holy Office had burned at least 30,000 witches in the previous century and a half, thereby preserving the world from destruction.[8]

Eventually witch-hunting died down for some time—only to flare up briefly again and again. In America, a particularly sordid outbreak was the spell of witchcraft mania in Salem, Massachusetts in 1692–93, when a number of hysterical young girls, some of whom seem to have really believed their fantasies, accused several old women of bewitching them. When the accusations succeeded—the old women were arrested and held for trial—the girls widened the scope of their charges more and more. Within a matter of months hundreds had been arrested and tried, many of whom, hoping to save themselves, confessed to minor improprieties but accused others of serious and even abominable practices; eventually, fourteen women and five men were hanged, and one man, who particularly exasperated the court by refusing to plead either guilty or not guilty, was subjected to the dreadful medieval penalty of being pressed to death by heavy weights. But when the witchfinders began to accuse prominent people such as the Boston clergy and wealthy merchants, the frenzy was called to a halt; at the urging of Increase Mather and other influential clergymen, the Massachusetts assembly dissolved the special court and released some 150 prisoners awaiting trial, most of whom would likely have been condemned to death. Twenty years later, looking back on the outbreak with perspective, the Massachusetts courts annulled the convictions of the condemned witches and indemnified their relatives.[9]

Although Sigmund Freud had nothing in common with either the fifteenth-century Inquisitors or the Salem accusers, he, too, briefly believed in the reality of induced narrations of vile experiences. In the 1890s, when he was first developing psychoanalytic therapy, he suspected that sexual problems were the cause of many or most of the neurotic disorders of his patients. By means of persistent questioning he was repeatedly able to get patients to recall, after considerable effort, that in childhood they had been sexually molested by adults in ways ranging from being fondled to being raped. The perpetrators were domestic servants, teachers, older brothers, and, most shockingly, fathers.[10]

Freud, amazed, thought that he had made a major discovery and made his findings known in a lecture and a published paper, but his so-called seduction theory was ill-received by the medical community and temporarily all but ruined his practice. He himself slowly came to doubt the validity of his theory, one reason being that he was having only limited success treating patients who had unearthed such recollections, another reason that he was finding it ever harder to believe that molestation by fathers of their own daughters could be as widespread as his patients' recollections made it seem. He finally concluded that the memories his patients were unearthing were not of actual events but of childhood fantasies and desires of being seduced by males important in their lives, especially their fathers.

Freud published this radically different interpretation of his patients' seduction memories in part in 1900, and more fully in 1905, and his new view of the matter was widely accepted by Freudians and other practitioners of talk therapies for many decades. But in the mid-1980s there was a remarkable outbreak of child-abuse cases in this country, much of it at first consisting of accusations that day-care workers had sexually abused the children in their care, not only copulating with them or making them do so with each other, but committing such bizarre acts as making the children drink urine, inserting knives and other objects into their sexual organs, and forcing them to witness the torture of animals and take part in satanic rituals.[11] In most cases, the children did not remember the abuse until questioned by therapists or other investigators who patiently and repeatedly asked suggestive and leading questions, eventually producing what were believed to be recovered memories.

From day-care workers, the roster of the accused grew and grew; it came to include parents, siblings, and other adults as malefactors who had subjected children to sexual acts, often perverse and horrific, which the children had totally repressed but which they recalled in therapy many years later. Hundreds of lawsuits were instituted by adult children against their parents and others whose depraved treatment of them they had had no notion of over the years until, under the guidance of recovered-memory therapists, they retrieved lost memories of them. Thousands of people discovered they had had such experiences, and rape relief organizations asserted that one in four women and one in six men had been sexually abused as children.[12] The memories of such abuse, although totally buried in the unconscious until recovered, were identified by the therapists as the source of the patients' symptoms of emotional disorder, although, strangely, in a number of cases the disorders grew worse rather than better after the alleged memories had been retrieved.

Two social phenomena that burgeoned and coalesced in the 1980s, the women's movement and the growth of day care, provided the environment in which recovered-memory therapy became a fad and claims of remembered sexual abuse became epidemic. Sexual abuse was a focus of the women's movement because, say researchers Janice Haaken and Astrid Schlaps, "It represented the convergence of clinical knowledge and feminist consciousness. Feminist analyses of abuse within the family and feminist challenges to authoritarian practices became a palpable presence in the discourse on sexual abuse."[13] At the same time, the rising divorce rate and increasing entry of mothers of young children into the workplace was greatly expanding the need for and facilities for day care; the expansion inevitably increased the number of reports or accusations of the sexual abuse of children in day-care centers. With the development and widening use of techniques of eliciting repressed and presumably recovered memories, some of these cases produced a crop of sensational and revolting details that were widely and repeatedly presented in the popular media.

* * *

The opposition to researchers like Loftus and their work thus come from three sources: militant feminists, for whom the recovered-memory syndrome is a potent weapon in their political struggle; recovered-memory therapists, for whom the retrieval of repressed memories is good business and offers important opportunities to make one's name known (and many of whom are deeply convinced of the reality of the memories they elicit); and survivors, for whom the discovery of the presumable source of their personal problems is, or promises to be, a great liberation, and who are furious when anyone, even a respected and scrupulous researcher, casts doubt on the reality of their recovered memories.

As the recovered-memory movement caught on, a number of therapists, motivated by conviction and rage, developed methods of evoking memories that violate the canons of accepted and ethical psychotherapeutic technique. They suggest to the patient that she (or he) may have had such experiences but repressed them; they tell patients that their symptoms sound very much like those produced by child abuse; they advise them that the very denial of such abuse or the inability to recall it is itself an indication that it happened (and that the memories are repressed); they offer details of specific acts and urge their patients to try hard to remember that they happened.[14] In some cases, recovered memories of sexual abuse have been corroborated by other witnesses or by evidence such as medical records showing trauma to the child's sexual parts, but many or most cases have no such confirmation.[15] (One measure of the frequency of corroboration: the South Dakota Department of Social Services reported that in 1994, of more than 10,000 reports of child abuse, only 1,923—19 percent— could be substantiated.[16])

The Council on Scientific Affairs of the American Medical Association, after studying the retrieval of memories of childhood abuse, deplored the use of leading questions and suggestions in the effort to recover repressed memories of abuse:

> It is well established for example that a trusted person such as a therapist can influence an individual's reports, which would include memories of abuse. Indeed, as the issue of repressed memories has grown, there have been reports of therapists advising patients that their symptoms are indicative—not merely sug-

gestive—of having been abused, even when the patient denies having been abused.[17]

The Council recommended that the AMA adopt, among other findings of the Council,

- That the AMA recognize that few cases in which adults make accusations of childhood sexual abuse based on recovered memories can be proved or disproved and it is not yet known how to distinguish true memories from imagined events in these cases....

- That Policy 515.978 be amended by insertion and deletion to read as follows: The AMA considers recovered memories of childhood sexual abuse to be of uncertain authenticity, which should be subject to external verification. The use of recovered memories is fraught with problems of potential misapplication.

Less tactfully, the sociologist Richard Ofshe, who has closely studied the recovered-memory movement, has called it "one of the century's most intriguing quackeries."[18]

In a recent critical overview of the recovered-memory phenomenon in the *New England Journal of Medicine*, Fred Frankel of Boston's Beth Israel Hospital and Harvard Medical School, points out that the case for repression of traumatic memories rests largely on anecdote, that "there are no compelling findings to support the practice of a therapy aimed specifically at the recovery of memories that have been totally unsuspected and absent since childhood," and that there is a "lack of evidence that any special type of psychological procedure or practice is capable, even in trained hands, of leading people to recover memories that can be accepted as valid without corroboration."[19]

* * *

That being the case, it is obvious that further research is urgently needed. But those whose research casts doubt on the authenticity of any, let alone many, recovered memories have experienced intense hostility, often in the form of unethical and destructive acts intended to harm the careers and halt the work of the researchers. A few examples:

- The veteran sex researcher Vern Bullough writes:

   Recently I attended the CSICOP conference (Committee for the Scientific Investigation of the Claims of the Paranormal) and found that all those attending the conference had received a letter denouncing Paul Kurtz, myself, and the magician Randi, for pedophilia, largely because we have been critical of some of the books and articles on recovered memory.[20]

- A number of skeptics and critics of the recovered-memory phenomenon have been castigated in articles and popular books written by the practitioners of repressed-memory recovery, charged with using their research "to hide truths and support lies," and accused of "antisurvivor" prejudice ("survivors" are persons who are said to have been sexually abused in childhood and, as adults, have symptoms suggestive of repressed memories).[21]

- Dr. Harold Lief, a distinguished sex therapist and professor emeritus of psychiatry at the University of Pennsylvania, was invited by McGill University in 1993 to deliver a lecture on "True and False Accusations by Adult 'Survivors' of Childhood Sex Abuse." He came prepared to offer research data in a temperate, evenhanded approach, but the audience was thoroughly infiltrated by survivors and activist members of the Canadian Psychological Association's Section on Women and Psychology (SWAP) who were determined to prevent any presentation of data casting doubt on their claims. A gleeful report of the occasion by one of the activists in a SWAP newsletter reads, in part:

  > At McGill, Dr. Lief didn't stand a chance. He was drowned out, reduced to a whisper, by the jeering, whistling, coughing, shouts and rattling noisemakers of survivors.... Using his wits, or at least any wits he had left, Dr. Lief went on, "There are some fools here. Some people with small minds, who are intent on disrupting freedom. They may succeed, but at a price to themselves and others who came to hear me speak." That really won the audience over. Utter chaos ensued. For five minutes. Now there was no way of pacifying the audience.... Now they could stand and shout, "No more!" And that's exactly what they did.[22]

- Pamela Freyd, executive director of the False Memory Syndrome Foundation (about which more below), says that virtually every conference at which the false memory syndrome is to be discussed and research presented is attacked in the media and on the Internet as biased, unscientific, and prejudiced against survivors, and the participating speakers are harshly criticized and defamed.[23] Although disruptive demonstrations do not occur at every such conference, they are common.

- Elizabeth Loftus, having continued to do research on the distortion and confabulation of memories, and to present her evidence at many trials of people accused of sexual abuse of children on the basis of recovered memories, has been subjected to more acts of hostility by survivors, recovered-memory therapists, and feminist activists than almost anyone else in the field. She has been called a whore in a courthouse hallway, labeled "prejudiced" and "a sloppy researcher" in the *Harvard Mental Health Letter*, assaulted by a fellow passenger on an airplane (the middle-aged woman sitting next to her, on learning who she was, began swatting her on the head with a rolled-up newspaper), accused in hate mail of collaborating with satanists and of being akin to extremist bigots who say the Holocaust never happened, threatened with lawsuits and with violence, and obliged to have armed guards at some of her lectures.[24] "The hatred of my enemies has grown and magnified in the last few years," she says. "It's as though

I'm a symbol of something that is beyond me and who I really am." If she were not made of tough stuff (beneath her genial and warm exterior) and did not have a substantial income as an expert witness, she would have had to abandon the fight long ago.

* * *

There are, however, some indications that the recovered-memory fad is beginning to abate, which suggests that opposition to the work of researchers like Loftus is likely to wane in the future.

An increasing number of survivors have retracted their accusations and characterized them as false memories, and some have sued their therapists.[25] A 1997 survey by the False Memory Syndrome Foundation found that 7 percent of adult accusers said they had retracted their accusations, and about 25 percent had returned to their families but declined to discuss what had happened.[26]

A number of convictions based on recovered memories have recently been reversed on various grounds. Two of the most notorious persons convicted on such testimony, George Franklin and John Quattrocchi, have both been released from prison; Franklin has filed suit against his daughter and the expert witness in the case. A minister in New York was freed after ten years, as were two couples in California after fourteen years, in each case because of decisions that were tardily overturned.[27]

Some accused parents have sued recovered-memory therapists, a few winning substantial damages, and some patients treated by recovered-memory methods have won major damages from those who treated them. In 1996 a Missouri church agreed to pay $1 million to a woman who, under the guidance of a church counselor, came to believe that her father had raped her and, when she became pregnant, aborted her with a coat hanger (in fact, she was still a virgin and her father had had a vasectomy).[28] In a 1996 California case, parents who had been accused of sexual abuse on the basis of recovered memory won $1.9 million in damages, and in a 1997 Wisconsin case parents similarly accused won $2.4 million. Most recently and spectacularly, in late 1997 a woman named Patricia Burgus won a $10.6 million settlement in her case against Rush-Presbyterian-St. Lukes Medical Center of Chicago and two of its doctors. While undergoing psychiatric therapy at the hospital from 1986 to 1992, including the use of hypnosis and medication, Burgus had become convinced that as a child she had taken part in ritual murders, cannibalism, and Satan worship, and had often been sexually abused and tortured by family members—all of which she later concluded had been false memories instilled in her by the doctors.[29]

In various states, an increasing number of convictions based on re-membered abuse have been appealed to higher courts. Such courts have regularly overturned the convictions by refusing to extend the statute of limitations for repressed-memory accusations, or have ordered trial courts to explore the reliability of the claims before allowing the cases to proceed.[30] In contrast to the upsurge in appeals scheduled to be heard in higher courts, there are now hardly any new remembered-abuse cases at the trial level. (Some new cases, however, are being brought on the grounds that only now has the appellant recognized the damage done long ago by recovered-memory therapy.[31])

Pamela Freyd, an educator, and her husband Peter Freyd, a professor of mathematics at the University of Pennsylvania, were accused by their daughter some years ago of numerous sexual abuses when she was a child, her evidence being recovered memories. (The daughter, Jennifer Freyd, is a professor of psychology at the University of Or-egon.) After a number of attempts at reconciliation failed, in 1992 Pamela Freyd decided to combat the recovered-memory movement by establishing the False Memory Syndrome Foundation to gather and disseminate legal and research developments in the field in its ten-issues-per-year publication, *FMS Foundation Newsletter*. The need for such a foundation can be gauged by its success: It has attracted nearly 3,000 member families, been contacted by more than 18,000 families that say they have had problems with recovered memories, has an an-nual budget of $750,000 from dues and contributions (it has no other support), and has a professional advisory board of some fifty eminent psychologists and psychiatrists, including Aaron Beck, Rosalind Cartwright, Frederick Crews, Rochel Gelman, Henry Gleitman, Lila Gleitman, Richard Green, Ernest Hilgard, Harold Lief, Ulric Neisser, Martin Orne, and Thomas Sebeok.

And, of course, Elizabeth Loftus.

10

Harming Harm-Reduction Research

Because substance abuse has become so serious a problem in our society, one might suppose that research testing a new way to lessen the damage it does or evaluating the benefit/harm ratio of that way would encounter no political opposition. Who, after all, could be against such research?

The answer is, regrettably, all too many people, namely, the members of organizations already established in the fight against substance abuse. If the research supports a form of treatment different from theirs, or yields evidence that theirs is not very effective, they will try to discredit the methodology, blacken the reputation of the researchers, cut off their funding, or use any other method of opposition that can interfere with the acquisition of findings they do not want to hear of, and want no one else to hear of.

The issue is not so much one of political ideology as of the challenge to dominance of their turf. In both cases to be presented here, researchers investigated "harm reduction" methods of dealing with addiction; in one they espoused it, in the other, found fault with it, but in each case they challenged a preferred, institutionalized approach and brought down on themselves, in one instance, a hailstorm of vilification, and in the other, administrative measures that cost them their jobs and ended their research funding.

The Controlled-Drinking Rhubarb

The Eighteenth Amendment, establishing prohibition and ratified in 1919, was an effort to impose abstinence on all Americans. It failed and was repealed in 1933, but because alcoholism was a severe social problem, the alternative advocated after the repeal of prohibition was the promotion of total abstinence for those who could not control their drinking or their behavior when they drank. Problem drinking, no longer illegal and not generally regarded as immoral, as in the temperance days, was redefined as a symptom of an underlying disease that made the alcoholic unable to control his or her use of alcohol; the alcoholic was not a wrongdoer but a helpless victim.[1]

Two social institutions promulgated this view. One was the medical community: The American Medical Association first labeled alcoholism a disease in 1956, and the details of the "disease model" of alcoholism, elaborated over the next several decades, were summarized in the *Journal of the American Medical Association* in 1992 by the Joint Committee of the National Council on Alcoholism and Drug Dependence and the American Society of Addiction Medicine. In that statement, alcoholism was defined as a "primary, chronic disease with genetic, psychosocial, and environmental factors influencing its development and manifestations."[2]

The other institution promoting the disease model of alcoholism was Alcoholics Anonymous, which had been founded in 1935 and, after a long period of slow growth, blossomed into a major national movement in the 1960s. The AA doctrine is that the disease, though incurable, is controllable—but only through total abstinence, which is achieved through a twelve-step program that must be adhered to religiously.

Both within the medical establishment and AA, the disease model became the orthodox conception of alcoholism, embraced with much of the fervor of the nineteenth-century temperance movement. According to this view, one either has or does not have the disease—there is no middle ground—and there is no alternative treatment. However, a dissenting minority opinion has long existed that sees drinking not as an either-or phenomenon but as a variety of behaviors ranging along a continuum from the least harmful to the most harmful. In this view, the goal of the treatment of problem drinking should be "harm reduction"— the modification of the drinker's behavior from the very harmful to the less harmful or even harmless. For many problem drinkers (though not the most severe ones), harm reduction is said to be achievable through behavioral training aimed not at total abstinence but at controlled, limited drinking.[3]

* * *

The continuum view had been espoused two centuries ago by none other than the great Dr. Benjamin Rush, the eminent physician (and signer of the Declaration of Independence), although he had no research evidence that a problem drinker could be taught to drink within socially acceptable boundaries. The first such evidence was offered in 1962 by D. L. Davies, a British physician and alcohol researcher at the Maudsley Hospital in London; Davies had conducted a follow-up study of ninety-three male alcoholics, seven to eleven years after treatment; although the hospital's program had promoted total abstinence, seven of the ninety-three reported that they had come to use alcohol in a normal, controlled fashion.[4] It was a startling finding that controverted accepted beliefs; the evidence, however, was very limited. For one thing, seven out of ninety-three was not much to brag about; for another, the therapy they had received had not been intended to yield normal, controlled drinking, so that it remained unclear that such a result could be deliberately brought about. A later reevaluation of Davies' paper also suggested that the patients were not really, as Davies had indicated, "gamma" alcoholics, which cast further doubt on its implications for treatment.*[5]

But in 1969, two young researchers, Mark Sobell, a heavily and darkly bearded twenty-six-year-old graduate student of psychology at the University of California at Riverside, and his attractive twenty-two-year-old girlfriend and wife-to-be, Linda, an undergraduate—both went on to earn doctorates in psychology—started a small but potentially significant research project at Patton State Hospital, a psychiatric facility in San Bernardino operated by the State of California. Forty men addicted to (physically dependent on) alcohol agreed to participate in an experiment in which they were randomly assigned either to an experimental group or to a control group. Those in the experimental group received seventeen sessions of behavioral training (behavior modification was, at that time, a relatively new and promising form of therapy). The training took place in a special setting, constructed within the hospital, resembling a living room and a bar. The treatment conducted by the Sobells and six members of their staff consisted of videotaping the participants' behavior when they were intoxicated and having them view the tapes later, teaching them problem-solving and other skills for handling anxiety-producing situations by means other than drinking, training them to drink in moderation (no gulping), administering aversive conditioning (electrical shock therapy) when they did gulp, and generally educating them about drinking and the effects of alcohol.[6] The

---

*Gamma alcoholism is characterized by physical dependence with withdrawal symptoms and loss of control.

patients in the control group, in contrast, received only the conventional abstinence training provided by the hospital.

After the patients were discharged from the hospital program, Linda Sobell and several staff members followed them up for a year (Linda Sobell continued the follow-ups for a second year), primarily by telephone but also by means of objective public data such as records of hospital admissions, jail admissions, and driving violations, plus interviews with collateral informants. Although the experimental and control groups were small, the difference in outcomes was large enough to be statistically significant (that is, very unlikely to have been due to chance): During the first follow-up year, the twenty patients who had had controlled-drinking treatment functioned well an average of 71 percent of all days, the twenty who had had abstinence training only 35 percent, and during the second year the controlled-drinking trainees functioned well 85 percent of all days, the abstinence trainees 42 percent. The Sobells cautiously refrained from concluding that controlled drinking was the panacea for alcoholism, suggesting only that it might be a preferable treatment goal for some alcoholics.[7]

They published their first findings in 1973 in the journal *Behavior Therapy*, their further findings in 1976 in the journal *Behavior Research Therapy*, and their first decade's results in a 1978 book, *Behavioral Treatment of Alcohol Problems*. From 1973 on, their work aroused growing and eventually widespread interest among behavior therapy researchers, some of whom undertook similar studies, and among behavior therapists, many of whom adopted the Sobells' methods and inaugurated treatment programs. But in the traditional treatment community the Sobells' work was scorned and even reviled, although seldom at important conferences and meetings—not out of good manners but because the treatment community ignored their work and all but ostracized them. Mark Sobell comments:

> The twelve-step abstinence program dominated the field and our work was opposed with great ideological fervor. There were no demonstrations against us, but we had a number of distinctly unpleasant personal discussions with people who would brook no deviation from the party line. But we weren't invited to meetings and conferences like those of the National Council on Alcoholism; we were persona non grata. The ideological fervor took the form of dreadful things that people throughout the treatment community would say about us and about our work, and that we heard about only at second hand; we'd speak somewhere and afterwards people would come up to us and tell us what was being said about us by traditionalists in the field. We had had no idea that our work would arouse such fierce opposition.

If we had known, would we have undertaken such research? In hindsight, yes—but maybe I say so because our research did work out and helped advance the field, although of course we couldn't have known in advance that that would be the case.

* * *

Unhappily for the Sobells, the ideological fervor also took another and far worse form. At the time of their first research project, the chairman of the department of psychology at UCLA was a psychologist named Irving Maltzman, who, like the Sobells, was particularly interested in behavioral conditioning, a field he had worked in for some years. After the Sobells' 1973 report of the successful outcome of their experiment in controlled drinking, Maltzman received a proposal from an assistant professor in his department who was applying for a training grant based on the Sobells' method. Maltzman was both interested and troubled:

> I'd heard vaguely about their work and it interested me because my career had been in the area of learning and conditioning. The grant proposal sounded fascinating—finally there was some practical application of conditioning studies.' But I was bothered by the idea, in the applicant's proposal, that undergraduate students would go into sleazy bars with patients and train them to control their drinking by telling them things like, "Don't drink straight whiskey," "Don't drink when you're alone," and so on. I wouldn't let one of those kids train my dog, let alone take a Korean War veteran into a bar to train him. It didn't seem reasonable.
>
> So I called a former student of mine, Mary Pendery, who'd gotten her Ph.D. in 1968 and was doing treatment of alcoholics, and I asked her what she thought of this project. She and I went to the hospital to see what we could learn, but by then the Sobells had closed down their simulated bar and left. However, people on the staff told us they saw many of the treated people coming back for further treatment. Mary said maybe we should do a follow-up study, and the hospital approved it—but we found that the records had disappeared.

Mark Sobell's recollection:

> In 1973 we learned from the hospital that there was a request for a list of the subjects' identities for a follow-up study, and that Pendery and Maltzman were the ones who wanted to do the study. But due to cutbacks, the hospital had destroyed the research records when we closed down the project. We had the identities in our own files, of course, but we didn't know what Pendery and Maltzman had in mind, and we questioned the advisability of having independent follow-ups, since we were still completing odds and ends of our own follow-up study and felt that another follow-up would interfere with our research. But we were basi-

---

'Maltzman's recollection is inaccurate; behavior therapy, using conditioning techniques, had become well established in the 1960s.

cally pretty open-minded about it at the time, and we contacted Maltzman and arranged to meet with him and Pendery.

Maltzman recalls the meeting:

> Mark Sobell called me and was quite upset that we had proposed to do a follow-up study without consulting him. I apologized, and we had a meeting in San Diego in 1973. In our proposal we named the counselor who would do the follow-up work, and Mark said that we could work together but that he and Linda objected to our choice of counselor. They said that that person had poor evaluations, and was untrustworthy as to confidentiality. We couldn't agree on the matter, and ended the meeting without resolving the situation.

Now there was deep distrust on both sides. The Sobells suspected that Maltzman and Pendery had more of an agenda than merely an independent follow-up, and they were right. Maltzman and Pendery were by now convinced, he as a behavior psychologist and she as an alcoholism therapist and former alcoholic, that it had been "a lousy study" (Maltzman's words); they suspected that there was something fishy about the Sobells' refusal to cooperate and that an independent follow-up might expose serious weaknesses in the reported success of controlled-drinking treatment.

Maltzman and Pendery decided to carry out their own follow-up without the Sobells' cooperation. It took them a couple of years of legal maneuvering to extract the list of names of the treated people from state agencies, but finally they had the list and Pendery, rather than the counselor they had originally planned to use, was about to start follow-up interviews with the former patients, when she, Maltzman, and the director of the hospital were sued for invasion of privacy in a class action suit initiated by the subjects of the study at the Sobells' urging. That froze the Maltzman-Pendery investigation for a long while, the suit dragging on until 1976. Pendery and Maltzman were represented in the continuing action at no cost to them by the U. S. Attorney General and the California Attorney General, but the Sobells were represented by their own lawyer at their expense, and in view of his estimate that it would cost them $50,000 to $60,000 to get to trial, they finally dropped the suit.

Thus freed to go ahead, Pendery set out to do what she had been itching to do for almost four years and soon found what she was looking for in the form of a statement by one of the former patients that Linda Sobell had called him only two or three times over a two-year follow-up period and had asked only, "How are you doing?" (The

Sobells' published studies give a very different account: The average patient was contacted monthly for two years and interviewed in detail. Mark Sobell later amended this, saying the average patient had been contacted fifteen times in the course of the two-year follow-up.[8]) Maltzman continues his account:

> Then a second and a third patient said much the same thing. One of them told us he'd gotten a letter from a lawyer telling him that he was going to be asked for an interview and that if he was disturbed by the invasion of his privacy, he should get in touch with the Sobells' lawyer. That's when we realized there was fraud.

Or at least that was Pendery and Maltzman's interpretation of the patients' recollections of the follow-up interviews. The Sobells say that the patients' recollections of the follow-up calls, so many years afterward, were subjective and inaccurate but that their own records of the calls are objective and accurate.

By 1982, Pendery and Maltzman had completed their follow-up study and were ready to fire pointblank. As a target, the Sobells were far more important than they had been nine years earlier, when they published their first report on the controlled-drinking project; since then they had published a number of other articles in important journals, written or edited three books, given a number of invited presentations, won a number of awards and citations, and achieved considerable renown and acceptance among behavior therapists, teachers, and nontraditional segments of the alcohol treatment community. They had also been subjected to considerable harsh and even virulent criticism, as Alan Marlatt, a professor of psychology at the University of Washington, who also had been doing research in controlled drinking, recalls:

> After the publication of the Sobells' 1978 book and a book of proceedings of a 1977 controlled drinking conference in Norway with material in it by me and the Sobells and others, criticism started to mount. Disease model people and AA people and treatment center people all accused us of being murderers. They said that alcoholics can never drink, so that what the Sobells and I were advocating was in effect murder. The Sobells drew most of the fire at first; later I came in for a lot of it.

None of this abuse and saber-rattling had prepared the Sobells for the published attack by Pendery and Maltzman, who, acting as the unofficial SWAT team of the "abstinence lobby" (as the proponents of the disease model are sometimes called), wrote a report of their follow-up study (co-authored by L. Jolyon West, a colleague at the UCLA School of Medicine) that torpedoed and very nearly sank the Sobells' reputation and the controlled-drinking approach. The article, "Controlled Drinking by Alcoholics? New Findings and a Reevaluation of a Major Affirmative Study," appeared in the AAAS's weekly flagship journal *Science* in July, 1982, after an earlier draft had been rejected as libelous. The authors' answer to the question they posed in the title was a definite No. Pendery et al. had been able to track down some of the subjects, gather data on hospitalizations and arrests on some others, and locate death reports on four others. In the ten years since the end of the Sobells' experiment, they reported, only one patient had maintained a pattern of controlled drinking; the others had either relapsed or had had to resort to abstinence, or died. Pendery et al. also charged that the treatment and control groups had not been genuinely comparable and that the treatment group should, if anything, have fared better than it had. Their harsh conclusion:

> Reports of the Sobells' study have influenced some clinicians, researchers, teachers, and students to believe that controlled drinking is not only feasible for a significant proportion of *gamma* alcoholics, but also for some may even be more attainable and safer than a goal of abstinence.
>
> The results of our independent follow-up of the same subjects, based on official records, affidavits, and interviews, stand in marked contrast to the favorable controlled drinking outcomes reported by the Sobells.... [and others]. Our follow-up revealed no evidence that *gamma* alcoholics had acquired the ability to engage in controlled drinking safely after being treated in the experimental program.[9]

Maltzman later went much further, repeatedly and publicly characterizing the Sobells' 1973 study as fraud.[10]

* * *

The Sobells were both sickened by the article and aggrieved by *Science's* handling of it; the journal had not, as is customary in academic publishing, shown them the article in advance nor offered them space for a rebuttal. They did, however, reply elsewhere; in several detailed articles they painstakingly dismantled the case made by Pendery et al. and pinpointed a number of misinterpretations, distortions, and errors in their article. As they sum up their rebuttal in an article in *Behaviour Research and Therapy*:

> The Pendery et al. critique *gave the appearance* of being a refutation by presenting findings for only one group of Ss in a comparative study. In this response, it is shown that the experimental and control Ss [subjects] were justifiably classified as *gamma* alcoholics, that Ss were randomly assigned to groups, and that the two groups were comparable in terms of pretreatment characteristics. Moreover, as

regards the originally reported 2-yr treatment outcome findings, it is shown that Pendery et al. reported no specific events which were not already documented in the original study records.... Finally, even in terms of long-term outcomes, i.e., mortality rates 10–11 yr after treatment, the experimentally-treated group (20% mortality) continued to fare better than the traditionally-treated group (30% mortality).... The attack on the IBTA study [the Sobells' study] can be meaningfully viewed as a reflection of the scientific revolution presently underway in the alcohol field.[11]

The Pendery et al. conclusion that there is no evidence that controlled drinking treatment works has also been called in question by the research findings of a number of other researchers, some of them, Alan Marlatt among them, of considerable distinction, who also have reported success in studies of controlled drinking treatment. As for the charges that the Sobells' follow-up was fudged and made to look far more thorough than it was, three later investigations found to the contrary. One, a five-month investigation of all available documents and records conducted by the Dickens Commission, an independent committee appointed by the Sobells' then employer, the Addiction Research Foundation of Toronto, concluded, "The Committee finds there to be no reasonable cause to doubt the scientific or personal integrity of either Dr. Mark Sobell or Dr. Linda Sobell."[12] Later, because the Sobells were receiving federal funding for their continued research, the Subcommittee on Investigations and Oversight of the U. S. House Committee on Science and Technology conducted its own review of the matter, and its investigator, James Jensen, summed up his conclusions in a letter to the Sobells that read, in part:

> Based on my review of the evidence, I have concluded that there is no evidence to support the allegation that your study was based upon fallacious, falsified or otherwise invented data...
>
> My review of all available [evidence] supports the findings of the Commission convened by the Addiction Research Foundation (also known as the "Dickens Commission") and fully supports their conclusions.[13]

As if that had not settled the issue, ADAMHA, the federal health agency that had supported the Sobells' work, had an investigation of its own conducted by a team from PHS and NIMH. The highlights of the team's twenty-seven-page report:

> Based on the investigative team's necessarily limited review, the Steering Group did not find evidence to demonstrate fabrication or falsification of data reported by the Sobells. However, we did note some errors and use of ambiguous terminology in their publications which indicate to us that the Sobells were careless in preparing their manuscripts for publication....

The affidavits of some former study subjects and their relatives, which have been referred to by Pendery, Maltzman, Miller and others, were obtained several years after the events in question. While these affidavits may state the subjects and/or collaterals were not contacted as frequently as the Sobells reported and/or were not asked for specific information about drinking patterns, such affidavits should be considered in the context of their timing following the study and the Sobells' explanations of how they estimated the subjects' "daily drinking dispositions." In addition, Maltzman was quoted as saying "Our evidence is not simply based upon the verbal reports of these patients. If that's all we had it would be a tempest in a teapot." Unfortunately, even though Pendery and Maltzman said they had other documents to support their allegations, they never permitted the investigative team to examine the documents.[14]

Until these investigative reports appeared, however, the Sobells were subjected to a torrent of mudslinging and character assassination in the press and elsewhere, plus a huge class-action damage suit by some of their former patients, all inspired by the Pendery et al. article. A handful of typical headlines:

"Data Said To Be Falsified In Major Alcoholism Study"—*San Diego Union*, June 27, 1982
"Social-drinking report contained falsified data, alcoholics charge"—Riverside, CA, *Press Enterprise*, June 27, 1982
"Intemperate Experiment.... a shocking story"—*Discover*, September 1982
"Experiment in Controlled Drinking For Alcoholics Is a Dismal Failure"—*International Herald Tribune*, July 2, 1982
"Alcoholism Study Draws More Fire: Congressman's Query Hints Possible Penalty for Patton Researchers"—*San Diego Union*, September 16, 1982
"Controlled drinking gets rough review at NCA [National Council on Alcoholism Forum]"—*U. S. Journal of Drug and Alcohol Dependence*, April 1983
"'Controlled drinkers' sue Sobells"—*APA Monitor*, September 1983
"Study participants seek $40 million"—*Riverside (CA) Press-Enterprise*, July 21, 1983

After the Dickens Commission report, a few publications ran small stories about the refurbishing of the Sobells' reputation and the reappraisal of their work. Some examples:

"Report to foundation supports the Sobells"—*APA Monitor*, November 1982
"Researchers cleared in alcohol study"—Toronto *Globe and Mail*, November 5, 1982
"Alcohol study not deceptive, inquiry says"—Toronto *Star*, November 5, 1982
"Panel supports integrity of alcoholic study"—San Bernardino *Inland Empire*, November 10, 1982
"No Fraud Found in Alcoholism Study"—*Science*, November 19, 1982
"'Controlled drinking' theory gains influence and respect"—Providence *Journal*, November 24, 1983

* * *

The final outcomes of the controlled-drinking brouhaha:

- The damage suit by Sobell patients was thrown out of court.
- Irving Maltzman has continued to fight what he sees as the good fight: This has become my major interest. I've had to give up other research. I'm concentrating on this, even though I've had difficulty getting my articles published because Sobell and Marlatt are on the boards of editors of almost every journal I would try to publish in.* Now I'm trying to write a book on it.
  (In 1989 the Sobells, in *Journal of Studies on Alcohol*, proposed a moratorium to Maltzman, but clearly without success.)
- Mary Pendery had a rendezvous with one of her former alcoholic patients several years ago that ended tragically in her murder.
- Although neither the abstinence-treatment community nor AA has ever yielded an inch to the controlled-drinking approach, it is gaining ground elsewhere: Several free self-help programs, such as Moderation Management, now exist and have groups in a number of cities; commercial programs, such as Drink Wise (in Michigan) are beginning to be available; and the National Academy of Scence's Institute of Medicine has recommended that there be more of these moderation-stage programs.[15] Considerable evidence has accumulated as to the effectiveness of behavior therapy used in the controlled drinking approach.[16]

Controlled drinking as an answer to alcoholism is far more common, the Sobells believe, than the data of therapists and treatment centers indicates because, they say, many people with drinking problems teach themselves to drink in moderation. "I think self-recovery is a much more common experience than most of us think," says Mark Sobell. "If people want to change badly enough, they find a way. And controlled drinking is one such way." The Sobells continue to take a keen interest in the subject of controlled drinking, although they have long expanded their horizons to include research on assessment of addiction and on natural recovery from addiction. They are now at Nova Southeastern University in Fort Lauderdale, where, with an ADAMHA grant of $135,000 a year for three years, they are doing research and development on facilitating self-change, a key part of which is the problem drinker's own choice of goal (either controlled drinking or abstinence). The Sobells have been devoted nearly thirty years to this area of research, although conceivably, had they known before they ever

---

*Mark Sobell comments: "Maltzman's difficulty in getting published is because journals do not want to commit libel."

started down this road how rocky it would be, they might have chosen a smoother one—and never done their valuable work.

A Dirty Secret About Clean Needles

The Sobells experienced a firestorm of opposition because their research supported a harm-reduction approach to alcohol addiction; the sociologist Mary Utne O'Brien encountered one because her research, to the contrary, found that another harm-reduction approach—needle exchange as a way of lessening the damage done by needle-sharing among drug addicts—was somewhat flawed in ways that had been neither anticipated nor previously reported.

In recent years, needle-sharing among addicts has been the major source of new HIV infections in the U.S.[17] But for some time there has been considerable evidence that if drug users had easy access to clean needles, they would be less inclined to share needles, thereby cutting down on the transmission of AIDS and other communicable diseases.

In Scotland in the 1980s, for instance, Edinburgh and Glasgow, with similar epidemics due to drug use, put different needle availability policies into effect and got different results. Edinburgh, in an effort to reduce drug use, made it illegal to buy syringes without a prescription; addicts, instead of shooting up less often, simply increased their needle sharing, resulting in the rapid spread of HIV and an epidemic of hepatitis. Glasgow, in contrast, which put no restrictions on needle availability, had a low rate of HIV positives among its drug injectors and no HIV or hepatitis epidemic.[18]

In the U.S., St. Louis, Seattle, and certain other cities that allowed needles to be bought without prescription had lower rates of HIV among drug-injecting addicts than did cities where needle purchase was illegal. Some cities went further and actively sought to promote the use of clean needles by instituting needle-exchange programs in which addicts who surrendered dirty needles were given clean ones free in exchange. When studies made in some of these cities reported that the annual number of new HIV cases decreased, the practice of needle exchange spread, and by 1994, fifty-five U.S. cities had a total of seventy-six needle-exchange programs in operation.[19] Still, that barely scratched the surface; 95 percent of the more than 1,200 U. S. cities of over 25,000 population had no such programs and an estimated 90 percent of intravenous drug users had no opportunity to obtain free sterile needles.[20]

In most American cities and states, and in Congress, political conservatives have consistently and adamantly opposed needle-exchange
programs because they believe that the programs make drug use cheaper
and easier, and therefore increase it.*[21] Since 1988 Congress has passed
at least six laws, in addition to the ADAMHA Reorganization Act of
1992, that contain provisions prohibiting or restricting the use of federal funding for needle-exchange programs and activities.[22] Ironically,
many black physicians, clergy, and politicians side with the conservatives, though on different grounds: They oppose giving addicts free
needles because they see it as a cheap and degrading substitute for
serious drug treatment programs and major efforts to eliminate poverty
and racial discrimination.[23]

Federal health officials, however, and their moderate and liberal supporters in Congress, say that the evidence contradicts the charge that
needle-exchange programs increase drug use; on the contrary, it supports the belief that needle exchange reduces the spread of AIDS. But
in order to gain the support of a majority of representatives and senators for needle exchange programs, federal health agencies needed research data that might sway committees and have an impact on the
floors of the House and Senate. Toward that end, in the late 1980s NIDA
and CDC funded some $40 million dollars' worth of research programs
to determine what effects needle-exchange and bleach (disinfectant)
distribution programs were having on the incidence of drug use and on
the spread of HIV.

*　*　*

Mary Utne O'Brien was one of the needle-exchange researchers.
She had joined an existing research group at the University of Illinois
at Chicago in 1991 as research director of Professor Wayne Wiebel's
study, funded by a $2.4 million NIDA grant, of large samples of addicts
in neighborhoods across Chicago over a five-year period. O'Brien then
brought in grants of her own from CDC, the American Foundation for
AIDS Research (AmFAR), and other sources. Pooling the samples from

---

*In September, 1997, William Weld, former governor of Massachusetts, withdrew
his nomination by President Clinton to become ambassador to Mexico because Senator Jesse Helms, head of the Senate Foreign Relations Committee, refused to schedule a hearing on the nomination, his reason being that Weld was unsuited to the job
because, among other things, he favors needle exchange and therefore, in Helms'
view, is "soft on drugs."

these projects in order to study even larger groups of addicts, O'Brien devised a plan to study needle exchange, which was due to arrive in Chicago shortly. Specifically, she meant to find out what effects needle exchange programs had on drug use frequency and HIV infection rates among roughly 1,000 injecting drug users not receiving other treatment.

O'Brien, though still in her thirties when she began leadership of this important project, had solid credentials. In addition to a number of years in evaluation research, she had been a survey director, and later a senior survey director, at NORC, one of the country's major social science research centers, at the University of Chicago. O'Brien, a cheery, charming, attractive young woman, had originally been interested in doing research on love and intimate relations, but for some reason she found herself drawn to grimmer social phenomena—crime, violence, poverty, problem drinking, and, in particular, drug use—and over the years had taken part in a couple dozen surveys in these areas. NSF and four federal health institutes, including NIMH, thought enough of her expertise to enlist her services as a proposal reviewer; half a dozen major professional journals relied on her as a consulting editor and reviewer; and in 1991 the University of Illinois School of Public Health appointed her an associate professor.

O'Brien's three grants for the study of drug addicts enabled her to design an ambitious research program that took her and her half-dozen colleagues into three inner-city neighborhoods in Chicago, one mostly black, another largely Puerto Rican, the third mixed, the populations of all three of which had high levels of drug use by injection. The field work was hardly what one would expect a good-looking, well-educated, middle-class woman like O'Brien to find congenial or comfortable: She and her colleagues had to hang out on slum-area street corners, in "copping" (drug sales) alleys, and in "shooting galleries" to persuade 850 intravenous drug users (IDUs) to take part in the research. Later, they added others to make a total of 1,091 IDUs in the research sample.[24]

The behavior of the IDUs had been tracked for about three years under Wiebel's grant, and O'Brien's team followed them for another three years, during which a needle-exchange program was launched and operated in Chicago by a volunteer group called the Chicago Recovery Alliance (CRA). O'Brien's research plan was to compare the drug use and HIV incidence of IDUs who did not make use of needle exchange with those who did. CRA started its first needle exchange program in 1992 from a card table set up on a sidewalk two hours a week, later from a van, and by 1994 at six different sites. O'Brien and her team members sat in on the exchange proceedings and interviewed the IDUs in detail as to how often they injected, whether they used only clean needles or needles previously used by others, whether or not they "backloaded"—drew blood into the syringe before injecting—and how much money they were spending on drugs. The team members also handled the voluminous paperwork and scheduling of blood tests of the IDUs who made use of needle exchange and those who did not.

By 1995, O'Brien and her team had enough longitudinal data to come up with some tentative answers as to the effects of needle-exchange programs, and fed their data and analytic program into the computer. The results surprised and distressed them. Needle exchange was believed to be an AIDS-prevention strategy, and supposed not to increase drug use, but the data dashed both expectations. O'Brien's recollection:

> We found that needle-exchange users were just as likely to report sharing dirty needles as were addicts who did not use needle exchange. And we also found that 80 percent of those who used needle exchange got more needles than they used— three times more! Even though it's a one-for-one exchange, you can get as many as you bring in, and when we asked them how many they were using, it turned out they were using only part of what they exchanged. We realized that the extra needles they were getting were a resource commodity—something they could sell to buy more drugs. Bad news![25]

In the more formal language of a report that she and her colleagues later wrote:

> Needle exchange use had no relationship with the risk behaviors examined. Exchangers obtained three times more needles than they consumed, this number unrelated to number of IDU associates [acquaintances who were users]. Injecting frequency was found to be positively associated with the number of needles exchanged....
>
> Economic factors appear to be an important motivator of needle exchange use. In Chicago, free needles are not associated with reductions in risk behavior, but are associated with increases in injection drug use. Exchange operations must recognize conflicting pulls on IDUs to use free sterile syringes for safe injections versus as an economic resource, and work to motivate exchangers to use them as part of risk reduction.[26]

The most troubling finding was thus that free needles were being acquired in surplus in order to support increased drug purchase and use. This had not appeared in other studies of needle-exchange programs, perhaps because other researchers had not asked the particular questions that could yield that result. O'Brien, who had not expected any such outcome, was dismayed:

> It turned out that the best predictor of increasing injection was the extra needles

an IDU had acquired the previous week. Needle exchange was associated with an increase in drug use. And that would be the kiss of death to any hope of getting federal funding for needle exchange programs. Just as bad, we did not find that needle exchange reduced the risk behavior of IDUs. There was no reduction in needle sharing, in giving away used needles, or in having risky sex.

It was very galling to me, as an old-style liberal do-gooder, to come out with data that seemed to be on the side of the Jesse Helmses and the Newt Gingriches. But we had done a careful study—not a perfect study but close enough, not tight science but the best that's out there—and that's what our data showed, like it or not.

At this time, O'Brien submitted a new $2.4 million proposal to NIDA for a grant for another five-year needle-exchange study (which she eventually got) and in the "Preliminary Studies" section of the application reported her findings thus far—the first formal statement of the disturbing data. To her surprise, the revelation was seen as deliberately hostile to needle exchange:

Jim Murray—my chief data analyst—and I were not out to nail needle exchange; we were out to support CRA and to do good studies, and I was pretty alarmed when I saw the lack of impact on risk behavior and the increase in drug use. I reported what we had found not only to NIDA and CDC but in December [1994] I shared the findings with the local needle-exchange group.

As, of course, she had to. But although she knew that nobody at NIDA, CDC, her university (through which the grant money flowed), or CRA would be pleased with the findings, she never expected the reactions they produced. Everything started coming apart after her project officers at NIDA and CDC asked if they could send out copies for critical review and, although the report she had submitted was a rough draft without the necessary qualifications and cautions, she gave her permission. And then:

Suddenly all kinds of people, advocates of needle exchange as well as researchers, had copies, and suddenly I wasn't in the loop on the planning of a conference at Johns Hopkins in February. I called up and was told that the program was full. I thought, "Whoa! I'm being shut out!" Finally I did get invited, and I walked into this meeting and everyone was talking about my study—and when they saw me they turned away and started talking about other things. I felt like a gate crasher.

I wasn't on the agenda, either, but when one speaker said that needle exchange was one of the few effective solutions to HIV transmission, I got up and said that in Italy, where needles are readily available in the supermarkets, they have one of the highest rates of infection among addicts and that we have data from Chicago showing that we can't think of needle exchange as a simple, mechanical fix because people are always cleverer than our interventions assume, they'll use the needles for their own purposes. When I sat down, there was silence, dead silence, and then they continued on as if I had never said a word.

Then, Chicago Recovery Alliance notified NIDA that they were pulling out of the newly funded project unless they had veto power over the studies that had already come out of the project and all the studies that would come out of it for the next five years. They'd been coached to do that by a number of senior needle-exchange researchers in New York and San Francisco—people who were very pro-needle-exchange. We said that as a matter of academic freedom, we couldn't allow them veto power, but we offered them a way to collaborate with us on the reports. While we were trying to work out something with them, we got really bad news: NIDA sent word that they wouldn't be giving us the money unless we did work it out with CRA. We said we had another group we could work with, but that didn't seem to help.

Next, at a senior staff meeting of my research group the three ethnographers on the staff, who were very pro-needle-exchange, said that they wanted me to fire Jim Murray—my chief data analyst, my number one day-in-day-out colleague, my close friend—and Wayne Wiebel, the group's overall director, sided with them. I was blown away. I asked why. They said that Jim was undeniably brilliant but that "philosophically" he didn't "fit in," and he had to go.

What the three meant by Murray's "philosophically not fitting in" was, apparently, that instead of a strong bias in favor of needle exchange, he had a commitment to what his data analysis showed. O'Brien dug in her heels, refused to dump him, and shortly was summoned to a conference with Susan Scrimshaw, the new dean of the School of Public Health. The dean's approval of O'Brien's stance was crucial: Grant money does not go directly to researchers but to the institutions for which they work and, through the institutions, to them. The dean's view therefore carried a great deal of weight—and hers was that Murray had to go. The reason, as she made fairly clear, was that the other research staff members and she herself considered his statistical analysis reactionary, or racist, or at least not in harmony with the do-good philosophy behind needle exchange. But there was still more, as O'Brien explains:

> The conflict was both ideological and monetary. People who had been fighting for social justice issues in the sixties and seventies didn't have an issue to rally around in the nineties, and needle exchange became the vehicle for helping indigent drug addicts. Many were old longhairs, and the public health rubric was almost incidental to the idea of doing good to help poor addicts (rich addicts didn't count). So Jim Murray was seen as a troublemaker and I was seen either as another one or as okay but saddled with Jim. The dean told me that all money for AIDS research at the School of Public Health was in jeopardy because of my reports, and that I was never to attempt to publish them, and that I had to fire Jim, if the situation was to be salvaged.

O'Brien feistily replied that her contract with the university gave her explicit hire and fire authority over her research staff. Dean Scrimshaw, scowling, snapped that she had already consulted university lawyers, that O'Brien's contract was not legally binding, and that if she didn't get rid of Murray, Scrimshaw would not renew O'Brien's contract as an associate professor—in other words, would fire her—when it ran out in a few months. Behind all this was a simple economic reality: The university badly wanted and needed the $2.4 million grant, and the political forces in Washington and Chicago arrayed against the O'Brien-Murray findings made it necessary to dump Murray, or better yet, both Murray and O'Brien, so that the university could patch things up with CRA and reestablish good relations with NIDA and CDC. (After a year and a half of negotiations, the University did get a go-ahead from NIDA to continue the needle-exchange study on the $2.4 million grant.) O'Brien, reflecting on the dean's demands, comments:

> I think the people at every level who were promoting needle exchange wanted a head on the platter. I'm well-liked, a hard worker, not a likely target, so Jim was the target. No one expected me to walk away from a big grant—by then it was two big grants, because another one had just come through—but I wouldn't give in. So my head had to be on the platter too. And because I wasn't tenured, the dean was able to fire me. That ended my connection with the project, I was locked out of my office, and even my voice mail was turned off. I was devastated, I didn't try to appeal, I just wanted to go hide, I was literally sick to my stomach for months. All those people I had worked with were politically correct, and they abandoned me.
>
> I had no interest in going back there. But I did want to tell my story to the university's vice chancellor for research, Mi Ja Kim, I wanted her to know what such an experience does to anyone trying to do high-quality research in a visible policy arena. She reacted with horror, dismay, why hadn't I come to her sooner? But when I mentioned that the topic of my Sunday School class last week had been public versus private morality, she became radiant and proclaimed, "God will bring justice in the end!" Then she said she envied me for now being at home with my children. "My husband and I weep, Mary," she said, "we weep real tears, as we see how the years have passed and we can never have back the time we lost with our children. God works in mysterious ways. This may be a blessing that you can recognize only as time goes on." I left her office dazed, not knowing whether I had just deeply connected with a sincere woman or been finessed by a canny administrator. Probably both.

* * *

The 1992 ADAMHA Reorganization Act directed the Secretary of Health and Human Services to have NAS review the evidence of the impact of needle exchange and bleach distribution programs on drug use behavior and the spread of HIV. The NAS's Institute of Medicine and the National Research Council assembled a panel of thirteen experts to conduct the review. The panel gathered data from five major sources, including two previous reviews of the evidence, a group of studies published after those reviews had been completed, and two sets of recent studies from Tacoma, Washington, and New Haven, Connecticut. Its conclusions, thoroughly affirmative about needle exchange, directly contradicted O'Brien's and Murray's findings:

> There is no credible evidence to date that drug use is increased among participants as a result of programs that provide legal access to sterile equipment.
> The available scientific literature provides evidence based on self-reports that needle exchange programs do not increase the frequency of injection among program participants and do not increase the number of new initiates to injection drug use.[27]

But what of the findings in the two reports by O'Brien, Murray, and their team? (O'Brien and Murray had split their original, overlong report into two shorter ones.) The panel consigned discussion of the reports to one of three appendixes of its book-length review, along with studies by researchers in San Francisco and Montreal that also questioned the effectiveness of needle exchange. All these negative or less-than-positive reports were, and remain, unpublished, and the panel justified discussing them only in an appendix on the grounds that "as unpublished findings, these studies lack the authority provided by the peer review and publication process."[28]

O'Brien's research project had, of course, been peer-reviewed in the grant-making process, though the reports had never been submitted to a journal and peer-reviewed at that stage. But as for the authority the reports are said to lack, it could have been supplied by the panel itself, which was fully capable of evaluating the methodology and findings—and did so, in the appendix, a convenient place to denigrate and bury them. There the panel devoted ten pages to the two O'Brien-Murray reports, giving two reasons for "concern" about the soundness of the conclusions: first, the failure to present alternative explanations of the findings, and second, the lack of an adequate sampling strategy, which, the panel said, may have resulted in biased estimates of various components of the IDU population in Chicago.

The panel, having depreciated the unpleasant evidence, did, however, conclude, in notably obfuscatory prose, that the negative findings of the San Francisco, Montreal, and Chicago studies "should be further studied with proper study designs, measurements, and analytical methods to properly investigate the tenability of such causal relationships."[29] In plain English: There might be something to it.

* * *

Mary Utne O'Brien, abruptly cut off from her research project and ousted from the university, sought to distract herself with other busy-work: For some months she busied herself with tennis lessons and an evaluation project for her children's school district, and considered several job offers from NORC, the Chicago Health Department, and others that came in unsolicited as result of publicity about her firing, all of which she turned down in order, as she told friends, "to sit back for a bit and figure out what I want."

But one option—early retirement from research—was never a possibility. "I have never not worked since I was fifteen," she says. "Just two months out with each kid, then back at it." And she is, now, back at it: She is working as an independent consultant, her most recent clients being the National Black Commission on AIDS, and the Russell Sage Foundation, for which she is designing an experimental study on "diversity intervention" (increase in minority representation) in large corporations.

As for research on needle exchange, she has no plans to resume that, but she keeps an eye on what's happening and recent news seems to support the findings of her ill-fated project. Two and a half years after O'Brien's initial (and still unpublished) report to her sponsors, *AIDS* published a report from Vancouver that corroborated many elements of her findings in Chicago, specifically the fact that needle exchange does not automatically decrease needle sharing and HIV transmission. From the Vancouver report:

> Our data are particularly disturbing in light of two facts: first, Vancouver has the highest volume NEP [needle exchange program] in North America; second, HIV prevalence among this city's IDU population was relatively low until recent years. The fact that sharing of injection equipment is normative, and HIV prevalence and incidence are high in a community where there is an established and remarkably active NEP is alarming...[and suggests] that the concept of harm reduction requires a broader perspective beyond NEP alone.[30]

O'Brien's comment: "It just shows, as we had shown, that needle exchange isn't the only answer, that needle exchange is a lot more complex than we had thought."

Her mistake, if one can call it that, is to have been a messenger bringing bad news; as the Earl of Northumberland says, in Shakespeare's *Henry IV, Part Two*, "The first bringer of unwelcome news/ Hath but a losing office."

11

Unhand That Rat, You Rat!

Ethics versus "Speciesism"

I invite you, Reader, to play the role of scientist for a moment by conducting a little thought experiment in which you imagine a situation that I specify, and observe your own probable reaction. This may strike you as not a very scientific way to gather evidence, but some of Einstein's most momentous discoveries resulted from just such *Gedankenexperimenten*, as he called them. He tried to visualize, for instance, what would happen if a man, in a box falling down a long shaft, took coins and keys out of his pocket and released them, and sensed that since they would already be falling at the same rate as the man himself, they would remain next to him, an intuitive recognition that played an important part in Einstein's theorizing about gravity.

So, on to your experiment: You are aboard an acquaintance's sailboat—you are a good swimmer, he is a poor one—when a sudden gust causes the boat to heel sharply and his baby and dog both fall overboard. You leap over, but because of the choppy water and other difficulties you realize that you can save only one of them. Which do you save?

Your answer, of course, is the baby. Most of the world's people, and certainly most Western people, have always believed that the life of a human being is worth more than the life of an animal. But beginning in the late 1970s and increasingly in recent years there has been a growth of interest in Buddhism and certain other Eastern belief systems in which the life of every creature is held to be of equal value; or, put another way, in which every living thing has an equal right to life.[1] Ingrid Newkirk, co-founder of People for the Ethical Treatment of Animals (PETA), has said, "Animal liberationists do not separate out the human animal, so there is no rational basis for saying that a human being has special rights. A rat is a pig is a dog is a boy."[2] Any attitude or action that values a human life above that of an animal is viewed by animal activists as an expression of an -ism as detestable as racism or sexism: "speciesism."

The most familiar behavioral outcome of the belief in the equality of all living things is vegetarianism, which in its strictest form holds that it is unethical for human beings to kill any animal, fish, or fowl for food; the belief is also expressed in the antifur, antileather, and similar movements. Some believers in animal rights extend the doctrine to include insects and will not kill flies, mosquitoes, or even crop-destroying pests. (Logically, the doctrine could include bacteria and viruses, although none of the many animal advocacy movements in America goes that far.)

Our concern here is not with vegetarianism or the antifur and antileather movements but with the impact of the doctrine of animal rights on behavioral and social science research using animals. (Biological and physiological research that has no implications for behavioral or social science is outside our field of view.) Initially, the goal of the animal-protection movement was essentially compassionate; the Society for the Prevention of Cruelty to Animals, founded in 1869, and the many humane societies formed in succeeding decades militated against inhumane treatment of animals—and some against vivisection—but said nothing about animal experimentation as a violation of the rights of animals. Even the expanding animal welfare movement of the 1950s made no such claim. But the civil rights movement of the 1960s and the antiestablishment attitudes of the Vietnam War protests created a different intellectual atmosphere; critics of our society saw its uses of animals as heartless commercialism and extended their moral defense of the rights of all human beings to include nonhuman creatures.[3] The doctrine of animal rights transformed the goals and activities of the animal welfare movement, as the social scientists James Jasper and Dorothy Nelkin point out:

> The moral language of rights has helped to radicalize animal protection. Because rights are dichotomous—one either has full rights or none at all—the very concept establishes a moral imperative. Applying the concept of rights to animals generated demands for the abolition of all uses of animals, increasingly disruptive tactics, and the inclusion of more and more species in the animal rights agenda.[4]

Some contemporary animal-advocacy organizations try to halt all uses of animals and animal products; others, most notably In Defense of Animals (IDA), concentrate on halting or limiting scientific research using animals.[5] The more moderate organizations agree that in some cases animal experimentation is morally defensible, but the radical groups maintain that experimentation on animals should be totally abolished. As Priscilla Feral, president of Friends of Animals, has said, "Animal experimentation is just plain wrong. Human beings have no right to the knowledge gained from experimentation on animals, even if it is done painlessly."[6] The definitive expression of animal-rights luddism was made by Tom Regan, author of *The Case for Animals Rights* and a leader of the radical animal rights movement:

> On the rights view, we cannot justify harming a single rat merely by aggregating "the many human and humane benefits" that flow from doing it[7].... The rights view will not be satisfied with anything less than total abolition [of animal experimentation]. If it means there are some things we cannot learn, then so be it. We have no basic right not to be harmed by those natural diseases we are heir to.[8]

* * *

An in-depth ethical analysis of animal rights doctrine and response to it would require far more time and space than can be allotted to it here, but two relatively brief observations may cast enough light for us to see our way.

The first is that "rights" are not a natural entity but a human artifact, a notion generated by the thinkers of the Enlightenment and embodied in our Constitution. In other times and places custom and law have conferred some rights on some people, few or none on others; the statement of our Declaration of Independence that rights are the gift of the Creator to all men is a noble philosophic dictum but not an empirical datum. Rights are a human concept that nonhuman creatures, lacking language and philosophy, are incapable of understanding or believing in; to say that they possess rights is anthropomorphism on a par with attributing nobility to the hive-defending bee or wickedness to the bird-killing cat.* The humane treatment of beasts of burden, animals raised for food, and animals used in experiments is an expression of human decency and is justifiably mandated by law, but the claim that animals have the same rights as human beings and therefore should be "liberated" from all such uses is as fanciful and groundless as the belief in ghosts.

The second observation is that evolution has generated many forms of life that can survive only by taking the lives of other forms. The

---

*Tom Regan, however, argues that rather than a capacity for conceptual thought, what entitles any creature to rights is its capacity to feel pleasure or pain (Regan 1983, quoted in Oliver 1990: 4).

snake that seizes and swallows a mouse, the spider that traps and eats a fly, the cougar that catches and devours a hare, are neither behaving immorally nor depriving their prey of their rights. If some supernatural force could be invoked to prevent predators from killing their prey, it would deprive the predators of their right to live—if predators, like prey, could be said to have any such right. Only in biblical fantasy shall the leopard lie down with the kid and the lion eat straw like the ox; the big cats would die if they had to give up preying on other animals. The drives and drive-generated behavior of animals, their needs and the abilities with which they meet them, were fashioned by evolution and are not based upon rights theory. Human beings, too, have drives and needs of evolutionary origin; our teeth and digestive tracts make it clear that we are omnivores, and not by our own choice; many strict vegans have discovered that it is difficult, sometimes impossible, for them to remain healthy and vigorous on a diet, however admirably ethical, totally devoid of animal, fowl, or fish protein.

The morality of eating other creatures was succinctly epitomized long ago by Benjamin Franklin. As a young man he was on his way by ship from Boston to Philadelphia, and having recently been converted to vegetarianism on moral grounds, felt that the crewmen, who were fishing for cod while becalmed, were committing murder. But as he later wrote in his *Autobiography*:

> I had formerly been a great lover of fish, and when this came hot out of the frying pan, it smelled admirably well. I balanced some time between principle and inclination till I recollected that when the fish were opened, I saw smaller fish taken out of their stomachs. "Then," thought I, "if you eat one another, I don't see why we mayn't eat you." So I dined upon cod very heartily and have since continued to eat as other people.[9]

More central to our concern, however, than the morality of eating other living things is the morality of scientific research using other living things. A cogent justification of such research was offered some years ago by the experimental psychologist Charles Gallistel of UCLA in an address to the Society for Neuroscience in which he spelled out the principles that research scientists, as contrasted to antivivisectionists, swear allegiance to:

> We believe, first, that the pursuit of scientific understanding is among the noblest of all human goals. Like the pursuit of great art, like the preservation of a beautiful wilderness, it is good in and of itself. It needs no good beyond itself to be justified as a pursuit. We further believe, however, that this pursuit has conferred more benefit upon humankind than has any other human pursuit.

> It follows...that the harm we cause to animals in the course of this pursuit is in no way wanton; it is in no way disregardful of the canons of judicious custodianship [of the world's creatures], and it is in no way morally wrong.[10]

It was through animal studies, he reminded his audience, that William Harvey, Robert Boyle, and other seventeenth-century physiologists had discovered the principles of circulation and respiration; in doing so, they had unavoidably inflicted pain, to their own distress, on many animals, but what they learned formed the basis of much modern medical practice. Gallistel concluded:

> We as biomedical scientists believe that it is *not* morally wrong to cause an animal pain, but it is morally wrong to cause an animal pain wantonly, recklessly, or for no good scientific reason.... The interfering with the pursuit of scientific truth on the part of antivivisectionists is itself the immoral and cruel act of the fanatic, the fanatic who believes that his/her superior view of moral truth permits the setting aside of the moral perceptions of the overwhelming majority of their fellow men. The antivivisectionist movement interferes with one of the noblest pursuits of mankind and condemns humankind to the continued suffering that is the necessary consequence of continued ignorance.

But unlike seventeenth-century experimentalists, contemporary researchers can almost always avoid inflicting pain. As the experimental psychologist William Greenough of the University of Illinois, Urbana-Champaign, recently pointed out, in most modern animal experimentation researchers are able to administer anesthetic and analgesic drugs that were unavailable to Harvey and other pioneers. Fortunately so, since, he said, animal experiments are essential to the understanding of the biology and behavior of living systems in health and disease. Within the realm of behavioral science alone, animal research was in large part the source of such important advances, Greenough said, as the use of psychotropic medications to combat mental illnesses; treatments for stroke, neurological disorders, and acute neural trauma; the alleviation of chronic pain; the treatment of Parkinsonism by drugs and by neural transplantation; and a number of others. He concluded that the most serious cost of the animal rights movement is "the reduced progress of biomedical research, and the consequent suffering and death of human victims of still incurable diseases and disorders."[11]

The American Psychological Association, in a lobbyist's "Briefing Sheet" for fiscal year 1998 appropriations, provides a long list of gains that owe much to animal research, among them improvements in infant and pediatric care, new treatments of Alzheimer's and Parkinson's Diseases, improvement of the quality of life for people with mental disabilities, methods of intervention in substance abuse, and the increase of automobile and aviation safety. Nor could these have been achieved by in-vitro or other methods short of animal experimentation:

> Whenever possible, behavioral researchers look for alternatives to using animals in research. However, alternatives are often unavailable or inadequate. Plants lack a nervous system and cannot be used to learn about behavioral phenomena. Tissue cultures cannot develop depression, alcoholism, autism, learning disorders, memory impairments or other psychologically relevant problems. Studies typically use animals when time requirements, risk, the need to control behavioral history, or other conditions make it impossible to use human beings.
>
> When there are clear practical or ethical reasons not to use human beings, the knowledge gained from animal research provides an essential benefit to the mental and physical health of our nation.[12]

All of which makes perfect sense—unless you value a dog as much as a baby, a rat as much as a human being.

Drug Abuse Researchers Under Fire: Two Illustrative Stories

1

"The day my kids came home crying, about six or seven years ago, I was ready to quit my job," says Dr. Marilyn Carroll, an attractive, wholesome-looking, and usually cheerful mid-Westerner in her late forties. "They were three, six, and ten at the time, and on the way home in the school bus the other kids had been taunting them, saying, 'Your mother tortures animals.' They got that idea from brochures PETA had been handing out to our whole neighborhood. My kids had known all along what my husband and I do, and why we do it, and we had taken them to the lab to see the monkeys and how we work with them. But on the bus the other kids were so nasty and mean that it made my kids cry."

What kept Carroll from resigning was that some sympathetic colleague put a note about PETA's actions on the Internet, and as the word rapidly spread throughout the psychological research community, messages of support poured in from researchers, federal agency people, the heads of university pharmacology and psychology departments, and many others. Carroll says, "I guess it was all that support that counteracted my experience and made me able to keep doing what I was doing."

Carroll, professor of Psychiatry and Neuroscience (she is a psychologist) at the University of Minnesota, has been conducting drug-abuse research with animals for nearly twenty years. Her doctoral dissertation was basic research on the feeding behavior of rats, but she soon moved on to studies with a more urgent and practical purpose: gaining understanding of the biochemical mechanisms of addiction in order to find ways to control it, a goal that has earned her generous grants from NIDA and a NIDA Merit Award. She recently told a reporter how she moved toward this kind of research:

> After I completed my Ph.D. on feeding behavior in rats, I really wanted to do something that had direct relevance to human suffering. I was struck by how little we know about drug abuse, yet how much human misery and destruction it causes. My interest was in identifying ways to reduce voluntary drug taking by humans.
> To do that, I had to switch to primates. Rats are very finicky about what they take in their mouths because they can't regurgitate. So the only way to give them drugs is intravenously. That allows us to study some variables controlling drug abuse, but the procedures don't last long enough to study many aspects of voluntary drug use. So I had to go to monkeys because, like humans, they will voluntarily take things that don't taste good if the reward—the effect of the drug—is desired.[13]

Three of her numerous significant discoveries:

• Rats with injection equipment surgically implanted in the jugular vein learned to press a lever to inject themselves with cocaine and rapidly developed a drug habit. But when their food included L-tryptophan, an amino acid that increases the level of the neurotransmitter serotonin in the brain, they voluntarily reduced their self-administered intake of cocaine by 50 percent.[14]

• Rhesus monkeys that had developed addiction to any of various drugs that they voluntarily took by mouth—among them, cocaine, nicotine, alcohol, and amphetamines—reduced their drug intake when they were given pleasing food, especially a desired treat such as saccharine. The harder they had to work to earn their drug fix and the easier it was for them to get the pleasurable nonaddicting treat, the stronger the counter-addictive effect. In the case of human beings, Carroll suggests, the "competing reinforcer" could even be social rather than gustatory; this method has recently been successfully applied in treatment of cocaine dependence.[15]

• Monkeys given a punch-flavored drink containing caffeine became caffeine-addicted, in which condition they were highly motivated to work for food by pressing a lever that delivered one pellet per push. But when their heavy caffeine intake was cut down, they developed withdrawal symptoms: They became listless, would not feed themselves (although they were hungry enough to eat if fed by hand), and functioned poorly at tasks requiring intelligence. The findings had important implications for parents: Children who drink a lot of soft drinks get considerable caffeine from them; if their intake is then curtailed by limited access to such drinks at school, they may suffer worrisome symptoms for some time, including fatigue, listlessness, headache, and learning and performance deficits.[16]

Carroll's many years of harassment by animal activists began in late April of 1984. Members of the University's Animal Rights Club had become aware of her research, probably by asking the university's Office of Research Administration for copies of grant proposals then in effect on campus. Their ambitious goal, in common with other groups throughout the country taking part in "World Animal Week," was to "wipe out animal research by the year 2000." At the University of Minnesota, this took the form that first year of nothing more serious than a small demonstration by several dozen students who marched around for hours in a circle in front of Carroll's laboratory building, shouting and chanting slogans. But year by year the annual demonstration escalated in intensity, and after a while the marchers were carrying signs accusing Carroll and others of "sentencing monkeys to death" and of killing a total of 130,000 animals. One year, a mob of about seventy-five students tried to force their way into Carroll's animal experimentation rooms—it was not clear what they intended to do there—but an assistant bolted the door from the inside and held the fort for five hours. The campus police were notified but the university's president, Ken Keller, declared that the demonstrators had every right to be wherever they wanted to be, including inside the laboratory, and the police were unable to act. The dean of the School of Medicine, David Brown, disagreed with Keller and refused to order Carroll to let the demonstrators in. After long and heated talks with the students, Brown got them to agree to end the siege if Carroll came to a press conference with them and answered their questions. She recalls that event:

> They asked questions and let me answer, but they were rude and disorderly and nasty. I was about eight and a half months pregnant, and they shouted things like, "Why don't you just have that baby and put it in a cage and do your experiments on your own kid?" I wasn't afraid that they'd be violent with me, but they were aggressive and hard to handle, and despite my condition I had to put up with it because that was the deal I made.

By 1989, PETA had joined the action; a cadre of its members went to Carroll's neighborhood on a Sunday morning and distributed copies of a PETA publication containing gory full-color pictures of sacrificed animals (not Carroll's) with a note stapled to each copy that read, in part: "Did you know that your neighbor, Marilyn Carroll, makes her living torturing monkeys at the University of Minnesota? Ask her to justify this cruelty and waste of the tax-payers' money. Her address is _____.* Call her. Ask for an explanation." (That was the year Carroll's children came home crying and nearly steered her into some other line of research.) The following year, PETA members picketed her home on holidays and on Sunday mornings until Carroll got her town to pass an anti-picketing ordinance. Carroll:

> For the next several years I didn't hear a thing because they were going after fur and factory farming. But in the last three years they've decided that their main priority once again is drug-abuse research in primates. Last year PETA went around putting signs on every telephone pole on campus saying that I've spent millions of dollars trying to solve the problem of drug abuse when we already have the solution. We do? I'd like to know what it is.

At the same time another animal-protection group, IDA, staged a demonstration on the main mall of the university; the protesters carried the usual kinds of signs bearing slogans such as "Taxes for treatment, not torture" and "Three animals die every second in U.S. laboratories." Heidi Greger, a sociologist and vice president of the Animal Rights Coalition of Minneapolis, told the crowd, "Our voices will be heard today and will not be silenced until Marilyn Carroll's federally funded research is stopped!"

In September, 1996, another group, the Student Organization for Animal Rights (SOAR), held a protest rally on campus, its members carrying signs saying that animal research is "scientific fraud" and distributing leaflets that called Carroll's work "cruel and useless," named her "Vivisector of the Month," and listed her home and work phone numbers. (Carroll and a veterinarian colleague got death threats by phone later that day.) SOAR also besieged Carroll at home, getting around the antipicketing ordinance by "lurking," a form of harassment used to plague abortion clinics and abortion doctors: Cars passing in front of Carroll's house would slow down and inch along, one after another, making the whole family acutely uncomfortable and Carroll herself anxious about the safety of her children. On Halloween several members of SOAR showed up, one of whom, a man in a black mask, identified himself as a member of Animal Liberation Front (ALF) and suggested that he and the SOAR cadre might burn down Carroll's home. She has since had to live with a restraining order against them and

---

*Omitted here at Carroll's request.

security provided by both the university and local law enforcement officials.[17]

Surprisingly, Carroll speaks of all this in a relatively dispassionate and calm fashion; as one fellow faculty member says, "Marilyn is made of tough stuff." Toughness, not usually thought of as a necessary attribute of the researcher, seems to be essential nowadays if one is seeking to help humankind by studying drug reactions in rats and monkeys.

2

Ronald Wood, an experimental psychologist, believes that for over a dozen years he has been performing a valuable service for his fellow human beings. He has been studying, under controlled laboratory conditions, the kinds of behavior that inhaling certain chemical vapors, particularly crack cocaine, causes through the changes it produces in various organs, especially the central nervous system. His assumption has always been that such fundamental knowledge will eventually be of value to society in its efforts to combat the horrendous effects of crack and other inhaled drugs.* Wood has good reason to believe in the worth of what he is doing: Since 1986 NIDA has found his research proposals valuable enough to warrant a series of grants totaling nearly $2 million.

Wood's only error (if one can call it that) is that he hasn't experimented on human beings but on macaque and squirrel monkeys, which he has made inhale the smoke of crack and other aerosols. The members of two animal activist organizations view this as atrociously barbaric, cruel, and impermissible, and have mounted crusades against him, one of which has gone on for four years.

Beginning in his graduate days Wood was interested in the general question of the bodily and behavioral changes produced by inhalation of vapors and chemicals common in everyday life, as revealed by laboratory studies using animals, but developments in American society steered him toward a far more urgently needed inquiry into the behavioral effects of intentionally inhaled drugs. He explains:[18]

> While I was still a graduate student, I got interested in the behavioral effects of marijuana smoking and wrote a grant proposal with my professor, Bernard Weiss, to study it in animals. I had trained monkeys to puff cigarettes, using juice as a

---

*Part of Wood's story was briefly sketched in chapter 1; it is more fully told here.

reward (they wouldn't smoke for tobacco alone). Just then a series of papers suggested that monkeys would probably not self-administer pot smoke because, it had been found, they wouldn't self-administer the effective agent intravenously. So we decided to convincingly demonstrate self-administration by the inhalation route. And we did. We trained animals to self-administer nitrous oxide ("laughing gas"), and this was a great success; every monkey leaped at the opportunity. These and other experiments led us to a series of studies of inhalation of other chemicals, including toluene and its effects on behavior.

With this background, I moved to the NYU Institute of Environmental Medicine in 1986 just as the crack epidemic was breaking out. An animal model of crack smoking offered a fine opportunity to master aerosol generation and measurement techniques (solvents and volatile anesthetics are a simple problem in comparison to condensation aerosols, smokes, fogs, and smogs), and thereby to grow as a scientist and inhalation toxicologist who could make a contribution toward dealing with the crack crisis.

I proposed such a project to NIDA, which funded it, and all was well—but not for long. In 1988 an animal activist group called Trans-Species Unlimited had a spectacular success against a researcher named Michiko Okamoto at Cornell and got her to cancel her project,* and, feeling their power, they took on my case. They put on a demonstration with about a thousand people in the street at NYU and posters all over Manhattan, and eighty-seven of their people were arrested. It was unnerving for me to walk through Grand Central Station and find activists distributing leaflets protesting my research program, and to see my name on plywood all over Manhattan and find every major local TV channel giving an account of the demonstration against my research. You can imagine my horror.[19]

Wood, although much troubled by these events, remained deeply committed to his research. His distress was renewed the following year, when Trans-Species Unlimited (TSU) prepared to mount a second campaign against him. This time, NYU asked the NIH to take action to counter the demonstration and to try to neutralize the bad publicity, and Louis Sullivan, secretary of HHS, responded by issuing a statement affirming the importance of animal research, as did Frederick Goodwin, then head of ADAMHA, Charles Schuster, head of NIDA, and James Wyngarden, director of NIH, who expressed "deep outrage" at activist attacks on biomedical research.[20] NYU also put out a press packet and arranged for Wood to be interviewed by the *Village Voice* (the article, unfortunately, was fiercely hostile to his work) and to discuss animal research at various AMA and other professional events. All this, except for the *Village Voice* article, went far to contain the TSU campaign but had some negative consequences for Wood:

> With my profile thus heightened, I found it more difficult to participate in professional meetings. In New York City I got crank calls in my hotel room in the middle

---

*Some details of Okamoto's story are in the next section of this chapter.

of the night right before a presentation. Whenever my name appeared in a program, I was likely to have a busload of demonstrators show up in front of the hotel in animal costumes and waving banners. And of course there was hate mail. But at least I wasn't worried about my family, because they lived in another city from which I commuted to the NYU Medical School laboratories at Sterling Forest, forty miles north of New York.

After several years of this, Wood had become more or less inured to his position as a target of animal activists. But in October 1993, when he was deeply involved in his latest NIDA-supported project, "Behavioral Pharmacology of Abused Aerosols: Crack," a new and far more ominous threat appeared: His project director at NIDA notified him that PHS's Office for Protection from Research Risks (OPRR) had received a letter from Susan Roy, program director of IDA, lodging a formal complaint that Wood was committing a number of serious violations of PHS's Policy on Humane Care and Use of Laboratory Animals. Wood knew enough about animal activists, IDA in particular, to recognize that this was only the first step in what would surely be a long and torturous struggle, but he had no idea how long and torturous or to what extent it would disrupt his work and his life.

OPRR replied to IDA's first letter of complaint by asking Ms. Roy to back up the charges with specific evidence; she and the headquarters staff of IDA did so over the next fourteen months in the form of thirteen more letters citing a long list of allegations of inhumane practices, including the use of restraint chairs, inhalation chambers, and water deprivation, inadequate veterinary care and botched surgery that resulted in the suffering and/or death of various monkeys, guinea pigs, and rabbits, and so on. For good measure, Roy claimed that Wood's work was outdated, duplicative of other work, and a waste of money. The letters were accompanied by a mass of copies of easily misinterpreted and seemingly incriminating internal memos, letters, and minutes of meetings—all leaked to IDA by someone with access to NYU Medical Center files—plus copies of newspaper articles by writers who had received materials from IDA and written what were in effect unverified IDA press releases.

The accusations repeatedly made by IDA in its press releases were exceedingly defamatory and shamelessly false (most would eventually be contradicted by OPRR after an investigation lasting more than a year and a half). One such press release, for instance, was headlined:

Pulling the Plug on NYU's Infamous Ron Wood

and asserted:

For over 20 years, Ron Wood has forcibly exposed and addicted untold numbers of monkeys, dogs, possums, chickens, rats and mice to toxic substances, including solvents, narcotics and crack cocaine. In the solvent experiments, Wood seals animals inside old refrigerators, as concentrated fumes of toluene and other toxic substances are funneled in.

In crack-smoking experiments, Wood deprived monkeys of water for up to 21 hours a day, terming this "modest water restriction," before placing them in restraining chairs—helmets strapped to their heads....

For years, these experiments have been criticized by scientific and drug treatment experts as being inhumane, irrelevant and wasteful of $500,000 per year....

In early 1993, sources inside NYU leaked internal documents to In Defense of Animals (IDA) showing extreme animal cruelty and scientific misconduct.[21]

The release added that Wood, whom it referred to as a "perpetrator," was guilty of scientific fraud, had "committed unspeakable cruelties on innocent animals," and had conspired with NYU officials to violate state and federal laws about animal experimentation.

During the first months of OPRR's investigation of Wood's research operation, his daily life at the laboratory was frequently subjected to disruptive inspections and investigations by people from OPRR and the NYU Medical Center's Animal Care and Use Committee (ACUC), and made miserable by numerous alarming communiqués from the U. S. Department of Agriculture (USDA), which oversees the Animal Welfare Act, and from NIH. Wood had to spend a great deal of his time assembling documents and writing reports rebutting the IDA charges and answering the queries of OPRR and ACUC; to keep his laboratory secure from intrusion by activists NYU installed security devices on the doors of the laboratory and offices, so that every passage from one room to another meant arming and disarming the devices, as well as unlocking and relocking one or several doors. He also had to dodge demonstrations in front of the laboratory by groups of activists and reporters, at one of which the leader said to those present that although she herself would never commit violence, she would understand if someone took a potshot at Ron Wood.[22]

Bad as all that was, worse was to come: The Medical Center's ACUC ordered Wood to suspend his research program while the OPRR investigation was going on. Wood had to shut down his research for eight months, during which time he had to maintain his professional staff and feed the animals without reaping any benefits; he estimates that as a result his project lost about $220,000. He says, bitterly, "There is no mechanism for recovering funds lost as a result of a suspension during an investigation of wrong-doing, even if the investigation clears the researcher, as it did in my case. But the financial loss is secondary in importance to the disruption, anger, frustration, and anguish that occur because of such attack."

During those eight dismal months in limbo, Wood, feeling that the situation at NYU would never again be a happy one, hunted for some other home for himself and his animal research. But when ACUC lifted its suspension, he and the staff resumed work at full speed and proceeded until the grant money was exhausted. Meanwhile, OPRR completed its investigation and issued its report in August, 1995; contrary to IDA's charges, it rated Wood's use of inhalation chambers and restraint chairs acceptable, and found most other allegations by IDA to be without merit. The report did note some shortcomings in the University's provisions for veterinary care, record-keeping, and certain administrative matters, all of which, it said, had already been satisfactorily corrected by NYU officials.[23]

Thus substantially exonerated, Wood filed for a grant renewal and got it. But as planned, he left NYU and took his grant to the University of Rochester—his alma mater, as it happens—where he set up his laboratory and resumed research in 1996. There he tried to maintain a low profile, hoping against hope that IDA would not quickly discover where he was. But of course IDA did (the research grants of every federal agency, and the identities and locations of the grantees, are a matter of public record and easily available on the Internet), and it has continued its efforts to halt his work. IDA has mounted demonstrations, generated mail protests by alumni, and, despite OPRR's report, has churned out news releases boldly misstating and misrepresenting OPRR's findings. Typically, a recent release refers to Wood as a "convicted animal abuser" and makes numerous slanderous and totally false statements— repeated in many media reports—such as "Ron Wood['s]...crack-smoking experiments on primates were halted after the U. S. Department of Agriculture (USDA) found him guilty of abusing animals."[24] The release also quotes Suzanne Roy, program director for IDA, as saying that Wood is a "disgraced researcher who is demonstrated to have committed scientific fraud."

Wood has had to endure this without making any legal counterattack. He writes me:

Although I continue to exist as a private person outside the unrelenting glare of public attention, some animal activist attorneys nonetheless might argue that I have become a "public figure." If this is, in fact, so, the applicable statutes and case law severely impair my ability to limit damage done by IDA's attempts to harass me and disrupt my life. Activists like this thrive on scientific illiteracy and will use unethical methods to pursue their agenda. They can indulge in slander and libel with impunity because the likelihood that the one attacked will respond with litigation is small—the investment of dollars ($125,000 and up) and time (perhaps two years) is so daunting that the activists can proceed with little fear of facing any consequences of their action.

With an unwritten but almost audible sigh, he adds, "There seems to be no end to this."

Means and Ends

The two preceding case histories are illustrative of only some of the means used by animal activists to interfere with, disrupt, and sometimes totally halt programs of animal research in the behavioral and social sciences. A definitive account of their techniques and operations would fill at least one, perhaps several, fat tomes; in brief, however, the 400 organizations radically oriented toward animal rights and the many hundreds of other animal advocacy groups combat animal research by methods ranging from the use of existing laws on the care of laboratory animals to threats of personal violence, break-ins, destruction of files and equipment, and kidnapping or release of research animals. In between is a wide array of other practices, including propagandistic publicity, posters and graffiti, demonstrations, disruptions of conferences, propaganda techniques such as the use of horrifying descriptions and color photos of experimental animals in brochures, and the defaming of researchers' characters in press releases, letters, and on the Internet.

A handful of examples of a few of these methods and goals follows, along with some suggestions as to the extent to which they have been obstructing research.

First, an acknowledgment: Much of the work of animal advocates is aimed not at research but at hunting, trapping, animal farming, and the slaughter of animals for food, and has the admirable goal of reducing needless animal suffering; the nineteenth-century ethical purpose of the movement to promote the humane treatment of animals remains as valid as ever. However, a great deal of the currently much-expanded activity of animal activists seeks not the humane treatment of animals but their total "liberation" from all uses by human beings, including the wearing of fur and leather, eating of meat and poultry, and keeping of pets. The ethical and social value of these latter-day goals and the means by which they are pursued is outside the scope of this book.

Our concern is far more limited and my stance as to the ethical and social merits of opposition to animal research in the behavioral and social sciences has already been made abundantly clear. Here, then, are a few indicators of the scope and magnitude of animal advocate interference with animal research, particularly in the behavioral and social sciences.

• *Working through existing laws and regulations* is the principal modus operandi of the Animal Legal Defense Fund (ALDF), which seeks to achieve its goals through negotiation or, when that fails, litigation.[25] The most important such law, on a federal level, is the Animal Welfare Act, originally passed in 1966 and later amended and strengthened a number of times; it governs and regulates all animal research funded by NIH and other agencies within PHS (but does not exercise control over the research treatment of rats and mice, which make up by far the largest number of research animals).[26] ALDF has had a number of significant victories, mostly in the area of the humane treatment of wild and farm animals, but some in the area of research.

Other far more confrontational and aggressive organizations, including PETA and IDA, also often use laws and regulations in addition to their more overtly aggressive methods, sometimes to great effect. It was IDA, as we have seen, that worked through OPRR, an office established under the Animal Welfare Act, to temporarily shut down Ronald Wood's research.

A historic case of the use of existing law to bring down a researcher and his project took place in 1981 (there have been many others since, though not as dramatic or totally successful from the animal advocates' viewpoint). Alex Pacheco, a lab technician at the Institute for Biomedical Research in Silver Spring, Maryland, filed a complaint with Montgomery County police to the effect that his boss, Edward Taub, was violating the humane treatment requirements of the Animal Welfare Act. Taub was conducting experiments on macaque monkeys to see whether, when a main nerve to the arm was severed, they could be trained to use the arm by means of other nerve circuits. Pacheco (who later was a co-founder of PETA) surreptitiously took gruesome colored photographs at night when no one else was around, filed his complaint, and succeeded in getting the police to confiscate the monkeys and turn them over to an associate of his, abruptly ending Taub's research. (Later, the monkeys were transferred to a primate center.) Taub was indicted on 113 counts of cruelty to animals, tried twice, and eventually exonerated on all but one trifling charge. The legal struggle over who should determine the animals' care and ultimate fate dragged on and on, but six years after the confiscation several NIMH researchers won the court's permission to examine the monkeys and found that, as Taub had hoped, some degree of cortical reorganization had taken place—not enough to restore arm control but enough to suggest that mechanisms exist which might some day be used to recreate muscular control in a limb with a severed nerve.[27] Taub, later applying what he had learned in his monkey experiments to brain reorganization in human stroke victims, has been able to restore some arm function in 25 percent of stroke victims who had lost the use of their arms.[28]

Some extremist animal advocates, rather than favoring legal regulation, reject it on the grounds that it controls rather than abolishes the use of animals. In 1985 Senator Robert Dole proposed amendments strengthening the Animal Welfare Act, and although many animal protection groups supported his bill, others opposed it, California's Society Against Vivisection saying, for instance, "Those who are for the 'regulation' of animal experimentation either don't understand what vivisection is all about or, worse yet, have a vested interest in keeping it going while pretending that they care."[29]

Propaganda, relying on photographs and descriptions of animals being used for research, has proven extremely effective not only in fund-raising but in arousing large numbers of animal lovers to write, phone, fax, and e-mail protests to their representatives and senators and to federal agencies, and to turn out for mass demonstrations. Propaganda is, of course, carefully and intentionally distorted to create the desired effect,[30] and although most of us are well aware of the common use in political propaganda of misleading allusions, half-truths, quotations attributed to sources that cannot be named, and either appealing symbols (babies, dogs, brides) or repellent ones (the fearsome-looking serial murderer, the body of a child caught in a drug shoot-out, the battered victim of police brutality), we do not expect such devices to be used in the publications of organizations with ostensibly noble motives, and accordingly are apt to believe what we read.

Many brochures, handouts, and other publications of animal advocacy groups include color photographs showing animals that the captions describe as being in misery; animal lovers, of course, read into the faces of the animals whatever they fear to find there. Whenever possible, the activists use photos showing animals that have undergone surgical procedures—a wound or a splotch of blood is worth a thousand words—or appear to be ailing in some way. The captions and text often, perhaps usually, grossly misrepresent what is illustrated; for instance, a great many animal advocacy publications, posters, and placards describe at length and in sickening detail the agonies researchers inflict on their animals, yet the USDA (which, as already noted, oversees the Animal Welfare Act) reports that 61 percent of laboratory animals suffer no pain, another 31 percent have their pain relieved by anesthesia, and only 6 percent experience pain, almost always because they are part of pain research.[31] Again: A typical ad prepared by IDA attacking a study at Rockefeller University said that researcher Alan Miller, investigating how the brain controls balance function and nausea, dosed cats with chemicals to make them vomit and that "one cat was forced to vomit 97 times in a four hour period," an experiment IDA called "horrific." What IDA researchers knew (or should have known) but did not mention was that Miller had experimented with hundreds of cats over more than a decade and that all but one of them had been totally unable to feel pain, being either decerebrate through surgery or deeply anesthetized. Furthermore, the cats did not actually vomit; the research recorded the nerve signals normally sent to the brain and muscles involved in vomiting, but under anesthesia the muscles did not contract. Only one cat was ever made to vomit without surgery or anesthesia; Miller had to be certain that the neuron activation in the anesthetized cats was comparable to that in a nonanesthetized cat.[32]

• *Confrontational and disruptive techniques* such as demonstrations, picketing, defacing of laboratory walls by graffiti, invasions of scientific meetings, shouting and other kinds of noise-making at conferences or in the vicinity of laboratories, and the like, are favored by many of the more aggressive animal advocacy groups, including IDA and PETA. A notable instance of the use of such methods to bring about the abandonment of a valuable and well-funded research program was a campaign mounted by Trans-Species Unlimited against a project at Cornell Medical School. In 1987, a year before its first attack on Ronald Wood, TSU selected Michiko Okamoto, a pharmacology researcher at Cornell, as a likely target. For years, she had been studying the effects of barbiturates on the brain by means of electrodes implanted in the skulls of cats. Both NIDA, which funded her work, and Cornell Medical School considered her project to be of major importance and her methods within ethical guidelines. But TSU widely distributed a brochure containing photos of the electrode-implanted cats, horrifying and outraging cat lovers; the brochure enabled TSU to mount a protest on April 24, 1987 (World Day for Laboratory Animals) that drew 350 demonstrators, fifty-six of whom were arrested for civil disobedience, and to have people in the streets outside the Medical School for months on end, protesting against the "horrors of the cat lab." TSU also networked with sixty-five other organizations which together generated 10,000 written protests to NIDA and drew inquiries from eighty congressional offices. Eventually the heads of the Medical School lost their nerve and told TSU that Okamoto's research would be terminated; Okamoto, who had stood her ground resolutely, now felt betrayed and wrote to NIDA, saying, "Recent developments both outside and inside the University have made it difficult for me to proceed with the experiments as proposed in my renewal grant.... I have decided reluctantly to decline the grant award as stipulated in the award notice."[33] The grant Okamoto gave up would have totaled $600,000 over a five-year period; she abandoned her addiction research using cats, but with a small temporary grant from the university itself turned to experimentation with rats.[34]

• *Militant tactics*, including those just described but going much farther, are sanctioned and advocated by groups in the animal rights wing of the movement. Such groups used to be the extremists of the movement, but in recent years animal rights ideology has been infiltrating even the centrist and moderate groups. The tactics include personal violence, break-ins, sabotage of equipment and research data, and kidnapping of the animals. Spokespersons for animal rights groups assert that it is morally justifiable to use any and all such methods to interfere with or halt such research.[35] An animal-rights movement document published on the Internet misdefines vivisection as "any use of animals in science or research that exploits and harms them,"* denounces any such use as immoral, says "vivisection" should be abolished, and lists the following as legitimate forms of animal rights activism:[36]

Sit-ins and occupations.

Obstruction and harassment of people in their animal-exploitation activities.... The idea is to make it more difficult and/or embarrassing for people to continue these activities.

Spying and infiltration of animal-exploitation industries and organizations. The information and evidence gathered can be a powerful weapon for AR activists.

Destruction of property related to exploitation and abuse of animals (laboratory equipment, meat and clothes in stores, etc.). The idea is to make it more costly and less profitable for these animal industries.

---

*According to *Webster's Third New International Dictionary*, vivisection means "the cutting of or operation on a living animal"; the animal-rights misdefinition includes any procedure that "exploits" an animal and in so doing harms it, whether or not the harm is painless.

Sabotage of the animal-exploitation industries (e.g., destruction of vehicles and buildings). The idea is to make the activities impossible.

Raids on premises associated with animal exploitation (to gather evidence, to sabotage, to liberate animals).[37]

Endorsing such activities, PETA co-founder Ingrid Newkirk told an animal rights convention, "I wish we would all get up and go into the labs and take the animals out or burn them down," and co-founder Alex Pacheco has said that arson, property destruction, burglary, and theft are "acceptable crimes" when used for the animals' cause.[38]

A few activists openly advocate the use of threats of personal violence or, better yet, actual violence. Vivien Smith, a leading female activist in ALF, has said, "I would be overjoyed when the first scientist is killed by a liberation activist." Activist Kevin Beedy, a political scientist, finds terrorism entirely acceptable: "Terrorism carries no moral or ethical connotations. It is simply the definition of a particular type of coercion....It is up to the animal rights spokespersons either to dismiss the terrorist label as propaganda or make it a badge to be proud of wearing."[39]

ALF has been the major user of violence in the war against research. Since 1979, when it broke into a laboratory at the New York University Medical Center and made off with two dogs, two guinea pigs, and a cat, ALF has conducted over a hundred operations in North America, freeing or kidnapping some 5,000 animals and causing several million dollars worth of damage.*[40] To be sure, many of ALF's raids have been directed against ranchers, butchers, fur retailers, and other commercial users of animals, but a California study indicates that about a fifth of ALF actions are directed at research facilities.[41] Some of its successful raids have done away with extremely valuable findings and halted important research. Two notable instances:

• On Christmas Eve in 1982 three ALF operatives broke into a lab at Howard University in Washington, D.C., where a research team was using thirty cats to study the effects of drugs on nerve transmission. The team photographed the cats (many of which were dragging their hind legs), made off with them, and gave them to a veterinarian, who treated them and put them up for adoption. The ALF team handed its photos over to PETA, which made effective use of them in its propaganda.[42]

---

*These are 1992 data (the latest available, as of this writing); by now, however, the figures are undoubtedly considerably higher.

• On Memorial Day weekend in 1984, five ALF infiltrators broke into the laboratory of Thomas Gennarelli at the University of Pennsylvania Medical School, where he was conducting a research project using baboons to investigate the effects of head injuries, such as those caused by whiplash in car accidents, on the brain and on cognitive functions. The break-in team destroyed a good deal of equipment, stole sixty hours of videotapes documenting the experiments, and, because ALF is illegal—the FBI has designated it a "terrorist" group—gave the videotapes to PETA, which is not. PETA edited them down into a twenty-minute film in which the researchers were made to seem, according to Jasper and Nelkin, "callous, even sadistic, and so brutal that discussion with them about their methods would be useless," the implication being that "direct action against such research was the only appropriate response."[43]

A report to Congress on terrorism in animal enterprises by the Department of Justice and the USDA said that from 1977 to 1993 there were 313 reported incidents of animal rights terrorism, and that, ominously, there was a growing tendency for the terrorists to victimize scientists themselves: Forty-three (almost 14 percent) of the documented incidents involved the victimization of individuals or their personal property, and twenty-nine cases involved personal threats ranging from intimidation and harassment to threats of bodily injury or death.[44] The victimized individuals were, primarily, research scientists using animals and working in the field of biomedical research. Of all reported incidents, 59 percent involved vandalism, 25 percent the theft or release of animals, 11 percent arson and firebombing, and 9 percent threats to the individual researchers and/or their families.[45]

* * *

The foregoing data reflect a surprising trait of some of the extremists in the animal rights movement, namely, misanthropy; their compassion for animals does not extend to humankind, which some of them apparently despise. Some relevant statements:

• George Cave of Trans-Species Unlimited (now renamed Animal Rights Mobilization): "Human beings are the only creatures that sit in smoke-filled rooms and plot the destruction of their own species."

• Ingrid Newkirk of PETA: "We're the biggest blight on the face of the earth[46].... Even if animal research resulted in a cure for AIDS, we'd be against it."[47]

• Chris DeRose, founder and director of Last Chance for Animals:

"If the death of one rat cured all diseases, it wouldn't make any difference to me."[48]

As for the thought experiment offered at the beginning of this chapter, Tom Regan, when asked whether he would save a dog or a baby if a boat capsized, said: "If it were a retarded baby and a bright dog, I'd save the dog."[49]

In contrast, most researchers, though often caricatured as dispassionate and cold-blooded, are genuinely pro-human. To quote Charles Gallistel once again:

> Restricting research on living animals is certain to restrict the progress in our understanding of the relation between the nervous system and behavior. Therefore, one should advocate such restrictions only if one believes that the moral value of this scientific knowledge and of the many human and humane benefits that flow from it cannot outweigh the suffering of a rat.[50]

Dr. Michael E. DeBakey, the distinguished heart surgeon and chancellor of Baylor College of Medicine, has said that the American public will decide whether "the rights of animals supersede a patient's right to relief from suffering and premature death. Let us hope that they reach a decision that is based on facts, reason, and good will."[51] And C. Everett Koop, the principled and compassionate former U.S. surgeon general, has succinctly said, "I care about animals. But I care about people more."[52]

12

A Miscellany of Assaults on Research

A complete account of attacks on behavioral and social research by advocacy groups in between the extremes of the political spectrum would call for many more chapters than the foregoing three. But I am mindful of that famous reaction to authorial thoroughness, the Duke of Gloucester's boorish comment when Edward Gibbon presented him with the third volume of *The Decline and Fall of the Roman Empire*: "What! Another damned, thick, square book! Always scribble, scribble, scribble! eh, Mr. Gibbon?" I therefore add here only a sampling of other instances to suggest the extent to which many kinds of advocacy groups today not only try to obstruct or halt research that might challenge their values and interests but consider their infringements on freedom of research legitimate and commendable.

Thou Shalt Not Speak Ill of Day Care

Speak ill of day care?—but who on earth would, and why? Certainly no one with any common sense; it would be like bad-mouthing Christmas, Social Security, or baseball. And Jay Belsky, a developmental psychologist, neither set out to nor supposed he would gather research data critical of day care; indeed, he thought he was doing the very opposite but negative data kept turning up in his research. A timid or cautious man would have ignored them and turned his attention elsewhere, but Belsky is neither timid nor cautious; acquaintances have described him as brash and contentious, and he himself says that having grown up in "a high-conflict family" in Manhattan's garment district, he has been able to tolerate controversy and to speak out even when he has a message that he knows will be ill received.[1] "I'm not willing to say all the right things," he has said with some pride; accordingly, he boldly informed the psychological community of his findings, and suffered the consequences.

Belsky, only thirty-four when he lit the fuse under himself in 1986, was already a full professor of human development at the Pennsylvania State University, winner of awards from APA and NIMH, recipient of research grants from NIMH, NICHD, and NSF, and author of numerous journal articles—clearly, a scientist well on the way to a distinguished career. Curly-haired, darkly bearded, and handsome in a classically Mediterranean fashion, Belsky had been interested in day care for many years. When he was an undergraduate and still unsure what he wanted to do with his life, one day he saw a fellow soccer player pass by accompanied by a gaggle of children and asked him, "Where'd you get those?" The other youth said, "Oh, I'm volunteering up at the Georgetown University Hospital day care center." For some reason, the idea appealed to Belsky, and he went to the center and volunteered to spend two or three mornings a week there. "It turned my life around," he has said. "It was the emergence of a set of interests I never knew I had."[2]

Those interests proved to be far broader than day care; the volunteer experience started him on the road to the study of child development, the discipline in which he would do his graduate and doctoral work at Cornell and in which, over the years, he has contributed a wide variety of research findings on topics ranging from the factors making for early childhood friendships to the effects of different marital and parenting styles on the child's personality, especially on the capacity to form healthy "attachments."

But Belsky's experiences in day care led him to take a particular interest in research on that topic during his graduate student years. He became a research assistant to the eminent psychologist Urie Bronfenbrenner, who had a federal contract to review what was known about the effects of child care; they conducted the review in 1976, at which time, Belsky recalls, "We didn't see much cause for concern." Although they laced their conclusions with a number of caveats, they found the evidence of most studies of day care reassuring, despite the fact that some child-development experts, most notably Britain's John Bowlby, were highly critical of day care and felt that it was far inferior to maternal care.[3]

Although the weight of professional opinion and of the evidence Belsky and others reviewed during the 1970s and early 1980s continued to be favorable to day care, the divorce rate was rising, more and more mothers of young children were going to work, and children were being put into day care at ever-younger ages, a trend that troubled Belsky.

"In the early seventies," he told a *New York Times* reporter in 1987, "we used to debate the effects of child care on children under six years of age. By the end of the seventies, we were wondering about the under-three's. In 1987 it's now children under one year of age."[4]

The trend also worried certain other developmental psychologists and mental health officials, and many studies of the effects of day care were conducted during those years, but there were so many variables that it was hard to draw conclusions. Belsky, who kept being invited to write articles and book chapters reviewing the latest findings, continued to find the effects of day care generally benign, but he could not help noticing some disturbing indications that very young children in day care twenty or more hours a week did more hitting, kicking, swearing, and shoving as first-graders than children who had had fewer hours of day care per week, and by third grade the children who had had a great deal of day care in their first year were seen by their peers as troubled. In 1985, as he prepared to give a talk at the University of Minnesota on day care and the data of the latest studies, he had a distressing epiphany:

> There was a slow, steady trickle of evidence. I would acknowledge the disconcerting evidence and, like everyone else, I would explain it away.... All of a sudden I realized, why am I spending all this time explaining away every piece of disconcerting evidence? A lot of energy was going into explaining away data, and every year there's more explaining away to be done.[5]

In that talk, and later that year in another one before the American Academy of Pediatrics, he said that the data suggested to him that more than twenty hours per week of day care in the first year of life increased the likelihood that the child would have attachment difficulties and that between three and eight the child was likely to be aggressive and noncompliant.[6] In the audience at the second talk was an editor of *Zero to Three*, a bulletin published by the National Center for Clinical Infant Programs, an organization that reports to policymakers on matters of concern regarding young children. She urged him to write a piece for them on his new view of day care; he did so, it appeared in 1986, and his life has never been the same since.

In the article, Belsky carefully reviewed the accumulating evidence that infants who were in day care over twenty hours a week, particularly if the care was not of high quality, were apt to have developmental problems, especially related to attachment. He candidly admitted that there were good grounds for disputing this view, but said that there were also good grounds for giving it careful consideration:

The point of this essay, and my reason for writing it, is not to argue that infant day care invariably or necessarily results in an anxious-avoidant attachment and, thereby, increased risk for patterns of social development that most would regard as undesirable, but rather to raise this seemingly real possibility by organizing the available data in such terms. I cannot state strongly enough that there is sufficient evidence to lead a judicious scientist to doubt this line of reasoning; by the same token, however, there is *more than enough* evidence to lead the same judicious individual to seriously entertain it and refrain from explaining away and thus dismissing findings that may be ideologically disconcerting.[7]

Belsky had thought that *Zero to Three* was a minor and little-noticed publication and that his unpleasant conclusions would pass almost unnoticed, but he was quite wrong. The editors knew how to make the most of what they considered the most controversial article they had ever published: Copies of the issue landed on the desk of every congressman and congresswoman, and Belsky and his controversial views were featured in a number of newspaper and magazine articles. Although he had carefully hedged his conclusions, he immediately became the target of intense ideological flak, since raising concerns about day care could be interpreted as hostile to feminist goals and to the pro-day-care stance of the National Institute of Child Health and Human Development (NICHD). One developmental psychologist, Tiffany Field, publicly characterized Belsky's views as "bunkum," Jerome Kagan of Harvard said that to suddenly read that day care is bad made him "symbolically cry," and Sandra Scarr called Belsky's article part of the "backlash against the women's movement" and of the effort to drive women out of the work force.[8] A number of journal articles were harshly critical of his work, and many people in the day-care and child-development field heard and repeated grotesquely distorted versions of what he was saying, such as, "Belsky says that if a child is in day care he'll be really screwed up" or "scarred for life," and "Belsky hates day care and says that day care is like death."[9]

Soon Belsky felt that he was being "effectively marginalized." As he later told clinical psychologist and author Robert Karen: "By 1985 [before the *Zero to Three* article], if I went to a child development meeting, I had lots of people coming up to me, wanting to talk to me about my work, wanting to talk about their work.... Now I walk through a meeting like Hamlet's ghost. Nobody sees me, nobody comes up to me.... I'm a pariah."[10] He had co-authored a successful textbook with his friend Larry Steinberg, but the publisher's sales force reported that now female professors were saying, "I don't want a book by Belsky," and the publisher of his next textbook, also a collaboration, said they would not publish the book with his name on it, though they would (and did) publish it omitting his name and concealing the fact that he was a co-author.[11]

Hadn't he realized, I asked, that he would stir up such a hornet's nest?

> Well, no. I was completely astounded. It sounds ridiculously naïve in retrospect not to have expected it. Until the article appeared in *Zero to Three*, I had a stellar reputation in my field—and it simply evaporated. Whatever credibility I had disappeared completely. I returned as good as I got, but what I found depressing was what it revealed to me about a field I had gone into willingly, happily, and was devoted to. It turned out that it was as much if not more politics than science. I was crushed by the fact that instead of disagreeing with me intellectually, people accused me of being against women, against day care, of implying that the quality of day care had no bearing. I had violated the Eleventh Commandment of Developmental Psychology—Thou Shalt Not Speak Ill of Day Care, whatsoever, ever.

Had his critics so disheartened him that he turned to other things?

> No, no. I just dug in. I felt many of the critiques were intellectually superficial, I lost respect for many of my adversaries. There have been times when I said to myself, "I ought to get out of this business," but then part of me would come back and say, "I don't want them to define my interests, my life, what I do with it." So for the most part I didn't let it get me down, and I continued to work in this field.

Had his enemies been able to interfere with his work or his funding?

Yes, to some degree. He is still a professor with many graduate students and still gets grants for big studies, but since 1986 "it's been a steep climb." Currently, NICHD is sponsoring an ambitious multisite consortium of day-care studies and Belsky is one of the principal investigators, but he almost got left out of the project: During NICHD's peer review discussion of studies that might be part of the project, his proposal, unlike the others, was critiqued in a hostile fashion and ranked too low to be included. But later, NICHD administrators apparently decided, or so Belsky believes, that the project would have greater credibility if he were part of it rather than made up entirely of women researchers known to be in favor of day care, so they enlarged the consortium to make place for him.

Belsky can take pride in the fact that his research helped make policymakers see parental leave as more important than they had realized and played some part in the passage of the parental leave bill in the opening months of the Clinton administration.[12] Paradoxically, however, he has been dismayed that some political conservatives have misused his findings to support anti-child-care arguments. "All I've said," he protests, "is that day care can be a risk factor. My purpose was not to castigate the institution but just to raise concerns about the institution as it exists today in this country."

The day-care hostilities continue: Belsky is still the person the media contact when they want a negative view of day care, and he is often embroiled in heated verbal and published clashes and still relatively alienated from many of his colleagues. But the trickle of data from which he derived his first cautionary critique of day care has become a steady stream.[13] Belsky comments:

> In 1994 I told the *New York Times* that the sorry state of day care in America is one of our best-kept secrets, and in 1995 and 1996 a whole slew of studies came out that confirmed my position, especially as to low-quality day care and as to the effects of over-reliance on day care for very young children. So all of a sudden it's okay to say not-nice things about day care.

Notwithstanding which, it is still okay, in academic and feminist circles, to say not-nice things about Jay Belsky, who, for all his toughness and bravado, would prefer to be respected, liked, and supported by his colleagues in his unpopular work.

Ancient Bones:
Rites of Native Peoples vs. Rights of Anthropologists

In July 1996, on a Sunday afternoon, two college students taking a shortcut along the banks of the Columbia River in Kennewick, Washington were startled to see a human skull protruding from the sand.[14] They dug it up, hid it in the bushes, and immediately notified the police, who called in Floyd Johnson, the Benton County coroner; Johnson, in turn asked James Chatters, a forensic anthropologist and owner of a consulting firm, Applied Paleoscience, to examine the skull and render an opinion as to whether it was that of a murder victim or had come from an Indian burial site.

Chatters studied the skull and was struck by certain features, particularly the worn-down crowns of the teeth and the color of the bone, both of which suggested to him that it was a remarkable find; it was the skull of a prehistoric Indian. He and Johnson went to the discovery site, painstakingly dug around in the mud and sand, and retrieved a large number of bones comprising nearly all of what had been a complete skeleton that apparently had fallen out of the river bank during recent flooding.

Because the bones might be those of a Native American, Chatters was obliged to report the find to the Army Corps of Engineers, which controls the part of the river where the bones were found. A 1990 federal law, the Native American Graves Protection and Repatriation Act (NAGPRA), empowers any federal agency that controls an area where Native American remains are found to take charge of them and requires the agency to return them to whatever tribe can make a convincing claim to them, the usual outcome of such return being reburial. Chatters asked the Corps, however, for permission, before it took any action, to have a radiocarbon dating performed as one step in determining the age and race of the skeleton. The Corps gave its approval and Chatters sent a tiny bone from the left hand to a laboratory at the University of California at Riverside, where technicians determined that the skeleton was between 9,300 and 9,600 years old.

This was stunning news; it meant that Kennewick Man—Chatters could tell that the skeleton was that of a male—was one of only about six or seven well-preserved remains that old to be found in North America. All of the previous finds had "Caucasoid" features (the term does not mean "Caucasian" but refers to certain biological features found in some south-Asian groups as well as Europeans); if Kennewick Man too were Caucasoid, the skeleton would be a valuable source of additional evidence as to where the earliest human beings to inhabit the Americas had come from. Of comparable importance, modern biochemical analysis and DNA analysis could reveal a great deal about Kennewick Man's diet, health, way of life, and blood ties to other peoples.

Before such studies could get under way, however, Chatters got a call from Johnson, the coroner, who said, to Chatters' dismay, "I'm going to have to come over and get the bones." It turned out that the Army Corps of Engineers had now decided that the radiocarbon dating proved the bones to be those of a Native American and therefore would have to be "repatriated" to whatever tribe could make the case that the skeleton was that of one of its ancestors.

On September 9, 1996 a coalition of Columbia River tribes headed by the Umatillas of northeastern Oregon, and including the Yakama, Colville, Nez Percé, and Wanapum, filed a formal claim to the skeleton and announced that they intended to bury it in a secret site where it would never again be available to science. But before the Corps could hand over the bones to the Umatillas—the law requires a thirty-day waiting period for legal protests—eight anthropologists from various western states filed suit against the repatriation of the skeleton on the grounds that Kennewick Man might not be a Native American and thus not subject to NAGPRA, since according to one anthropological view Native Americans had been relative latecomers who drove the original Caucasoid inhabitants out of the area.[15] Dennis Stanford, the chairman of the Department of Anthropology at the Smithsonian's National Museum of Natural History, said that if Kennewick Man were reburied before being studied, the loss to science would be "incalculable" and that the skeleton had "the potential to change the way we view the entire peopling of the Americas." Because the lawsuit prevented further action by the Corps for the time being, the Corps had the bones locked away in a vault at the Pacific Northwest National Laboratory in Richland, Washington, where no scientist could have access to them; if the decision in the lawsuit were to go against the anthropologists, the bones would be handed over to the Umatillas and lost to science forever.

The Umatillas, meanwhile, issued a public statement written by Armand Minthorn, a tribal religious leader, defending their position in hard-line fundamentalist terms:

> Our elders have taught us that once a body goes into the ground, it is meant to stay there until the end of time.... From our oral histories, we know that our people have been part of this land since the beginning of time. We do not believe that our people migrated here from another continent, as the scientists do.... Some scientists say that if this individual is not studied further, we, as Indians, will be destroying evidence of our history. We already know our history. It is passed on to us through our elders and through our religious practices.[16]

"We're not afraid of the truth," Minthorn has said, "We already know our truth."

Nine months later, on June 27, 1997, the U. S. District Court in Portland finally handed down a fifty-two-page opinion that "stayed" the scientists' lawsuit until the Army Corps of Engineers, as ordered by the court, gathered certain additional evidence and reached a new decision consistent with the facts and the law. But the opinion did not include a determination of the larger and more crucial question as to whether scientists have a constitutional or statutory right to study ancient remains and archeological objects held in agency and museum collections; the court did say, however, that this issue warranted greater consideration than the Corps had given it to date.

And that is where matters stand as of this writing. If the Corps eventually decides that Kennewick Man is a Native American, the bones will be lost to science; if the Corps decides otherwise, the bones will not go to the Umatillas and anthropologists will be free to study them—

a victory, to be sure, but a very limited one, since scientists will not have gained an inch in their fight against the repatriation and reburial of Native American remains.[17]

* * *

If Kennewick Man were a unique case and ultimately decided against the scientists, it would represent a substantial but not crippling loss to research on the origins of the prehistoric peoples of America. But it is far from unique. Since the passage of NAGPRA in 1990, 874 museums and federal agencies holding over 5,000 thousand Native American remains and 200,000 associated funerary objects—most of them not yet studied by modern technological methods—have had to draw up inventories of their collections and share them with "lineal descendants, Indian tribes, and Native Hawaiian organizations" by publishing notices of the inventories in the *Federal Register*.[18] As a result, during the past few years many tribal officials have obtained printouts of the inventories and scores of tribes—the first wave of what promises to be a flood—have filed repatriation demands with the museums and agencies. In most cases, the skeletal remains that will soon be lost to science have not yet been studied by modern biochemical and biogenetic methods and never will be, and in the future many or most new archeological finds will, like Kennewick Man, be claimed by tribes.

In fairness, it must be said that the proponents of NAGPRA were seeking to right old wrongs. In the past, anthropologists and archeologists were often high-handed and insensitive to the deepest feelings of native peoples: They dug up and looted new or recent graves, and bought, sold, traded, and exhibited bones and funerary objects without regard for tribal sentiments and customs. Dr. James Ridingin of Arizona State University calls hunting for bones, skulls, and artifacts, and displaying them, "extremely disrespectful," and Armand Minthorn terms digging up and studying Native American remains "desecration of the body and a violation of our most deeply-held religious beliefs." (It is easy for most people to understand and sympathize with Native Americans who are upset and angered by the exhumation and analysis of the remains of a known ancestor, but difficult to sympathize with them when they claim to feel that way about the retrieval and study of bones centuries old and not identifiable as those of any known individual.)

Representative Morris Udall, a liberal Democrat, introduced H.R. 5237, the Native American Grave Protection and Repatriation Act, on July 10, 1990, and later that month the House Committee on the Interior and Insular Affairs held a hearing at which witnesses on both sides of the controversy testified. Indians spoke of the tribes' rights to the remains and objects, some asserting that the spirits of their ancestors would not rest until they were returned to their homeland, a belief they said had been generally ignored by the museums that hold the remains and objects. Scientists stressed the importance of the remains to the scientific study of the origins and ways of life of prehistoric American peoples, and expressed great concern that if remains were reburied now, they would be lost to science forever and unavailable for study when more sophisticated research techniques were developed in the future.[19]

As has been true for other minority groups, the rights of Indians had long had the support of many liberals, but the bill was enacted into law because the liberals had the support of unlikely allies. Udall and Democratic Senator Daniel Inouye collaborated on compromise language with conservative Republican Senator John McCain, and although some large museums opposed the bill, lobbying groups for most museums and archeologists deemed it politic to support representatives of the tribes. Surprisingly, the pro-native and liberal forces also had the support of conservative Christians; as Douglas Preston explains in his account of the Kennewick case in the *New Yorker*, "Fundamentalists of all varieties tend to object to scientific research into the origins of humankind, because the results usually contradict their various creation myths.... A novel coalition of conservative Christians and liberal activists was important in getting NAGPRA through Congress." Fundamentalist support was welcome to the Indians, whose own views are thoroughly fundamentalist, according to Dr. Martin Sullivan, director of the Heard Museum in Phoenix, who for over a decade has been a negotiatior and mediator in disputes over cultural property:

> Vine DeLoria Jr.'s recent book *Red Earth, White Lies: Native Americans and the Myth of Scientific Fact* (1996) emphatically rejects commonly held scientific hypotheses regarding the origins of North America's indigenous peoples, and DeLoria supports Native origin beliefs that others call creationist. I have listened carefully to Native American traditional leaders who've made public testimony to the NAGPRA Review Committee during the past 4 years in every region of the US. Almost all have sided forcefully with DeLoria's position that science has little or nothing to offer in the debate over human remains. To them, the Umatilla position stems from a different preference as to what should be known and what should be unknown or unknowable.[20]

The unknown and unknowable already includes far more than Kennewick Man. Ever since the passage of NAGPRA, the *New York Times* reported in late 1996:

American Indian creationism, which rejects the theory of evolution and other scientific explanations of human origins in favor of the Indians' religious beliefs, has been steadily gaining in political momentum. Adhering to their own creation accounts as adamantly as biblical creationists adhere to the Book of Genesis, Indian tribes have stopped important archaeological research on hundreds of prehistoric remains.[21]

A few examples:

• The Buhl Burial, the skeleton of a woman more than 10,000 years old found in Idaho together with grave goods—one of the oldest remains yet found in North America, and valuable evidence as to the origins of the peopling of the continent—has been repatriated by the Shoshone-Bannock tribe and reburied without being adequately studied.[22]

• Another of the earliest specimens, the Hourglass Cave skeleton from the Colorado Rockies, has been reclaimed and reburied by the Southern Utes.[23]

• A third very early specimen, a mummy from Spirit Cave in Nevada, has been claimed, though not yet reburied, by the Northern Paiute tribe.[24]

• The Nevada State Museum formally asked permission of the Nevada Bureau of Land Management to make radiocarbon and DNA analyses of forty-two of the best-documented burials (including the Spirit Cave mummy) in that state's Great Basin—studies it regards as indispensable to unveiling the prehistory of that region—but as of this writing it appeared that the request would be denied. All these specimens may eventually be claimed for repatriation, a prospect that dismays the museum's researchers:

> Without the adequate analysis of the biological matter, we can never know anything about the genetic relationship between these and any other humans, including the modern claimants for repatriation. Without a minimal sample of human tissue preserved for future research, new advances in scientific method cannot be applied to the only large sample of human remains there will ever be from the one area of the US known to have a preserved perishable record of human occupations over 10,000 years in duration.[25]

• The Osage Nation Elders' Council, along with Four Directions (a Native American student organization at Missouri University), has been pressing the university to return the bones of nearly 1,500 individuals held by the university's museum to whatever tribes can make a proper claim to them. Last year the chancellor's chief of staff appointed a faculty committee to consider the matter and recommend a course of action.[26] (The outcome is not known at this time.)

• Several years ago the Hopi tribe in Arizona demanded a complete moratorium on access by researchers to field notes, photographs, sound and video recordings, and other archival materials about their tribes held at museums, research libraries, and universities. Martin Sullivan refers to this as "the first such action," which implies that others will follow.[27]

• Douglas Preston, in his *New Yorker* report on the Kennewick case, says that in the 1980s the American Museum of Natural History had an estimated 20,000 or more human remains of all races and the Smithsonian some 35,000 sets of human remains, about 18,000 of them Native American, but that now "angry Native Americans, armed with NAGPRA and various state reburial laws, are emptying such museums of bones and grave goods."[28]

Not surprisingly, even anthropologists and archeologists who empathize with the Indians' feelings are aghast at the prospect of the permanent loss of access to so much knowledge. Mike O'Brien, an anthropologist at Missouri University, says that returning bones is like burning books; Amy Dansie and Donald Tuohy of the Nevada State Museum write in *Anthropology Newsletter*, "Despite the general assumption that science is free to inquire where it will, science is no longer free in the realm of human prehistory"; and Victor Mair, an archeologist and orientalist at the University of Pennsylvania, says that "the gravest peril to the precious remains of our ancestors, whoever they may have been, is due to closed minds, minds that do not want to know."[29]

Shakespeare's Brutus says that the good that men do "is oft interred with their bones," to which we must now add "as is the knowledge of who their predecessors were, how they lived, and what that might add to our understanding of human nature and culture."

Fairness in Testing

Americans like tests that tell them about themselves; *Reader's Digest*, *Parade*, and other popular publications often run articles that include little questionnaires with titles like "How Honest Are You?", "What's Your E.Q. (Emotional Quotient)?", and "How Healthful a Life Do You Lead?" What Americans do *not* like and increasingly resist by legal and other means is the use of tests that have practical impact on their lives, such as those that influence or determine what education or employment they are qualified for.* (The routine use of such tests is not

---

*Some aspects of this phenomenon, particularly resistance to IQ testing in the 1960s and the controversy over race-norming in tests of job skills, have already been discussed; see pages 72 and 95–99.

basic research—the kind involved in most of the foregoing discussions—but as a means of gathering information on which decisions are based it constitutes applied research.)

In contrast to nearly all of what we have seen so far, opposition to testing comes not only from groups at the far ends of the political spectrum but is relatively ubiquitous. Many leaders of unions and minority groups see preemployment tests as a means by which employers deprive minority people of equal opportunity or by which business and government control and exploit the common man and woman; many liberals and centrists consider such tests invasions of constitutionally protected privacy; and a number of moderates and conservatives view tests that have been modified to eliminate cultural biases favoring whites as Trojan horse devices by which minority people of lower competence unfairly invade the job market.

All these and other viewpoints can be found in the reports published in *FairTest Examiner*, a quarterly newsletter published by the National Center for Fair & Open Testing (FairTest, in brief) of Cambridge, Massachusetts. FairTest is a nonprofit, nonmember organization supported by the Ford Foundation, the Rockefeller Family Fund, three other foundations, and individual contributors. It was founded in 1985 by a collection of education reformers, civil rights and student activists, feminists, and miscellaneous liberals, but its initial funding was provided by Pat Rooney, a libertarian conservative.[30] FairTest is devoted to "defending the rights of test-takers," that is, opposing testing seen as unfair to minorities, women, and employees in general, but on some issues, such as President Clinton's national testing proposal (see page 332 below), it has pulled together what its Public Education Director, Robert Schaeffer, calls a "strange bedfellow coalition" of groups opposed to the Clinton plan ranging from civil-rights activists to far-right Republicans.

In the past dozen years, FairTest and a number of educator, employee, and civil rights organizations, including Common Cause, have criticized and lobbied against many kinds of standardized testing, most notably SAT and ACT (ACT is an alternative to SAT), which are taken by high school seniors and weigh heavily in the reckoning of college admissions officers. The anti-SAT movement is having results: Nearly 300 colleges now have optional admissions policies in which applicants need not submit SAT scores but can offer other forms of qualification; several states have ended scholarship competitions based on SAT scores; and a growing number of journal articles have questioned the validity of the SAT and other standardized higher-education admissions tests, arguing that they are racially and culturally biased against most nonwhites.[31]

Opponents of standardized tests claim that with the present drift away from affirmative action, which had partly offset the influence of the SAT, to make SAT again a major determinant for admission to colleges and professional schools could wipe out a generation's worth of social gains for minorities and lead to the resegregation of higher education. Advocates of SAT, per contra, argue that although personality, accomplishments, and other factors should be counted in, use of SAT and other standardized tests is essential because of the large volume of applicants, the limited budgets for evaluating them, and the tendency of college-ranking guides to emphasize test scores.[32] The arguments of both sides are complex and muddied by multiple confounds, and it is currently moot whether decreasing reliance on SAT and other standardized tests by institutions of higher education will work to the benefit of American society or will prove, like open admission, to be ethically admirable but damaging to the institutions that implement it and to the society that relies on the skills of their graduates.

The same is true of preemployment tests: Many law suits have challenged, some successfully, the validity, fairness, and necessity of the preemployment exams administered by local governments and private employers, but it is far from clear whether the resulting changes that have been made in such testing have been, or will prove to be, good or bad for the nation. In 1992, as mentioned in an earlier chapter, conservative forces in Congress banned the use of race-norming (the adjustment of preemployment test scores to offset minority disadvantages) by the United States Employment Service, but as yet there is no proof that this has raised the general level of employee competence, as foes of race-norming said it should. Nor, on the other hand, is there evidence that the successful challenges to preemployment testing by employee advocacy organizations have lowered the general level of employee competence.

Yet conservative forces and employee/minority groups, as different as their aims are, are alike in one important sense: They are motivated not by a desire for higher-quality research but by purely political ends, and their efforts are thus, by and large, harmful to science. A handful of examples may be illuminating:

• Many personality tests have been developed and validated in recent decades; their use in research and diagnosis is widely accepted by psychologists and psychotherapists, and employers often use them to determine whether applicants have the traits needed for the job. Recently, however, this latter use has been successfully attacked, not on scientific grounds but as an invasion of privacy. In November 1989 a man named Sibi Soroka applied for the job of security officer at a Target Store in California and was required to take two personality tests, the Minnesota Multiphasic Personality Inventory and the California Psychological Inventory, both long widely regarded as reliable and valid, and often used to screen out emotionally unstable persons from "safety sensitive" positions.

Over the years, Target Stores had given the tests to 2,500 applicants for security jobs, but Soroka was the first to sue its owner, Dayton Hudson, for making him take the tests, which, he charged, invaded his privacy and caused him distress because they included true-false items such as "I have never indulged in any unusual sex practices," "I feel sure there is only one true religion," and "I have had no difficulty starting or holding my bowel movements." Previously, many employees had brought privacy-invasion suits over drug testing in employment settings, but the claim that standard personality tests invaded privacy broke new ground. After many delays, a trial, and an appeal, Dayton Hudson agreed in 1993 to pay damages of over $2 million. From a legal viewpoint, the settlement is a landmark; from a scientific viewpoint, an ominous defeat.[33]

• "Integrity tests" (honesty tests) are paper-and-pencil questionnaires that usually include 100 to 200 items such as "Do you think it is stealing to take small items home from work?" and "How easy is it to get away with stealing?", or, more subtly, "How much do you dislike doing what someone tells you to do?" and "True or False: I like to take chances."[34] By one estimate, 5,000 to 6,000 business establishments in the United States use such tests to screen and select job applicants in an effort to weed out at least some of the one-third of employees who steal from their employers and are responsible for $15 to $25 billion annual losses to business.[35] Integrity tests have existed since the early 1950s, but interest in and use of them has increased sharply in the past decade and a half. Many studies have sought to determine whether they are valid, that is, whether they do in fact predict honest and dishonest behavior; the studies have disagreed, but a 1991 meta-analysis combined and analyzed the data of seventy-five such studies and concluded that the tests are indeed valid.[36]

Nonetheless, their use has been criticized by civil rights advocates and a number of blacks and females have challenged them in court on the grounds that the tests unfairly discriminate against them.[37] The evidence presented has been mixed, and although some trials have found against the tests, as yet there has been no landmark win comparable to the Soroka *v.* Dayton Hudson case.[38] It may, however, be an indication of which way the wind is blowing that in recent years Minnesota, Massachusetts, and Rhode Island have enacted laws restricting the use of honesty tests, and Wisconsin's Fair Employment Law prohibits "unfair" honesty testing.[39]

• Polygraph tests ("lie-detector tests), best known for their use in criminal investigations and trials, have been recommended by polygraph technicians as a way of assaying the honesty of prospective employees. The central notion behind lie-detector testing is that anxiety about lying, particularly when the subject is asked questions he or she does not want to answer truthfully, speeds the heart rate, accelerates breathing, and increases skin conductance, all of which the machine measures and records. But many studies have raised serious doubts about the validity of polygraph testing and controlled studies have found error rates ranging anywhere from 25 to 75 percent.[40] One possible reason: The polygraph measures anxiety, not lying, and even honest people may feel anxious when taking such a test.[41]

The error rates and their potential for unjust discrimination against honest job applicants (and against innocent persons accused of crime) have led to many successful challenges of polygraph tests in court and to a 1988 federal law prohibiting most employers from using polygraph tests to screen employees and job applicants.[42] Proponents continue to insist that polygraph testing is scientific and valid, and that further research on the kinds of questions asked and the techniques of measuring responses will significantly improve its accuracy; however, because of the legal limits on such testing, almost no scientific research is now being done on it.[43]

Ironically, research revealing the shortcomings of polygraph testing was, for a time, all but buried by a different kind of political pressure. A major experimental study of polygraph testing conducted by the Department of Defense Polygraph Institute in 1989 and using simulated espionage cases found that polygraph tests yielded false conclusions in only 3 percent of the "innocent" cases but in a startling 66 percent of the "guilty" ones.[44] But because the DoD wanted to continue using polygraph testing in espionage cases, the study's lead author, Gordon Barland, was forbidden to present the results at scientific meetings or to publish them in the scientific literature, and the second author, Charles

Honts, was prohibited from publishing the findings while he remained at DoD.[45] (Honts did later publish them, and the DoD report, though not widely disseminated, is unclassified and obtainable.[46])

• For some time, a number of educators have been developing and urging the use of "performance assessment" tests that measure the ability of students to creatively use their knowledge to solve problems or write essays, often deeply personal, in contrast to the more traditional and standardized multiple-choice exams. Some school systems have adopted these tests and in 1993, after two years of development of the California Learning Assessment System, the state mandated its use in its schools. But conservative and centrist groups mobilized to stop the trend and to maintain the use of multiple-choice tests, their arguments being that performance assessment tests are subjective, invasive of privacy, and part of liberal "social engineering." The opponents succeeded killing off the California Learning Assessment System: Governor Pete Wilson vetoed its reauthorization in 1994. A continuing drive against other applications of performance assessment is being carried on in a variety of jurisdictions by means of the usual media appeals, mailings, and filing of law suits by legal advocacy groups; the outcome, FairTest's Schaeffer says, will probably not be clear for a decade or more.[47]

• The National Collegiate Athletic Association (NCAA) has long decreed the minimum SAT and ACT scores college students need to be eligible to play first-year college sports and to receive athletic scholarships. In 1994 the McIntosh Commission, a panel of independent scholars, reviewed available data and protested to NCAA that its policy made black student-athletes ineligible at six times the rate of white student-athletes. NCAA rejected the findings, but a legal activist team in Washington filed a class action suit seeking an injunction to halt NCAA's use of the minimum test score requirement. In 1997 the suit had progressed to a federal court; as of this writing it seem unlikely to come to trial until mid-1998 or later.[48]

• California has long required would-be teachers to qualify for employment by taking the California Basic Educational Skills Test (CBEST). In 1992 a class-action suit was filed on behalf of the Association of Mexican-American Educators, the California Association for Asian-Pacific Bilingual Educators, and eight individual teachers; their complaint was that the CBEST violated their civil rights by measuring skills other than those needed on the job, the result being that minorities had far lower passing rates than whites. The State's Commission on Teacher Credentialing thereupon modified the test to eliminate the non-job-related items and raised the passing score to adjust for the changes, but the results remained unfavorable for the minorities, the pass rates for the revised test being whites 73 percent, Asians 53 percent, Latinos 49 percent, and blacks 38 percent. The plaintiffs continued their suit, a California district court ruled in 1995 that the modified test was a reasonable exercise of state power, and the plaintiffs have appealed that ruling.[49]

• In 1997 the Clinton Administration proposed a national program to annually test reading in grade 4 and math in grade 8, using exams that would be about 80 percent multiple-choice. Reactions by educators' organizations were mixed, but as mentioned above, an unusual constellation of civil rights, liberal, and conservative advocacy groups blocked passage of the proposed legislation. Phyllis Schlafly's Eagle Forum and other conservative organizations militated against it and enlisted support from Representative William Gooding, chair of the House Committee on Education and the Workforce; the NAACP Legal Defense and Education Fund and other civil rights groups voiced their opposition; and some black and Hispanic members of Congress expressed deep mistrust of the tests. By early November, 1997 a face-saving compromise was worked out with the Administration: The use of the test was put on hold until NAS can conduct studies of the matter; Congress is to take it up again next year, but if at that time antitesting forces in the House or Senate are able to deny funding, the proposal will die.[50]

A Shotgun Blast at Mental Health Research

In March, 1995, shortly before the House Labor, Health and Human Services Appropriations Subcommittee was to take up the 1996 appropriations bill for NIMH, its members—and all other members of Congress—received a disturbing two-page fax. It came from Citizens Against Government Waste (CAGW), a 600,000-member national lobbyist organization, primarily conservative but with some centrist support, whose purpose is to identify what it sees as wasteful federal government operations and press Congress to take corrective measures.

The fax presented a list of twenty—later expanded to twenty-three—research programs funded by NIMH that CAGW called "wacky, even sinister science-fair experiments" and a waste of taxpayer money. Or far worse: Tom Schatz, president of CAGW, said that taxpayers "should be angered and appalled...especially [by] a $1.3 million study of known sex offenders that could have needlessly put children at risk," a charge spelled out in the fax and later CAGW press releases as "a four-year study in which known child molesters were allowed to prey on children without law enforcement officials being notified."[51]

Other research projects itemized in the CAGW fax and press releases, though they were not that horrifying, seemed frivolous, absurd, and having no purpose other than to fatten the purses of the researchers. Among the studies listed (the following descriptions are CAGW's words):

- A thirty-two-year study on the chemical reactions in the jaw muscles of pigeons to find reasons for eating disorders in humans. (Over $1,200,000)

- A nine-year study of the brain circuits which control mounting and receptive sexual behavior of the unisex whiptail lizard. (Over $1,400,000)

- A five-year study of red-winged blackbirds to determine how humans make choices of mates, dwelling, reproductive areas, escape routes and foraging areas. (Over $539,000)

- A seventeen-year study of slang terms used by Puerto Ricans in New York City when under stress. ($4.7 million)

A number of members of Congress were understandably incensed and eager to demonstrate to their constituents that they would tolerate no such boondoggles and most certainly not a project that allowed sex offenders to freely prey upon children. Three especially infuriated Republican congressmen were in a good position to do something about it: Ernest Istook of Oklahoma, Ed Royce of California, and Henry Bonilla of Texas were all members of the subcommittee that was about to consider NIMH's 1996 appropriations, and any one of them could draft an amendment cutting NIMH's appropriation, ostensibly as part of the general budget-cutting being carried on that season but actually as punishment for funding such projects. If the amendment failed to be approved by the subcommittee, any representative or senator could offer one when the appropriations bill later came to the floor of the House or Senate unless an amendment-limiting procedure were in effect. The word going around on the Hill was that the House committee might recommend up to a 10 percent cut in NIMH's appropriation and that some members of the Senate Budget Committee were thinking of a draconian 25 percent cut.[52]

NIMH officials were greatly alarmed, as were the officers of APA and APS, the two national organizations of psychologists. Alan Kraut, executive director of APS says, "We were scared to death," and for good reason; in fact, for two good reasons. One: CAGW had shown itself capable of exerting considerable lobbying power and in the previous ten years had played a part, in some cases a major one, in cutbacks or terminations of federal projects running to many millions and even billions of dollars. The other reason: The CAGW attack was actually the latest and most worrisome stratagem of a powerful and adamant foe of all mental health research. Dr. Rex Cowdry, acting director of NIMH, identified that foe when he testified before the subcommittee several days later at the hearing on the appropriation bill:

> The NIMH portfolio has come under attack in a coordinated campaign, which frankly I would describe as disinformation, initiated by the Citizens Commission on Human Rights...a group sponsored by the Church of Scientology, and the Commission's campaign echoes the themes of Scientology. Scientologists believe that mental disorders can be treated by an expensive program of so-called auditing, using the E-meter, a device available from the Church of Scientology, to guide the removal of engrams and to advance to higher stages of being.
>
> The church has consistently attacked major advances in psychiatric treatment. They focus particular attention on medications which relieve the profound symptoms of psychosis and depression. Their latest assault on mental illness research comes under the guise of alleged waste, fraud and abuse.... There is an underlying self-serving agenda, I believe, that would deny millions of Americans the hard-won fruits of successful treatments resulting from our biomedical and behavioral research. [53]

A number of other knowledgeable people, including Kraut and Frederick Goodwin, former head of NIMH, likewise had reason to believe that CAGW's attack was mounted on behalf of, or at least based on materials furnished by, the Church of Scientology. David Williams, director of research at CAGW, whom I asked about the charge, answered carefully: "We have not received any money from Scientologists as a group. I can truthfully tell you that there was no conspiracy here. We are not a front for Scientology." His statement may have been accurate as far as it went, but Goodwin told me that the list of NIMH research projects that CAGW considered wasteful, absurd, or reprehensible was in fact drawn up by Joe Winkelman, a member of CAGW's research staff—whom Goodwin had interviewed and who was indeed a member of the Church of Scientology.[54] Williams acknowledged that Winkelman had prepared the list but said, "He had a particular interest in the NIMH, and he had a list of grants, but I don't know how he got the information," a remark which, coming from the director of research of CAGW, seems somewhat disingenuous.

At the subcommittee hearing Cowdry presented detailed explanations and justifications of each of the twenty projects CAGW regarded as wasteful, wacky, or sinister. Several days earlier, as soon as word reached NIMH of the CAGW fax to the members of Congress, Richard Nakamura, then chief of NIMH's Behavioral and Integrative Neuro-science Research Branch, aided by members of the institute's Science Policy Office, had begun preparing an emergency counterattack. Nakamura had contacted all principal investigators of the studies on the CAGW list, asking them to drop everything and immediately provide a brief description of their work and an explanation of its relevance to NIMH's goals. Within three days, working day and night, the NIMH staff had gathered thirty-eight pages of write-ups from the researchers, rewritten them to make them more comprehensible to laypersons, had the resulting twenty-two-page document printed, and delivered copies to Cowdry and to the subcommittee's members. Nakamura comments:

> Given the atmosphere and the importance to Congress of paring down the budget at that time, NIMH was under a clear threat, and CAGW had a good track record of getting agencies' funding cut. We took very seriously the news that they were targeting us. It was incumbent on us to show that even weird-sounding grants—and there's no question that this list had strange-sounding grants on it—were worth the funding we were giving them. We had to take complex ideas and turn them into language that Congress could accept.

The NIMH document's accounts of the challenged studies made it clear that CAGW's descriptions were artful selections or distortions of project language that either trivialized or grossly misrepresented the research. For instance, CAGW had said that one project was, as quoted above, "a nine-year study of the brain circuits which control mounting and receptive sexual behavior of the unisex whiptail lizard." Silly stuff, clearly—until one reads the NIMH response:

> The brain mechanisms underlying many complex behaviors have been preserved throughout evolution, thus making animals, including reptiles such as lizards, appropriate choices for research intended ultimately to clarify certain aspects of human behavior.... Dr. Crews' research focuses on hormonal influences on sexual behavior. The species of whiptail lizards used in Dr. Crews' research include parthenogenetic species: that is, animals that reproduce without getting genetic material from partners. Such animals show sexual behavior but each individual animal can play both male and female roles. Thus, these lizards offer unusually apt models in which to study how hormones influence behavior....
>
> Dr. Crews' research has demonstrated that behavioral differences observed in animals of the same species need not be based on structural differences in the brain; rather, animals with the same brain structure but different environmental factors will behave differently, a finding that challenges prevailing scientific understanding of animal behavior. Additionally, the research has shown that proges-

terone, considered to be a female hormone, plays an important part in male sexual behavior. These findings have stimulated reexamination of progesterone's role in human reproductive behavior.[55]

Another project was identified by CAGW as "a seventeen-year study of slang terms used by Puerto Ricans in New York City when under stress. (4.7 million)" A costly and seemingly worthless diversion—but not when adequately explained. NIMH, through a grant to the Hispanic Mental Health Research Center at Fordham University, was funding a large-scale many-faceted research effort to learn how to assess and treat mental disorders in U. S. Hispanics, and one component of that project—the study listed by CAGW—was a study seeking to develop psychological "scales" (tests) for measuring mental health among New York Puerto Ricans. Without such tests—existing mental health scales, based on Anglo culture and language, were of little use—health agencies could neither assess the extent and severity of psychological disorders among Puerto Ricans in New York nor knowledgeably develop programs to deal with them. As summarized in the NIMH presentation for the subcommittee:

> The specific study referred to in the CAGW document refers to a project concerned with how the interaction between the culture that Puerto Ricans bring with them to the U.S. mainland, and the mainstream culture they confront, is related to immigrant Puerto Rican psychological wellbeing and distress. The objectives of Dr. Rogler's study are to develop and validate two psychological scales: a measure that will assess biculturality, and a measure of the idioms that Puerto Ricans use to express psychological distress...[in order to be able to gather] data vital to the Nation, the State and the City in setting health delivery systems. [56]

Cowdry, in his appearance before the subcommittee, eloquently presented the material prepared by Nakamura but often in far more outspoken terms than Nakamura had used in the response document, saying, for instance:

> The allegation that NIMH has supported a 17-year New York study of slang terms used by Puerto Ricans when under stress is an outrageous summary of our Hispanic Research Center at Fordham University, in the Bronx.... The use of the words "slang terms" is a total distortion of an attempt to study the words that Hispanic individuals use to express psychological distress, which may not be nice, simple diagnostic terms like panic, for example, or even depression, necessarily.... The study, for example, looks at...term[s] like—it wasn't slang terms— "ataque de nervios," which is in some Hispanic cultures a term that's used to describe a panic-like syndrome. And part of the importance is to understand how such a term as this might be similar to panic, and how it turns out to be a more inclusive term. We must know this to be sure that we deliver the right treatment.[57]

As for CAGW's characterization of the study of child molesters, Cowdry was even more vehement:

> In the most egregious example of misrepresentation, they claim that we funded a "four-year study in which known child molesters were allowed to prey on children without law enforcement officials being notified."
>
> In truth, this study concerns a sex offender assessment and treatment study that was conducted at the Florida Mental Health Group in Tampa...[and] approved by local authorities to treat child molesters who were required to receive such treatment as a condition of probation or parole. Obviously, these sex offenders were all known to the local legal authorities....
>
> Rather than endangering the community, I think you can make a strong case that the NIMH research program probably contributed to enhanced safety in this setting by offering the best available treatment in a well-organized, intensive and extended format. By carefully monitoring the participants in the research program, the risk of re-offending by a participating child molester was probably reduced.... This project had a local advisory board of victim advocates, attorneys, police and others, who carefully reviewed and supported the procedures in this project....
>
> It is this kind of misrepresentation of facts and the purpose of the research that I think frankly characterize a good many of the specific materials developed by the Scientologists. [19]

Despite some sharp questioning by Representative Bonilla and needling by Representative Istook, Cowdry's testimony and the NIMH document plus the testimony of several other high-ranking officials from NIH and HHS defused the attack on the twenty NIMH research projects, and the NIMH appropriations bill was approved without the cuts advocated by CAGW. At NIMH, APA, and APS, there was a guarded sense of relief—guarded because neither CAGW nor the members of Congress who were most sympathetic to its stand on NIMH research had given up. Months later, Winkelman was still contacting members of Congress he thought might be sympathetic to the CAGW/Scientology viewpoint, and in late July, he conferred with Representative Royce and in a follow-up letter offered him an expanded list of NIMH studies in the hope that Royce would offer an amendment reducing NIMH funding to the Labor/HHS bill, which had been reported out from the appropriations committee to the House.

A few days later Royce, who had been preparing such an amendment, dropped the idea because, aides said, he had too much else going on. Perhaps so, or perhaps he thought it was a losing cause. CAGW did not think so; it continued to send faxes to members of Congress, a typical one charging that NIMH works "hand-in-hand with an army of social engineers who have been busy redefining mental illness over the past 30 years" and is "wasting taxpayer dollars to define normal behavior as pathology and create new victim groups."[59] David Williams, whom I interviewed more than a year after the committee hearing, said that CAGW had not given up on the effort to get the twenty-three projects defunded. "We're continuing to work on the NIMH thing," he said. "We will being making presentations on it."

Thus, although the CAGW/Scientology threat to NIMH may not be imminent, apparently it is immanent.

A Penultimate Script

Not a postscript, please note, but a next-to-last word; next-to-last for a reason I will give shortly. But first to the business of this Penultimate Script:

In addition to the cases presented thus far, various informants have called to my attention a number of other instances of egregious political intrusion on scientific freedom. Most are in areas of science outside the concern of this book, though some include or at least touch upon the social sciences. But we have already seen so much that rather than present any more detailed case histories, I will merely cite four other notable cases in brief to further illustrate political opposition by persons and groups not at the extremes of the political spectrum.

• In 1995 Congress killed off one of its own major research agencies, the Office of Technology Assessment. OTA had long been conducting high-quality original studies and research reviews in response to congressional requests; about half of its output either dealt with social sciences or examined behavioral and social issues associated with technological innovations. In the hearings and debate about closing down OTA, the main issue seemed to be whether the studies took too long and cost too much, but knowledgeable observers say there was a hidden agenda: OTA had originally been started by Democrats, many Republicans disliked its considerable interest in social sciences, and the drive to junk it was headed by a conservative Republican, Senator Connie Mack, and a mainline Republican, Representative Robert Walker.[60]

• In 1979 psychiatrist Herbert Needleman of the University of Pittsburgh School of Medicine analyzed the lead content of children's discarded first teeth, correlated the data with their cognitive abilities, and reported that those who had elevated lead in their teeth scored lower on tests of IQ, speech and language function, and measures of attention. Two scientists who were or shortly became grantees of the lead industry association publicly accused Needleman of having deliberately manipulated the data, and for the next ten years Needleman was harassed and criticized by lead-industry friends and his continuing investigation of the behavioral effects of low-level exposure to lead crippled by coordinated attacks on his work at scientific meetings and by the skillful use of the procedures for investigating scientific misconduct. Not until 1992 did the federal Office of Research Integrity clear Needleman of misconduct (although it did recommend that he publish some corrections to his data).[61]

• For many years, Stanton Glantz, a professor in the School of Medicine, University of California, San Francisco, has investigated the effects of second-hand smoke on the heart, and, at greater peril to his work, the influence wielded by tobacco companies on state and federal legislators' actions on tobacco issues. The tobacco industry has waged a continuing war against his research through the votes of legislators to whom it has made campaign contributions. Two instances:

1. Under California's Proposition 99, passed in 1988, nearly half a million dollars of cigarette tax money was allocated to Glantz's research, a small part of which consisted of studies of the influence of the industry's political contributions on tobacco legislation. Most members of the Assembly had previously voted with tobacco interests on some issues, and Willie Brown, then Speaker of the Assembly, had been a major recipient of tobacco industry campaign donations. In 1990 Brown said to university officials that if Glantz's study were not shut down, "you're going to have trouble with me on every single appropriation." The university stood fast. Governor Wilson then vetoed a bill authorizing continued spending of Proposition 99 revenues on research projects, and in 1994 and 1995 the legislature voted to divert Proposition 99 funds from research into health care for the poor. (Eventually, the courts restored the funding.)

2. By the time the California Legislature had cut off the Proposition 99 research program, Glantz had won a grant from the National Cancer Institute (NCI) supporting the continuation and expansion of his work. But in 1995 the long arm of the tobacco industry reached into the House Appropriations Committee, the majority of whose members were Republicans and recipients of tobacco industry contributions; the Committee, considering renewal of NCI's appropriation, voted to cut off NCI funding for Glantz's project, the only time the Committee has ever singled out a specific NCI research grant for defunding. (After much harrumphing and posturing, Congress ignored the Committee's recommendation and the grant has continued.)[62]

• In the 1980s, a number of experiments involving fetal-tissue transplantation promised significant help for sufferers of two cognitive disorders, Parkinson's and Alzheimer's diseases. But in 1988, mindful of (or perhaps reminded of) Presidents Reagan's and Bush's debts to anti-abortion forces, the leadership of HHS ordered a moratorium on federal funding for all research using fetal tissue from elective abortions (the major source of such tissue; spontaneous miscarriages could supply only a minimal amount). Efforts by liberal and centrist forces in Congress to end the ban were defeated again and again. In 1992 a bill that would have lifted the ban finally passed both houses but President Bush vetoed it and the House failed by fourteen votes to override the veto. *Science* magazine, in an editorial, said, regretfully, "The sooner this game of politics is ended, the better. Research on fetal tissue has great promise of benefit to all." But federal funding for such research remained unobtainable until President Clinton took office; even he, however, banned funding for research that would have created in-vitro embryos in order to harvest and use the tissue experimentally.[63]

* * *

And so on, and on. But perhaps, adapting Mies van der Rohe's famous apothegm, more would be less, and it is time to conclude.

So, now, my reason for calling this section a next-to-last word: Having displayed at length the increasing infringements on freedom of research in the social sciences by political forces of all kinds, I must confront the difficult question, previously answered only in brief, as to whether such opposition is ever justified; or to put it another way, whether there are or should be any limits to freedom of research in these sciences. A few observations on this crucial question, in the following epilogue, will, I promise, be the last word.

Epilogue:
The Boundaries of Freedom of Research:
Second Thoughts

A common and deeply troubling experience of childhood is the recognition that there are some things we are not supposed to ask about, some kinds of knowledge that are forbidden. What are our parents doing at night that sounds so odd? How much money does our family have? Why did God make Grandpop suffer so before he died? Why are the people two houses away, who go to that other church, so unfriendly?

Later we learn the answers, but we never outgrow the sense that there are some things we are not supposed to know and that learning the truth about would harm us. The motif is deeply embedded in both Judeo-Christian and Greek culture: Adam and Eve ate of the forbidden fruit of the tree of the knowledge of good and evil and were expelled from Eden; Pandora (or, in some versions of the legend, her husband) opened the box that was supposed to remain shut and let evils out upon the world; Lot's wife, disobeying divine instructions, looked back to see Sodom being destroyed by God and was turned into a pillar of salt; Orpheus, rescuing his wife Eurydice from the underworld, turned around, against Pluto's orders, to be sure she was following him, and so lost her; Psyche, visited only in the dark by her lover, Cupid, and overcome by her desire to know if he was the monster she feared would marry her, brought an oil lamp to where he slept and let a drop of hot oil fall on him, whereupon he fled because of her lack of trust in him (though later Jupiter took pity on them, turned her into a goddess, and reunited the lovers).[1]

In the era of science the ancient theme has taken the form of cautionary tales about researchers who, daring to invade territory reserved for the Maker, create or modify life itself, with disastrous consequences: *Frankenstein, or The Modern Prometheus*, *The Strange Case of Dr. Jekyll and Mr. Hyde*, and in recent years *Jurassic Park* and other stories in which the hubris of scientists brings down horror upon them and innocent bystanders. Thus, both childhood experience and cultural tradition predispose us to fear that scientists who dare to discover truths beyond their proper ken will unleash upon the world evils created by their forays into forbidden territory.

But fear of the consequences of probing too deeply into the unknown is expressed not only in legend, fiction, and popular superstition; it is the source of the intellectually retrograde and socially harmful efforts of political advocacy groups to obstruct and forbid scientific inquiries that some of them fear will disadvantage their members, others see as undermining their belief systems and values, and still others believe will prove ruinous to the entire nation.

This book, arguing for the primacy of freedom of scientific research, has portrayed politically motivated opposition to research as at best unenlightened and misinformed, at worst bigoted, antiintellectual, and tyrannical, but it is only fair to ask if there are not some kinds of research that should be forbidden. A proper answer to that question would fill a massive tome; what follows is only a hint of what it would contain.

* * *

First, it is necessary to distinguish between two meanings of the word "science" to which the concept of freedom applies: the first, the methodology of research, and the second, the knowledge being sought and acquired by it.[2]

The first meaning will not occupy us long: There is little disagreement within the scientific community and the society around it that some kinds of methodology are either (1) impermissible on ethical grounds or (2) so dangerous to the subjects of the research or society, or both, as to warrant suppression by the government or other institutions.

1. *Impermissible on ethical grounds*: The ultimate exemplars of unethical research methodology are the abominable experiments, mentioned earlier, performed by Nazi doctors on hapless concentration camp prisoners. Conducting research procedures on human subjects who have not voluntarily and knowingly agreed to undergo what is done to them has been forbidden by civilized nations been since the drafting of the Nuremberg Code. The key proviso of the code is that the subjects must freely give their "informed consent"; anything done to them without it violates their right to determine what is done to their bodies and minds.

The Nazi doctors' experiments were primarily biomedical, but the same ethical principle applies to psychological and social research with human subjects, and recipients of federal research grants in those fields have long been obliged to observe the informed-consent principle by

HHS regulations. In particular, deceptive social-psychological research—studies in which subjects are misinformed about the situation they will be exposed to in order to elicit their natural reactions—is authorized by Institutional Review Boards only if the research "could not practicably be carried out" without deception and if there will be "minimum risk to the subject."[3] Much of the deceptive research conducted several decades ago went far beyond those bounds and could not be replicated today if federally funded; even if funded by private sources, it might be blocked by the universities with which the researchers are affiliated.

Research with animal subjects, however, is not constrained by the informed-consent principle, since, obviously, animals can neither understand nor consent to an experiment. Nor does research invade their rights, since, as already pointed out, a right is a human artifact, a concept comprehensible only to an intelligence capable of verbal abstractions. Nonetheless, the great majority of researchers using animals treat them humanely, both out of compassion and in compliance with federal requirements for the humane care of experimental animals. Contrary to the propaganda of PETA, IDA, and other animal activist groups, researchers, as noted earlier, do not inflict pain in the vast majority of experiments using laboratory animals.

2. Impermissible because unduly dangerous: Society, in the interests of self-preservation, obviously has a right to limit or forbid inordinately dangerous research methodology. Most research involving serious danger lies outside our area of interest; examples are experiments with pathogenic organisms where safeguards against their escape beyond the laboratory are inadequate, tests of pest control in which predators of the pests are released into the environment without sufficient knowledge of their possible adverse impact, and of course tests of nuclear explosions that leak radioactivity into the environment. But even within the social sciences some research methods, though not involving deception, may impose undue risk to participants—experiments, for instance, that impose severe stress on subjects (noise, threats, apparent danger, simulated accidents), intense forms of aversive therapy that psychologically traumatize the subjects, the supposed recovery of dreadful memories through therapists' persistent suggestions and the use of hypnosis, and so on. Appropriately, most research involving such risks is now either controlled by federal, state, or institutional regulations of one kind or another or by the codes of ethics of professional societies.

* * *

So much for limitations on freedom of methodology.

The far more salient question is whether certain kinds of scientific investigation ought to be banned because the knowledge they seek is inherently harmful to humankind.

But who can reliably predict that acquiring some particular form of scientific knowledge will harm humankind—or, for that matter, benefit it? The history of science is replete with examples of astonishingly erroneous predictions by the very people one would think best qualified to see into the future. A single example will serve: In 1930, the Nobel Laureate physicist Robert Millikan, who had determined the charge on the electron, rebutted alarming speculation by the physical chemist Frederick Soddy (also a Nobelist) that atomic energy might some day yield weapons of terrible power:

> Since Mr. Soddy raised the hobgoblin of dangerous quantities of available sub-atomic energy, [science] has brought to light good evidence that this particular hobgoblin—like most of the hobgoblins that crowd in on the mind of ignorance—was a myth.... The new evidence born of further scientific study is to the effect that it is highly improbable that there is any appreciable amount of available sub-atomic energy to tap.[4]

So said the Nobel Prize winning physicist only fifteen years before Hiroshima and Nagasaki.

Although scientists sometimes commit such howlers, usually they are able to make somewhat better guesses than lay persons about the knowledge that might be gained through proposed research. Such informed guesses, though not an ideal basis on which to decide what kinds of research are allowable and what should be banned, are the best we have. Imperfect though the scientists' guesses are, the uninformed guesses of nonscientists are a far poorer guide for making such decisions. Today's "New Know-Nothings," as I have called them, dogmatically assert that certain kinds of new knowledge will have dire consequences or that the social costs of the knowledge will greatly outweigh the possible benefits, but their predictions are based on political and religious beliefs, not on empirical evidence. While they have a right to their beliefs, they do not have a right to force scientists to abstain from seeking knowledge that may challenge those beliefs.

* * *

Since lay predictions of the effects of the knowledge sought by proposed research are worth little and scientists' predictions are only informed guesswork, is there any other basis on which to answer the question whether any kinds of knowledge should *not* be sought?

Some scientists have answered that question with a categorical No: No kind of knowledge should be considered impermissible. Many physicists have regretted that the research that produced the atomic bomb was ever conducted, but others have argued that the knowledge of how to obtain nuclear reactions has had immensely valuable applications, and some have taken the extreme position that whether or not the knowledge was of practical value, we were right to seek it: As the combative physicist Edward Teller asserted unequivocally a few years ago, "There is no case where ignorance should be preferred to knowledge—*especially* if the knowledge is terrible."[5]

Teller's dictum, however, seems more a declaration of faith than a reason-based appraisal. Could anyone prefer knowledge of how to create a more virulent form of anthrax for use in biological warfare to ignorance of how to create it? Or favor knowledge of how to make a more devastating nerve gas over the lack of such knowledge? There are, surely, some kinds of research that yield knowledge of no value other than a foundation for certain horrendous applications. Not only should scientists shun such research for ethical reasons but governments should forbid it, despite the grave problem of how to prevent it from being conducted by unethical researchers in rogue states such as Iraq.

Clear enough; but the situation is less clear in the case of the kind of social research said by those politically opposed to it to be harmful to some segments of society and productive of social conflict. This was the case with J. Philippe Rushton's studies of racial differences in intelligence, parental behavior, incidence of criminal behavior, and other traits. Black and civil rights activists said that his findings were not only seriously flawed but would be psychologically and socially harmful to blacks, provide bigots with ammunition to use in legislative chambers, increase racial animosity, and incite violence and social disorder.[6]

But is it certain or even likely that these results would ensue? And even if they did, that they would clearly outweigh any possible benefits that might come from having a factual basis for policy development? Many reputable social scientists have said that Rushton's work is grossly faulty and others, equally reputable, that it is sound, but whether it is faulty or sound is not relevant to whether or not it should be suppressed. The only approach to such research consonant with the principle of freedom of thought and expression is not suppression but disproof. The philosopher of science Sir Karl Popper said that "the business of science is falsification," implying that researchers should be free to produce what they consider new knowledge and that scientific progress is made by trying to disprove their findings, most of which will, indeed, prove false— but we should rely on science, not censorship, to prove them so.[7]

And yet, must we not pay heed to the predictions of the political opponents of research such as Rushton's that it will do serious social damage? Yes, we should consider what they say if it is anything more than mere dark speculation. But such predictions, at least all that I have read, are based not on hard evidence such as historical precedents or extrapolations of sociological data but on the predictors' political beliefs. Even if one considers their beliefs admirable, even if one understands and sympathizes with the feelings of those who are alarmed and infuriated by Rushton's research, their forecasts of disaster are inadequate grounds on which to obstruct or ban it.

The same is true of political opposition to research on the biological components of gender differences, the harm done to infants by overlong hours of day care, the sources of teenage sexual attitudes and behaviors, and many another case that we have looked at. In all of them, the assertions that the research will be socially damaging and therefore should be prohibited are predictions without evidence; they are guesswork, agitprop, political rodomontade. And even if there are some grounds to think that the findings could generate social tensions, these outcomes may be outweighed by the possible value of the findings— but who is to weigh the good and bad possible outcomes, and how, since both the harm and benefit of new knowledge are often unknown and unsuspected until the knowledge is available?

Since weighing such imponderables against each other is so uncertain a procedure, we must seek a better way of appraising the legitimacy of research that offends some groups and which, they say, will have harmful consequences. And in fact there are two better ways, both of them consonant with Popper's doctrine and with the ethos of freedom of research. One is to reanalyze the controversial or upsetting data by more sophisticated methods than the original researcher employed and to show that his or her conclusions are incorrect. The other is to perform better primary research on the same subject, producing findings that disprove those alleged to be wrong and harmful. The lively and open interchange of ideas and findings, not the suppression of those that some people find repugnant, is the essential mechanism by which humankind advances from ignorance to understanding, from passive control by fate to active control of its own fate.

Still, what if the acquisition of some kinds of knowledge is likely to unfairly harm some people? The Human Genome Project may well make it possible to easily identify individuals bound to develop hereditary physical or mental disorders during adulthood, and this could cause them to be classified as uninsurable by insurance companies, unemployable by potential employers, and undesirable by potential mates. In the social sciences, comparable harm may arise from knowledge: Research indicating a biological tendency in women to be less aggressive than males might obstruct their efforts to rise to top-level management positions, and studies showing that Hispanics, blacks, and Native Americans score lower than whites on tests of various cognitive skills could limit their employment opportunities and chances of career success.

Should society halt research that generates such knowledge? Are special-interest groups justified in trying to do so? Organizations of people who believe they will be harmed by such research findings, and some ethicists, say yes to both questions, but some scientists argue that the cure, suppression, may be worse than the disease; we may never learn things that would eventually improve the human condition. Bernard Davis says of biobehavioral research (his comments are equally applicable to psychological research):

> In the long run increased insight into the biological roots of our behavior should aid us in meeting the crisis. If we should cut off the flow of such insights, in order to sidestep immediate problems, we may pay dearly—not only through deprival of valuable knowledge but also through damage to the ideals of an open society....
>
> If we build policies on assumptions that contradict reality, nature will have the last word, and our policies will not be effective or durable. Hence freedom of inquiry in this area...can be defended on long-term pragmatic grounds—as well as on grounds of admiration for the cultural value of creative intellectual activity.*[8]

J. Richard Udry, whose major sex survey was killed by HHS Secretary Sullivan in response to right wing pressures, grants that opponents of his work have a right to their view and sees the conflict between the proponents and opponents of sex research not as a battle between the forces of good and evil but as a "genuine and legitimate political battle between two groups in the population who hold diametrically opposed policy views." In that legitimate battle, however, conservatives have overcome the efforts of science administrators, researchers, and Con-

---

*Davis made these comments in 1986, before the launching of the Human Genome Project, but they are as pertinent today as they were then.

gress to protect the peer review system, perverting the scientific enterprise itself and seriously jeopardizing the peer review system, the most important safeguard of freedom of research. Referring to the conservatives' halting of SHARP and the American Teenage Study, Udry says:

> The political victory over these high profile sex research projects has had a chilling effect on the plans of other researchers to seek funds for sex research. This was inevitable, and the chill must be gratifying to the victors.... We should make cause with the entire scientific research community to insulate peer review from being undermined. This means that we must be organized for political action to defend peer review.

But, he adds, the peer review system has also been seriously eroded by political forces of the liberal-left side, with results equally harmful to science, which is why he concludes, "We and our political defenders must be ready to defend peer review against political violations by those with whose politics we agree."[9]

* * *

Thus far we have found that while certain kinds of research methodology are themselves either despicable or dangerous and not to be tolerated, the only areas of scientific knowledge, and therefore of scientific research, that by their very nature should be forbidden are those that yield only purely and predictably destructive knowledge. Aside from that, we have found no other blanket justification for forbidding the search for knowledge. Nothing about scientific research merits a modern equivalent of the kind of taboo of knowledge of the primitive Israelites whose God told them that they dared not see His face, or of the early Christian theologians who declared that some central issues in their religion were mysteries that had to be taken on faith ("I believe it because it is absurd," said Tertullian, and then outdid himself: "It is certain because it is impossible"[10]).

Roger Shattuck, in the appendix of his intriguing book *Forbidden Knowledge*, names six kinds of knowledge that, he suggests, should be forbidden. Most of these concern literary, religious, political, or other nonscientific matters, but within the sciences he cites, as examples, the atomic bomb, recombinant DNA research, and the Human Genome Project. But despite the title of the appendix ("Six Categories of Forbidden Knowledge"), he does not recommend that research in such fields actually be forbidden; rather, he urges scientists to voluntarily take an oath, similar to the *Primum non nocere* of physicians, binding them "to assess scrupulously the consequences of their work, to study pertinent cases in the history of science, to avoid the co-option of their work by inappropriate agencies, and to produce a more principled profession."[11] In short, they are forbidden nothing, but enjoined to avoid research that will yield harmful applications and to prevent the results of their work from being applied in harmful ways:

> The knowledge that our many sciences discover is not forbidden in and of itself. ...[But] the free market may not be the best guide for the development of knowledge. State planning has not always served us better.... In this era of liberation and permissiveness, it may well be that a judicious oath for scientists will help to prevent us from acting like the Sorcerer's Apprentice.[12]

Shattuck's recommendation is admirable in intent but hardly practicable; scientists are too heterogeneous and too jealous of their independence to band together and require an oath binding upon all who mean to become researchers. Even if the AAAS, the umbrella association of the sciences in America, were to militate for such an oath, it is unreasonable to expect scientists to foresee all the ways in which their research findings might be used for ill ends or to prevent them from being so used. As Robert K. Merton pointed out sixty years ago, the scientist "does not or cannot control the directions in which his discoveries are applied"—a reason, he added with prescience, for the antipathy toward science in every society where it has reached a high stage of development.[13]

Jay Belsky, in discovering that infants who are given over too much to day care are likely to develop poorly, did not anticipate that antifeminists would find his data useful. Sandra Scarr and Richard Weinberg, in studying transracial adoption, did not know in advance that their finding that biology was a more powerful determinant of the child's development than the adoptive home would be denounced by blacks and liberals as useful to racists and reactionaries. Researchers of aversive conditioning did not foresee that in the third world their techniques would be used to physically control political prisoners. Sleep researchers did not anticipate that their work would lend itself to brain washing and cult indoctrination.[14] In all these cases, even had the researchers foreseen the antisocial uses of their findings, the information they were acquiring has had and will continue to have important prosocial outcomes, of which perhaps the most valuable, though indeterminable, is an increase in the scientific understanding of human nature.

In sum, scientists, though they should avoid research aimed at wholly and predictably malign outcomes such as biological weapons research, must feel free, and be free, to inquire into whatever other matters they find interesting. Rather than calling on scientists to take an oath to do no harm—which obliges them to try, individually, to judge the potential harm of their work—it would be more practicable to have impartial panels of scientists and ethicists speculate about the problems likely to be caused by certain kinds of research and offer recommendations for minimizing potential harm.

Indeed, just such a group, the Recombinant DNA Advisory Committee, chartered by NIH, provides oversight and guidelines to the agency's reviewers of grant proposals, and in mid-1997 the Hastings Center (a bioethics institute) and others convened a conference of genetics researchers, ethicists, and legislators in Washington to discuss the ethical implications of mammalian cloning and make recommendations as to how to proceed cautiously with further research.[15] These examples may be indicative of a trend to develop resources to advise and assist scientists about areas of research that involve serious risk of harmful outcome.

* * *

In the final analysis, there appear to be few cases in which research, particularly in the social sciences, ought to be banned or which it is legitimate for political advocacy groups to try to block. Although some limits to methodology, and safeguards of the rights of research subjects, are wise and ethically obligatory, it is damaging to science and to our society, which is so dependent on it, for religious, political, or other groups to try to halt research that offends their sensibilities or threatens their value systems. To the extent that humankind has advanced from primitivism to civilization, from brute ignorance to some degree of understanding of itself and the cosmos, it has not done so by means of revelation, magic, or divination but through rational scientific inquiry and the light it casts into the darkness.

To conclude:

Of the many observations about the nature of freedom that I have come across, I find none as movingly idealistic and yet (I believe) realistic as the statement, quoted earlier, by Justice Oliver Wendell Holmes: "If there is any principle of the Constitution that more imperatively calls for attachment than any other, it is the principle of free thought—not free thought for those who agree with us but freedom for the thought we hate."[16]

And of the statements specifically about freedom of research that I have read, I find none more stirring and yet (I believe) more utilitarian than one made in 1949 by J. Robert Oppenheimer: "There must be no barriers to freedom of inquiry. There is no place for dogma in science. The scientist is free, and must be free, to ask any question, to doubt any assertion, to seek for any evidence, to correct any errors."[17]

Notes

Quotations without citation in the following notes are from interviews with the person quoted.

Preface

1. Lysenko's views are detailed in Graham 1987: 126–36.
2. Details of the 1948 conference: Graham 1987: 123–24; M. Hunt 1949. (I. V. Michurin, a Russian horticulturist, claimed that changes in an organism created by the environment would be passed on hereditarily to its offspring.)
3. My Internet postings were on some dozen listservs; these are sites serving special-interest groups, in this case social scientists of one stripe or another. All subscribers to a given listserv automatically receive any notice posted to it; the sender does not know their names or addresses, and those who reply identify themselves only if they choose to. I present no data in this book from unidentified and unverified sources.
4. Two typical attacks on the Pioneer Fund are Mehler 1994, and Adam Miller 1994. Detailed rebuttals can be found on Pioneer's home page, HTTP://WWW.PIONEERFUND.ORG., and in the thoroughly documented Weyher 1997.

Chapter 1: A Clear and Present Danger

1. *Criminal Justice Newsletter*: 23(16): August 17, 1992.
2. Breggin letter of May 26, from Center for the Study of Psychiatry, Inc., to members of his center and others; Breggin letter in *Washington Post*, August 31, 1992; interviews with David Wasserman. For a detailed treatment of the story, see chapter 5.
3. Udry 1993 and Udry, personal communication; Sullivan's reason for cancellation: *New York Times*, July 25, 1991: B8. The story is told in more detail in chapter 6.
4. U.S. Public Health Service, Office for Protection from Research Risks 1995.
5. Wood, telephone interviews and personal communications. The story is told in more detail in chapter 11.
6. Quoted in Boorstin 1983: 325–26.
7. Boorstin 1983: 325–27; White 1960 [1896], vol. 1, chapter III; the story of the whisper came into existence only in 1761, according to *Chambers's Biographical Dictionary* (New York: St. Martin's Press, 1962).
8. *New York Times*, Oct. 31, 1992: sec. 1: 1.
9. White 1960 [1896], vol. II: 50–55; Boorstin 1983: 351–60.
10. Graham 1987: 124–50.
11. Ibid.: 165, 214–16.
12. Stanley 1996.

13. *Chambers's Biographical Dictionary* 1962: "Freud."
14. Alexander and Selesnick 1966: 407–08; the Jung articles: Introduction to Göring, *Zentralblatt für Psychotherapie, 6* (1933): 139, and *7* (1934): 11.
15. Watson and Raynor 1920.
16. Dennis 1935, 1938.
17. Lifton 1986; Caplan 1992b; Annas and Grodin 1992 (includes transcripts of the opening statement of the prosecution before the Nuremberg Tribunal I and the Court's judgment of the evidence).
18. Jones 1981; Katz 1987.
19. Milgram 1963.
20. Hunt 1985: 178–82; Cleary 1987; Cohen and Ciocca 1992.
21. U.S. Department of Health, Education, and Welfare. "Protection of Human Subjects. Institutional Review Boards." *Federal Register 43* (November 30, 1978): 56186, 56191.
22. "Code of Federal Regulations," *Federal Register 46:16* (January 26, 1981): 8389.
23. Hunt 1985: 185.
24. Loehlin, personal communication.
25. Horowitz 1995.
26. Skolnick 1969: 6.
27. Heclo 1996: 39–42.
28. Gross and Levitt 1994: 33.
29. Halpern et al. 1996: 260.
30. Hamilton 1996b: 400.
31. Gitlin 1995; Heclo 1996; Hamilton 1996b; and interviews with Frederick Goodwin and Philip Smith.
32. Halpern et al. 1996: 260.
33. Heclo 1996: 55.
34. The survey: Swazey et al. 1993; the *New York Times* article: Hilts 1993.
35. Gardner and Wilcox 1993; Gross and Levitt 1994: 42–53, 88–91; "All knowledge...": Gottesman 1994: 26; see also Menand 1993.
36. *Schenck* v. *United States,* 249 U.S. 52, 1919.
37. Paul H. Harvey and Robert M. May, "Out for the Sperm Count," *Nature, 337:* 508–9 (February 9, 1989).
38. Chomsky 1973: 294–95.
39. E. Goode 1997: 421.
40. Halpern et al. 1996: 267.
41. Laumann et al. 1994a: xxviii–xxix.
42. *United States* v. *Schwimmer,* 279 U.S. 654–655, 1929.

Chapter 2: The Roots of Illiberal Liberalism

1. Galton 1907 [1874]: 12.
2. The pundit: Leon Wieseltier, literary editor at the *New Republic*, in Fraser 1995: 156.
3. *The Federalist*, Number 10, quoted in Parrington 1927, 1930, vol. 1: 287–288.
4. "booted and spurred": letter to Roger Weightman, June 24, 1826; "aristocracy": Mayo 1942: 77–78.
5. Thomas Jefferson, *Autobiography* (New York: Modern Library, 1944): 51.
6. Thomas Jefferson, *Notes on the State of Virginia*, quoted in Dumas Malone, *Jefferson and His Time* (Boston: Little, Brown, 1950), vol. 6: 31.
7. Biographical details are from Galton 1908, and Forrest 1974.

8. Galton 1865.
9. Galton 1892 [1869]: 79.
10. Quoted in Forrest 1974: 89.
11. Fancher 1979: 293–94.
12. Galton 1907 [1883]: 17n.
13. Article in *Frazier's* magazine, quoted in Forrest 1974: 136.
14. Mongolians...Indians: Galton 1865, Part II: 321; the Negro...[Jews]: letter to Swiss botanist Alphonse de Candolle, quoted in Hirsch 1970.
15. Davenport 1911: 216, 218–19, 221–22.
16. Terman 1916: 91–92.
17. Ibid.: 6–7.
18. Cravens 1978: 53.
19. *Buck* v. *Bell*, 274 U.S. 200–08 (1927).
20. Kevles 1995 [1985]: 111–12.
21. Goddard 1917.
22. U. S. Congress. House 1922: 741; and 1924: 1318 and 1339.
23. *Encyclopaedia Britannica*, 1935 edition: "Migration," vol. 15: 468.
24. See, for instance, Gould 1981; Kevles 1995 [1985]; and Shipman 1994.
25. Selden 1995: 55, and passim.
26. Kevles 1995 [1985]: 63–4.
27. Sanger 1922.
28. Shipman 1994: 151.
29. Kevles 1995 [1985]: 122–23.
30. Huxley 1936.
31. Muller et al., 1939.
32. Watson 1913.
33. Watson 1924: 104.
34. Gregory Kimble, in Koch and Leary 1985: 316.
35. On Nazi practices: Kevles 1985: 116–17; on death of eugenics, Carlson 1973.
36. Shipman 1994: 162.
37. UNESCO, *Statement on Race*, 1950, quoted in Shipman 1994: 163–64.
38. Dobzhansky 1962: 258.
39. Reprinted in Dobzhansky 1981.
40. Shipman 1994: 219.
41. Scarr 1988.
42. Jim Holt, "Anti-Social Science," *New York Times*, October 19, 1994.
43. Over 99 percent in humans: Siebert 1995: 54; and in chimpanzees: Shipman 1994: 269.
44. Horgan 1993.
45. Lewontin 1994.
46. Lewontin et al. 1984: ix–x.
47. Whitney 1995b.
48. Schachter 1980.
49. Ibid.
50. The studies are reviewed in Whalen and Simon 1984.
51. Ibid.
52. Ibid.
53. Galton 1908: 294–95.
54. Wright 1995: 49.
55. Lykken et al. 1992.
56. Carey 1994; Gottesman and Goldsmith 1994; Lyons et al. 1995.
57. Bouchard 1994a.

58. Pearson 1993: 283–88.
59. Mehler 1994.
60. Open letter of March 10, 1995, to Professor Irvin Schonfeld, seven colleagues, and "interested parties."
61. Plomin and Daniels 1987: 2.
62. The IQ study: Skodak and Skeels 1949; the four personality traits studies are cited and summarized in Plomin and Daniels 1987: 5.
63. Scarr and Weinberg 1976: 726; Loehlin et al. 1985.
64. Scarr 1988.
65. Scarr 1981: 524–25.
66. Scarr and Weinberg 1976.
67. The ten-year follow-up study: Weinberg et al. 1992.
68. Scarr and McCartney 1983.
69. Ibid.; Scarr and Weinberg 1983; Scarr et al. 1981.
70. Maccoby interview.
71. Oden and MacDonald 1978.
72. Kamin, "Commentary," in Scarr 1981: 468, 482.
73. Jean Walker Macfarlane, "Perspectives on Personality Consistency and Change from the Guidance Study," *Vita Humana*, vol. 7 (1964): 115–26.
74. Thomas et al. 1963.
75. Chess and Thomas 1986: appendix B.
76. Watson and Crick 1953; Plomin, in Plomin and McClearn 1993: 476.
77. Plomin, in Plomin and McClearn 1993: 478.
78. Ibid.: 228; Horgan 1993; Goleman 1996.
79. Plomin, in Plomin and McClearn 1993: 480.
80. *Science, 235*: 1445.
81. Plomin 1994: 3–4.
82. Scarr and McCartney 1983.
83. Bouchard et al. 1990a.
84. Bouchard 1997.
85. Plomin 1994: 2.
86. Scarr and McCartney 1983.
87. Plomin 1994: 153–68.
88. Turkheimer and Gottesman 1991; see also Dobzhanksy 1973, in Scarr 1981: 253; Gottesman 1981.
89. Kevles 1995 [1985]: 253–54, 257–58; "communal and social welfare": Magnus 1997.
90. See entries for Brimelow, for Rushton, and for Vining in References Cited.
91. Nelkin and Lindee 1995: 101, 126.
92. Dorothy Nelkin, "Biology Is Not Destiny," *New York Times*, September 28, 1995.
93. Lewontin 1994.
94. Bouchard 1994b.
95. Scarr 1981: 531.

Chapter 3: The IQ Wars

1. Hothersall 1984: 323–24; Garrett 1951: 244; Block and Dworkin 1976: 2–3.
2. Lippmann 1922–23.
3. Snyderman and Rothman 1988: 17–18.
4. But Snyderman and Rothman (1988: 19) maintain that the Army data played little part in the passage of the act, which would have been passed in any case.

5. The survey: Snyderman and Rothman 1988: 93, table 3.1; "Great majority": 94 percent said they regard the data as evidence of the heritability of IQ in white Americans, but because far fewer studies exist from which heritability in American blacks can be derived, only a quarter felt a reasonable heritability estimate could be made for them.

6. Biographical details: Jensen interviews; Krawiec 1974, v. 2, chapter 5; an unpublished Jensen autobiography; and Pearson 1993, chapter 4.

7. Quoted in Krawiec 1974, v. 2: 222.

8. Jensen 1997a.

9. Jensen 1997b.

10. Dobzhansky 1973.

11. Jensen, in Krawiec 1974, v. 2: 233.

12. Jensen 1969: 82.

13. Hunt 1971.

14. Ibid.

15. Astin et al. 1975: 2–15.

16. Lewontin, in *Bull. of the Atomic Scientists,* March 1970.

17. Snyderman and Rothman 1988: 2.

18. Hirsch: the addresses and articles are listed in Hirsch 1975, where the above statement is repeated; "holy war": *Harvard Educ. Rev.,* Spring 1969: 592, 338; "perversion": Grove 1989.

19. Block and Dworkin 1974: 517–18.

20. Merton 1942.

21. Jensen interviews.

22. Jensen 1972: 55.

23. Ibid.

24. Rowan, in Pearson 1993: 179; "fifteen letters": Jensen 1972: 13, 17; *Daily California;* Jensen 1972: 13, 17, 21 22.

25. Jensen 1972: 44–45.

26. Letter of April 4, 1990 from Jensen to the Appeals Committee, University of Western Ontario, in the case of J. Philippe Rushton.

27. Jensen 1972: 1.

28. Following examples are from Pearson 1993: 167–84, verified by Jensen, personal communication.

29. Jensen 1972: 48.

30. Ibid.: 48–50.

31. Unpublished Jensen autobiography, 1974, quoted in Krawiec 1974: 241.

32. Jensen 1970: 99.

33. Jensen 1969 (in Jensen 1972: 202–03).

34. Shaughnessy 1994: 141.

35. Barber 1979 [1952]: 340.

36. Gottesman 1974.

37. Canada Federal Code, chapter c-46, section 319; Ontario Human Rights Code, 1981, section III, "Ontario Policy on Race Relations."

38. Korwar 1995.

39. Ibid.; Rushton 1994: 273.

40. Rushton et al. 1986.

41. The paper was published later: Rushton 1992a.

42. Ibid.

43. MacArthur and Wilson 1967; Wilson 1975.

44. In Rushton's 1989 paper (Rushton 1992a) the only cited reference on genetic distance is Stringer and Andrews 1988, but Rushton also said in the 1989 paper

that he had cited a number of other sources in his own earlier papers; these studies are summarized and cited in Rushton 1995: 220–22.

45. Rushton 1992a. The same argument is made by anthropologist Christopher Stringer of the Natural History Museum in London in Stringer 1990.
46. Pedersen interview.
47. Quoted in Paula Adamick, "Racial Theory Attacked," *Toronto Star*, February 20, 1989.
48. Pedersen interview.
49. Letter to Rushton from Collins, February 9, 1989.
50. Rushton interviews.
51. Criminal Code, section 319(2).
52. *London Free Press*, November 4, 1989: C1, C2
53. Rushton 1994: 272; Pedersen interview.
54. Szathmary interview.
55. Letter of September 25, 1989 to Rushton from Greg Moran, chairperson of the Departmental Personnel, Promotion, and Tenure Committee.
56. Rushton was supported in this work by a grant from the Pioneer Fund.
57. Lerner 1992: 147.
58. Szathmary interview.
59. Rushton interviews; Pearson 1993: 241–43.
60. Section IIIb of the Code states, "All doctrines and practices of racial superiority are scientifically false, morally reprehensible and socially destructive, are contrary to the policies of this government, and are unacceptable in Ontario."
61. Ontario Human Rights Commission Complaint No. 20–618S, and letter of Aug. 26, 1991 to Rushton from Walter J. Burns, manager, Southwestern Region, Ontario Human Rights Commission.
62. Letter of November 24, 1995 from J. Christopher McKinnon, acting case coordinator, Southwest Region, Ontario Human Rights Commission, to Andrew Pinto of Scott and Aylen, counsel for the complainants, stating that the Commission considered the case "abandoned."
63. Rushton 1994: 277.
64. Gottesman interview.
65. Snyderman 1994.
66. Sperling 1994.
67. Rushton 1995: 257.
68. Horowitz 1995.
69. Jensen 1991: 179.
70. Snyderman and Rothman 1988: 250.
71. "about half": Snyderman and Rothman 1988: 140–41; "lost the benefits": Herrnstein 1982.
72. *New York Post*, January 23, 1996.
73. Ibid.
74. Jacoby and Glauberman 1995: xiv.
75. Murray 1996.
76. Ibid.
77. Ibid.
78. Ibid.
79. Ibid.
80. Ibid.
81. Blits and Gottfredson 1990a: 19; Blits and Gottfredson 1990b: 4.
82. Hartigan and Wigdor 1989: 20–21; Blits and Gottfredson 1990a: 20.
83. Gottfredson 1986: 379–80.

84. Gottfredson and Blits 1991: 2.
85. Gottfredson 1986: 385–86.
86. Gottfredson 1988: 316.
87. Details from Gottfredson and Blits 1991.
88. Ibid.: 7–8.
89. *Wilmington News Journal,* April 30, 1992; *Washington Times,* May 1, 1992, A, p.3; *Science, 256*: 962.
90. Gottfredson interview.
91. Gottfredson 1996a.
92. Gottfredson 1996b.
93. Lamb 1997.
94. Ibid.
95. Susan Spilka, Manager of Corporate Communications of Wiley, quoted in Holden 1996.
96. Holden 1996.
97. Brand, in an e-mail widely distributed by him.
98. Quoted in Holden 1996.
99. Lamb 1997.
100. Murray, in Herrnstein and Murray 1996: 533.

Chapter 4: Anatomy is Destiny

1. Plato, *The Republic,* Book V.
2. Aristotle, *De generatione animalium,* iv, 6.
3. Demosthenes, "Against Neaera."
4. Lord Chesterfield, *Letter to his son,* Sept. 5 (O.S.), 1748.
5. Woodhull is quoted in Paulina W. Davis, *History of the National Woman's Rights Movement* (New York: Journeymen Printers' Co-op Assn., 1871): 118.
6. The apothegm is in Freud 1910: 189; the quoted exegesis is in Freud 1950 [1927].
7. James McKeen Cattell's count in 1903 is cited in Fausto-Sterling 1985: 14–15.
8. Learning theory, social modeling, and cognitive theories are three latter-day explanations of the psychosocial forces determining the sex roles of today's women, see Halpern 1992: 187–91.
9. Hunt 1994: 383.
10. Winthrop, *History of New England,* II, 216, 235 (New York, 1908 [1825–1826]).
11. Deutsch 1944: 220f.
12. Quoted in Hunt 1962: 28.
13. Halpern 1992: 2–3.
14. Ibid.: 2–3.
15. Educational Testing Service, public information office.
16. Engineers: 1990 Census, cited in National Science Board 1996: table 3–7; airline pilots: estimate by Gary DiNunno, editor-in-chief, *Air Line Pilot* (Air Line Pilots Association journal); Congress: roughly one-tenth in House and in Senate of 105th Congress, by actual count; board members: *Select,* June 1997 (via www.selectgroup.com/staffing/press/pr97/women.htm); N. Y. Stock Exchange: NYSE Membership Services.
17. Halpern 1992: 174.
18. Deaux 1985: 56–7.
19. Kimura and Hampson 1993, 1994.
20. Kenrick 1988.
21. Epstein 1988: 98.

22. Fausto-Sterling 1985: 8–9.
23. Fausto-Sterling 1985: 10.
24. Halpern 1992: 16.
25. Ibid.: 17.
26. Halpern 1994: 524.
27. McHugh et al. 1986; Baumeister 1988.
28. Fausto-Sterling 1985: 221–22.
29. Halpern 1992: 2.
30. Flanagan et al. 1961, as reported in Maccoby and Jacklin 1974, vol. 1: 85, and table 36; and sources cited in Benbow and Stanley 1980, note 1.
31. Stanley 1996.
32. Benbow and Stanley 1980.
33. Details in the paragraph are from a letter of Jan. 29, 1996 from Stanley to me; the editorial in *Science*: Schafer and Gray 1981.
34. Benbow 1988a: 169–83.
35. Benbow 1988b: 217.
36. American Psychological Association 1995.
37. Zita 1989:189–90, 205.
38. Kimura, personal communication.
39. Lewis and Horn 1991.
40. These and other related issues are reviewed in Halpern 1992: 141–45 and 164–70. See also Kimura 1992, and Kimura and Hampson 1993, 1994.
41. Quoted in column by Rory Leishman, *London (*Ontario*) Free Press*, September 23, 1993: 3.
42. Halpern 1992: 164.
43. Halpern et al. 1996.
44. Ehrhardt and Money 1967; Ehrhardt and Baker 1974.
45. Hall and Kimura 1995.
46. Ibid.; LeVay 1991, 1995.
47. Bleier 1987: 117.
48. University of New Orleans "Research News," Fall 1996, v. XVI, no. 2.
49. Farganis 1992: 209, 212
50. Gruen 1993: 64.
51. Lynda Birke, in Adams and Donovan 1995: 43.
52. Carolyn Merchant, *Radical Ecology*, quoted in Gross and Levitt 1994: 162.
53. Lewontin 1988.
54. Gross and Levitt 1994: 132.
55. Wilson 1995 [1994]: 285.
56. Ibid.: 328.
57. Ibid.: 309–10.
58. Ibid.: 239, 312.
59. Wilson 1979: 17.
60. Wilson 1975: 3–4.
61. Ibid.: 4.
62. Wilson 1995 [1994]: 332–33.
63. Ibid.: 333.
64. Joseph Alper et al., in Caplan 1978: 478.
65. Wilson 1995 [1994]: 337.
66. The letter is by L. Allen et al.
67. Quoted in Wade 1976.
68. Wilson 1975: 548.
69. Wilson 1995 [1994]: 339.

70. Sociobiology Study Group 1976; Sociobiology Study Group, in Ann Arbor Science for the People 1977: 135.
71. The petition: Segerstråle 1986; *Harvard Crimson,* December 1975, quoted in Segerstråle 1986.
72. Wade 1976; Segerstråle 1986.
73. Lewontin 1974.
74. Wilson 1995 [1994]: 331.
75. Montagu 1980: 4.
76. Ibid.: 26.
77. Richard Alexander, in Betzig et al. 1988: 317. The episode took place in 1981.
78. Liesen 1995: 145.
79. Fausto-Sterling 1985: 166; for the sociobiological view of rape that Fausto-Sterling is attacking, see Thornhill 1994; Furlow and Thornhill 1996; and Thornhill and Thornhill 1983, 1984.
80. Personal communication.
81. Joseph Alper, Jon Beckwith, and Lawrence G. Miller, in Caplan 1978: 484–86.
82. Lumsden and Wilson 1981: 2.
83. Wilson 1995 [1994]: 350–51.
84. Grove 1989: 91.
85. Gould 1991.
86. van der Dennen and Falger 1990: 18.
87. Irons interview; *Politics and the Life Sciences, 14(2):* 191.
88. In a review of Robert Plomin's *Genetics and Experience* in *Politics and the Life Sciences, 14(2):* 300 (1995).
89. Wilson 1995 [1994]: 364.

Chapter 5: Unmapped Country: Genetic Influences on Behavior

1. *Memories and Studies* (1911): 301 (emphasis added).
2. Kretschmer 1925.
3. Sheldon et al. 1940; Sheldon and Stevens 1942.
4. Ibid.
5. Mill 1869: 162.
6. Rousseau: *Discours sur les sciences et les arts.*
7. Lipsey 1992.
8. Crowell and Burgess 1996: 54.
9. Levine and Rosich 1996: 25.
10. LeVay 1995.
11. Rapaport 1989.
12. Diamond and Sigmundson 1997.
13. Scarr 1992; Plomin 1994: 18–23, 160–68.
14. Harris et al. 1996.
15. Mehlman et al. 1994.
16. Nelson et al. 1995.
17. Raine 1993.
18. Rushton 1996; Mednick et al. 1984.
19. Comings et al. 1994.
20. The studies are summarized and cited in Blangero 1995.
21. Plomin 1994: 159–68.
22. Biographical details: Shipman 1994: 225–27.
23. Wasserman 1991.

24. FBI data for 1990: I. Reiss and Roth 1993: 72, table 2–5.
25. Goodwin 1992.
26. Shipman 1994: 241.
27. Ibid.: 242.
28. Genome Study Section, "Summary Statement on Application Number 1 R13 HG00703-01," 1991 (quoted in Shipman 1994: 234).
29. Shipman 1994: 243, quoting U. C. Leid, "Inner-City Children Targeted for 'Intervention,'" *City Sun, 10(2)*: 4.
30. Toufexis 1993: 61.
31. *Washington Post*, August 19, 1992.
32. AAAS *Professional Ethics Report*, Summer 1992: 2.
33. University of Maryland *Diamondback*, September 17, 1992: 1.
34. *Science, 257*: 739.
35. *Providence Journal*, August 22, 1992: A10.
36. *Baltimore Evening Sun,* September 30, 1992.
37. Quoted in "The Blue Sheet," F.D.C. Reports, Inc., August 26, 1992.
38. Details in this paragraph are from various newspaper reports, and from Shipman 1994: chapter 13.
39. Letter in the *Washington Post*, August 31, 1992: A18.
40. *Science, 258*: 212 (October 9, 1992).
41. *San Francisco Weekly*, July 15, 1992: 13.
42. *Washington Post*, September 5, 1992: A1.
43. *New York Times*, September 5, 1992: 1, 8; Shipman 1994: 255.
44. *Chronicle of Higher Education*, September 10, 1992.
45. Ibid., September 23, 1992.
46. Undated release, "Frequently asked questions about the upcoming conference on *The Meaning and Significance of Research on Genetics and Criminal Behavior*," Institute for Philosophy and Public Policy, University of Maryland.
47. *New York Times*, September 19, 1995, C1.
48. *Sacramento Bee*, September 19, 1995, article by Deborah Blum.
49. Ibid., September 24, 1995, article by Deborah Blum.
50. Ibid., September 19, 1995, article by Deborah Blum.
51. *Philadelphia Inquirer*, September 23, 1995.
52. Roush 1995.
53. Beardsley 1995a: 22.
54. Wheeler 1995.
55. Sacks: *Washington Times*, September 24, 1995: A3; Miller: *USA Today*, September 25, 1995: 5A; *Bangor Daily News*, October 20, 1995; "Such research"; Roush 1995.
56. Green: *USA Today,* September 25, 1995: 5A; also, Rhein 1995; *Probe, 4(9)*; and Maass 1995a; "paranoid delusions": Rhein 1995, and Maass 1995a.
57. Rhein 1995.
58. Roush 1995.
59. Owen Jones, in "Symposium: Genetics and Crime," *Politics and the Life Sciences*, March, 1996: 101.
60. Roush 1995.
61. Wheeler 1995.
62. *Biotechnology Newswatch*, October 2, 1995: 3.
63. Wasserman 1995b.
64. Wasserman 1996.
65. Ibid.
66. Wasserman 1995b.
67. Wheeler 1995.

68. *New York Times*, September 18, 1992.
69. *Washington Post*, Aug. 19, 1992: A4.
70. *New York Times*, September 18, 1992.
71. Peter Breggin, "The 'Violence Initiative'—A Racist Biomedical Program For Social Control." *Rights Tenet: Summer 1992.*
72. *Professional Ethics Report*, AAAS Committee on Scientific Freedom and Responsibility, Summer 1992: 2.
73. Wheeler 1995.
74. Richard Stone, "HHS 'Violence Initiative' Caught in a Crossfire." *Science, 258*: 212 (October 9, 1992).
75. "From the Editor," *Journal of NIH Research, 4*: 10 (November 1992).
76. Ibid.
77. *Science, 258*: 212 (October 9, 1992).
78. "From the Editor," *Journal of NIH Research, 4*: 10 (November 1992).
79. For an appraisal of needed research, see the National Research Council's two-volume report, *Understanding and Preventing Violence* (I. Reiss and Roth 1993, 1994), which recommends a multidisciplinary program of research very much along the lines of the Violence Initiative.
80. Butterfield 1997.

Chapter 6: Keeping Sex a Mystery

1. Quoted in introduction (by F. S. Klaff, translator) to Richard Krafft-Ebing, *Psychopathia Sexualis* (New York: Bell, 1965).
2. Bullough 1985b.
3. Bullough 1985a.
4. See, for instance, Kinsey et al. 1948: 201 ("It is unwarranted to believe that particular types of sexual behavior are always expressions of psychoses or neuroses. In actuality, they are more of an expression of what is biologically basic in mammalian and anthropoid behavior"); also ibid.: 580; and Kinsey et al. 1953: 230–31, 448.
5. Udry 1993.
6. Bullough 1985b.
7. di Mauro 1995: 8.
8. Interview with sociologist Julia Erickson of Temple University, author of a forthcoming history of sex research.
9. Pomeroy 1972: 285.
10. Laumann et al. 1994a: 45.
11. Udry 1993.
12. Udry 1993; Laumann et al. 1994b.
13. Rubin, personal communication; *Science, 192*: 450.
14. Rubin, personal communication.
15. Rubin and Henson 1976.
16. Philip Smith (former head of NAS), interview.
17. di Mauro 1995: chapter 2.
18. Details on the history of SHARP: Laumann et al. 1994b, and Gagnon interview.
19. Laumann et al. 1994b.
20. Fay 1989.
21. Laumann et al. 1994b.
22. Letter from Dannemeyer in *Science, 244*: 1530 (1989).
23. Laumann et al. 1994b.
24. Erickson interview.

25. Laumann et al. 1994b.
26. Ibid.
27. Quoted in Laumann et al. 1994b.
28. *Congressional Record*, September 12, 1991, S12861, S12862.
29. Laumann et al. 1994b.
30. Ibid.
31. Ibid.
32. Ibid.
33. On 1996: Dan Ralbovsky, public information officer of NIH, by phone.
34. 1996 Udry interview.
35. Gardner and Wilcox 1993.
36. Udry 1993; Udry 1993 and 1996 interviews.
37. Udry 1993 interview.
38. Price 1991.
39. Dannemeyer letter of July 22, 1991, "18 MILLION TO STUDY SEX HABITS OF TEENAGERS!"
40. Dannemeyer press release of July 22, 1991, "TEN REASONS WHY NIH WANTS TO SPEND $18 MILLION ON A TEEN SEX STUDY."
41. Price 1991.
42. Gardner and Wilcox 1993.
43. Ibid.
44. Udry 1993; *New York Times,* July 25, 1991: B8; Gardner and Wilcox 1993.
45. Charrow 1991.
46. APA *Psychological Science Agenda*, Sept/Oct. 1991, p. 4.
47. ASA Press Release, September 5, 1991.
48. *New York Times*, Sept. 25, 1991: A21.
49. Laumann et al. 1994a: 41.
50. Public Law 103–43, June 10, 1993, Title 10, Subtitle D., Sec. 1031, paragraph titled "Prospective Longitudinal Study of Adolescent Health."
51. *Science, 263*: 1688 (25 March, 1994).
52. Knight 1994: 11.
53. Udry 1993.
54. National Family Planning and Reproductive Health Association, personal communication.
55. Bancroft interview, and statement issued by the Kinsey Institute for Research in Sex, Gender, and Reproduction, Indiana University, May 8, 1996, "Kinsey's reported evidence of children's sexual responsiveness," signed by John Bancroft, MD, director.
56. di Mauro 1995: 51.
57. Pierce interview.
58. Laumann et al. 1994a: xxix.
59. Gardner and Wilcox 1993.
60. Udry 1993; see also Gardner and Wilcox 1993.
61. Udry 1993.
62. Ibid.

Chapter 7: Just Say No

1. See discussion in Sieber 1992, chap. 5.
2. Hunt 1985: 103–4.
3. Ibid.: 104.
4. Hauser 1975: 9–10.

5. Hunt 1985: 105.
6. Hauser 1975: 108.
7. *Congressional Record*, August 4, 1939: 11092–11093.
8. "Surveys and Privacy," a brochure published by the American Statistical Association and available on the Internet.
9. Hunt 1985: 127.
10. Steeh 1981; for recent years (1978–1996), Julie M. Antelman, NORC, personal communication; for NORC's General Social Survey, see T. Smith 1995, where the refusal rate from 1990 to 1993 ranged from 19.1 to 14.6 per cent.
11. "What Is a Survey?", a brochure by R. Ferber et al., published by the American Statistical Association and available on the Internet.
12. Julie Antelman, Public Information Coordinator, NORC, personal communication. Some experts say it is not clear how much of the non-response rate is due to refusals and to not finding someone at home or able to respond; see Bradburn 1992.
13. Ellickson and Hawes-Dawson 1989.
14. History of the bills is sketched in U.S. Congress, House 1995c.
15. Kearney, Hopkins et al. 1983, and other studies cited in Moberg and Piper 1990. See also discussion below of testimony presented at the hearings on H.R. 11 and H.R. 1271.
16. Levine 1995b; U. S. Congress, House 1995b.
17. Ibid.
18. U. S. Congress, House 1995b.
19. Ibid.
20. The following account of the hearing is based on U. S. Congress, House 1995a.
21. U.S. Congress, House 1995b.
22. Events of April 4th, 1995 described in following paragraphs are based on *Congressional Record* for that date, pp. H4125ff.
23. APA *Psychological Science Agenda*, November/December 1995.
24. Following details are from the printed record of the hearing; see U. S. Congress, Senate 1995c.
25. U. S. Congress, Senate 1996.
26. Action Alert! from 3PRES3ER@bssl.umd.edu
27. E-mail of July 8, 1997 to me from Angela Sharpe, assistant director for governmental affairs at COSSA.

Chapter 8: The War Against Social Science Research

1. *National Science Foundation Budget Summary, Fiscal Year 1996*: 4, 43–49 (in U.S. Congress, House 1995g: 26, 64–70).
2. National Science Board 1996: A136–A137.
3. Lippmann 1965 [1922]: 234–35.
4. Ibid.
5. R. Miller 1982a.
6. Merton 1938.
7. Bush 1980 [1945].
8. R. Miller 1982a; Geiger 1993: 12–19; Kleinman 1995: 101
9. England 1982: 50.
10. D. Johnson 1992a.
11. Marrett interview; David Johnson 1993.
12. Such was the view of Harold Varmus, head of NIH; see COSSA Annual Report 1994: 2.

13. The events narrated in this and the following section are drawn from David Johnson 1992a, 1992b, 1992c, and David Johnson 1993; R. Miller 1982a, 1982b, and 1987; Larsen 1992; and interviews with Roberta Miller, David Johnson, and Howard Silver. A few quotations and controversial items in these two sections are individually annotated.
14. Johnson 1992b.
15. E.g., Nathan Glazer, *Affirmative Discrimination* (New York: Basic Books, 1976); Peter Steinfels, *The Neoconservatives* (New York: Simon & Schuster, 1980).
16. Miller 1987: 374.
17. *Additional Details on Budget Savings*, Executive Office of the President, Office of Management and Budget, April 1981 (quoted in Miller 1987: 375–76).
18. Miller 1987: 376.
19. D. Johnson 1993: 1.
20. National Science Foundation 1996: tables 2, 2A.
21. *National Science Foundation Budget Summary, Fiscal Year 1996*: 48 (in U. S. Congress, House 1995g: 69).
22. Details in this paragraph and the rest of this section are drawn from an interview with David Johnson, executive director of the Federation of Behavioral, Psychological, and Cognitive Sciences, and written accounts provided by him (David Johnson 1992a, 1992b, 1992c, and David Johnson 1993); an interview with Howard Silver, director of COSSA; and other sources as indicated.
23. Quoted in May 17, 1995 (misdated 1994) *Update* from the Federation of Behavioral, Psychological, and Cognitive Sciences to all members.
24. National Science Foundation *Budget Summary, Fiscal Year 1996*: 2, 48 (in U.S. Congress, House 1995g: 24, 69).
25. Petersen 1996b.
26. Wydler interview.
27. Quoted in "May 22 Update from David Johnson Regarding `Elimination,'" one of a series of e-mail updates he sent to members of the Federation of Behavioral, Psychological and Cognitive Sciences.
28. Kraut Update of May 22 [1995] (on website psych.hanover.edu).
29. U. S. Congress, House 1995g: 136.
30. *Federation News*, June/July 1995: 2 (a periodical newsletter of the Federation of Behavioral, Psychological and Cognitive Sciences).
31. Kraut, NSF Update, June 10, 1995.
32. Petersen 1996a.
33. U. S. Congress, House 1995f: 9, 20.
34. Ibid.: 31ff.
35. Kraut NSF/NIMH Update, 7/19/95.
36. Ibid.
37. U. S. Congress, House 1996a: 59.
38. Ibid.: 2.
39. U. S. Congress, House 1996b: 28.
40. Kraut NSF Update, 12/16/95.

Chapter 9: The Assault on Memory Research

1. Loftus 1975.
2. Loftus 1974.
3. Loftus and Ketcham 1994: 3.
4. Ibid.
5. Loftus 1980: 49.

6. James 1890, vol. 1: 373–74.
7. Neimark 1996a.
8. Hunt 1994: 192–99.
9. Samuel Eliot Morison, *The Oxford History of the American People* (New York: Oxford University Press, 1965): 124–25.
10. Freud 1896.
11. Neimark 1996a.
12. Loftus and Ketcham 1994: 140.
13. Haaken and Schlaps 1991, quoted in Ofshe and Watters 1994: 10.
14. Ofshe and Watters 1993: 9–12; P. Freyd 1995; Loftus and Ketcham 1994: chap. 9.
15. Report of the Council on Scientific Affairs, American Medical Association, CSA Report 5-A-94.
16. *FMS* [False Memory Syndrome] *Foundation Newsletter*, July/August 1996: 4.
17. Report of the Council on Scientific Affairs, American Medical Association, CSA Report 5-A-94.
18. Quoted in Loftus and Ketcham 1994: 146.
19. Frankel 1995.
20. Personal communication.
21. See, for instance, E. Sue Blume, *Secret Survivors* (New York: Ballantine Books, 1990).
22. *SWAP Newsletter,* 20(2) [n.d.].
23. Freyd interview.
24. Neimark 1996a; Loftus and Ketcham 1994: 36, 205–12.
25. See, e.g., *FMS Foundation Newsletter*, July/August 1996: 3, where eight lawsuits against one therapist, and one suit against another, are cited.
26. Ibid., May 1997: 3.
27. Ibid., September 1996: 1.
28. *New York Times*, November 6, 1997: A1.
29. *FMS Foundation Newsletter,* October 1996: 13; April 1997: 8; and on the Burgus case, ibid., December 1997: 9, and *New York Times*, November 6, 1997: A1.
30. *FMS Foundation Newsletter,* September 1996: 1.
31. Freyd interview.

Chapter 10: Harming Harm-Reduction Research

1. Marlatt et al. 1993.
2. Morse and Flavin 1992.
3. Marlatt et al. 1993.
4. Davies 1962.
5. Edwards 1985.
6. Sobell and Sobell 1973a, 1973b, 1976, 1978.
7. Ibid.
8. Monthly: Sobell and Sobell 1973a, 1973b; "fifteen times": Mark Sobell, quoted in article "Panel supports integrity of alcoholic study," San Bernardino (CA) *Inland Empire*, November 10, 1982.
9. Pendery et al. 1982.
10. Maltzman interview.
11. Sobell and Sobell 1984.
12. Doob et al. 1982.
13. Letter to the Sobells from James E. Jensen, Investigator, House of Representatives, Congress of the United States, March 23, 1983.

14. ADAMHA 1984: 2, 26.
15. Marlatt interview.
16. Hester and Miller 1989; Miller and Hester 1986.
17. Holmberg 1994.
18. Marlatt and Tapert 1993: 260–61.
19. "decreased": ibid.; "55 U.S. cities": Normand et al. 1995: 74.
20. Bauman 1995.
21. Marlatt and Tapert 1993: 261
22. Facts on File News Services 1996; U.S. General Accounting Office 1993.
23. Bauman 1995; Facts on File News Services 1996.
24. O'Brien et al. 1995a, 1995b.
25. Uncited comments by O'Brien here and later are from two interviews with her and from a long letter to a colleague which she shared with me.
26. O'Brien et al. 1995b.
27. Normand et al. 1995: 4.
28. Ibid.: 281.
29. Ibid.: 304–5.
30. Strathdee et al. 1997: F63–F64.

Chapter 11: Unhand that Rat, You Rat!

1. A lengthy Internet document, "Animal Rights Frequently Asked Questions," says, in answer to Q#1: "Animals have the RIGHT to be free from human cruelty and exploitation, just as humans possess this right. The withholding of this right from the nonhuman animals based on their species membership is referred to as 'speciesism.'"
2. Quoted from *Vogue*, September 1989, in "Animal Rights Movement Quotations."
3. *Animal People* 1995: 1.
4. Jasper and Nelkin 1992: 170–71.
5. Ibid.: 32–33.
6. Quoted in Oliver 1990: 1.
7. Quoted in Jasper and Nelkin 1992: 95.
8. Quoted in Oliver 1990: 4.
9. Benjamin Franklin, *The Autobiography and Other Writings* (New York: Signet Classic, 1961): 48–49.
10. Gallistel 1983.
11. Greenough 1991.
12. "Advances in Psychological Science and Practice Based on Animal Research," [1998] F[iscal]Y[ear] Appropriations Briefing Sheet, Public Policy Office, American Psychological Association.
13. *Health Sciences* (University of Minnesota), Fall 1989: 19.
14. Carroll et al. 1990.
15. Carroll's work is reported in *Health Sciences* (University of Minnesota), Fall 1989, and Winter 1991; the application to cocaine users: Higgins, Budney, et al. 1994.
16. Anne Brataas, "Caffeine effects on kids focus of researchers," *Denver Post*, March 9, 1992.
17. "Animal Rights Activity Increases," on-line document from the American Psychological Association (www.apa.org/psa/janfeb97/animal.html).
18. Wood's statements in this section are from his e-mail messages to me.
19. The details are also documented in Jasper and Poulsen 1993: 650–52.
20. Holden 1989.

21. IDA press release (undated but internal evidence indicates 1995): "Pulling the Plug" etc.
22. "Potshot": quoted in interview with Christine Hartel, associate executive director, Science Directorate, APA, and formerly of NIDA.
23. U. S. Public Health Service, Office for Protection from Research Risks (OPRR) 1995.
24. IDA news release of September 18, 1996.
25. Jasper and Nelkin 1992: 35–36.
26. Ibid.: 134–35; Public Law 99-158, November 20, 1985; Animal Research Data Base 1994.
27. Palca 1991; Guillermo 1993; Pons et al. 1991.
28. Animal Research Data Base 1994.
29. Jasper and Nelkin 1992: 135.
30. Pratkanis and Aronson 1991, *passim.*
31. Animal Research Data Base 1994.
32. The ad: *Cat Fancy*, October 1996; the facts about Miller's experiments: P. Miller interview, and "Research Investigations by Alan Miller, Ph.D.," undated release from the Office of Public Affairs, Rockefeller University.
33. Letter to David Fennimore, NIDA, September 22, 1988.
34. Jasper and Poulsen 1993: 648–50.
35. "Animal Rights Frequently Asked Questions": Q#?
36. Ibid.; Q#77.
37. Ibid.: Q#87.
38. Newkirk: Animal Rights '97 Convention, reported in Americans for Medical Progress Intelligence Report, July 1997; Pacheco: The Associated Press, January 15, 1989, reported in Americans for Medical Progress advertisement in *Roll Call* (Capitol Hill newspaper), June 30, 1997.
39. "The Politics of Animal Rights," *Animals Agenda*, March 1990.
40. Jasper and Nelkin 1992: 33.
41. Ibid.: 33–34.
42. Reed and Carswell 1993.
43. Jasper and Nelkin 1992: 2–3.
44. Animal Research Data Base 1994.
45. Ibid.
46. Oliver 1990.
47. *Vogue*, Sept. 1989, in "Animal Rights Movement Quotations."
48. Animal Research Data Base 1994, quoting from undated issue of Fred Trost's *Outdoors Club Outdoor Digest.*
49. Q&A session following speech, "Animal Rights Human Wrongs," University of Wisconsin-Madison, October 27, 1989.
50. Gallistel 1981.
51. Quoted in Animal Research Data Base 1994.
52. Quoted in Animal Research Data Base 1994, from a statement made in Washington D.C. on April 29, 1991.

Chapter 12: A Miscellany of Assaults on Research

1. Karen 1994: 337.
2. Gorney 1987.
3. Karen 1994: 325.
4. Collins 1987.

5. Karen 1994: 328.
6. Karen 1994: 328–29.
7. Belsky 1986.
8. Karen 1994: 331–32.
9. Reported by a colleague of Belsky's in Karen 1994: 332.
10. Karen 1994: 337.
11. Ibid.: 338.
12. Ibid.: 339.
13. Ibid.: 340.
14. Details of the case of Kennewick Man: Preston 1997; Chatters 1997; Schneider 1997a.
15. Bonnichsen et al. v. US, Civil No. 96-1481 JE; Schneider 1997a.
16. Quoted in Preston 1997: 74.
17. Schneider 1997b.
18. Letter from National Park Service and National Conference of State Historic Preservation Officers in *Anthropology Newsletter, 38 (5)* [May 1997]: 6–7; *Anthropology Newsletter, 38 (1)* [January, 1997]: 4.
19. U.S. Congress, House 1990.
20. Sullivan 1997: 4.
21. Johnson 1996.
22. Preston 1997: 75, 81.
23. Ibid.
24. Ibid.
25. Dansie and Tuohy 1997.
26. *The Maneater: The Student Voice of MU,* February 9, March 29, and December 6, 1996.
27. Sullivan 1997: 4.
28. Preston 1997: 81.
29. O'Brien: *The Maneater: The Student Voice of MU*, February 9, 1996; Dansie and Tuohy 1997; Mair 1997: 11.
30. *FairTest Examiner,* Fall/Winter 1995–96; Schaeffer interview.
31. *FairTest Examiner*, Summer 1997: 5; Bronner 1997: A12.
32. Bronner 1997: A1.
33. Hunt 1993: 618–19; Soroka v. Dayton Hudson Corp., CA Ct. App., No. A052157, 1993.
34. U. S. Congress, Office of Technology Assessment 1990: 31–32.
35. Hermann 1994; U. S. Congress, Office of Technology Assessment 1990: 1, 21.
36. Many studies: U. S. Congress, Office of Technology Assessment 1990; the metaanalysis: Ones, Viswesvaran, et al. 1991.
37. Murphy 1996.
38. The latest available review of such cases is somewhat dated (U. S. Congress, Office of Technology Assessment 1990: 68–69), but Murphy 1996, summarizing opposition to the tests, makes no mention of recent court cases successfully challenging them.
39. Minnesota, Massachusetts, Rhode Island: Murphy 1996; Wisconsin: Wisconsin Fair Employment Law (Chapter 111.31-111-395), 1980 amendment.
40. Saxe 1994.
41. Saxe 1991, 1994.
42. Successful challenges: Peterson 1996; 1988 federal law: Saxe 1994; Employee Polygraph Protection Act of 1988 (Public Law 100-347).

43. Further research: Peterson 1996: 16–22; almost no current research: Leonard Saxe interview.
44. Berland, Honts, and Barger 1989: iii.
45. Honts 1994: note 5, and Honts interview.
46. Honts' later publications: Honts 1991, 1994.; the DoD report: Barland, Honts, and Barger 1989.
47. *FairTest Examiner*, Summer, 1994; Schaeffer interview.
48. *FairTest Examiner*, Winter, 1996–1997; Schaeffer interview.
49. *FairTest Examiner*, Fall, 1996; Schaeffer interview.
50. *FairTest Examiner*. Summer, 1997; Schaeffer interview.
51. Citizens Against Government Waste press release, March 22, 1995, "Watchdogs Call on Congress to Probe 'The Secrets of NIMH.'"
52. So reported by Rep. Istook and Sam Donaldson on "PrimeTime Live," May 17, 1995.
53. U. S. Congress, House 1995h: 1167–68, 1171.
54. Frederick Goodwin interview.
55. Nakamura 1995a (the project: Investigator David Crews, Grant number 5 R37-MH41770-08).
56. Ibid. (the project: Investigator Orlando Rodriguez, previously Lloyd H. Rogler, Grant number RO1 MH-30569).
57. U. S. Congress, House 1995h: 1171–72.
58. Ibid.: 1168–69.
59. *Washington Fax*, "Life Science," July 28, 1995.
60. Fred Wood (former senior associate project director at OTA) interview.
61. "The Messenger Under Attack—Intimidation of Researchers by Special-Interest Groups," *New England Journal of Medicine, 336 (16)* (April 17, 1997): 1176–80; "ORI Clears Lead Scientist of Misconduct," *Science, 263* (March 11, 1994): 1363; Needleman 1992.
62. *Cancer Letter 22 (18)*, (May 3, 1996); Wiener 1996; Dreyfus 1996; Stanton Glantz, personal communication.
63. "Aborted Research," *Scientific American*, February 1990: 16; "Fetal Tissue Research," *Science, 256* (June 26, 1992): 1741; Beardsley 1992.

Epilogue

1. Shattuck 1996 is an entertaining compendium of examples of the theme in Western myth and literature.
2. Davis 1986: 18–19, distinguishes among three meanings: methodology, the knowledge base of science, and value-laden choices as to what to study and how to study it; I have collapsed the latter two.
3. "Code of Federal Regulations," *Federal Register 46:16* (January 26, 1981): 8389, 8390.
4. Millikan 1930.
5. Shattuck 1996: 176–77.
6. See pp. 91–93 above, and Gabor and Roberts 1990.
7. Letter by Theodore Rockwell in *American Scientist, 77* (1989): 520.
8. Davis 1986: 233, 244.
9. Udry 1993.
10. *De Carne Christi*, 5.
11. Shattuck 1996: 224.

12. Ibid.: 225.
13. Merton 1938.
14. Scarr 1988.
15. McGee 1997.
16. *United States* v. *Schwimmer,* 279 U. S. 644, 653 (1928).
17. *Life*, October 10, 1949.

Glossary of Acronyms

AAAS   American Association for the Advancement of Science
ACUC   Animal Care and Use Committee
ADAMHA Alcohol, Drug Abuse, and Mental. Health Administration
ALDF   Animal Legal Defense Fund
ALF   Animal Liberation Front
APA   American Psychological Association
APS   American Psychological Society
ASA   American Sociological Association
ATS   American Teenage Study
BGA   Behavior Genetics Association
CAGW   Citizens Against Government Waste
CBEST   California Basic Educational Skills Test
CDC   Centers for Disease Control
COSSA   Consortium of Social Science Associations
EMR   educationally mentally retarded
HEW   Department of Health, Education and Welfare
HGP   Human Genome Project
HHS   Department of Health and Human Services
IDA   In Defense of Animals
INCAR   International Committee Against Racism
IRB   Institutional Review Board
NAGPRA Native American Graves Protection and Repatriation Act
NAS   National Academy of Sciences
NCAA   National College Athletic Association
NCI   National Cancer Institute
NHSLS   National Health and Social Life Survey
NICHD   National Institute of Child Health and Human Development
NIDA   National Institute on Drug Abuse
NIH   National Institutes of Health
NIMH   National Institute of Mental Health
NORC   National Opinion Research Center
NRC   National Research Council
NSF   National Science Foundation
OCD   obsessive-compulsive disorder
OHRC   Ontario Human Rights Commission

OMB	Office of Management and Budget
OPRR	Office of Protection from Research Risks
OSRD	Office of Scientific Research and Development
OTA	Office of Technology Assessment
P.C.	politically correct, or political correctness
PETA	People for the Ethical Treatment of Animals
PHS	Public Health Service
PMS	premenstrual tension
SBE	Directorate for Social, Behavioral, and Economic Sciences
SES	socioeconomic status
SHARP	Survey and Health and AIDS-Related Practices
SMPY	Study of Mathematically Precocious Youth
SOAR	Student Organization for Animal Rights
SSRC	Social Science Research Council
TSU	Trans-Species Unlimited
USDA	U.S. Department of Agriculture

References Cited

ADAMHA: *See* Alcohol, Drug Abuse, and Mental Health Administration.

Adams, Carol J., and Donovan, Josephine, eds., 1995. *Animals and Women: Feminist Theoretical Explorations.* Durham, NC: Duke University Press.

Alcohol, Drug Abuse, and Mental Health Administration [of the National Institutes of Health], 1984. "Report of the Steering Group to the Administrator...Regarding Its Attempts to Investigate Allegations of Scientific Misconduct Concerning Drs. Mark and Linda Sobell. August. Unpublished document.

Alexander, Franz G., and Selesnick, Sheldon T., 1966. *The History of Psychiatry.* New York: Harper & Row.

American Psychological Association, 1995. *Intelligence: Knowns and Unknowns.* Report of a Task Force Established by the Board of Scientific Affairs of the American Psychological Association Science Directorate. Washington, DC.

Animal People, 1(3) (1995). Editorial. "Remembering the Aim." April.

Animal Research Data Base, 1994. In website www.looksmart.com.

Animal Rights Frequently Asked Questions. In website www.envirolink/org/arrs/faqtop. Html.

"Animal Rights Movement Quotations." In website www.ampef.org/activist.htm.

Ann Arbor Science for the People Editorial Collective, 1977. *Biology As a Social Weapon.* Minneapolis, MN: Burgess Publishing Company.

Annas, George J., and Grodin, Michael A., eds., 1992. *The Nazi Doctors and the Nuremberg Code: Human Rights in Human Experimentation.* New York: Oxford University Press.

Astin, Alexander; Astin, Helen; et al., 1975. *The Power of Protest.* San Francisco, CA: Jossey Bass Publishers.

Barber, Bernard, 1979 [1952]. *Science and the Social Order.* Westport, CT: Greenwood Press.

Barland, Gordon H; Honts, Charles R.; and Barger, Steven D., 1989. "Studies of the Accuracy of Security Screening Polygraph Examinations." [Washington, DC:] Research Division, Department of Defense Polygraph Institute.

Bauman, Norman, 1995. "In a State of Denial." *New Scientist, 148* (October 7): 12f.

Baumeister, Roy F., 1988. "Should We Stop Studying Sex Differences Altogether?" *Amer. Psychologist, 42*: 756–57.

Beardsley, Tim, 1992. "Aborting Research." *Scientific American*, August: 17–18.

———, 1995a. "Crime and Punishment." *Scientific American*, December: 19–22.

———, 1995b. "For Whom the Bell Curve Really Tolls." *Scientific American*, January: 14–17.

Belmont Report. *See*: National Commission for the Protection of Human Subjects of Biomedical and Behavioral Research, 1979.

Belsky, Jay, 1986. "Infant Day Care: A Cause for Concern?" *Zero to Three, 6 (5)*: September: 1–7.

Benbow, Camilla Persson, 1988a. "Sex Differences in Mathematical Reasoning Ability in Intellectually Talented Preadolescents: Their Nature, Effects, and Possible Causes." *Behavioral and Brain Sciences, 11*: 169–83.

————, 1988b. "Author's Response." *Behavioral and Brain Sciences, 11(2)*: 217–32.

————, and Stanley, Julian C., 1980. "Sex Differences in Mathematical Ability: Fact or Artifact?" *Science, 210 (4475)*: 1261–64.

————, eds., 1983. *Academic Precocity: Aspects of Its Development*. Baltimore, MD: The Johns Hopkins University Press.

Betzig, Laura; Mulder, Monique Borgerhoff; and Turke, Paul, eds., 1988. *Human Reproductive Behavior: A Darwinian Perspective*. Cambridge: Cambridge University Press.

Blangero, John, 1995. "The Genetic Analysis of Complex Traits: Implications for the Behavioral Genetics of Violence." Paper delivered at 1995 Crime and Genetics Conference, Queenstown, MD.

Bleier, Ruth, 1987. "A Polemic on Sex Differences Research." In Farnham, 1987.

Blits, Jan H., and Gottfredson, Linda S., 1990a. "Employment Testing and Job Performance." *The Public Interest, 98*: 18–25.

————, 1990b. "Equality or Lasting Inequality?" *Transaction/SOCIETY, 27(3)*: 4–11.

Block, N. J., and Dworkin, Gerald, 1974. "IQ, Heritability, and Inequality." *Philosophy and Public Affairs, 3(4)*: 331–409.

————, eds., 1976. *The IQ Controversy: Critical Readings*. New York: Pantheon Books.

Boorstin, Daniel J., 1983. *The Discoverers*. New York: Random House.

Bouchard, Thomas J., Jr., 1986. "Diversity, Development and Determinism: A Report on Identical Twins Reared Apart." In *Bericht ber den 35. Kongress der Deutschen Gesellschaft für Psychologie*, Manfred Amelang, ed. Gttingen: *Verlag fr Psychologie*, 417–35.

————, 1994a. "Genes, Environment, and Personality." *Science, 264*: 1700–01.

————, 1994b. "Ideological Obstacles to Genetic Research: Tales from the Nature-Nurture Wars." Paper presented to the seminar "Science and the Powers," Swedish Ministry of Education and Science, Stockholm, March 16.

————, 1997. "The Genetics of Personality." In *Handbook of Psychiatric Genetics*, K. Blum and E. P. Noble, eds. (Boca Raton, FL: CRC Press).

Bouchard, Thomas J. Jr.; Lykken, David T.; et al., 1990a. "Sources of Human Differences: The Minnesota Study of Twins Reared Apart." *Science, 250*: 223–28.

Bouchard, Thomas J. Jr.; Segal, Nancy L.; and Lykken, D. T., 1990b. "Genetic and Environmental Influences on Special Mental Abilities in a Sample of Twins Reared Apart." *Acta Genet. Med. Gemellol., 39*: 193–206.

Bradburn, Norman M., 1992. "A Response to the Nonresponse Problem." Presidential address, American Association for Public Opinion Research, St. Petersburg Beach, FL, May 18.

Brimelow, Peter, 1994. "For Whom the Bell Tolls." *Forbes*, October 24: 153–58.

Bronner, Ethan, 1997. "Colleges Look for Answers to Racial Gaps in Testing." *New York Times*, November 8: A1, A12.

Brooks-Gunn, Jeanne, and Klebanov, Pamela, 1996. "Ethnic Differences in Children's Intelligence Test Scores: Roles of Economic Deprivation, Home Environment, and Maternal Characteristics." *Child Development, 67*: 396–408.

Buck v. *Bell*, 274 U.S. 200–208 (1927).

Bullough, Vern L., 1985a. "Problems of Research on a Delicate Topic: A Personal View." *J. of Sex Research, 21(4)*: 375–86.

————, 1985b. "The Rockefellers and Sex Research." *J. of Sex Res., May*: 113–25.

Bush, Vannevar, 1980 [1945]. *Science—The Endless Frontier*. Washington, DC: National Science Foundation.

Butterfield, Fox, 1997. "Homicides Plunge 11 Percent in U.S., F.B.I. Report Says." *New York Times,* June 2: A1.

Caplan, Arthur L., ed., 1978. *The Sociobiology Debate.* New York: Harper & Row.

————, 1992a. "Twenty Years After: The Legacy of the Tuskegee Syphilis Study." *Hastings Center Report: November-December:* 29–32.

————, 1992b. *When Medicine Went Mad: Bioethics and the Holocaust.* Totowa, NJ: Humana Press.

Carey, Gregory, 1994. "Genetics and Violence." In Reiss and Roth, 1994.

Carlson, Elo Axel, 1973. "Eugenics Revisited: The Case for Germinal Choice." *Stadler Symp., 5:* 13–14.

Carroll, M. E.; Lac, S. T.; et al., 1990. "IV Cocaine Self-Administration in Rats is Reduced by Dietary L-tryptophan." *Psychopharmacology, 100:* 293–300.

Chambers's Biographical Dictionary, 1962. New York: St. Martin's Press.

Charrow, Robert P., 1991. "Sex, Politics, and Science." *J. of NIH Research, 3:* 80–83.

Chatters, James C., 1997. "Encounter With an Ancestor." *Anthropology Newsletter, 8(1):* 9–10.

Chess, Stella, and Thomas, Alexander, 1986. *Temperament in Clinical Practice.* New York: Guilford Press.

Chomsky, Noam, 1973. "The Fallacy of Richard Herrnstein's IQ." *Cognition, 1(1).*

Citizens Against Government Waste, 1995. "Watchdogs Call on Congress to Probe 'The Secrets of NIMH'." News release, March 22, 1995. Washington, DC: Citizens Against Government Waste.

Cleary, Robert E., 1987. "The Impact of IRBs on Political Science Research." *IRB,* May/June: 6–10.

Cohen, Richard L., and Ciocca, Alexander J., 1992. "The Institutional Review Board: Ethical Gatekeeper." In *Research Fraud in the Behavioral and Biomedical Sciences,* David J. Miller and Michel Hersen, eds. (New York: John Wiley & Sons, Inc.)

Collins, Glenn, 1987. "Day Care for Infants: Debate Turns to Long-Term Effects." *New York Times,* November 25.

Comings, D. E.; Muhleman, D.; et al., 1994. "The Dopamine D2 Receptor Gene: A Genetic Risk Factor in Substance Abuse." *Drug and Alcohol Depend., 34:* 175–180.

Consortium of Social Science Associations, 1995, 1996, 1997. *Annual Report, 1995, 1996, 1997.* Washington, DC: Consortium of Social Science Associations.

COSSA: *See* Consortium of Social Science Associations.

Cravens, Hamilton, 1978. *The Triumph of Evolution: American Scientists and the Heredity-Environment Controversy.* Philadelphia: University of Pennsylvania Press.

Crowell, Nancy A., and Burgess, Ann W., eds., 1996. *Understanding Violence Against Women.* Washington, DC: National Academy Press.

Dansie, Amy, and Tuohy, Donald R., 1997. "What We Can and Can't Know About Great Basin Prehistory." *Anthropology Newsletter, 38 (1):* 52f.

Davenport, Charles B., 1911. *Heredity in Relation to Eugenics.* New York: Henry Holt.

Davies, D. L., 1962. "Normal Drinking in Recovered Alcohol Addicts." *Quart. J. of Studies on Alcohol, 23:* 94–104.

Davis, Bernard, 1986. *Storm Over Biology: Essays on Science, Sentiment, and Public Policy.* Buffalo, NY: Prometheus Books.

Deaux, Kay, 1985. "Sex and Gender." *Ann. Rev. Psychol., 36:* 49–81.

Dennis, Wayne, 1935. "The Effect of Restricted Practice Upon the Reaching, Sitting, and Standing of Two Infants." *J. Genet. Psychol., 47:* 17–32.

————, 1938. "Infant Development Under Conditions of Restricted Practice and of Minimum Social Stimulation: A Preliminary Report." *J. Genet. Psychol., 53*: 149–57.

Deutsch, Helene, 1944. *The Psychology of Women*. New York: Grune and Stratton.

Diamond, Milton, and Sigmundson, H. Keith, 1997. "Sex Reassignment at Birth." *Archives of Pediatric and Adolescent Medicine, 151*: 298–304.

di Mauro, Diane, 1995. *Sexuality Research in the United States. An Assessment of the Social and Behavioral Sciences*. New York: The Social Science Research Council.

Dobzhansky, Theodosius, 1962. *Mankind Evolving: The Evolution of the Human Species*. New Haven, CT: Yale University Press.

————, 1973. "Differences Are Not Deficits." *Psychology Today*, December.

————, 1981. "Genetic Diversity and Human Equality." In Scarr, 1981: 253–56.

Doob, Anthony; Warwick, O. Harold; Winegard, William C.; and Dickens, Bernard M., 1982. Report of the Committee of Enquiry into Allegations Concerning Drs. Linda & Mark Sobell. Toronto: Alcoholism and Drug Addiction Research Foundation.

Dreyfus, Robert, 1996. "Tobacco: Enemy Number 1." *Mother Jones, May/June*: 42–47.

Edwards, G., 1985. "A Later Follow-up of a Classic Case Series: D. L. Davies' 1962 Report and Its Significance for the Present." *Jour. of Studies on Alcohol, 46*: 181–90.

Ehrhardt, Anke, and Baker, S., 1974. "Fetal Androgens, Human Central Nervous System Differentiation, and Behavior Sex Differences." In R. Friedman, R. Richart, and R. Van de Wiele, eds., *Sex Differences in Behavior* (New York: Wiley and Sons).

Ehrhardt, Anke, and Money, John, 1967. "Progestin-Induced Hermaphroditism: IQ and Psychosexual Identity in a Study of Ten Girls." *J. of Sex Res., 3*: 83–100.

Eisenberg, Nancy; Shell, Rita; et al., 1987. "Prosocial Development in Middle Childhood: A Longitudinal Study." *Developmental Psychol., 23(5)*: 712–18.

Ellickson, Phyllis L., and Hawes-Dawson, Jennifer A., 1989. "An Assessment of Active Versus Passive Methods for Obtaining Parental Consent." RAND NOTE N-2935-CHF. Santa Monica, CA: The RAND Corporation.

England, J. Merton, 1982. *A Patron for Pure Science*. Washington, DC: National Science Foundation.

Epstein, Cynthia Fuchs, 1988. *Deceptive Distinctions: Sex, Gender, and the Social Order*. New York: Russell Sage Foundation.

Ericksen, Julia, 1996. *Kiss and Tell: The Revelations of Sexual Behavior Surveys*. Cambridge, MA: Harvard University Press.

Facts on File News Services, 1996. "Needle-Exchange Programs: An In-Depth Analysis." *Issues and Controversies On File*. www.facts.com/fofcd..htm.

Family Research Council, 1995a. "Dr. Kinsey and the Children of Table 34." *In Focus*, IF95C1HS. Washington, DC: Family Research Council.

————, 1995b. "Serious Flaws in the Kinsey Research." *In Focus*, IF95C9HS. Washington, DC: Family Research Council.

Fancher, Raymond, 1979. *Pioneers of Psychology*. New York: W. W. Norton.

————, 1985. *The Intelligence Men: Makers of the IQ Controversy*. New York: W. W. Norton.

Farganis, Sondra, 1992. "Feminism and the Reconstruction of Science." In Jaggar and Bordo, 1992.

Farnham, Christie, 1987. *The Impact of Feminist Research in the Academy*. Indianapolis: Indiana University Press.

Fausto-Sterling, Anne, 1985. *Myths of Gender: Biological Theories About Women and Men*. New York: Basic Books. Inc.

Fay, R. E., 1989. "Prevalence and Patterns of Same-Gender Sexual Contact Among Men." *Science, 243*: 338–48.

Fisher, R[onald] A., 1924. "The Elimination of Mental Defect." *Eugenics Rev., 16*: 114–16.

Forrest, D. W., 1974. *Francis Galton: The Life and Work of a Victorian Genius.* London: Paul Elek.

Frankel, Fred H., 1995. "Discovering New Memories in Psychotherapy—Childhood Revisited, Fantasy, or Both?" *The New England J. of Med., 333(9)*: 591–94.

Fraser, Steven, ed., 1995. *The Bell Curve Wars: Race, Intelligence, and the Future of America.* New York: Basic Books.

Freud, Sigmund, 1896. "Further Remarks on the Neuro-Psychoses of Defense." In Freud, 1953–1966, vol. 3: 164ff.

———, 1910. "On the Universal Tendency to Debasement in the Sphere of Love." In Freud, Sigmund, 1953–1966, vol. 11: 189ff.

Freud, Sigmund, 1950 [1927]. "Some Psychical Consequences of the Anatomical Distinction Between the Sexes." In Freud, Sigmund, 1953–1966, vol. 19: 253ff.

Freud, Sigmund, 1953–1966. *The Standard Edition of the Complete Psychological Works of Sigmund Freud,* ed. by James Strachey (London: Hogarth Press)

Freyd, Pamela, 1995. "False Memory Syndrome Phenomenon: Weighing the Evidence." *Court Review*, Spring: 16–21.

Furlow, E. Bryant, and Thornhill, Randy, 1996. "Orgasm Wars." *Psychology Today*, January/February: 42–46.

Gabor, Thomas, and Roberts, Julian, 1990. "Rushton on Race and Crime: The Evidence Remains Unconvincing." *Canadian J. of Criminology, 32*: 335–43.

Gallistel, C[harles] R., 1981. "Bell, Magendie, and the Proposals to Restrict the Use of Animals in Neurobehavioral Research." *Amer. Psychologist, 36(4)*: 357–60.

———, 1983. "Vivisectionist Ethics." Talk given at Annual Meeting of the Society for Neuroscience, November 9

Galton, Francis, 1865. "Hereditary Talent and Character." *Macmillan's Magazine, 12(68)*: 157–66, and *12(71)*: 313–27.

———, 1892 [1869]. *Hereditary Genius: An Enquiry into Its Laws and Consequences.* Cleveland, OH: World Publishing. Reprint of 1892 edition.

———, 1907 [1883]. *Inquiries into Human Faculty and Its Development.* London: Everyman's Library.

———, 1908. *Memories of My Life.* London: Methuen and Co.

Gardner, W., and Wilcox, B. L., 1993. "Political Intervention in Scientific Peer Review. Research on Adolescent Sexual Behavior." *Amer. Psychologist*, September: 972–83.

Garrett, Henry E., 1951. *Great Experiments in Psychology.* 3rd ed. New York: Appleton-Century-Crofts.

Geiger, Roger L., 1993. *Research and Relevant Knowledge: American Research Universities Since World War II.* New York: Oxford University Press.

Gitlin, Todd, 1995. "The Rise of 'Identity Politics': An Examination and a Critique." In. *Higher Education Under Fire*, Michael Bérubé and Cary Nelson, eds. (New York: Routledge).

Glantz, Stanton, 1995. "Dear Colleague (9/11/95.)" E-mail letter to various persons about the House Appropriations Committee's actions concerning Glantz's National Cancer Institute grant, "Effect of Tobacco Advocacy at the State Level."

Goddard, Henry H., 1917. "Mental Tests and the Immigrant." *The J. of Delinquency, 2*: 243–77.

Goleman, Daniel, 1996. "Forget Money; Nothing Can Buy Happiness, Some Researchers Say." *New York Times*, July 16, C9.

Goode, Erica E.; Schrof, Joannie M.; et al., 1991. "Where Emotions Come From." *U. S. News and World Report*, June 24: 54–62.

Goode, Erich, 1997. "Ideological, Ethical, and Moral Implications of Studying Deviance." Chapter 14 in Erich Goode, *Deviant Behavior*, 5th ed. (Englewood Cliffs, NJ: Prentice-Hall).

Goodwin, Frederick K., 1992. Transcript of untitled speech, February 11, at meeting of the National Mental Health Advisory Council.

Gorman, Christine, 1997. "A Boy Without a Penis." *Time*, March 24, 1997: 83.

Gorney, Cynthia, 1987. "How Young Is Too Young?" *Parenting*, October.

Gottesman, Irving I., 1974. "Exorcise or Excommunicate the IQ-Race-Class Controversy." [review of T. Dobzhansky, *Genetic Diversity and Human* Equality] *Contemp. Psychol., 19(8)*: 587–588.

———, 1981. "Developmental Genetics and Life-Span Orthogenetic Psychology." In *Prospective Longitudinal Research,* S. A. Medwick and A. E. Baert, eds. (Oxford: Oxford University Press).

———, 1994. "Schizophrenia Epigenesis: Past, Present, and Future." *Acta Psychiatr. Scand., 90 (Suppl. 384)*: 26–33.

———, and Goldsmith, H. Hill, 1994. "Developmental Psychopathology of Antisocial Behavior: Inserting Genes into Its Ontogenesis and Epigenesis." In Guze, S. G.; Earls, E. J.; and Barrett, J. E., eds., *Childhood Psychopathology and Development* (New York: Raven Press).

Gottfredson, Linda S., 1986. "Societal Consequences of the *g* Factor in Employment." *J. of Vocational Behav., 29*: 379–410.

———, 1988. "Reconsidering Fairness: A Matter of Social and Ethical Priorities." *J. of Vocational Behav. 33*: 293–319.

———, 1996a. "The New Challenge to Academic Freedom." *J. of Social Distress and the Homeless, 5(2)*: 205–12.

———, 1996b. "Racially Gerrymandered Police Tests." *Wall Street Journal*, October 24.

——— and Blits, Jan H., 1991. "Memorandum of Professors Linda S. Gottfredson and Jan H. Blits in Support of Their Grievance Against the University of Delaware." American Arbitration Association, June 20: Case No. 14 390 1935 90 A.

Gould, Stephen Jay, 1981. *The Mismeasure of Man.* New York: W. W. Norton.

———, 1991. "Exaptation: A Crucial Tool for an Evolutionary Psychology." *J. Of Social Issues, 47(3)*: 43–65.

Graham, Loren R., 1987. *Science, Philosophy, and Human Behavior in the Soviet Union.* New York: Columbia University Press.

Greenough, William T., 1991. "The Animal Rights Assertions: A Researcher's Perspective." *Psychological Science Agenda* (Amer. Psychological Assoc.), May/June: 10–12.

Gross, Paul R., and Levitt, Norman, 1994. *Higher Superstition: The Academic Left and Its Quarrels with Science.* Baltimore, MD: Johns Hopkins Press.

Grove J. W., 1989. *In Defence of Science: Science, Technology, and Politics in Modern Society.* Toronto: University of Toronto Press.

Grove, William M.; Eckert, Elke E.; et al., 1990. "Heritability of Substance Abuse and Antisocial Behavior: A Study of Monozygotic Twins Reared Apart." *Biol. Psychiatry*, 27: 1293–1304.

Gruen, Lori, 1993. "Dismantling Oppression: An Analysis of the Connection Between Women and Animals." In *Ecofeminism: Women, Animals, Nature*, Greta Gaard, ed. (Philadelphia, PA: Temple University Press).

Guillermo, Kathy, 1993. *Monkey Business: The Disturbing Case That Launched the Animal Rights Movement.* National Press.

Hall, J. A. Y., and Kimura, Doreen, 1995. "Sexual Orientation and Performance on Sexually Dimorphic Motor Tasks." *Arch. of Sexual Behavior, 24(4)*: 395–407.

Halpern, Diane F., 1992. *Sex Differences in Cognitive Abilities.* 2nd ed. Hillsdale, NJ: Erlbaum.

———, 1994. "Stereotypes, Science, Censorship, and the Study of Sex Differences." *Feminism and Psychol., 4(4)*: 523–30.

———; Gilbert, Richard; and Coren, Stanley, 1996. "PC or not PC? Contemporary Challenges to Unpopular Research Findings." *J. of Social Distress and the Homeless, 5(2)*: 251–270.

Hamilton, Neil W., 1995. *Zealotry and Academic Freedom.* New Brunswick, NJ: Transaction Publishers.

———, 1996a. "Foreword: Symposium on Zealotry and Academic Freedom." *William Mitchell Law Rev., 22(2)*: 333–55.

———, 1996b. "Contrasts and Comparisons Among McCarthyism, 1960s Student Activism and 1990s Faculty Fundamentalism." *William Mitchell Law Rev., 22(2)*: 369–413.

Harris, Julie Aitken; Rushton, J. Philippe; Hampson, Elizabeth; and Jackson, Douglas N., 1996. "Salivary Testosterone and Self-Report Aggressive and Pro-Social Personality Characteristics in Men and Women." *Aggressive Behavior, 22*: 321–31.

Hartigan, John A., and Wigdor, Alexandra K., 1989. *Fairness in Employment Testing.* Washington, DC: National Academy Press.

Hauser, Philip M., 1975. *Social Statistics in Use.* New York: Russell Sage Foundation.

Heclo, Hugh, 1996. "The Sixties' False Dawn: Awakenings, Movements, and Postmodern Policy-Making." *J. of Policy Hist., 8 (1)*: 34–63.

Hermann, Susan, 1994. *Hiring Right.* Thousand Oaks, CA: SAGE Publications.

Herrnstein, Richard J., 1982. "IQ Testing and the Media." *Atlantic Monthly,* August: 68–74.

———, and Murray, Charles, 1996 [1994], *The Bell Curve: Intelligence and Class Structure in American Life.* New York: Free Press Paperbacks.

Hester, R. K., and Miller, W. M., 1989. *Handbook of Alcoholism Trteatment Approaches.* New York: Pergamon Press.

Higgins, S. T.; Budney, A. J.; et al., 1994. "Incentives Improve Outcome in Outpatient Behavioral Treatment of Cocaine Dependence." *Arch. of General Psychi., 51*: 568–76.

Hilts, Philip J., 1993. "Misconduct in Science Is Not Rare, a Survey Finds." *New York Times,* November 12: A22.

Hirsch, Jerry, 1970. "Behavior-Genetic Analysis and Its Biosocial Consequences." *Seminars in Psychiatry, 2*: 89–105.

———, 1975. "Jensenism: The Bankruptcy of 'Science' Without Scholarship." *Educational Theory, 25 (1).* 3–27.

Holden, Constance, 1989. "A Preemptive Strike for Animal Research." *Science, 244*: 415–16.

———, 1996. "Wiley Drops IQ Book After Public Furor." *Science, 272*: 644.

Holmberg, S., 1994. "Emerging Epidemiologic Patterns of HIV in the United States." *AIDS Research and Human Retroviruses, 10 (Supplement 2)*: S1.

Honts, Charles R., 1991. "The Emperor's New Clothes: Application of Polygraph Tests in the American Workplace." *Forensic Reports, 4*: 91–116.

———, 1994. "Psychological Detection of Deception." *Current Directions in Psychol. Science, 3 (3)*: 77–82.

Horgan, John, 1993. "Eugenics Revisited." *Scientific American, 270(6)*: 122–31.

Horowitz, Irving Louis, 1987. "Disenthralling Sociology." *Transaction/SOCIETY, 24* (January/February): 48–55.

————, 1989. "Sociology and Subjectivism." *Transaction/SOCIETY, 26* (July/August): 49–54.

————, 1995. "The Rushton File: Racial Comparisons and Media Passions." *Society, 32:* 7–17.

Hothersall, David, 1984. *History of Psychology.* Philadelphia: Temple University Press.

Hunt, Earl, 1995. *Will We Be Smart Enough? A Cognitive Analysis of the Coming Workforce.* New York: Russell Sage Foundation.

Hunt, Morton, 1949. "Dr. Muller and the Million Human Time-Bombs." *Science Illustrated,* May: 46ff.

————, 1962. *Her Infinite Variety: The American Woman as Lover, Mate and Rival.* New York: Harper & Row.

————, 1971. "The Intelligent Man's Guide to Intelligence." *Playboy,* February.

————, 1985. *Profiles of Social Research: The Scientific Study of Human Interactions.* New York: Russell Sage Foundation.

————, 1993. *The Story of Psychology.* New York: Doubleday.

————, 1994 [1959]. *The Natural History of Love.* New York: Anchor Books.

Huxley, Julian, 1936. "Eugenics and Society." *Eugenics Rev., 28(1):* 11–31.

Jacoby, Russell, and Glauberman, Naomi, eds., 1995. *The Bell Curve Debate: History, Documents, Opinions.* New York: Times Books.

Jaggar, A. M., and Bordo, S. R., eds., 1992. *Gender/Body/Knowledge: Feminist Reconstructions of Being and Knowing.* New Brunswick, NJ: Rutgers University Press.

James, William, 1890. *The Principles of Psychology.* New York: Henry Holt and Company.

Jasper, James M., and Nelkin, Dorothy, 1992. *The Animal Rights Crusade.* New York: The Free Press.

————, and Poulsen, Jane, 1993. "Fighting Back: Vulnerabilities, Blunders, and Countermobilization by the Targets and Three Animal Rights Campaigns." *Sociological Forum, 8(4):* 639–57.

Jensen, Arthur R., 1969. "How Much Can We Boost IQ and Scholastic Achievement?" *Harvard Educ. Rev., 39:* 1–123.

————, 1970. "Race and the Genetics of Intelligence: A Reply to Lewontin." *Bull. of the Atomic Scientists,* May: 93–106.

————, 1972a. *Genetics and Education.* London: Methuen & Co., Ltd.

————, 1972b. "The IQ Controversy: A Reply to Layzer." *Cognition, 4:*427–52.

————, 1991. "Spearman's g and the Problem of Educational Equality." *Oxford Rev. of Educ., 17(2):* 169–87.

————, 1994. "Race and Sex Differences in Head Size and IQ." *Intelligence, 18:* 309–33.

————, 1997a. "'Spearman's Hypothesis.'" Spearman Lecture, Spearman Seminar, University of Plymouth, England, July, 1997. MS copy.

————, 1997b. "What We Know and Don't Know About the g Factor." Keynote address, Convention of the International Society for the Study of Individual Differences, Aarhus, Denmark, July, 1997. MS copy. I

Johnson, David, 1992a.. "Next to Nothingness and Being at the National Science Foundation" Part I: *Psychol. Science 3(3):* 145–49; 1992b: Part II: *3(5):* 261–65; 1992c: Part III: *3(6):* 323–27.

————, 1993. "Next to Nothingness and Being at the National Science Foundation: Part IV." *Psychol. Science, 4(1):* 1–6.

Johnson, George, 1996. "Indian Tribes' Creationists Thwart Archeologists." *New York Times,* October 22: A1f.

Jones, James H., 1981. *Bad Blood: The Tuskegee Syphilis Experiment.* New York: Free Press.

Kamin, Leon, 1974. *The Science and Politics of I.Q.* Potomac, MD: Erlbaum.

Karen, Robert, 1994. *Becoming Attached: Unfolding the Mystery of the Infant-Mother Bond and Its Impact on Later Life.* New York: Warner Books.

Katz, Jay, 1987. "The Regulation of Human Experimentation in the United States— A Personal Odyssey." *IRB, 9(1)*: 1–6.

Kearney, Kathleen A.; Hopkins, Ronald H., et al., 1983. "Sample Bias Resulting from a Requirement for Written Parental Consent." *Public Opinion Quarterly, 47*: 96–102.

Kenrick, Douglas T., 1988. "Biology, Si; Hard-wired Ability, Maybe No." *Behavioral and Brain Sciences, 11*: 199–200.

Kevles, Daniel J., 1995 [1985]. *In the Name of Eugenics: Genetics and the Uses of Human Heredity.* Cambridge, MA: Harvard University Press.

Kimura, Doreen, 1992. "Sex Differences in the Brain." *Scientific American*, September: 119–25.

———, and Hampson, Elizabeth, 1993. "Neural and Hormonal Mechanisms Mediating Sex Differences in Cognition." In *Biological Approaches to the Study of Human Intelligence*, P. A. Vernon, ed. (Norwood, NJ: Ablex Publishing Corp.).

———, 1994. "Cognitive Pattern in Men and Women Is Influenced by Fluctuations in Sex Hormones." *Current Directions in Psychol. Science, 3(2)*: 57–61.

Kinsey, Alfred; Pomeroy, Wardell B.; and Martin, Clyde E., 1948. *Sexual Behavior in the Human Male.* Philadelphia, PA: W. B. Saunders.

Kinsey, Alfred; Pomeroy, Wardell B.; Martin, Clyde E.; and Gebhard, Paul H., 1953. *Sexual Behavior in the Human Female.* Philadelphia, PA: W. B. Saunders.

Kleinman, Daniel Lee, 1995. *Politics on the Endless Frontier: Postwar Research Policy in the United States.* Durham, NC: Duke University Press.

Knight, Robert, 1994. "Dr. Kinsey and the Children of Table 34." Washington, DC: Family Research Council.

Koch, Sigmund, and Leary, David E., eds., 1985. *A Century of Psychology as Science.* New York: McGraw-Hill.

Kolata, Gina, 1980. "Math and Sex: Are Girls Born with Less Ability? A Johns Hopkins Group Says 'probably.' Others Are Not So Sure." *Science, 210*: 1234–35.

Korwar, Arati, 1995. *War of Words: Speech Codes of Colleges and Universities in the United States, 1995.* Nashville, TN: Freedom Forum First Amendment Center (on the Internet).

Krawiec, T. S., ed., 1974. *The Psychologists.* New York: Oxford University Press.

Kretschmer, Ernst, 1925. *Physique and Character.* New York: Harcourt Brace.

Lamb, Kevin, 1997. "IQ and PC." *National Review*, January 27.

Larsen, Otto N., 1992. *Milestones and Millstones: Social Science at the National Science Foundation, 1945–1991.* New Brunswick, NJ: Transaction Publishers..

Laughlin, H[arry H.], 1922. "Model Eugenic Sterilization Law." In *Eugenic Sterilization in the United States, A Report of the Psychopathic Laboratory of the Municipal Court of Chicago* (Municipal Court of Chicago, 1992): 446–52, 454–61.

———, 1939. *Conquest by Immigration.* A report of the Special Committee on Immigration and Naturalization of the Chamber of Commerce of the State of New York.

Laumann, Edward O.; Gagnon, John H.; Michael, Robert T.; and Michaels, Stuart, 1994a. *The Social Organization of Sexuality: Sexual Practices in the United States.* Chicago: The University of Chicago Press.

Laumann, Edward O.; Michael, Robert T.; and Gagnon, John H.; 1994b. "A Political History of the National Sex Survey of Adults." *Family Planning Perspectives*, January/February: 34–38.

Layzer, David, 1973. "Science or Superstition?" *Cognition, 1(2)*: 265–99.

Lerner, Richard, 1992. *Final Solutions: Biology, Prejudice, and Genocide.* University Park: Pennsylvania State University Press.

LeVay, Simon, 1991. "A Difference in Hypothalamic Structure Between Heterosexual and Homosexual Men." *Science, 258*: 1034–37.

————, 1995. *The Sexual Brain.* Cambridge, MA: MIT Press/Bradford.

Levine, Felice J., 1995a. "Consent for Research on Children." *Chron. of Higher Educ.,* November 10: B1–2.

————, 1995b. Testimony on behalf of The Research and Privacy Coalition before the Senate Committee on Governmental Affairs, November 9. Washington, DC: [American Sociological Association].

————, and Rosich, Katherine J., 1996. *Social Causes of Violence.* Washington, DC: American Sociological Association.

Lewis, Carol M., and Horn, Joseph M., 1991. "Premenstrual Changes and Neuroticism: A Twin Study." *Personality and Indiv. Diff., 12(11)*: 1205–12.

Lewontin, Richard C., 1974. "The Analysis of Variance and the Analysis of Causes." *Amer. J. of Human Genetics, 26*: 400–11.

————, 1988. "Science for the People in Action: An Expert Witness Makes His Case." *Science for the People,* November/December: 6–7.

————, 1994. "Women Versus the Biologists." *New York Review of Books,* April 7: 31–35.

————; Rose, Steven; and Kamin, Leon, 1984. *Not in Our Genes.* New York: Pantheon Books.

Liesen, Laurette T., 1995. "Feminism and the Politics of Reproductive Strategies." *Politics and the Life Sciences 14(2)*: 145–162.

Lifton, Robert J., 1986. *The Nazi Doctors—Medical Killing and the Psychology of Genocide.* New York: Basic Books.

Lippmann, Walter, 1922–23. "The Abuse of the Tests" and "A Future for the Tests," reprinted in Block and Dworkin, 1976: 4–44.

————, 1965 [1922]. *Public Opinion.* New York: The Free Press.

Lipsey, Mark, 1992. "Juvenile Delinquency Treatment: A Meta-Analytic Inquiry into the Variability of Effects." In *Meta-Analysis for Explanation: A* Casebook, Thomas Cook et al., eds. (New York: Russell Sage Foundation).

Loehlin, John C., 1987. "Twin Studies, Environmental Differences, Age Changes." *Behavioral and Brain Sciences, 10(1)*: 30–31.

————; Horn, Joseph M.; and Willerman, Lee, 1981. "Personality Resemblance in Adoptive Families." *Behav. Genetics, 11(4)*: 309–30.

————; Lindzey, G.; and Spuhler, J.N. *Race Differences in Intelligence.* San Francisco, CA: Freeman.

————; Willerman, Lee; and Horn, Joseph M., 1985. "Personality Resemblances in Adoptive Families When the Children are Late-Adolescent or Adult." *J. Personality and Soc. Psychol., 48(2)*: 376–92.

————; Willerman, Lee; and Horn, Joseph M., 1987. "Personality Resemblance in Adoptive Families." *J. Personality and Soc. Psychol., 53(5)*: 961–69.

Loftus, Elizabeth F., 1974. "The Incredible Eyewitness." *Psychol. Today,* December.

————, 1975. "Leading Questions and the Eyewitness Report." *Cog. Psychol., 7*: 560–72.

————, 1980. *Memory.* Reading, MA: Addison-Wesley Publishing Company.

————, 1993. "The Reality of Repressed Memories." *Amer. Psychologist, 48(5)*: 518–37.

————, and Ketcham, Katherine, 1994. *The Myth of Repressed Memory.* New York: St. Martin's Griffin.

Lumsden, C., and Wilson, E. O., 1981. *Genes, Mind, and Culture.* Cambridge, MA: Harvard University Press.

Lykken, D. T.; Bouchard, T. J.; et al., 1990. "The Minnesota Twin Family Registry: Some Initial Findings." *Acta Genet. Med. Gemellol, 39*: 35–70.

Lykken, D. T.; McGue, M.; Tellegen, A.; and Bouchard, T. J., Jr., 1992. "Emergenesis: Genetic Traits That May Not Run in Families." *Amer. Psychologist*, February: 1565–77.

Lyons, M. J. et al., 1995. "Differential Heritability of Adult and Juvenile Antisocial Traits." *Arch. of General Psychi., 52*: 906–15.

Maass, Peter, 1995a. "Crime, Genetics Forum Erupts in Controversy." *Washington Post*, September 24, 1995.

———, 1995b. "Conference on Genetics and Crime Gets a Second Chance." *Washington Post*, September 22, 1995.

MacArthur, Robert H., and Wilson, E. O., 1967. *The Theory of Island Biogeography.* Princeton, NJ: Princeton University Press.

Maccoby, Eleanor E., and Jacklin, Carol Nagy, 1974. *The Psychology of Sex Differences.* Stanford, CA: Stanford University Press.

Magnus, David, 1997. "Lock Out 'Back Door Eugenics.'" *Penn Bioethics, 3 (1),* (Center for Bioethics, University of Pennsylvania).

Mair, Victor, 1997. "Whose Ancestors Are They?" *Anthropology Newsletter, 38 (1)* [January]: 11.

Marlatt, G. Alan; Larimer, Mary; et al., 1993. "Harm Reduction for Alcohol Problems: Moving Beyond the Controlled Drinking Controversy." *Behavior Therapy, 24*: 461–504.

Marlatt, G. Alan, and Tapert, Susan F., 1993. "Harm Reduction: Reducing the Risks of Addictive Behaviors." In *Addictive Behaviors Across the Lifespan*, J. S. Baer et al., eds. (Newbury Park, CA: Sage Publications).

Mayo, B., 1942. *Jefferson Himself.* New York: Houghton Mifflin.

McGee, Glenn, 1997. *Center for Bioethics Newsletter* (University of Pennsylvania), *2 (3),* (Spring).

McGue, Matt, and Bouchard, Thomas J., Jr., 1989. "Genetic and Environmental Determinants of Information Processing and Special Mental Abilities." In *Advances in the Psychology of Human Intelligence*, vol. 5, Robert J. Sternberg, ed. (Hillsdale, NJ: Lawrence Erlbaum Associates).

McHugh, M. C.; Koeske, R. D.; and Frieze, I. H., 1986. "Issues to Consider in Conducting Nonsexist Research." *Amer. Psychologist, 41*: 879–90

Mead, Margaret, 1972. *Blackberry Winter.* New York: Morrow.

Mednick, S. A.; Gabrielli, W. F.; and Hutchings, B., 1984. "Genetic Influences in Criminal Convictions: Evidence from an Adoption Cohort." *Science, 224*: 891–94.

Mehler, Barry, 1994. "In Genes We Trust: When Science Bows to Racism." *Reform Judaism*, Winter, 10ff.

Mehlman, P. T.; Higley, J. D.; et al., 1994. "Low CSF 5-HIAA Concentrations and Severe Aggression and Impaired Impulse Control in Nonhuman Primates." *Amer. J. of Psychiatry, 151*: 1485–1491.

Menand, Louis, 1993. "The Future of Academic Freedom." *Academe*, May-June: 11–17.

Merton, Robert K., 1938. "Science and the Social Order." *Philosophy of Science, 5*: 321–37. In Merton, 1973, chapter 12.

———, 1942. "The Normative Structure of Science." Originally published as "Science and Technology in a Democratic Order," *J. of Legal and Polit. Sociol., 1*: 115–26. In Merton, 1973, chapter 13.

———, 1973. *The Sociology of Science: Theoretical and Empirical Investigations.* Chicago: University of Chicago Press.

Michael, Robert T.; Gagnon, John H.; Laumann, Edward O.; and Kolata, Gina, 1994. *Sex in America.* New York: Little, Brown.

Milgram, Stanley, 1963. "Behavioral Study of Obedience." *J. Abnormal and Soc. Psychol. 67*: 371–78.

Mill, J. S., ed., 1869. Second ed. of James Mill's *Analysis of the Phenomena of the Human Mind*. London: Longmans.

Miller, Adam, 1994. "Professors of Hate." *Rolling Stone*, October 20.

Miller, Edward M., 1995. "Human Breasts: Evolutionary Origins as a Deceptive Signal of Need for Provisioning and Temporary Infertility." *Mankind Quarterly, 36(2)*: 135–50.

———, 1996. "*The g Factor*: The Book and the Controversy." *J. of Social, Polit. and Econ. Studies, 21(2)*:221–232.

Miller, Roberta Balstad, 1982a. "The Social Sciences and the Politics of Science: The 1940s." *Amer. Sociologist, 17(4)*: 205–09.

———, 1982b. "Federal Funding of Social Science: An Interview with Dr. Roberta Balstad Miller, Executive Director of the Consortium of Social Science Associations." *Amer. Sociologist, 17(4)*: 217–25.

———, 1987. "Social Science Under Siege: The Political Response, 1981–1984. In *Social Science Research and Government: Comparative Essays on Britain and the United States*, Martin Bulmer, ed. (Cambridge: Cambridge University Press).

Miller, W. M., and Hester, R. K., 1986. "The Effectiveness of Alcoholism Treatment." In *Treating Addictive Behaviours*, W. M. Miller and N. Heather, eds. (New York: Plenum).

Millikan, Robert A., 1930. "Alleged Sins of Science." *Scribners Magazine, 87 (2)*: 119–30.

Moberg, D. Paul, and Piper, Douglas L., 1990. "Obtaining Active Parental Consent via Telephone in Adolescent Substance Abuse Prevention Research." *Evaluation Rev., 14 (3)*: 315–23.

Montagu, Ashley, ed., 1980. *Sociobiology Examined*. New York: Oxford University Press.

Morse, R. M., and Flavin, D. K., 1992. "The Definition of Alcoholism." *J. of the Amer. Medical Assoc., 268*: 1012–14.

Muller, Hermann J., et al., 1939. "The 'Geneticists' Manifesto.'" *Eugenical News, 24*: 63–64.

Murphy, H. Lee, 1996. "Honesty Tests Measure Employee Integrity." *Franchise Times*, April, 1996.

Murray, David, 1996. "Racial and Sexual Politics in Testing." *Academic Questions, Summer 1996*: 10–17.

[Nakamura, Richard, 1995a]. "Allegations by Citizens Against Government Waste: NIMH's Response." Unpublished paper. [Rockville, MD: National Institute of Mental Health.]

[Nakamura, Richard, 1995b]. Unpublished paper; untitled; continuation of Nakamura, 1995a.

[Nakamura, Richard, 1995c]. "The NIMH Response to Recent Attacks." Unpublished paper. [Rockville, MD: National Institute of Mental Health.]

National Commission for the Protection of Human Subjects of Biomedical and Behavioral Research. OPPR Reports. 1979. *The Belmont Report. Ethical Principles and Guidelines for the Protection of Human Subjects of Research*. Washington, DC: U.S. Government Printing Office.

National Research Council, Panel on Research on Violence Against Women: *See* Crowell and Burgess, 1996.

National Science Board, 1996. *Science & Engineering Indicators—1996*. Washington, DC: U. S. Government Printing Office.

National Science Foundation, 1996. *Federal Funds for Research and Development:*

Federal Obligations for Research by Agency and Detailed Field of Science and Engineering: Fiscal Years 1973–96. NSF 96-319. Bethesda, MD: Quantum Research Corp.

NCOVR [National Consortium on Violence Research], 1996. "Violence." Draft brochure. [Pittsburgh, PA: Carnegie Mellon University].

Needleman, Herbert L. 1992. "Salem Comes to the National Institutes of Health: Notes From Inside the Crucible of Scientific Integrity." *Pediatrics, 90(6)*: 977–81.

Neimark, Jill, 1996a. "The Diva of Disclosure: Memory Researcher Elizabeth Loftus." *Psychology Today*, January.

———, 1996b. "Dispatch from the Memory War." *Psychology Today*, May/June.

Nelkin, Dorothy, 1995. "Biology Is Not Destiny." *New York Times,* September 28, 1995: A27.

———, and Lindee, M. Susan. *The DNA Mystique: The Gene as a Cultural Icon.* New York: W. H. Freeman.

Nelson, Randy J.; Demas, Gregory E.; et al., 1995. "Behavioural Abnormalities in Male Mice Lacking Neuronal Nitric Oxide Synthase." *Nature, 378*: 383–86.

Norman, Geoffrey, 1995. "Edward O. Wilson." *Modern Maturity, May-June*: 62–71.

Normand, Jacques; Vlahov, David; and Moses, Lincoln E., eds., 1995. *Preventing HIV Transmission: The Role of Sterile Needles and Bleach.* Report of the Panel on Needle Exchange and Bleach Distribution Programs, Commission on Behavioral and Social Sciences and Education, National Research Council and Institute of Medicine. Washington, DC: National Academy Press.

O'Brien, Mary Utne; Murray, James; et al., 1995a. "Needle Exchange in Chicago: The Effects of Exchange Use on HIV Risk Behavior and incidence." Unpublished research report, NIDA grant No. 5-RO1 DA 06589-04, two CDC grants, and grants from AmFAR.

———; Murray, James; et al., 1995b. "Needle Exchange in Chicago: The Demand for Free Needles and The Effect of Free Needles on HIV Risk Behavior and Injecting Frequency." Unpublished research report, NIDA grant No. 5-RO1 DA 06589-04, two CDC grants, and grants from AmFAR.

Oden, Chester W., Jr., and MacDonald, W. Scott, 1978. "The RIP in Social Scientific Reporting." Comment on Scarr and Weinberg, 1976. *Amer. Psychologist, 33*: 952–54.

Ofshe, Richard, and Watters, Ethan, 1993. "Making Monsters." *Society, 30(3)*: 4–16.

———, 1994. *Making Monsters: False Memories, Psychotherapy, and Sexual Hysteria.* New York: Charles Scribner's Sons.

Oliver, Charles, 1990. "Liberation Zoology." *Reason Magazine*, June.

Ones, Deniz; Viswesvaran, Chockalingam; and Schmidt, Frank L., 1991. "Meta-Analysis Shows Integrity Tests Are Valid Despite Moderating Influences." Paper presented at 1991 meeting of the American Psychological Society.

Palca, Joseph, 1991. "Famous Monkeys Provide Surprising Results." *Science, 252*: 1789.

Parrington, Vernon Louis, 1927, 1930. *Main Currents in American Thought.* New York: Harcourt, Brace and Company.

Pearson, Roger, 1993. *Race, Intelligence and Bias in Academe.* Washington, DC: Scott-Townsend Publishers.

Pendery, Mary L.; Maltzman, Irving M.; and West, L. Jolyon, 1982. "Controlled Drinking by Alcoholics? New Findings and a Revaluation of a Major Affirmative Study." *Science, 217*: 169–75.

Petersen, Anne C., 1996a. "The Psychological and Social Sciences in the Larger Scheme of Things." Address at annual meeting of American Psychological Association, August 11, Toronto.

———, 1996b. Untitled. address at meeting of Council of Graduate Departments of Psychology, Santa Fe, NM, March 3.

Peterson, Charles F., 1996. Brief of the Committee of Concerned Social Scientists as *Amicus Curiae* in Support of the Respondent. U. S. Supreme Court, October Term, 1996: No. 96-1133.

Pierce, Nancy T., 1993. *Bedford AIDS Task Force Parent Survey, April 1993.* Final Report. [Bedford, MA: Bedford AIDS Task Force.]

Plomin, Robert, 1994. *Genetics and Experience: The Interplay Between Nature and Nurture.* Thousand Oaks, CA: Sage Publications.

———, and Daniels, Denise, 1987. "Why Are Children in the Same Family So Different from One Another?" *Behav. and Brain Sciences, 10*: 1–60.

Plomin, Robert, and McClearn, Gerald E., eds., 1993. *Nature, Nurture, and Psychology* Washington, DC: Amer. Psychological Assoc.

Pomeroy, Wardell B. *Dr. Kinsey and the Institute for Sex Research.* New York: Harper & Row, 1972.

Pons, T. P.; Garraghty, P. E.; et al., 1991. "Massive Cortical Reorganization After Sensory Deafferentation in Adult Macaques." *Science, 252*: 1857–60.

Pratkanis, Anthony, and Aronson, Elliot, 1991. *Age of Propaganda: The Everyday Use and Abuse of Persuasion.* New York: W. H. Freeman and Company.

Preston, Douglas, 1997. "A Reporter at Large: The Lost Man." *New Yorker*, June 16: 70–81.

Price, Joyce, 1991. "Surprised Sullivan Says 'Whoa' to Teen Sex Survey." *Washington Times*, July 19.

Raine, Adrian, 1993. *The Psychopathology of Crime: Criminal Behavior as a Clinical Disorder.* San Diego, CA: Academic Press.

Rapoport, Judith L., 1989. "The Biology of Obsessions and Compulsions." *Scientific American*, March: 83–89.

Reed, Susan, and Carswell, Sue, 1993. "Animal Passion." *People*, January 18: 35–39.

Regan Tom, 1983. *The Case for Animal Rights.* Berkeley: University of California Press.

Reisman, Judith; Eichel, Edward; et al., 1990. *Kinsey, Sex, and Fraud: The Indoctrination of a People.* Lafayette, LA: Lochinvar-Huntington House.

Reiss, Albert J., Jr., and Roth, Jeffrey A., eds., 1993, 1994. *Understanding and Preventing Violence.* Washington, DC: National Academy Press.

Reiss, Ira L., 1993. "The Future of Sex Research and the Meaning of Science." *J. of Sex Res., 30(1)*: 3–11.

———, 1997. "Making a Living in Sex: An Autobiographical Account." In *"How I Got Into Sex,"* Bonnie Bullough et al., eds. (Amherst, NY: Prometheus Books).

Renzetti, Claire M., and Lee, Raymond M., eds., 1993. *Researching Sensitive Topics.* Newbury Park, CA: Sage Publications.

Rhein, Rex, 1995. "Amid protest, crime gene meeting held in Maryland." *Biotechnology Newswatch*, October 2, 1995.

Ridley, Matt, 1992. "Swallows and Scorpionflies Find Symmetry is Beautiful." *Science, 257*: 327–28.

Roberts, Julian V., and Gabor, Thomas, 1990. "Lombrosian Wine in a New Bottle: Research on Crime and Race." *Canadian J. of Criminology, 32*: 291–313.

Robinson, John K., and Woodward, William R., 1989. "The Convergence of Behavioral Biology and Operant Psychology: Toward an Interlevel and Interfield Science." *Behav. Analyst, 12*: 131–41.

Rodin, Judith, 1995. Letter, The Pennsylvania University *Almanac*, February 14: 7.

Rosen, Clare Mead, 1987. "The Eerie World of Reunited Twins." *Discover*, September: 36–46.

Roush, Wade, 1995. "Conflict Marks Crime Conference." *Science, 269*: 1808–09.

Rubin, H. B., and Henson, Donald E., 1976. "Effects of Alcohol on Male Sexual Responding." *Psychopharmacology, 47*: 123–34.

Rushton, J. Philippe, 1988a. "Race Differences in Behaviour: A Review and Evolutionary Analysis." *Personality and Indiv. Differences, 9(6)*: 1009–24.

———, 1988b. "The Reality of Racial Differences: A Rejoinder With New Evidence." *Personality and Indiv. Differences, 9(6)*: 1035–40.

———, 1991. Do *r-K* Strategies Underlie Human Race Differences? A Reply to Weizmann et al." *Canadian Psychol., 32(1)*: 29–42.

———, 1992a. "Evolutionary Biology and Heritable Traits (With Reference to Oriental-White-Black Differences): The 1989 AAAS Paper." *Psychol. Repts., 71*: 811–21.

———, 1992b. "Cranial Capacity Related to Sex, Rank, and Race in a Stratified Random Sample of 6,325 U. S. Military Personnel." *Intelligence, 16*: 401–13.

———, 1994. "The Equalitarian Dogma Revisited." *Intelligence, 19*: 263–80.

———, 1995. *Race, Evolution, and Behavior.* New Brunswick, NJ: Transaction Publishers.

———; Fulker, D. W.; et al., 1986. "Altruism and Aggression: The Heritability of Individual Differences." *J. of Personality and Soc. Psychol., 50(6)*: 1192–98.

———, et al., 1990. *On Rushton, Race and Academic Freedom: Responses from the Academic Community.* [letters supporting Rushton] London, Ontario: University of Western Ontario, Social Science Centre.

Sanger M[argaret], 1922. *Pivot of Civilization.* New York: Brentano's.

Saxe, Leonard, 1991. "Lying: Thoughts of an Applied Social Psychologist." *Amer. Psychologist, 46(4)*: 409–15.

———, 1994. "Detection of Deception: Polygraph and Integrity Tests." *Current Directions in Psychological Science, 3(3)*: 69–73.

Scarr, Sandra, ed., 1981. *Race, Social Class, and Individual Differences in I.Q.* Hillsdale, NJ: Erlbaum.

———, 1988. "Race and Gender as Psychological Variables: Social and Ethical Issues." *Amer. Psychologist, 43(1)*: 56–59.

———, 1992. "Developmental Theories for the 1990s: Development and Individual Differences." *Child Development, 63*: 1–19. Presidential address to the biennial meeting of the Society for Research in Child Development, April 20, 1991.

———, and McCartney, Kathleen, 1983. "How People Make Their Own Environments: A Theory of Genotype-Environment Effects." *Child Development, 54*: 424–35.

Scarr, Sandra; Webber, Patricia L.; Weinberg, Richard A.; and Wittig, Michele A., 1981. "Personality Resemblance Among Adolescents and Their Parents in Biologically Related and Adoptive Families." *J. Personality and Soc. Psychol., 40(5)*: 885–98.

Scarr, Sandra, and Weinberg, Richard A., 1976. IQ Test Performance of Black Children Adopted by White Families." *Amer. Psychologist, 31*: 726–39.

Schachter, Stanley, 1964. "The Interaction of Cognitive and Physiological Determinants of Emotional State." *Advances in Experimental Soc. Psychol., 1*: 49–80.

———, 1980. "Non-psychological Explanations of Behavior." In *Retrospections on Social Psychology,* Leon Festinger, ed. (New York: Oxford University Press).

Schafer, Alice T., and Gray, Mary W., 1981. "Sex and Mathematics." *Science, 211*: 231.

Schneider, Alan L., 1997a. "Why Kennewick Man Is in Court." *Anthropology Newsletter, 38 (2)*: 17–18.

Schneider, Alan L., 1997b. "Court Rules on Kennewick Man Case." *Anthropology Newsletter, 38 (6)*: 37–38.

Schneider, Allen M., and Tarshis, Barry, 1980. *An Introduction to Physiological Psychology*. New York: Random House.

Segal, Nancy L., 1984. "Cooperation, Competition, and Altruism Within Twin Sets: A Reappraisal." *Ethol. and Sociobiol., 5*: 163–77.

———, 1987. "Cooperation, Competition, and Altruism in Human Twinships: A Sociobiological Approach." In *Sociobiological Perspectives on Human Development*, Kevin MacDonald, ed. (New York: Springer-Verlag).

———, 1990. "The Importance of Twin Studies for Individual Differences Research." *J. Counseling and Development: 68*: 612–22.

Segerstråle, Ullica, 1986. "Colleagues in Conflict: An 'In Vivo' Analysis of the Sociobiology Controversy." *Biol. and Philos., 1*: 53–87.

———, 1990. "The Sociobiology of Conflict and the Conflict about Sociobiology: Science and Morals in the Larger Debate." In van der Dennen and Falger, 1990.

Selden, Steven, 1995. "Popularizing and Resisting Genetics in Early twentieth century America." Paper delivered at 1995 Crime and Genetics Conference, Queenstown, MD.

Shattuck, Roger, 1996. *Forbidden Knowledge: From Prometheus to Pornography*. New York: St. Martins Press.

Shaughnessy, Michael F., 1994. "An Interview with Arthur R. Jensen." *The School Field, 4(1/2)*: 129–54.

Sheldon, William, and Stevens, S. S., 1942. *The Varieties of Temperament: A Psychology of Constitutional Differences*. New York: Harper and Brothers.

Sheldon, William; Stevens, S. S.; and Tucker, W. B., 1940. *The Varieties of Human Physique: An Introduction to Constitutional Psychology*. New York: Harper and Brothers.

Shipman, Pat, 1994. *The Evolution of Racism: Human Differences and the Use and Abuse of Science*. New York: Simon & Schuster.

Sieber, Joan, ed., 1984. *NIH Readings on the Protection of Human Subjects in Behavioral and Social Science Research*. Albuquerque, NM: University Publications of America.

Sieber, Joan E., 1992. *Planning Ethically Responsible Research*. Newbury Park, CA: SAGE Publications.

Siebert, Charles, 1995. "The DNA We've Been Dealt." *New York Times Magazine*, September 17: 50ff.

Singh, Devendra, 1993. "Adaptive Significance of Female Physical Attractiveness: Role of Waist-to-Hip Ratio." *J. of Personality and Soc. Psychol., 65(2)*: 293–307.

———, 1994. "Body Fat Distribution and Perception of Desirable Female Body Shape by Young Black Men and Women." *Internat. J. of Eating Disorders, 16(3)*: 289–94.

———, 1995. "Female Health, Attractiveness, and Desirability for Relationships: Role of Breast Asymmetry and Waist-to-Hip Ratio." *Ethology and Sociobiology, 16*: 466–81.

Skodak, M., and Skeels, H., 1949. "A Final Follow-up Study of Children in Adoptive Homes." *J. of Genetic Psychol., 75*: 85–125.

Skolnick, Jerome, 1969. *The Politics of Protest: Violent Aspects of Protest*. A Staff Report to the National Commission on the Causes and Prevention of Violence. [Washington, DC]: The National Commission on the Causes and Prevention of Violence.

Smith, Philip M., and Torrey, Barbara Boyle, 1996. "The Future of the Behavioral and Social Sciences." *Science, 271*: 611–12.

Smith, Tom W., 1995. "Trends in Non-Response Rates." *Internat. J. of Public Opinion Res., 7(2)*:157–71.

Snyderman, Mark, 1994. "How to Think About Race." Review of Shipman, 1994, and Rushton, 1995. *National Review,* September 12: 78–80.

Snyderman, Mark, and Herrnstein, R. J., 1983. "Intelligence Tests and the Immigration Act of 1924." *Amer. Psychologist,38*: 986–95.

Snyderman, Mark, and Rothman, Stanley, 1988. *The IQ Controversy: The Media and Public Policy.* New Brunswick, NJ: Transaction Publishers.

Sobell, Mark B., and Sobell, Linda C., 1973a. "Individualized Behavior Therapy for Alcoholics." *Behavior Therapy, 4*: 49–72

———, 1973b. "Alcoholics Treated by Individualised Behaviour Therapy." *Behav. Res. and Ther., 11*: 599–618.

———, 1976. "Second Year Treatment Outcome of Alcoholics Treated by Individual Behavior Therapy: Results." *Behavior Res. and Ther., 14*: 195–215.

———, 1978. *Behavioral Treatment of Alcohol Problems.* New York: Plenum.

———, 1984. "The Aftermath of Heresy: A Response to Pendery *et al.'s* (1982) Critique of 'Individualized Behavior Therapy for Alcoholics.'" *Behav. Res. Ther., 22(4)*: 413–40.

———, 1989. "Moratorium on Maltzman: An Appeal to Reason." *J. of Studies on Alcohol, 30(5)*: 473–80.

———, 1993. *Problem Drinkers: Guided Self-Change Treatment.* New York: The Guilford Press.

Sociobiology Study Group of Science for the People, 1976. "Sociobiology—Another Biological Determinism." *BioScience, 26(3)*: 182, 184–186.

Sperling, Susan, 1994. "Beating a Dead Monkey." Review of Rushton, 1995, and Shipman, 1994, *Nation,* November 28.

Stanley, Alessandra, 1996. "Freud in Russia: Return of the Repressed." *New York Times,* December 11: A1, A10.

Stanley, Julian C., 1996. "In the Beginning: The Study of Mathematically Precocious Youth (SMPY)." In *Intellectual Talent: Psychometric and Social Issues*, Camilla Benbow and David Lubinski, eds. (Baltimore, MD: Johns Hopkins University Press).

Steeh, Charlotte G., 1981. "Trends in Nonresponse Rates, 1952–1979." *Public Opinion Quarterly, 45*: 40–57.

Strathdee, Steffanie A.; Patrick, David M; et al., 1997. "Needle Exchange is Not Enough: Lessons from the Vancouver Injecting Drug Use Study." *AIDS, 11 (8)*: F59–F65.

Stringer, Christopher B., 1990. "The Emergence of Modern Humans." *Scientific American,* December: 98–104.

———, and Andrews, P., 1988. "Genetic and Fossil Evidence for the Origin of Modern Humans." *Science, 239*: 1263–68.

Sullivan, Martin, 1997. "Cultural Property Issues: The Unknowns and the Unknowables." *Anthropology Newsletter, 38 (1)*: 1, 4–5.

Swazey, J. P.; Anderson, M. S.; and Lewis, K. S., 1993. "Ethical Problems in Academic Research." *Amer. Scientist, 81*: 542–53.

Tellegen, Auke; Lykken, David T.; et al., 1988. "Personality Similarity in Twins Reared Apart and Together. *J. Personality and Soc. Psychol., 54(6)*: 1031–39.

Terman, Lewis M., 1916. *The Measurement of Intelligence.* Boston, MA: Houghton Mifflin.

Thomas, Alexander; Chess, Stella; and Birch, Herbert G., 1963. *Temperament and Behavior Disorders in Children.* New York: New York University Press.

Thornhill, Randy, 1994. "Is There Psychological Adaptation to Rape?" *Analyse & Kritik, 16*: 68–85.

————, and Thornhill, Nancy Wilmsen, 1983. "Human Rape: An Evolutionary Analysis." *Ethology and Sociobiology, 4*:137–73.

————, 1992. "The Evolutionary Psychology of Men's Coercive Sexuality." *Behavioral and Brain Sciences, 15*: 367–79.

Toufexis, Anastasia, 1993. "Seeking the Roots of Violence." *Time*, April 19: 60–61.

Turkheimer, Eric, and Gottesman, Irving I., 1991. "Individual Differences and the Canalization of Human Behavior." *Developmental Psychol., 27(1)*: 18–22.

Udry, J. Richard, 1993. "The Politics of Sex Research." *J. of Sex Res.*, May: 103–10.

U. S. Congress, House. 1922. Hearings before the Committee on Immigration and Naturalization, 67th Congress, Third Session, November 21.

————. 1924. Hearings before the Committee on Immigration and Naturalization, House of Representatives, 68th Congress, First Session, March 8.

————. 1990. Committee on Interior and Insular Affairs: Report: Providing for the Protection of Native American Graves, and for Other Purposes.

————. 1994. Committee on Appropriations, Subcommittee on VA, HUD, and Independent Agencies. Hearings, Appropriations for 1995, Part 8.

————. 1995a. Subcommittee on Government Management, Information & Technology. Hearing on Title IV of H. R. 11, the Family Reinforcement Act. March 16.

————. 1995b. Committee on Government Reform and Oversight. Report on H. R. 1271, the Family Privacy Protection Act of 1995. Report 104-94.

————. 1995c. H.R. 1946: Parental Rights and Responsibilities Act of 1995.

————. 1995d. H.R. 1271: Family Privacy Protection Act of 1995.

————. 1995e. Committee on Appropriations, Subcommittee on VA, HUD, and Independent Agencies. Hearings, Appropriations for 1996, Part 3.

————. 1995f. Subcommittee on Basic Research and Committee on Science: Transcript from Legislative Markups, Report 104-231.

————. 1995g. Committee on Science: Subcommittee on Basic Research. Hearings, February 22, March 2.

————. 1995h. Committee on Appropriations, Subcommittee on VA, HUD, and Independent Agencies. Hearings, Appropriations for 1995, March 22.

————. 1996a. Committee on Science: Subcommittee on Basic Research. Hearing, March 22.

————. 1996b. Committee on Science: Omnibus Civilian Science Authorization Act of 1996. Report 104-550, Part 1.

U.S. Congress, Office of Technology Assessment, 1990. *The Use of Integrity Tests for Pre-Employment Screening*. OTA-SET-442. Washington, DC: U. S. Government Printing Office.

U. S. Congress, Senate. 1995a. S. 984: Parental Rights and Responsibilities Act of 1995.

————. 1995b. H.R. 1271: Family Privacy Protection Act of 1995.

————. 1995c. Committee on Governmental Affairs: Hearing on H.R. 1271, Family Privacy Protection Act of 1995; November 9.

————. 1996. Committee on Governmental Affairs, Report on H.R. 1271, the Family Privacy Protection Act of 1995. Report 104-351.

U.S. General Accounting Office, 1993. "Needle Exchange Programs—Research Suggests Promise as an AIDS Prevention Strategy."

U. S. Public Health Service, Office for Protection from Research Risks (OPRR). 1991. "Protection of Human Subjects: Title 45, Code of Federal Regulations, Part 46.

————. 1992. "Information of Interest About the Office for Protection from Research Risks (OPRR) and the Protection of Human Subjects Who Are Involved in HHS-Supported Research." Packet containing two OPRR Reports and other materials.

————, 1995. "Report on Investigation of Allegations of Noncompliance with the Public Health Service Policy on Humane Care and Use of Laboratory Animals at New York University Medical Center."

van der Dennen, Johan M. G., and Falger, Vincent S.E., eds., 1990. *Sociobiology and Conflict: Evolutionary Perspectives on Competition, Cooperation, Violence and Warfare*. London: Chapman and Hall.

Vernon, Philip A., ed., 1993. *Biological Approaches to the Study of Human Intelligence*. Norwood, NJ: Ablex Publishing Corporation.

Vining, Daniel R., Jr., 1995a. Letter, The Pennsylvania University *Almanac*, March 28: 3.

————, 1995b. Letter, *The Pennsylvania Gazette*, March: 10.

Wade, Nicholas, 1976. "Sociobiology: Troubled Birth for New Discipline." *Science, 191*: 1151–55.

Wasserman, David, 1991. "Genetic Factors in Crime: Findings, Uses, and Implications." Grant proposal to the National Center for Human Genome Research, National Institutes of Health.

————, 1995a. "Genetic Predispositions to Violent and Anti-Social Behavior: Responsibility, Character, and Identity." Paper delivered at 1995 Crime and Genetics Conference, Queenstown, MD.

————, 1995b. "Science and Social Harm: Genetic Research into Crime and Violence." Report from the Institute for Philosophy & Public Policy. Queenstown, MD: University of Maryland.

————, 1996. "Research into Genetics and Crime: Consensus and Controversy." *Politics and the Life Sciences, 15 (1)*.

Watson, James D., and Crick, Francis H. C., 1953. "Molecular Structure of Nucleic Acids: A Structure for Deoxiribose Nucleic Acids." *Nature, 171*: 737–38.

Watson, John B., 1913. "Psychology As the Behaviorist Views It." *Psychol. Rev., 20*: 158–77.

————, 1924. *Behaviorism*. Chicago: University of Chicago Press.

————, 1961 [1936]. "John Broadus Watson." In *A History of Psychology in Autobiography*, C. Murchison, ed. (Worcester, MA: Clark University Press).

————, and Rayner, Rosalie, 1920. "Conditioned Emotional Reactions." *J. of Experimental Psychol., 3*: 1–14.

Watters, Ethan, 1995. "Claude Steele Has Scores to Settle." *New York Times Magazine, September 17*: 45ff.

Weinberg, Richard A.; Scarr, Sandra; and Waldman, Irving D., 1992. "The Minnesota Transracial Adoption Study: A Follow-Up of IQ Test Performance at Adolescence." *Intelligence, 16*: 117–35.

Wells, William G., 1982. "Politicians and Scientists: An Uneasy Alliance." *American Behavioral Scientist, 26*: 235–49.

Weyher, Harry, 1997. "The Pioneer Fund." Paper submitted to *J. of the Hist. of the Behavioral Sciences*.

Whalen, Richard E., and Simon, Neal G., 1984. "Biological Motivation." *Ann. Rev. Psychol., 35*: 257–76.

Wheeler, David L., 1995. "The Biology of Crime." *Chron. of Higher Educ., 42(6)*: A10f.

White, Andrew Dickson, 1960 [1896]. *A History of the Warfare of Science With Theology in Christendom*. New York: Dover Publications, Inc.

Whitney, Glayde, 1995a. "Genetics and Human Behavior I. Scientific and Research Issues." In *Encyclopedia of Bioethics*, 2nd ed., W. T. Reich, ed. (New York: Macmillan).

————, 1995b. "Ideology and Censorship in Behavior Genetics." Presidential address, 25th Annual Meeting of Behavior Genetics Association, Richmond, VA, June 2.

Wiener, Jon, 1996. "The Cigarette Papers." *Nation*, January 111–18.

Wilson, Edward O., 1975. *Sociobiology: The New Synthesis.* Cambridge, MA: Harvard University Press.

———, 1976. "Academic Vigilantism and the Political Significance of Sociobiology." *BioScience, 26(3)*: 183, 187–90.

———, 1979 [1978]. *On Human Nature.* New York: Bantam Books.

———, 1995 [1994]. *Naturalist.* New York: Warner Books.

Wright, Lawrence, 1995. "A Reporter at Large: Double Mystery." *New Yorker*, August 7: 45–62.

Zimbardo, Philip G.; Haney, Craig; Banks, W. Curtis; and Jaffe, David, 1974. "The Psychology of Imprisonment: Privation, Power, and Pathology." In *Doing Unto Others*, Zick Rubin, ed. (Englewood Cliffs, NJ: Prentice-Hall, Inc.).

Zita, Jacquelyn N., 1989. "The Premenstrual Syndrome: 'Dis-easing' the Female Cycle." In *Feminism and Science*, Nancy Tuana, ed. (Bloomington: Indiana University Press).

Index